S0-BAH-215

SHOW ME THE MONEY

Show Me the Money is the definitive business journalism textbook that offers hands-on advice and insights into the job of a business journalist. Chris Roush draws on his experience as both a business journalist and educator to explain how to cover businesses, industry and the economy, as well as where to find sources of information for stories and how to take financial information and make it work for a story.

Updates to the third edition include the following:

- Timely issues related to real estate;
- Additional examples from websites and other nontraditional business media such as BuzzFeed and Quartz;
- Tips from professional business journalists including Andrew Ross Sorkin of the *New York Times* and Jennifer Forsyth of the *Wall Street Journal*.

Essential for both undergraduate and graduate courses in business journalism and professional business journalism newsrooms, *Show Me the Money* is a must-read for reporters, editors and students who want to learn the ins and outs of how to cover public and private companies. Additional materials, including a sample syllabus and additional links and tips for students can be found at https://www.routledge.com/products/9781138188389

Chris Roush is the Walter Hussman Sr. Distinguished Professor in Business Journalism at UNC–Chapel Hill, where he has taught since 2002. In 2010, he was named Journalism Teacher of the Year by the Scripps Howard Foundation and the Association for Education in Journalism and Mass Communication. His business journalism students work throughout the industry for organizations such as CNBC, the *New York Times*, the *Wall Street Journal*, MarketWatch, Bloomberg News and Reuters; websites such as BuzzFeed and Business Insider; and American City Business Journals newspapers.

SHOW ME THE MONEY

Writing Business and Economics Stories for Mass Communication

THIRD EDITION

Chris Roush

Routledge
Taylor & Francis Group

NEW YORK AND LONDON

Third edition published 2017
by Routledge
711 Third Avenue, New York, NY 10017

and by Routledge
2 Park Square, Milton Park, Abingdon, Oxon OX14 4RN

Routledge is an imprint of the Taylor & Francis Group, an informa business

First edition published 2004 by Lawrence Erlbaum Associates, Inc.

Second edition published 2011 by Routledge

Library of Congress Cataloging-in-Publication Data
Names: Roush, Chris, author.
Title: Show me the money : writing business and economics stories for mass communication / Chris Roush.
Description: Third edition. | New York : Routledge, 2017. | Includes index.
Identifiers: LCCN 2016006517| ISBN 9781138188372 (hardback) |
    ISBN 9781138188389 (pbk.) | ISBN 9781315642376 (ebk.)
Subjects: LCSH: Journalism, Commercial.
Classification: LCC PN4784.C7 R68 2017 | DDC 070.4/4965—dc23
LC record available at http://lccn.loc.gov/2016006517

ISBN: 978-1-138-18837-2 (hbk)
ISBN: 978-1-138-18838-9 (pbk)
ISBN: 978-1-315-64237-6 (ebk)

Typeset in Classical Garamond
by Apex CoVantage, LLC

CONTENTS

FOREWORD

For many budding journalists, business and economics is a mysterious realm filled with arcane numbers, puzzling graphs and incomprehensible documents. It seems thick with brainy academics whom no one can understand, venal executives squinting in the Klieg lights on their way to trial, and little else. Worse, to many newcomers the topic fills a section somewhere toward the back of the newspaper or the end of the newscast, far from the consequential stuff of politics, warfare and crime.

My, how wrong these naifs are.

As Chris Roush shows throughout this book, business and economic journalism is a vital and vibrant arena filled with drama, conflict and color. Far from dabbling in the inconsequential, financial reporters cover the news that really matters. The stories behind politics, warfare and crime—along with sports, health, science and other staples of coverage—are often tales of dollars and cents, of maneuverings driven by economic and commercial concerns. Financial wellbeing, or the lack of it, drives much of the news.

Journalists who can tell readers and viewers lively, intelligent and intriguing stories about businesspeople and their companies, about trends and innovations, and about the global markets that influence them all are coveted by editors. They get jobs because this corner of journalism is still healthy and the specialized knowledge they bring is valuable. Financial journalists are the soothsayers and entrails-readers editors turn to when they need someone to explain the latest unemployment report, spell out the meaning of a stock market slide, or tell people about what that big corporate deal means.

Oh, and such journalists nowadays often get on the front page, lead the newscast, or dominate the website. The reason: The news they cover affects people's lives. It hits them in the wallet, a place not far from the heart for most folks.

Despite the popular misconceptions among some editors (and students), business and economic journalism is not rocket science. Following the numbers and understanding economic developments and corporate strategy is a matter of applying common sense, practical experience and a bit of book learning. Who is making money and why? Who is losing and why? What needs are being filled and what needs remain? Such are the basic questions that business reporters seek to answer.

But it is necessary, of course, to understand the tools that businesspeople and economists use to grapple with such questions. That's where books such as this one come in. Corporate financial reports may seem like so much impenetrable agate type, but it's easy to shake them down if one knows the templates they follow. Economic trends may seem inscrutable until one understands the approaches economists and policymakers take. The pronouncements of even the most eggheady business analyst or economist can be translated into terms an ordinary reader can grasp, if one just knows the language.

This book will guide the diligent student through the thicket of issues that sometimes obscures economic and commercial discussions. It shines a bright light on the field and equips the aspiring journalist to do the same for readers and viewers. Such mysterious matters as Form 10-K filings and off-balance sheet transactions are rendered understandable. Wonder whether a trade surplus or deficit makes a difference, or why anyone cares about global trade, anyway? Curious about what drives mergers? This book is for you.

Financial journalists—or journalists of all stripes, for that matter—dig into complex and often chaotic affairs and break them down so nearly any reader or viewer can grasp them. We translate the arcane into the comprehensible. We dig into specialized niches and depict them in ways the average citizen can get. Just what are those futures traders doing in front of their dazzling computer screens and what does that have to do with the price of eggs, literally? What do the gyrations of the Dow Jones Industrial Average mean for Main Street? How do statisticians count the jobless?

To do this work, the savvy journalist, whether a financial reporter or not, needs to understand how business and economic matters shape our lives. That journalist may want to explain why jobs are disappearing in some corners of American industry and popping up in Malaysia and Mexico, for instance—and why such shifts, surprisingly, can mean new and more rewarding jobs in the U.S. That reporter needs to understand global forces at play. Want to dissect the railings of an ambitious politician about world trade, unemployment rates, or federal spending? It's indispensable to understand the dynamics involved.

This text provides a foundation for financial journalists and generalists alike. Keep it at hand and mine it often, whether you cover politics or mergers. In the end, you'll find, it's all business and economics.

Joseph Weber
Associate Professor, University of Nebraska–Lincoln,
and former chief of correspondents for *BusinessWeek*

PREFACE

I can remember my first week as a business reporter like it was yesterday. At the Manatee County bureau of the *Sarasota Herald-Tribune* in May 1989, I spent the first week being trained by my predecessor, who was transferring to the newspaper's main office. After a week, she left. I panicked.

I had never been a business reporter before. My previous job was covering cops and courts in the Pasco County bureau of the *St. Petersburg Times*—a job, I might add, that I hated. I wanted to do anything else besides look at dead bodies. So I called a friend in Sarasota who told me about the business opening. I got over the panic and learned what to do—on the job, making some mistakes.

It was the break I needed, and the right career move. Becoming a business reporter put me in the fastest-growing part of editorial content in newspapers, magazines and later, the Internet, during the 1990s. Reporters who knew something about business were recruited by other publications, and my career took off.

After a year in Sarasota, the business editor at the *Tampa Tribune* called me. I had no idea who he was, or what stories of mine he'd seen. But he wanted to hire me, and he offered more money and the opportunity to work at a larger newspaper.

The trend continued. *BusinessWeek* needed someone in its Connecticut bureau who knew how to write about insurance. Bloomberg News wanted someone in its Atlanta office that had covered the beverage industry. A publishing company in Virginia hired a recruiter to find someone who could start an insurance magazine.

Business news, no matter what form, has been the growth industry of mass communication for the past 15 years. Yet during the entire time that my career progressed, I kept thinking back to that first job and my lack of experience. I learned on the job, just like many others in the field, about the difference between revenue and profits, and net income and operating income. I discovered public company filings the way other reporters did—someone with more experience told me about them and what they contained.

And as my career has transitioned into teaching, I've thought even more about how most business reporters get into the business. Why should they start off with little or no knowledge of corporate America?

The answer is they shouldn't. The public deserves to have information about the business world from all forms of mass communication written and edited by journalists who are knowledgeable and can explain the significance of stories to consumers in a way anybody can understand.

Yet higher education and mass communication have failed miserably in effectively training journalists for careers in business reporting. In a 2002 survey by Selzer & Co. for the American Press Institute and the Reynolds Foundation, not one journalism school administrator rated their program as doing an excellent job of training students for careers in business journalism. Only 28 percent said they do a good job. And news executives say business is the hardest beat to find qualified reporters for; just 38 percent of them say that business is a high priority in their newsroom, calling into question just how important that expertise is.

Universities and colleges across the country need to team with mass communication outlets to provide more training and teaching in business journalism. In some areas, this is happening. Business journalism programs exist at major schools such as Missouri, Northwestern, Columbia and Boston University, as well as others, including Illinois, Baruch College in New York and Washington & Lee University.

And newspapers, magazines, TV stations and websites are sending their reporters and editors to more and more conferences for training and tips. The Society of American Business Editors and Writers, the American Press Institute and the Reynolds Foundation are also making concerted efforts to improve business journalism education and knowledge.

And while there have been other books to help business reporters along the way, there's never been a guide to show them specifically how writing stories about companies and the economy should be done.

This book strives to be a guide for the beginning business reporter and one who has worked the beat for years, providing guidance on important topics and issues that everyone who writes a business-related story encounters. It starts off with a basic history lesson on the importance of business journalism to everyone and then teaches readers what every business reporter should know, from reading an income statement and balance sheet for a company to what to look for in SEC filings.

Those are the skills I wish I had back in 1989. Now, business journalists won't have to start their jobs without this knowledge.

While this book is primarily written from the viewpoint of the newspaper business editor, there are also excellent examples of business journalism from television, the Internet and magazines mentioned. All of the reporting techniques and methods discussed are relevant to any media.

Chris Roush
Walter E. Hussman Sr. Distinguished
Professor in business journalism,
School of Media and Journalism

1

BUSINESS JOURNALISM'S IMPORTANCE

If you want to understand why business journalism is so important, just look at the money being spent in the past decade to acquire or build news organizations that provide business and economic information.

In 2007, News Corp. spent $5 billion to acquire the parent company of the *Wall Street Journal*, MarketWatch.com and *Barron's*. Shortly thereafter, Thomson Corp. bought Reuters, primarily a financial news wire, for $17 billion.

Condé Nast, one of the largest magazine companies in the United States, spent $100 million to start a business magazine called *Portfolio*. Bloomberg acquired *BusinessWeek* magazine to expand its portfolio of business news products to a consumer audience. The company also spent millions expanding its news operation to include coverage of regulatory and government news that affect businesses.

More recently, Axel Springer, a German company, spent more than $340 million in 2015 to acquire a majority stake in Business Insider, the second-largest business news website in the United States. And in the same year, Japanese company Nikkei spent $1.3 billion to acquire the *Financial Times*, the second-largest business newspaper behind the *Wall Street Journal*.

Billions of dollars have been spent on acquiring business journalism organizations for one simple reason—it's the one news area that consumers can use to make money. And that makes it very valuable all over the world.

It's also why business journalism is gaining in prominence in the media world, and why journalists—whether they're interested in business and economics stories or not—would be wise to know something about how such stories are reported and written.

Business reporting is just like reporting any other beat. You have to know what you are writing about, which documents to look for and which sources to use. Even though the quality of business journalism has improved in the past 15 years, there are still concerns that reporters in the field are not fully knowledgeable about their topics.

Also, some business reporters and editors do not know the appropriate place to look for the information they need to get the story or to make the story they already have even better. Still others do not understand the basic principles of economics that help a company's profits rise and fall, and even more do not understand the importance of the stock market and trade relations to a business's future prospects.

Those that do understand how to find information about companies and the economy have a leg up on other journalists.

Business journalism is also almost every story in journalism. Government stories are about who is getting contracts to repair roads and build schools. Crime stories can be about why someone embezzled millions of dollars from a company. Health stories are about the escalating cost of taking care of the sick or injured, and what company is developing a new drug to treat cancer. Environmental stories are about how businesses are changing their operations to decrease their pollution into the air. And gender stories are about how some companies don't pay women as much as they pay men for the same job.

The skills of a business journalist pay off on these other beats. Knowing how to read an income statement and a contract, or a regulatory document, for news is a skill every journalist should know, whether they are covering a business and economic beat are not.

TIPS FROM THE PROS

Quartz reporter Melvin Backman advises new-comers to business journalism:

Read a lot. The half-life of a story idea has gotten dramatically shorter these past few years. You need to stay abreast of all the angles that are getting tackled when news breaks so that you can keep your writing original and serve the readers by showing them something they haven't already seen (or a new way to see it).

In other words, all journalism boils down to one statement: Show me the money. Show the reader or viewer or listener where the money is coming from, or where it is going, and you have a great story. And that is the essence of business journalism.

There's also more money involved for those who work in business journalism. A 2015 study by the Society of American Business Editors and Writers (SABEW) and the Talking Biz News website discovered that business journalists received a salary between $70,000 and $75,000 and that a majority of those surveyed had received a raise in the past year.[1]

In comparison, the mean salary for all reporters and correspondents in the United States is $45,800, according to the Bureau of Labor Statistics.[2]

And there's yet another strong reason to consider a career in business journalism: The jobs are plentiful. News organizations such as Bloomberg, Reuters, the *Wall Street Journal*, Business Insider, American City Business Journals, Crain Communications and others are constantly looking for business reporters and editors to work for them. Unlike other areas of journalism, their publications continue to grow in circulation and advertising, which means that they can hire more journalists.

Why is this happening? The reason goes back to why all of those companies are spending billions of dollars to own business news organizations. The readers of business and economics news are willing to pay for that information because it helps them make decisions on how to spend money, whether for personal reasons or for their companies. And these readers typically make more money than the consumers of other media, which means these companies can charge more for advertising than other media.

In the first part of the twenty-first century, the number of business journalism news outlets has proliferated, particularly online. Many of them only cover a specific industry, or a specific type of company. Others try to present business and economic news and information in a way that hasn't been done before. Still others are trying to cater to new demographics.

They're all responding to the decline in business news and information in daily newspapers across the country, where many consumers got their fill of company news each day. Many metro dailies cut back on their business sections when they stopped printing daily stock prices, and then they cut their staffs during the economic recession in 2008 and 2009.

TIPS FROM THE PROS

 Quartz reporter Melvin Backman advises newcomers to business journalism:

Ask where the chart is. You don't necessarily need to actually make a chart for every story you do, but it's always helpful to think about the numbers that might be behind it. How fast has this company grown? What kind of year is this asset class having? That kind of context can be key to help you establish a narrative or disprove one if need be.

For example, Business Insider was launched in 2009 by former Wall Street analyst Henry Blodget. By 2015, it had become the No. 2 business and financial website in the country, behind only Yahoo Finance, and had seen a 70 percent increase in readers in the previous year. The site also contained entertainment and sports news, but it targeted younger readers. It expanded to Europe and Australia and introduced a consumer tech site. Sixty percent of its readers used mobile devices.

Another site, 24/7 Wall St., was launched in 2006 by the former *Financial World* editor. Its content was also republished on other websites such as MSN Money, Yahoo Finance, AOL's Daily Finance, MarketWatch.com and the Huffington Post. It posted 30 articles daily, and its profit margin was higher than 50 percent, showing that an advertising-based business model can work for business news sites with strong editorial content.

Quartz, another business news website, was launched by the *Atlantic* in 2012 and is now breaking news. It launched sites in India and Africa, and it's primarily funded by advertising revenue and sponsors. In a unique move, Quartz has reporters and computer developers sitting beside each other in its offices.

The Information is a tech news site launched in 2013 by former *Wall Street Journal* reporter Jessica Lessin. A subscription to the site costs $400 per year, and Lessin had built a full-time staff of 15 by the end of 2015, covering what it believes are underreported stories.

NerdWallet.com launched in 2010 and is a personal finance site used by 30 million people in 2014. It combines personal finance articles with data about financial products such as credit cards and mortgages, helping its readers make the best financial decisions. Its funky name also helps attract readers.

American City Business Journals, which operates 40 weekly business newspapers across the country, launched BizWomen.com in 2014. The site provides news for women business leaders and gathers content from its other papers onto the site as well as creating original content.

Then there's my former student Aaron Kremer, who in the past decade has launched RichmondBizSense.com in Virginia and the BusinessDen.com in Colorado to provide business news to readers in those areas.

These examples, and many others like them, show that business journalism is not only alive and well, but growing. And it shows that the field needs more trained business reporters and editors.

Top 10 Business Journalism Stories of All Time

1. Ida Tarbell's coverage of the Standard Oil Co. in *McClure's.*
2. Upton Sinclair exposing the meatpacking industry in *The Jungle.*
3. Rachel Carson's exposé of the chemical industry in *Silent Spring.*
4. Ralph Nader's "Unsafe at Any Speed," which disclosed dangers of the Corvair.
5. John Spargo's reporting on coal mines using children as workers.

6. Edward R. Murrow's "Harvest of Shame," exposing working conditions of migrants.
7. Jessica Mitford's "American Way of Death," uncovering funeral industry abuses.
8. Houston station KHOU-TV reporting on problems with Firestone tires on Ford Explorer vehicles.
9. Barlett and Steele explaining how federal tax laws are applied unequally.
10. *Collier's* magazine's 1905 exposé of the patent medicine industry.

The History of Business Journalism

Business journalism has had a profound effect on the United States and the millions of people who interact with companies on an everyday basis by purchasing their goods, products and services.

Early settlers in America depended on newspapers to provide them with details of crop and livestock prices and information about which ships had entered the port and the goods they contained. By the nineteenth century, newspapers devoted solely to business news were established. The *Journal of Commerce* began in 1827. The *Wall Street Journal* came along in 1889. But some of the most important stories in business journalism during this time ran in mainstream papers.

TIPS FROM THE PROS

 Quartz reporter Melvin Backman advises newcomers to business journalism:

 Look for diverse experts. Business journalism, like most subject areas, isn't very diverse along race or gender lines. Reach out to women and minorities in order to build a more sophisticated worldview and bring underrepresented perspectives to your readership that can really enrich coverage.

In the late 1850s, Horace Greeley of the *New York Tribune* pushed for a railroad that would connect the East and the West. His stories were the first major push to combine the regional economies of a growing country. Greeley also wrote about the need for low-cost homestead lands, another important development in the U.S. economy. A decade later, the *New York Sun* exposed how the construction company that helped build the first intercontinental railroad had been formed by the railroad companies themselves, which were essentially making contracts with one another and bribing members of Congress to keep quiet by selling them shares in the company at a discounted price. The story led to the first major Congressional investigation into a corporation, foreshadowing later hearings on the downfall of Enron, WorldCom and others.

Newspapers also influenced how government regulated business. Around the same time Greeley was pushing for a railroad, another newspaper in New York, *Frank Leslie's Illustrated Newspaper,* exposed how bad milk was killing children. The article pushed regulators into passing laws banning swill milk. The milk exposé was not the first in journalism that took aim at a business or corporation. Throughout the late 1890s and the early part of the twentieth century, many newspapers directed reporters to investigate how companies were affecting the lives of people. In 1899, the *Chicago Daily Tribune* began publishing stories about how firecrackers and other explosives sold to celebrate the Fourth of July were killing people every year. Its stories led to restrictions on how fireworks were manufactured and sold.

The most famous examples of business journalism that led to business operation reforms are Upton Sinclair's novel *The Jungle,* which documented the unsanitary conditions of the meatpacking industry, and Ida Tarbell's *McClure's* magazine articles about how Standard Oil had forced its competitors out of business. After reading Sinclair's novel, Theodore Roosevelt ordered an investigation that culminated in the passing of the Pure Food and Drugs Act and the Meat Inspection Act in 1906. And in 1911, the U.S. Supreme Court ordered Standard Oil to be split up. After the turn of the century other articles in *McClure's* attacked the railroad industry, which led to laws limiting shipping charges on goods and products transported by rail. In *Cosmopolitan,* a 1906 article about child labor helped discontinue the abuse of young workers in factories across the country.

Journalists also turned their attention to investments. In 1920, the *Boston Post* uncovered the financial wrongdoings of Charles Ponzi, a local financial expert who promised huge returns to investors. Ponzi was arrested and convicted based on the articles and spent time in prison. His name, of course, lives on in the business world, as the term Ponzi scheme is now used to refer to any illegal pyramid scheme in which investors are paid with money from other investors, such as in the recent reporting of former New York investor Bernard Madoff.

BusinessWeek magazine was founded in 1929, just weeks before the stock market crash that led to the Great Depression. *Fortune* magazine, created by *Time* founder Henry Luce, followed a year later. Both publications, along with *Forbes,* spent the next seven decades defining business journalism in a magazine format, printing long articles about industries, Wall Street and labor—all important topics that gave readers a broad understanding of the effects of business on the country.

TIPS FROM THE PROS

Quartz reporter Melvin Backman advises newcomers to business journalism:

Ask how the money flows. When writing about business, it's always a good idea to ask how people get paid. Where do revenues come from? When does a business make a profit? Who are the vendors that actually make things happen and what's their cut? All of these will give you and your readers a more nuanced sense of what's going on behind the scenes.

New and interesting reporting styles also developed. In 1935, Sylvia F. Porter began writing a column in the *New York Post* on financial news. Her writing defined personal finance reporting, explaining to readers in simple terms how they should take care of their hard-earned money, and it landed her on the cover of *Time* in 1960. At the height of her career, Porter's column ran in more than 450 newspapers around the world, and her style spawned other well-known personal finance writers, such as Jane Bryant Quinn and Kathy Kristof, who today continue the tradition of bringing sound, basic personal finance advice to millions. Without these reporters, many people would have never understood how a 401(k) plan works or the difference between growth and value stocks.

In 1941, Barney Kilgore took control of the *Wall Street Journal* at the age of 32 and turned a newspaper that basically catered to a small subscriber base in New York City into an international newspaper that day in and day out publishes the best business journalism in the world. Kilgore, considered the father of modern business journalism, took a financial newspaper and turned it into a publication that explained the relationship between labor, capital and enterprise. "He also believed that those who had to deal with these problems would value a newspaper that informed them in depth and without sensation about the world they live in in all its variety," said Peter Kann, CEO of Dow Jones & Company, the newspaper's owner (Kann, 2000, p. 1). When Kilgore began running the paper, it had 41,000 subscribers. By the time he died in 1967, it had a circulation of more than 1.1 million.

More recently, publications have led the way to improved living conditions by educating consumers, thereby leading them to purchase safer products. For example, *Reader's Digest,* not known today for breaking stories or leading causes, was the first broad publication to expose the potential dangers of smoking and link it to cancer. The December 1952 article is credited with starting the antismoking debate and forcing the cigarette industry to admit its products were harmful.

With an article in the *Nation* in April 1959, well-known consumer advocate Ralph Nader began his investigation into automobile safety that eventually led to new federal regulations requiring seat belts, recalls, crash tests and air bags in most vehicles. His argument gained clout after it was disclosed that General Motors Corporation hired private investigators to track Nader.

In the 1960s, the *Des Moines Register* printed articles that led to Congress closing loopholes in inspections that allowed for diseased animals to be turned into meat sold in grocery stores. A 1977 article in *Mother Jones* exposed readers to the dangers of driving a Pinto, which, because of its poorly designed fuel tank, easily exploded when hit from behind. The article led to a recall of the Ford Motor Company's car and the end of its production. More than two decades later, a television reporter at KHOU in Houston found an unsettling pattern of crashes involving Ford SUVs with Firestone tires. The resulting coverage led to the recall of millions of tires.

TIPS FROM THE PROS

Quartz reporter Melvin Backman advises newcomers to business journalism:

Know who the big players are. Find out who the titans of your respective industry are, and you'll know who will be showing up in most of your headlines and where you should be trying to develop sources.

In 1970, Louis Rukeyser began hosting *Wall Street Week* on public television. It became the first show broadcast to millions of viewers that discussed nothing but the stock market and the economy. The program became the standard television show for understanding how Wall Street affected Main Street and was the precursor of other television shows and even networks such as Bloomberg Television, CNBC and Fox Business Network that now report exclusively about business and the economy. Viewers around the world now think nothing of turning on CNBC in their offices and leaving it on all day. Two decades ago, the mere thought of someone who wanted to constantly watch a television network devoted solely to business news would have earned that person a well-deserved leave of absence. Now, it is considered almost standard for large segments of society.

More recently, business journalism stories have regularly won the Pulitzer Prize, the highest award for journalism in the United States. In 2015, reporters at both the *Wall Street Journal* and Bloomberg News won Pulitzers for, respectively, using Medicare records to uncover how some health care providers are bilking the system and for disclosing how some companies want to move their headquarters overseas to avoid paying taxes. In 2013, there were three Pulitzers for business journalism. A Pulitzer for investigative reporting was awarded to David Barstow and Alejandra Xanic von Bertrab of the *New York Times* for their reports on how Wal-Mart used widespread bribery to dominate the market in Mexico, resulting in changes in company practices. The Pulitzer in explanatory reporting was awarded to the *New York Times* staff for its penetrating look into business practices by Apple and other technology companies that illustrates the darker side of a changing global economy for workers and consumers.

These articles were all researched and written by reporters who understood the importance of business in society and exposed the problems, warts and all. Some of these reporters were not specifically trained in understanding how businesses operate but learned the vital information about how companies work and how they make money, thus turning dogged reporting into stories that changed our economy and our lives. That is the standard that today's business reporters need to strive to match. Many other reporters and editors have changed business journalism during the last 100 years, evolving the art of reporting and writing about companies and the economy into arguably the most important journalism of the last 20 years.

Resources Every Business Journalist Should Have, Besides This Book

1. *Understanding Financial Statements: A Journalist's Guide.* The book by Chicago financial guru Jay Taparia is written in an easy-to-understand style.
2. A subscription to the *Wall Street Journal.* Simply the best business reporting, day in and day out. To be the best, read the best.
3. Access to a Bloomberg terminal. This machine can provide the data to make a story stronger, and contact information for sources across the globe.
4. The book *24 Days: How Two Wall Street Journal Reporters Uncovered the Lies That Destroyed Faith in Corporate America,* which details how reporters reported the story behind one of the biggest company failures in the past century.
5. Membership in the Society of American Business Editors and Writers. SABEW offers workshops and conferences where business journalists learn from others in the field.

Hits and Misses

For all of the advancements and impact brought upon society by reporting and writing that has focused on business and the economy, business journalism must also rightly take the blame for some of the problems in the world, past and present.

At the same time that the muckrakers were exposing unsanitary conditions in meatpacking plants and monopolistic business practices, companies were turning to experts to help them deal with the media. These forebears of public relations professionals brought a new twist to business journalism. CEOs attacked in newspaper stories wanted a way to respond. In the early twentieth century, major corporations such as General Electric and General Motors hired public relations experts to answer questions from the media and to try to persuade reporters that these for-profit businesses were not as evil as many believed. After World War II, public relations jobs proliferated as the economy grew. The task of public relations professionals was to tell the media the good things that their companies were doing.

TIPS FROM THE PROS

Quartz reporter Melvin Backman advises newcomers to business journalism:

Check your rearview mirror. What was a big deal in your industry five, 10, 20 years ago? Look through your outlet's archives and you might find something (or someone) worth revisiting. Even if there's not a story there, the exercise will give you a good historical background for evaluating new trends and developments.

In a way, the rise in public relations led to an overall down period for business journalism. In the 1950s and 1960s, the business desk became a place where newspapers put reporters who could not hack it covering city hall or state government. Older reporters were put out to pasture with an assignment to cover business. With a few notable exceptions, business reporting took a back seat to writing about the Vietnam War and the race riots.

The 1980s and 1990s were better. The quality of business journalism improved as reporters and editors gained experience, but major stories were still missed. And business reporting took some hits. Foster Winans wrote the popular "Heard on the Street" column for the *Wall Street Journal* in the early 1980s. The stories disclosed whether professional investors were bullish or bearish on certain stocks. Winans started leaking information before his stories were published and was eventually caught and served time in prison. A decade later, well-known business columnist Dan Dorfman was fired from *Money* magazine for failing to disclose his sources to his editor after reports in other publications noted his close relationship with investors.

Along the way, few reporters were warning readers about impending problems. There were no glaring headlines in early October 1987 urging investors to take their money out of the stock market before it fell. A decade later, business sections and magazines lauded the management of Enron in prose that now seems ludicrous. In the *Dallas Morning News,* Enron was dubbed in a headline as a "global e-commerce leader" (North, 2002). A reporter for the *Houston Business Journal* wrote, "Enron has shown a widely recognized knack for innovation that consistently generates additional sources of revenue, potential profits and more capital" (North, 2002).

The boosterism was not confined to local publications touting hometown companies. Even the magazines and publications that were the so-called experts in writing about these new industries and businesses missed out on notifying readers of the problems. "Too often the new magazines and Web sites acted as incurious cheerleaders, championing executives and innovative companies without questioning their books," said James Ledbetter, business editor of *Inc.* magazine and a former employee of the *Industry Standard,* one of the publications that chronicled the meteoric rise of many Internet companies without realizing that many of them were doomed to failure. "Do a search, for example, of the word 'Enron' in the databases of those publications prior to 2000 and you'll find little but praise for its market innovations" (Ledbetter, 2003, p. A17).

TIPS FROM THE PROS

Quartz reporter Melvin Backman advises newcomers to business journalism:

Who's going bust in the boom? Though not everything is zero-sum in business, the rise of a new company or business model often implies bad news for the incumbent. Find out how they're coping with lost market share and relevancy, or reveal that a disruption-driven narrative might be a bit overblown. Hint: This also works in reverse.

Even revered mass communication outlets failed in their watchdog role. The *New York Times* called Enron's president an "idea machine" (Salpukas, 1999, p. C1). "Not only did the press miss the Enron scandal, it actively helped create the Enron scandal," said Jeffrey Madrick, editor of *Challenge,* an economics magazine. "It not only missed the complications of Enron's fancy partnerships, which are indeed complicated, but it extolled Enron's virtues beyond almost any company. *Fortune* named Enron the most innovative company five or six years in a row, presumably without once checking the books" (Madrick, 2003, p. 3).

And even when mass communication outlets investigated serious business issues, such as the series run by the *New York Times* in March 1996 that examined why people around the country were losing their jobs despite strong economic growth, gaps remained. The series made faulty assertions, such as that the economy was not producing workers who stayed in the same jobs for long periods of time, that it was harder for a laid-off worker to find a new job, and that many of the jobs being created were low-paying service jobs, not higher paying manufacturing jobs.

"The problem with business coverage in the 1990s was not that journalists weren't smart enough to root out the corruption," wrote Charles Layton in *American Journalism Review* in March 2003. "Reading the coverage of the past half-decade, one is struck by how much certain reporters *did* uncover. But even within their own news organizations, their insights were lost in a cacophony of naive reportage that reassured us the system was sound, analysts and auditors and CEOs were basically trustworthy, and the market boom might go on forever" (Layton, 2003, p. 22).

In recent years, business journalists have had to answer tough questions about why they failed to warn consumers about the economic crisis that began in 2008 and was caused by problems, such as inflated prices, in the real estate market. However, a review of coverage from the past decade shows that business reporters and editors performed better this time around. They wrote numerous stories about the housing bubble and warned about the dangers of derivatives on Wall Street firms. A former Harvard Business School professor, Gregory Miller, found that nearly one-third of the accounting improprieties uncovered at companies are first discovered by business journalists.

Still, a number of major stories were missed, including the aforementioned Madoff scandal, in which one tipster sent documents to a *Wall Street Journal* reporter three years before the crime was uncovered. The story went unreported until charges were filed.

With a dose of reality now entering business reporting, is it any wonder that confidence in the quality of work by business journalists remains low, particularly among those who regularly read the business section, namely, corporate executives? Even in newsrooms and among journalists, business reporting is still considered a backwater in knowledge and expertise. In a 1992 poll by Louis Harris, 46 percent of executives rated the overall quality of business journalism as negative. Furthermore, 17 percent of executives felt that the quality of business journalism had actually declined since 1967.

In the same survey, more than three-fourths of executives—and nearly the same amount of journalism academics—agreed that too much emphasis was being placed on "personality" reporting, or writing stories about the CEO. Only 34 percent of journalists agreed, resulting in stories that made heroes of CEOs that later fell from grace as their companies faltered. But the most telling numbers are these: Ninety-two percent of executives and 72 percent of journalists and journalism academics were concerned about a reporter's knowledge of the businesses they were covering.

TIPS FROM THE PROS

Quartz reporter Melvin Backman advises newcomers to business journalism:

 Get specific. Editors and readers will always want to know more. When reporting, get the answer to every question raised by the information you uncover. What's left on the cutting room floor might make for a good story down the road. Same for the questions you can't get answers to.

Two years later, the Freedom Forum First Amendment Center published a study called *The Headline vs. The Bottom Line: Mutual Distrust Between Business and the News Media*. The study found that more than two-thirds of journalists believed that they did not make mistakes on the technical details of business stories. However, more than three-fourths of executives felt the opposite way (Haggerty and Rasmussen, 1994, p. 12). In addition, the same survey found that nearly half of all journalists believed they were not adequately trained for reporting about business, whereas 7 out of 10 executives were convinced that reporters did not have the business background they needed (Haggerty and Rasmussen, 1994, p. 10).

Ten years later, many of the same attitudes and beliefs exist about the value of business journalism. A survey conducted in the year 2000 by Selzer & Company for the Reynolds Foundation and the American Press Institute concluded that the nation's business leaders were unimpressed with the quality of business reporting in most daily newspapers and described business journalists as lacking a basic understanding of how businesses operate. "They don't ask questions that probe below the surface and so their reports do not convey the detailed information business leaders need," said the report (Selzer & Co., 2000, p. 2).

The survey also found that when newsroom executives rated five beats, business desk reporters earned the lowest ratings, and business was a low priority for resources in the newsroom, even though a number of solid—even brilliant—stories in business journalism have helped readers understand complex issues and warned them of future problems.

Why is business journalism held in such low esteem, given that the quality of stories and the content in business coverage has improved overall and is more objective than it was 50 years ago? Part of the problem is perception. Business stories are considered by many to be staid and unwieldy, with too many numbers and complicated topics to be of any interest to the average reader. Business is too often covered for managers and executives in business and not enough for the worker.

Business writing can—and should—be interesting to the masses, and it should be some of the best journalism today in newspapers and magazines, and on television. Virtually every person in the country spends time each day thinking about how much money they make, whether they have job security, or whether they should be looking for a new job. They want to know if now is the time to refinance a home mortgage, or whether the CEO of the company where they work is considering selling the business. They want to know which companies are in financial trouble so they do not invest in their stocks. And they want to know which businesses might be good places to work.

Simply put, they want better business coverage. That's what this book will help you do.

Understand and Analyze

TIPS FROM THE PROS

Quartz reporter Melvin Backman advises newcomers to business journalism:

Don't be afraid to go through the front door. A lot of journalists are adversarial by instinct. That can get you good stories, but it won't get you every story. Using PR folks to gain access to key executives can help you learn more about the companies you cover than you can on your own with a lot less work. That's not to say such a relationship doesn't come with constraints, but it has its uses.

The most important thing for business journalists around the world to do is to understand what they are writing about. A former business editor at a large metropolitan newspaper recoils at remembering his first story as a professional writer 15 years earlier, when he confused revenue with net income. That mistake, if it had not been caught by a careful editor, would have called into question the facts throughout that story and the entire business section.

But, as we've seen, mass communication outlets have never placed much emphasis on training and teaching their business reporters and editors the ins and outs of the business world. It is not just reporters on the business desk, unfortunately, who need this understanding of business topics and concepts. Reporters throughout every section of every newspaper magazine, Internet news site and television news station will eventually come across a story that involves money or business in some fashion. Without the knowledge to cover the story adequately, they will be doing a disservice to their audiences.

And it's not just the journalists. Public relations professionals also often do not understand many of the concepts and ideas that they are writing about in press releases for companies. They, too, have not gone to school to learn how to read a balance sheet or analyze an executive's compensation package.

There is so much for business journalists to learn to be effective reporters. They need to know how to report and write about the economy, government regulation and taxes affecting businesses. They need to understand how businesses operate and why some businesses make money, whereas others lose money. They need to know the role of executives and other managers inside a company and that some businesses do not exist to make money but to serve the community.

In addition, many reporters simply regurgitate what they have been told or have read regarding a business topic without questioning the validity of the meaning or fully understanding what they are writing about. And that can lead to problems for both the reporter and the reader or listener. As we have seen in numerous surveys, business executives and other readers can easily tell by reading a story when a reporter does not fully understand what he or she is writing. That should not be the case. True, newsrooms are places where deadline pressure prohibits reporters from spending a day or two researching a topic until they feel comfortable writing about it. But that is when an editor with the relevant knowledge should take the time and care to guide the reporter along, imparting his or her wisdom.

TIPS FROM THE PROS

 Quartz reporter Melvin Backman advises newcomers to business journalism:

Be nimble. Corporations are people, or at least they're made of them, and people are fallible. They'll make mistakes, turn things around, hide things that eventually come to light, and a million other actions. In that light, every trick and tip you're given will likely fail you at some point. Develop the ability to act in the moment when reporting and stay ethical while doing so.

Knowledge and understanding of business topics is vital not just for reporters, but for their editors as well. Reporters who cover county or city government have a basic understanding of how governments operate from their high school and college political science classes. And many sports reporters have spent countless hours as youths watching and playing the games that they now write stories about.

Yet few business reporters and editors ever took a class or majored in business to obtain the knowledge that they needed to do their job. "Nobody would send someone to cover the Red Sox who doesn't know what a shortstop is," said *New York Times* business columnist Floyd Norris at the 2003 SABEW annual conference. Yet "many people send reporters to cover business who are not real [*sic*] sure what earnings per share means" (Nelson, 2003, p. 6).

Business journalism has made great strides and has made the world a better place to live but still falls short of being as good as it can be. But small changes are occurring in business journalism. More editors and reporters have realized that they need more and better training to do their jobs.

Those interested in the quality of business journalism are taking steps to improve it. In 2008, the Reynolds Foundation gave a $5 million grant to Arizona State University to expand training programs offered by the Donald W. Reynolds National Center for Journalism. It also gave money to hire journalism professors focused on teaching business reporting at the University of Missouri and the University of Nevada–Reno. On college campuses across the country, more journalism schools are teaching business and economics reporting classes than ever before, giving students some basic training and understanding. Most importantly, however, there appears to be a newfound diligence on the part of newspapers, magazines, websites and television stations to be more critical in their business coverage.

Peter Carlson, who critiques magazines for the *Washington Post,* lauded this change of heart recently after reading two important articles: one in *Fortune* that exposed white-collar crime and another in *Business 2.0* that skewered American business. "Business magazines have turned into pit bulls, printing stories excoriating these once-deified entrepreneurs as crooked, mendacious, rapacious robber barons," wrote Carlson. "To tell you the truth, I much prefer these new stories," he added. "They're a lot more fun—and probably a lot more accurate, too" (Carlson, 2002, p. C4).

Harder, tougher, more thorough business reporting done by reporters who have been properly trained and who better understand what they are writing about will dramatically raise the quality of stories and topics discussed in mass communication today.

Many consider the 1990s a golden age for business journalism, a time in which coverage expanded dramatically and more stories were written. Others would argue that business journalism has yet to reach its peak. Quality reporting and editing is needed now more than ever, as more and more consumers cope with job losses and harder-to-find investment ideas. Business journalism has helped them in the past, but not as much as it could have.

"It is time for business journalists to be more ambitious," said Martin Baron, now editor of the *Washington Post,* "to set their sights higher, to routinely produce the finest journalism in America" (Baron, 2001).

The readers need and want better business journalism.

Notes

1. "Results of survey by Talking Biz News and SABEW are optimistic for business journalists," by Meg Garner. www.sabew.org/. Retrieved December 21, 2015.
2. www.bls.gov/oes/current/oes273022.htm. Retrieved December 21, 2015.

Suggested Exercises

1. Write a 500-word essay explaining how business has affected your life, from the products and services you purchase to where your parents work. How would your life be different without one or two of those businesses being in operation?

2. Review a newspaper's business section for a week. Bring in the sections and discuss with the class what stories you thought were informative and what stories you did not understand. What helped you understand the stories? What was hard to decipher?

3. With the rest of the class, discuss the relationship between a CEO and a business reporter. Should a CEO attempt to help educate a reporter that he or she sees is struggling with a topic?

4. In a group discussion, talk about the qualifications for being a business reporter or editor. What skills should they have? What should they know about how business and the economy operate? Where should they obtain that knowledge?

5. Write a one-page paper about what you have learned about the economy based on coverage you have read of the recent recession. Focus on economic concepts that you previously did not understand as well as personal finance strategies.

 Business Journalism Books

Dealy, F.X. (1993). *The power and the money: Inside the Wall Street Journal.* New York: Birch Lane Press.

Emery, E., & Emery, M. (1984). *The press and America.* Englewood Cliffs, NJ: Prentice Hall.

Quirt, J. (1993). *The press and the world of money.* Byron, CA: Anton/California-Courier.

Reed, R., & Lewin, G. (2005). *Covering business: A guide to aggressively reporting on commerce and developing a powerful business beat.* Oak Park, IL: Marion Street Press.

Rosenberg, J.M. (1982). *Inside the Wall Street Journal: The history and the power of Dow Jones and Company and America's most influential newspaper.* New York: MacMillan.

Roush, C. (2006). *Profits and losses: Business journalism and its role in society.* Oak Park, IL: Marion Street Press.

Scharff, E. (1982). *Worldly power: The making of the Wall Street Journal.* New York: Beaufort Books.

Taparia, J. (2003). *Understanding financial statements: A journalist's guide.* Oak Park, IL: Marion Street Press.

Thompson, T. (ed.) (2000). *Writing about business: The new Columbia Knight-Bagehot guide to economics and business journalism.* New York: Columbia University Press.

References

Barnhart, B. (2002, January). Downturn brings out the critics. *The Business Journalist*, p. 8.

Baron, M. (2001, October 15). Business journalism: Is the boom over? Speech to the Society of American Business Editors and Writers. Retrieved September 1, 2002 from www.sabew.org.

Caldwell, C. (1996, Fall). Trading places. *Forbes Media Critic*, Vol. 3, No. 4, pp. 80–86.

Carlson, P. (2002, March 26). Post-Enron, a reversal of fortune. *The Washington Post*, p. C4.

Fost, D. (2002, March 3). Stung by Enron, business journalists increase their vigilance. *San Francisco Chronicle*, p. Gl.

Haggerty, M., & Rasmussen, W. (1994). *The headline vs the bottom line: Mutual distrust between business and the news media*. Nashville, TN: Freedom Forum First Amendment Center, pp. 1–92.

Kann, P. (2000, March 14). Peter Kann talks about Barney Kilgore. *Princeton Packet*, p. 1.

Layton, C. (2003, March). Ignoring the alarm. *American Journalism Review*, Vol. 24, No. 2, pp. 21–28.

Ledbetter, J. (2003, January 2). The boys in the bubble. *New York Times*, p. A17.

Lewis Harris Poll. (1992). *The quality of business journalism in America*. [Brochure]. Boston: John Hancock Financial Services.

Ludwig, M. (2002, Spring/Summer). Business journalists need specialized finance training. *Newspaper Research Journal*, Vol. 23, No. 213, pp. 129–141.

Madrick, J. (2003, Winter). Financial reporting: Lessons of the Enron collapse. *The Harvard International Journal of Press/Politics*, Vol. 8, No. 1, pp. 3–7.

Nelson, D. (2003, July). It's a question of ethics. *The Business Journalist*, p. 6.

North, G. (2002, February 6). Enron, spawn of business journalism. LewRockwell.com. Retrieved December 11, 2002 from www.lewrockwell.com/north.

Pummer, C. (2002, August 29). How business media is failing its audience. CBS.MarketWatch.com. Retrieved September 1, 2002 from www.cbs.marketwatch.com/news.

Salpukas, A. (1999, June 27). Firing up an idea machine. *New York Times*, p. Cl.

Selzer & Co. (2000). *Business journalism surveys*. Reston, VA: American Press Institute.

Smith, T. (2002, February 19). Asleep at the switch. *News Hour with Jim Lehrer*. Retrieved November 25, 2003 from www.pbs.org/newshour.

2

SOME BUSINESS JOURNALISM BASICS

Defining Public and Private Companies

Read the business section of almost any major metropolitan newspaper, and you will find that most of the stories are written about large companies with stock traded on an exchange in New York.

One day, a typical front page of the business section of the *News & Observer* in Raleigh, NC, could feature an article on Bank of America, the Charlotte-based public bank. Inside the section would be articles about defense contractor Northrop Grumman and phone company Sprint, also public companies. All of these stories mention how big these companies are in terms of revenue or profits.

But read the business section of a paper in a smaller town or city, and the stories will likely be about small private companies that are not required to disclose information about their operations. For example, the front page of the business section of the *Huntsville Times* (Alabama) one day contained a story about Alterations & More, a one-woman alteration and sewing business. As a private company, this business was not required to disclose its revenue and profits. The reporter likely never even asked for them.

The dichotomy is evident. A public company sells stock to the public, and its stock is traded on an exchange. Because of this, the public company is required to file information with the Securities and Exchange Commission (SEC), making it easy for business reporters to obtain facts for their stories.

Securities and Exchange Commission (SEC): A federal agency that protects investors and ensures the integrity of the stock markets. The SEC regulates publicly traded companies, companies who trade stocks and investors. As part of its mission to protect investors and the investment community, the SEC requires public companies to file documents disclosing financial information and other material so that it can be read by anyone.

Private companies, for the most part, are not required to file such information. (You will learn later in the book where to find financial information about some private companies.) As such, reporters have access to few financial numbers to flesh out a story on a private company unless the company willingly discloses its performance. Still, it is valuable to learn how to read and dissect the financial information available on public companies. Public and private companies operate similarly. They are both in business to make money, and a CEO typically runs both.

There are advantages and disadvantages to both structures. Public companies are more easily able to raise cash to expand. However, they are also required to disclose their financial performance every three months. That can be a disadvantage, particularly after a bad quarter. In contrast, private companies often have a harder time raising the money to expand, which is a problem if they need to expand quickly to take advantage of a business opportunity. But if they have a bad quarter, few people know. That can be an advantage, particularly in businesses in which perception is important.

Bill Smartt, a former executive vice president and chief financial officer (CFO) at DHL Airways, a California-based airfreight carrier, said that private ownership allowed the company to maintain a low profile. If it had to file information with the SEC as a public company, competitors like Federal Express could analyze those facts and gain a competitive advantage. In the end, though, public and private companies are similar in how they measure success—that is, by increased sales or revenues and improved profits. Unfortunately, these are concepts that many inexperienced business reporters confuse.

This chapter explores some basic concepts that every business reporter and editor should know, beginning with how the business journalist does his or her job. Business reporting and editing is just like any other beat at a newspaper, a television or radio station, or even an Internet site. It requires knowledge of who the best sources are and where to find documents that will answer questions and provide the details to make great stories.

TIPS FROM THE PROS

Milwaukee Business Journal reporter Olivia Barrow on how she got started in business reporting:

Write for your mother. Conventional wisdom says you should write for an 8th-grade reading level, but I have a hard time remembering what I read in 8th grade. But I know that my mother, who has a master's degree in electrical engineering and has educated six kids from kindergarten to high school graduation, still zones out and loses interest in news stories if it's not abundantly clear within the first few paragraphs what the story is about, and why she should care. Even when my mom lives five states away from the local news outlet I work for, it's still possible to tell a business story in a way that captivates her interest by focusing on the human elements, or the transformation storyline, or illuminating trends that could hit her region.

Business reporting also requires knowing something about how business operates, much like the school reporter needs to know how the school board works and when it meets. Businesses have a reputation of being tight-lipped and unwilling to provide information. Knowing when they are required to provide information can give reporters an edge. Sources such as company executives will be more willing to talk when they see the reporter as a knowledgeable person.

public company: A business whose ownership includes stockholders that have purchased shares on Wall Street.

Sometimes, the worlds of public and private companies overlap, and not just for the business reporter. The CEO of a public company may also own private businesses that could be affected by the performance of the public corporation. When regulators went after former HealthSouth CEO Richard Scrushy for allegedly inflating earnings at the medical rehabilitation company, they sought to freeze the assets at his private businesses, too.

In another example, the owner of the Carolina Hurricanes hockey team was asked questions during a conference call about whether his public company (Compuware) was for sale and, if so, how that might affect his ownership of the privately held hockey business:

> Days after shutting down part of his youth hockey operation, Carolina Hurricanes owner Peter Karmanos said he had been approached about

selling part of his software company, Compuware. Karmanos confirmed he had spoken with other companies about a sale but had no interest in breaking up Compuware.

"The company is not up for sale, and divisions of the company are not up for sale," Karmanos said in a conference call with analysts Wednesday to discuss Compuware's fourth-quarter earnings. "Some people have inquired. That's about it. All kinds of people inquire. . . . There's no active discussion going on at this point in time." The Dow Jones news service reported that BMC Software and Texas Pacific Group were potential buyers for part of Compuware.

Over the past 3½ years, Karmanos has seen his net worth take a beating as Compuware's stock has plummeted. According to SEC filings, Karmanos owns 15.7 million shares of Compuware, worth about $75 million. Compuware is valued at about $1.8 billion.

Karmanos founded Compuware with two friends in 1973. Long a supporter of youth hockey in his hometown of Detroit, he purchased the Hartford Whalers NHL franchise in 1994 and moved the team to North Carolina to become the Hurricanes in 1997.[1]

Public and private companies interact with each other on a daily basis. Public companies sell their products and services to private companies, and vice versa. In many ways, the success of public companies and private companies are intertwined. If there is a business relationship, a company will want its business partner to succeed. If the business that a company is working with does not succeed, then it may not be able to pay its bills, which could hurt the company. And both types of companies are vitally important to the U.S. economy. There are many more private companies than there are public companies. Think of all of the small businesses in a community, whether they are one-person shops or factories with 1,000 workers. Virtually all of them are private companies.

But think about the companies providing products you may buy the most: shoes from Nike, clothes from the Gap, drinks from Coca-Cola, computers from Dell, software from Microsoft, cars from General Motors, a home from D.R. Horton, gasoline from Chevron. All of these companies are public companies with stock that is traded by investors every day.

How Public Companies Disclose Information

Most medium- and large-sized newspapers focus their business coverage on public companies. Internet news sites, such as MarketWatch.com and TheStreet.com, and television stations also focus on public companies. Newspapers in major metropolitan areas, such as New York and Washington, spend the bulk of their coverage on public businesses. The reason behind this is simple: For the reporters and editors, there is more information available with which to write stories about public companies than there is about private companies.

Public companies are required by law to disclose information. Many times, it is information that executives may not want to disclose. Most private companies are under no such restrictions.

As mentioned earlier, public companies are regulated by the SEC, a federal agency created in 1934 to provide protection for investors against unscrupulous companies who dupe people into buying worthless stock. One of the ways the SEC has gone about its job of protecting investors and maintaining the integrity of the stock markets is by requiring companies with publicly traded stock to provide information that anyone can read. For example, financial performance must be filed every quarter by a certain deadline. Public companies are also required to file documents with the SEC to disclose important events, such as mergers, acquisitions, or changes in auditors. In addition, the SEC regulates other parties involved in the investment industry, including companies who buy and sell stocks and mutual funds, like large money management companies who pool stock purchases into funds to limit the risk for investors. These companies are also required to disclose information to the public.

TIPS FROM THE PROS

 Milwaukee Business Journal reporter Olivia Barrow on how she got started in business reporting:

Ask good questions. Good writing is a by-product of good reporting, and good reporting means asking the right questions of the right people. And the right questions aren't usually the ones that make a source sit back with a chuckle and say, "Hmm, what a great question!" In my experience, that response usually precedes a completely useless, canned answer because the subject is out of their depth or unprepared to think of personal examples about their most embarrassing moment, or whatever the question may be. Good questions stay within the realm of the source's expertise, and should be easy for them to answer. Good questions sometimes make your source uncomfortable for reasons of emotion or privacy, but if you've developed a good rapport, you can break through that discomfort and get to the best responses. Good questions guide your understanding of the subject matter from broad overarching storyline into narrow, specific details that you can use to craft a focused story.

Although these filings are intended for investors to decide whether they want to put their money in the company's stock, the documents are available for anyone to read on the SEC's website at www.sec.gov. Increasingly, companies provide access to their SEC filings on their websites as well. These documents, detailed in later chapters, can be invaluable sources of information for reporters writing stories about companies and other business topics. They are often filled with interesting revelations, such as information about lawsuits and severance packages for departing executives, both of which companies are required to detail.

If the SEC believes, on the basis of the filings, that a company or someone has violated its rules, it will investigate. Often, the SEC will levy fines or set restrictions on the future involvement of that business or person in public companies or trading stocks. The staff of the SEC—overseen by five commissioners who are appointed by the president—writes rules when it determines that new regulations are needed. Once a rule is proposed, the SEC invites companies and others to comment on the proposal. These comments are available for review by any reporter and can often make for an interesting story, particularly if companies are opposed to the new regulations.

One of the most important rules—at least for reporters writing stories about public companies—passed by the SEC is Regulation Fair Disclosure (FD), which went into effect in 2000. Regulation FD requires public companies to provide information to every investor at the same time. This has resulted in companies providing access to discussions their managements have with investors and analysts by telephone or Internet and to more SEC filings. Reporters can listen to these earnings conference calls, attend presentations at investor conferences, and read the filings along with everyone else.

Another important SEC regulation provides business reporters with access to the inner workings of a company. Each public corporation is required to hold an annual meeting of its shareholders once a year. The invitation to the meeting is in the form of an SEC filing that is sent to every shareholder of the company, even if they just own one share of stock. In fact, many business journalists or business news departments in the past would purchase one share of stock for each company they covered to make sure they received this invitation.

> **annual meeting:** A meeting held once a year by public companies where shareholders are invited to attend and vote on matters. Company executives typically give presentations about the performance of the company at the meeting and answer questions from shareholders in the audience.

The annual meeting, as it is commonly known, is often held near or at the company's headquarters, but sometimes it may be held at another company location. Large corporations, such as Anheuser-Busch and General Electric, rotate the location of their annual meeting among their various locations. Anheuser-Busch, for example, prefers to hold its meetings at its theme parks and breweries. Although journalists are not specifically invited to annual meetings by law, virtually every public company allows reporters to attend the meetings.

> **proxy statement:** A document sent to shareholders of public companies to invite owners of the company's stock to its annual meeting. The proxy statement will include information about proposals to be voted on at the annual meeting and executive salaries.

At these meetings, the companies discuss some of their business. For example, an auditor may be elected to review the company's books, or new board members may be chosen. Each shareholder can vote on the proposals presented at the annual meeting, even if they do not attend the meeting. Shareholders can also make proposals to be voted on at the annual meeting, so it is important to do some homework before the event. These proposals are detailed in the invitation to the meeting, which is known as the proxy statement. In the proxy statement, the shareholders explain their proposal and why they think it is good for the company. The company usually responds and states whether it supports or opposes the proposal. Such conflict is common between public companies and shareholders, but these proposals often make good stories or serve as examples and anecdotes for a larger trend story. Here is an example of a shareholder proposal in Coca-Cola's (2015) invitation to its shareholders:

> John C. Harrington, President, Harrington Investments, Inc., 1001 2nd Street, Suite 325, Napa, California 94559, owner of 100 shares of Common Stock, submitted the following proposal:
>
> RESOLVED: Shareholders of Coca-Cola ask the board of directors to amend the bylaws to adopt a "proxy access" procedure whereby Coca-Cola shall include in any proxy materials prepared for a shareholder meeting at which directors are to be elected, the name, the Disclosure and the Statement (as defined herein) of any person nominated for election to the board of directors by a shareholder or group thereof (the "Nominator") that meets the criteria appearing below, and Coca-Cola shall allow shareholders to vote on such nominee on Coca-Cola's proxy card. The number of shareholder-nominated candidates in proxy materials shall not exceed one-quarter of the number of directors then serving. This bylaw should provide that a Nominator must:

(a)   have beneficially owned 3% or more of Coca-Cola's outstanding common stock continuously for at least three years before submitting the nomination;

(b)   give Coca-Cola written notice within the time period identified in Coca-Cola's bylaws of information required by the bylaws and rules of the Securities and Exchange Commission about (i) the nominee, including his or her consent to being named in the proxy materials and to serving, if elected; and (ii) the Nominator, including proof of ownership of the required shares (the "Disclosure"); and

(c)   certify that (i) it will assume liability stemming from any legal violation arising out of its communications with (company) shareholders, including the Disclosure and Statement; (ii) it will comply with all applicable laws if it uses soliciting material other than Coca-Cola's proxy materials; and (iii) to the best of its knowledge, the required shares were acquired in the ordinary course of business and not to change or influence control at Coca-Cola.

The Nominator may submit with the Disclosure a statement not exceeding 500 words in support of the nominee (the "Statement"). The board shall adopt procedures for promptly resolving disputes over whether notice of a nomination was timely, whether the Disclosure and Statement satisfy the bylaws and any applicable federal regulations, and the priority to be given to multiple nominations exceeding the one-quarter limit.

Supporting Statement

We advocate enhanced Board accountability and believe long-term shareholders should have a meaningful voice in nominating directors. The case for proxy access at Coca-Cola is compelling: Over the last decade, the company has been embroiled in numerous controversies alleging degradation in worker safety, the violation of human rights, misleading marketing tactics and worsening water conditions for farmers in many countries, including India and Mexico. Furthermore, proxy access has the potential to enhance board performance with little cost or disruption to companies.

By ignoring these issues, the Board has failed to insulate the company from regulatory pressure and reputational risks.

After reading this proposal in Coca-Cola's filing, a reporter might feel there is a story to be written examining the company's executive team. Or a reporter could use the proposal to examine the company's practice of hiring executives.

Annual meetings are also good for reporters to attend because the CEO and other executives will often make a presentation about the company's past performance and future direction and take questions from those in attendance. If the company is small, there might not be many shareholders in the audience and the reporter might be able to ask a lot of questions, getting more candid answers from executives than if the reporter had tried calling or going through the company's public relations staff. Other companies will set aside time after the annual meeting for its executives to meet with the media. These meetings can be valuable for a reporter to attend. The more time a reporter can show his or her face to an executive and demonstrate that s/he is interested in learning about a company and its operations, the more likely the CEO or president will answer questions the next time that reporter calls by phone.

Questions asked by the shareholders at the meeting can also elicit story ideas. The question-and-answer period at some large company annual meetings can last for hours. Some shareholders may be angry about a company's poor performance and may ask the CEO and president pointed questions about how they are going to turn it around. Others may want the company to take on an environmental cause. There are even shareholders who attend dozens of annual meetings a year simply to harangue executives and ask for better performance. The most famous of these is Evelyn Y. Davis, a Washington, DC, resident, who writes a newsletter for shareholders and who once told a CEO that he was better looking than his predecessor.

In addition, an annual meeting can often act as a barometer of a company's current standing. If there are many negative questions asked at an annual meeting, likely the business performed better in the past and shareholders would like the corporation to return to that level. If there are few negative questions, the company has likely been performing well financially and with the interest of its shareholders in the fore. Watch the mood of the attendees and the executives to get a feel for where a company is headed and where it has been.

Public companies are a vital part of news for any mass communication outlet, particularly regional or local publications, because many area residents are likely shareholders of the company. Because many companies offer their employees stock ownership plans, the workers are also likely shareholders who would want to know information about the company from an independent source. In Atlanta, for example, thousands of residents own stock in Coca-Cola, and Home Depot has made millionaires out of hundreds of its store employees. The same situation exists across the country in the Seattle area, where Microsoft's stock has made many people—in addition to Bill Gates—rich. Find out which stocks are owned by residents in your circulation or distribution area. Those are likely to be the companies that they will want to read about.

Private Companies Dominate Local Economies

Private companies, on the other hand, are not required to discuss disagreements with their shareholders in public, and they do not hold annual meetings that reporters can attend. Still, private companies are vital to the readers or

TIPS FROM THE PROS

Milwaukee Business Journal reporter Olivia Barrow on how she got started in business reporting:

Find patient sources. Even if you minor in business, you will face assignments or entire beats in business journalism that you have no background in, and your editors will likely only have a surface knowledge. Find sources in the community who are willing to explain the complex parts of accounting, or investing, or estate planning, or the Internet of Things to you on background. You can also go to these people to vet your story ideas. You may think you've stumbled on an alarming scandal, but you're 10 years late to the party, or you just don't understand the inner workings of the industry, and what you discovered is actually the norm. These people are also useful when condensing complex information into a non-jargony statement. I call these sources up and say, "May I read a phrase that I'm using in a story to you to make sure it accurately describes what's going on?" They may not have been able to articulate something at an 8th-grade level, but when they hear me read it back to them, they can point out any oversimplifications I've done and save me from a fact error.

viewers of any mass communication outlet that reports on business news. The largest private companies in the country include businesses such as accounting firms PricewaterhouseCoopers and Ernst & Young, candy maker Mars, and grocery store chain Publix Super Markets—all businesses that have touched our lives in one way or another. These are multibillion-dollar corporations equal or larger in size to many of their public competitors.

In fact, there are more than 440 private companies in the United States with more than $1 billion in annual revenue. According to *Forbes* magazine, these companies have more than 6.1 million employees combined and contribute more than $1.8 trillion in products and services to the country's economy.

Think again about the businesses that are part of your everyday life, such as the corner gas station, the local bank branch, or the restaurant downtown where you might eat dinner tonight. Chances are these businesses are privately held enterprises owned by maybe just one person or a handful of investors with no intention to ever sell shares of stock to the public. For every public company, there are likely to be dozens of private competitors. These companies, especially in small- and medium-sized towns and cities, could be the largest employers in the area. Many local hospitals are privately owned, as are factories and manufacturers. Yet despite their status as private companies, they can still make for compelling stories that readers and viewers will want to know about.

However, there is more work involved in finding information about private companies. In fact, many business journalism experts believe that it is easier to write stories about public companies because much of the information needed to explain a company and its strategy is available in SEC documents. Thus, a reporter can earn his or her stripes as a top-notch business journalist by writing a story about a private company because the information is much harder to find, and company executives may not want the exposure.

private company: A business whose ownership is confined to a handful of people, or whose ownership cannot be traded on a stock exchange.

There is still a lot of information to be found in public documents about private companies. It just may not necessarily be with the SEC, although there are many private businesses that do have to file documents with the federal regulatory agency. For example, private companies that have issued bonds to investors will file documents with the SEC although they are still considered private businesses. But there are plenty of other places to get information about private enterprises. All businesses have to incorporate themselves with the state in which they are operating. This is typically done with the secretary of state's office or a regulatory entity such as the State Corporation Commission, as it is called in Virginia. Documents filed with these entities will often tell a reporter who owns the business, who the executives are and where it is located.

Other state regulatory agencies also have plenty of information about private companies. Most businesses, from barbershops to banks, are regulated in some form or another by a state agency. Many of these state agencies will have information about the business's performance in their files. Federal agencies, such as the Occupational Safety and Health Administration (OSHA) within the U.S. Department of Labor, and the Federal Trade Commission (FTC), also have jurisdiction over thousands of private companies. They are worthy places to look for information if you are writing about a business with stock that is not publicly traded.

Although most small private businesses are owned by only one or two people, other private companies have solicited investors, just not in the same way that public companies sell stock to investors. Many private businesses seeking capital to expand will go to investment firms that specifically invest in small operations. These firms provide what is typically known as venture capital funding.

Venture capital firms give private companies money—sometimes millions of dollars—to expand their operations. In return, the owners of the private company give the venture capital operation an ownership stake in their business. The venture capital executives may want to have a say in how the company operates after they invest money. But they are hoping that the business will take their money and put it to good use, expanding their operations in a prudent manner and creating additional profits, making the private business more valuable. Often, a venture capital firm will sit on its investment in a private company for five to seven years and then sell it to another investor or sell its stake in the company to public investors in an initial public offering (IPO), making the private company a public operation.

TIPS FROM THE PROS

Milwaukee Business Journal reporter Olivia Barrow on how she got started in business reporting:

Find a way to network that fits your personality style. Reporting is all about developing relationships with key people in your industry. Large networking events can provide access to a lot of important people at once, but they can also be completely overwhelming and unproductive. I find that one-on-one connections developed from LinkedIn, referrals from other meetings and cold calls to small companies who haven't been covered in the media much are sometimes the best ways to develop sources. But don't pressure yourself to build your network in a way that only stresses you out unnecessarily.

In the 1990s, dozens and dozens of venture capital firms poured billions of dollars into private businesses in the hopes that the money would provide huge investment returns. Much of that money went into Internet, technology and telecommunications companies. However, because many of these companies went out of business, leaving venture capital investors with nothing in return, such investments are now done with closer scrutiny.

Below is a story from the *Kansas City Star* that explains the process many private companies in the Midwest went through to try to entice venture capital firms to invest money into their companies:

Money doesn't grow on trees the way it used to.

Venture capitalists have long since stopped scribbling out checks to companies they've just met. And in many instances they've stopped writing checks altogether.

According to a quarterly survey of venture capital investment by PricewaterhouseCoopers, only $3.8 billion in venture capital was invested in the first quarter. That's a five-year low, and a far cry from the $28.6 billion invested in the first quarter of 2000.

But those facts didn't seem to dampen the enthusiasm of the 20 companies on stage Thursday morning at InvestMidwest, a venture capital forum in Kansas City designed to link high-growth companies with investors.

The fourth annual event, which alternates between Kansas City and St. Louis, drew representatives from more than 30 venture capital firms. Companies from throughout the Midwest got 10 minutes each to introduce themselves and explain why they were looking for venture financing.

"If we would have had this venture conference last year in Kansas City, it would have been voices in the wilderness," said Abel Mojica, a partner with Kansas City Equity Partners. "No one would have been here to listen."

But Thursday morning, sitting around tables in a hotel ballroom at the Hyatt Regency Crown Center hotel, investors were listening—even if their pens weren't poised over blank checks.

"For three years they've hunkered down and covered their heads up and said, 'We're just going to cover ourselves,' " said David Lazenby of ScenarioNow Inc., a St. Louis technology company.

After making his presentation to investors, Lazenby said he was confident the situation was finally beginning to turn. Money has been piling up, he said, and investors are starting to uncover their heads.

Thomas Marshall, a partner with Hickory Venture Capital in Huntsville, Ala., said his firm was still very cautious and, like many venture firms, was likely to continue to be much more wary of risky early-stage investments.

His firm wants potential investments to already have at least $1 million in revenue. Not exactly early stage.

Doug Elliott, a partner with Duff & Phelps Capital Partners in Chicago, said venture firms had learned from the past two years. They're looking for better deals—a bigger ownership stake for their investments—which is easier to come by in lean times.

Of course, investors are also looking for the next big success story.[2]

Venture capital meetings are great places to meet owners of small, local, private businesses and to get a feel for the companies. At these meetings, private companies are essentially trying to sell their business to investors, much the same way a public company does when it sells stock to the public. If a private company gets an investment from a venture capital firm, it can be a story for the business reporter. What will the company do with the money? How much of an ownership stake are the venture capital investors receiving in return?

Ownership in private companies can come in all shapes and sizes. Private companies also often offer shares to their employees, just like many public companies do. One person can control ownership in a private company, such as an insurance agency or a barbershop. These owners can be valuable resources for stories—besides those about their companies. As business owners, they are often cognizant of the economy and make decisions on a daily basis such as whether they should spend money to expand or hold back until times get better. If a business reporter is writing a story about economic conditions in his or her community, private business owners can give the best interviews.

In addition, private business owners often band together in groups such as the local chamber of commerce. The business reporter should attend their functions and get to know them; one never knows when those contacts will come in handy. As mentioned earlier, private businesses far outnumber public companies in every community. The reporter should find out what these private businesses are and how they are doing, and he will likely get a better picture of the area than he would by talking to executives at a public company, which may only have a local subsidiary run by a manager who reports to higher-ups in another state or country.

Writing Business-Related Stories

Writing business stories appears daunting at first. They are filled with numbers and use terms, such as adjustable-rate mortgage or off-balance sheet financing, that the average reader may not understand. And then there is the whole idea of whom a business reporter must interview to get the information to write a story. CEOs and presidents of large corporations are busy people and sometimes appear curt in responding to questions because they have other topics on their mind—like running their company. Other sources in the business world are also difficult to reach and even harder to interview. Many of them do not have to talk to a reporter; it is not part of their job description. However, a reporter should not get discouraged. These people started out with limited knowledge of the business world as well. With a little experience and some training, the reporter will be able to talk like an expert with these sources, opening them up, and will begin writing stories that read as if the writer knows more about the copper tubing industry than the company executive does.

TIPS FROM THE PROS

Milwaukee Business Journal reporter Olivia Barrow on how she got started in business reporting:

Meet the decision makers. You only have a limited amount of time to develop your source network, so make it count. Don't settle for talking to a mid-level management person you met at an event; use that meeting to get you an audience with the CEO.

Business stories can come from a number of different places. Some of the best business stories are developed in a reporter or editor's mind by watching trends and understanding economic numbers or by tracking a company for months or years at a time. Great business stories are not always readily apparent. They can take time to report and write. The bulk of business stories written today come from basic sources, such as company news releases or releases from regulatory agencies. Stories can also come from regulatory filings made by companies or from lawsuits or other documents filed in a courthouse.

Stories can come from source tips provided by union officials or from people who overheard a conversation. Business stories can also come from attending meetings such as zoning or planning commissions. Reporters should be knowledgeable enough about their beats to write stories that show the audience that they know what they are discussing.

Understanding what a company or regulatory agency is saying in a release is part of the job. Sometimes, the hardest part is translating the release into a story that the average reader can understand. The problem with news releases is that they are sometimes written or approved by lawyers, so the language may not be clear. Or the release can be written in such a way as to downplay or hide the actual news. A company could issue a release announcing its quarterly dividend of 20 cents per share. But what the release does not state is that the dividend has been reduced from the 40 cents per share the company was paying its shareholders in previous quarters. Or a company could announce a new advertising campaign for its major product without disclosing that its commercials from last year were a total flop and the company slogan has been changed. It is important, therefore, for any writer to research the topic he is writing about. Even the most mundane and basic announcements could have a hidden news peg just waiting to be found.

Using numbers effectively and correctly in business-related stories is also key to making your writing understandable to readers and viewers. Make sure that numbers are used sparingly in most cases. Numbers can bog down a story and disinterest the reader. If a story, such as one about a company's earnings, requires a lot of numbers, make sure the numbers are spread out. Do not put revenue and earnings numbers in the same paragraph. Make sure to explain why the numbers rose and fell. Behind every number is a story.

Numbers can be tricky in other ways. Make sure you are comparing the right numbers. For example, it is not valid to compare earnings growth from the second quarter with that from the third quarter, but it is valid to compare earnings from the third quarter of one year with those of the third quarter from the previous year. Quarterly earnings can fluctuate for a variety of reasons. For example, Coca-Cola's revenues and earnings are stronger in the second and third quarters of a year because that is when the weather is hottest and consumers want to quench their thirst. It would not be meaningful to compare the company's earnings in the warm second quarter with earnings in the chilly first quarter, but a reporter could compare earnings at the second quarter of this year with those of last year.

TIPS FROM THE PROS

Milwaukee Business Journal reporter Olivia Barrow on how she got started in business reporting:

Make connections outside of your main beat. While meeting CEOs is still your priority, if you have the time, don't write off people who don't seem like an obvious source at first. If you ask the right questions, you can almost always find a way that both of you can help each other. Sometimes your best source is someone who used to work at Tech Company X and now owns a wine bar in retirement, but she still keeps up with the inner workings of the company. And younger sources can be useful as well, even though they are rarely in decision-making positions. If they're ambitious, they'll keep their ears [open] about what's happening in their company or industry, and they can provide much-needed insight.

Providing context for a number is an absolute necessity in business reporting. When writing a story about the number of newly unemployed workers in the country during a month, you must tell the reader the previous month's number so that they can determine whether and by how much the number is rising or falling.

Follow the money. How is the money being spent? Where is the money coming from? Who decides how the money gets spent? The business reporter who answers these questions will write a compelling story that will help explain an issue to readers. Thus, knowledge of key business terms is also critical. A reporter who does not know the difference between revenue and earnings should look the terms up. Misusing business terms can cost the media outlet, the reporter and the entire journalism community credibility.

Above all, a journalist taking on the task of reporting and writing a business story should write with as much clarity as possible. Explain in simple words what is going on, avoiding the jargon permeating the corporate world today. Do not write about a "reduction in force." Call it a "layoff" or a "firing."

When a company "agrees to divest certain assets," it's selling a business. Let your reader know what's happening in terms that they can understand.

Terms commonly used by corporations in releases that may need to be explained to average readers include market capitalization, takeover, joint venture, charges, forecasts, stock split, debt, liabilities, strategic alternatives, margins, shortfall and reserves. (We recommend the *SABEW Stylebook* for business journalists needing to know how to define these terms.)

 strategic alternatives: Anything up to and including the sale of a company.

Corporate America can seem daunting. However, virtually every business story comes down to money. Businesses are trying to make more money. The more money they make, the happier their shareholders—public or private— will be. Increased profits send up the stock price of public companies and make a private company more valuable, also increasing the value of a private shareholder's stake. The business world is fascinating. There are con artists and there are people trying to make the world a better place to live. The job is to write about both in a way that will attract the widest audience possible.

Labor and Consumer Issues

When writing business stories, the reporter should think about the impact the topic of the story is going to have on readers or viewers. Is the story about a large local company that has lost money? That could mean that the business might have to lay off some of its workers or that it might even be headed toward bankruptcy court. That is information that its workers and customers will want to know. Is a local company adding new jobs to its plant? That could mean more jobs for the community, improving the area's unemployment rate and boosting the economy by adding more workers to the area who have money to spend on groceries, housing and other goods and services. That is also information that people will want to read about.

All too often, business journalism forgets about the worker and the consumer. Yet, arguably, these two constituents are the most vital to writing about business and the economy. Without workers, companies would not have the ability to produce and sell their products and services, and without consumers going into stores every day, these companies would not have anyone to sell their goods and services to. The best business writers do not lose sight of this important fact. They write stories for the employees and consumers of a company, making sure readers understand the ramifications.

Merger and acquisition stories are not just about Company A purchasing Company B. In virtually every case, they are also stories about employees losing jobs as the two companies merge operations and no longer need two secretaries for the CEO—or two CEOs for that matter. A product recall story is not just about the millions of dollars an automaker will have to spend to fix a defective seat belt on its latest model. It is also a story about the consumers who purchased that car and were injured or killed when the seat belt did not properly protect them in an accident. Stories about store closings are not just about going-out-of-business sales. They are about competition, the workers who are losing their jobs, or the external forces that have caused a business's decline. The beginning of this story from the *Door County Advocate* in Sturgeon Bay, Wisconsin, is a classic example:

> The ailments of the aging Michigan Street bridge probably are the biggest reason Sturgeon Bay is losing a grocery store.
>
> Nick Swinarski said he hates to beat a dead horse but in this case, he can't help it. After 10 years of owning Nick's SuperValu in downtown Sturgeon Bay, Swinarski is bowing to the pressures of the long and frequent bridge closings.
>
> The bridge problems are the primary reason he and his wife, Cindy, are closing their Third Avenue grocery store.
>
> While it may be difficult for most residents to assign a dollar value to the inconvenience caused by the Michigan Avenue bridge closings, it's not difficult for business owners like Swinarski. Each time the bridge closed, Nick's SuperValu recorded a 35 percent drop in sales.
>
> Over the past three years, Swinarski was forced to slash his peak workforce of 40 to the 18 employees who currently work for him. The job cuts were directly attributable to eroding sales and decreased profits, a downward trend like a kind of snowball effect that all started when traffic flow across the bay was interrupted due to bridge repairs.

The story goes on to explain how many times the bridge has been closed by repairs, how many grocery stores will remain in the town—a vital piece of information for downtown grocery shoppers in Sturgeon Bay—and how Swinarski tried to sell his store but could not find any takers.

The best business writers think of what they would want to know if they were a consumer or an employee when they write such stories. The reporters who covered the Firestone tire recall pointed out how people could go out to their driveways and read the writing on their tires to determine if they had come from one of the factories that had been producing faulty tires. They explained this because they thought of their audience. Many reporters try to think of relatives, like their parents or grandparents, and write their stories on the basis of information they know those people would understand.

Business journalism is full of stories that help consumers and workers. Publications call these stories "news you can use" or personal finance reporting. This type of reporting offers advice on how to write resumés or how to go into a job interview prepared for the tough questions. It shows readers what to wear to work and teaches them proper e-mail etiquette. But, it is also much more. Personal finance journalism can run the gamut from picking the correct

TIPS FROM THE PROS

Milwaukee Business Journal reporter Olivia Barrow on how she got started in business reporting:

Make friends with your sources. Don't be afraid to meet sources for a casual drink after work if you felt a real connection to them during an interview. Leave business behind and get to know each other. You may gain a real-life friend, or you may just build a bond that will turn into trusted confidential information in the future. Just be careful that friendship doesn't keep you from being an objective reporter.

stocks in a down market to understanding a life insurance policy. Stories that provide a service to readers are valuable commodities in business journalism, and many publications and websites are devoted solely to this type of reporting. For more on personal finance stories, see Chapter 5.

Business reporters should also think about stories that may not even go in the business section. If a town can maintain its high credit ratings, it can borrow money at a lower rate than other cities and keep its residents' taxes down, as this local news story from the *Herald-Sun* in Durham, NC, explained:

> The city of Durham's financial health is good enough for three national agencies to give it their entire AAA credit rating, a status that allows the city to borrow money at lower interest rates.
>
> In fact, with the help of the ratings and unusually low interest rates, the city recently refinanced roughly $45 million in outstanding debt at 2.505 percent. Before, the city had been paying about 5 percent to 6 percent on the money.
>
> But one firm warned that the city should stop dipping into its savings account to cover operating costs, as it did last year.[3]

debt: An amount of money owed by a person or a company to another person or company.

Business reporters should think about the impact of every story on employees and consumers. An otherwise arcane story about Coca-Cola's earnings falling as a result of rising prices will have more meaning to consumers if the reporter explains that fewer grocery shoppers bought the company's 12-packs after it raised its prices in the last quarter.

Business Journalism Ethics

At one time or another, anyone involved in the reporting, writing, or editing of news will be faced with an ethical dilemma. It is no different in reporting on business and economic topics. In fact, some argue that because everyone who is involved with business reporting is an investor or a consumer of products, everything they do in their daily lives results in ethical questions. Is a reporter covering the beverage industry showing favoritism by drinking Pepsi instead of Coke? Can a reporter who only shops for groceries at Kroger write objectively about the Cincinnati-based company? These questions may seem silly, but they have been raised at business journalism seminars and conferences.

TIPS FROM THE PROS

Milwaukee Business Journal reporter Olivia Barrow on how she got started in business reporting:

Force your editors to coach/mentor you/keep you on track. One of the by-products of the dramatic shift in journalism economics is that editors don't have much time to spend actually editing. They're too busy planning, budgeting and meeting with the publisher to spend much time giving you feedback on your reporting or writing. Your only meaningful feedback could come just once a year during your performance review. But if you track them down in their office and ask pointed questions about your writing and reporting, you can often elicit a useful response.

One of the biggest potential areas of conflict for business journalists is Wall Street. Many business reporters and editors own stock in companies or shares in mutual funds. Should that prevent them from writing or editing stories about investing or stories about companies or industries in which they own stock? There is no clear-cut answer to this question, unfortunately. Media outlets handle it differently, and some handle it on a case-by-case basis. Bloomberg News, for example, allows reporters to write about events involving companies in which they have a financial interest as long as they disclose that interest to their supervisor and state that this interest will not prevent them from covering the topic in an unbiased manner.

The ethical guidelines at Dow Jones, the parent of the *Wall Street Journal* and *Barron's,* are strict. They state that staff members and their families can receive a financial gain "by acting on the basis of information obtained through Dow Jones employment before that information was available to the general public; such information includes hold-for-release material or publishing plans with respect to news, advertising, or other information" (Dow Jones & Co. Code of Conduct, 2015). The company says that its journalists cannot create and disseminate news or other information with a desire to affect the price of any investment.

Recode, a tech news website, goes one step further. It requires each of its editorial staff members to write an ethics statement about their investments that can be clicked on underneath their byline. Co-founder Walt Mossberg, a former *Wall Street Journal* staffer, discloses on his that he will "occasionally take a free t-shirt from these companies" and that he does not own "a single share of stock in any of the companies whose products [he] cover[s]" but that he does have a 401(k) plan.

The trustworthiness of a business reporter and editor is vital. If that trust is violated, the readers and viewers may not believe the next story. Reporters and editors who violate these rules have been fired or have left their jobs under pressure. MarketWatch.com tech columnist Bambi Francisco resigned in 2007 after criticism of her investment in a tech start-up that had clients she had written about. In 2005, former MarketWatch.com co-founder and commentator Thom Calandra settled with the SEC after it was discovered he had failed to disclose that he had held stocks that he had written about in a positive fashion and had sold shortly after publishing the stories. However, CNBC anchor Maria Bartiromo was backed by her network after it was disclosed she had taken a trip on the Citigroup jet in 2007 with one of the company's executives. The network reimbursed the company for the flight.

TIPS FROM THE PROS

Milwaukee Business Journal reporter Olivia Barrow on how she got started in business reporting:

Understand your value. Why do people read your paper? Why do they read your writing specifically? Figure out what you provide that helps your readers do their jobs better. Is it a lead for the business development director of a construction company, who will call the company you wrote about and offer his company's services? Is it insight into the quirky personality of one of your city's top CEOs who happens to be a major philanthropist, and will help your readers develop a rapport in their first meeting with him to ask for money for their nonprofit? If you know who your readers are and what they need from you, your reporting will be more focused and you won't waste time wondering if the press release you just received is worth your coverage.

Many journalism ethics codes, including the one for Dow Jones, the parent of the *Wall Street Journal*, prohibit any of its reporters from shorting stocks. Some publications go so far as to require their reporters and editors to disclose their financial holdings to their bosses. These financial holdings can include stocks, bonds and other securities. Some even require that reporters' spouses and immediate family also disclose investments.

Do such situations always result in an ethical conflict? Not necessarily. For example, when I was a reporter at the *Atlanta Journal-Constitution,* I inherited Southern Co. stock from my grandfather, and I was asked to cover a speech by the company's CEO on downtown redevelopment. I went to my boss and explained the stock ownership, telling the editor that I did not think a speech on downtown development had anything to do with my ownership of stocks. The editor allowed me to cover the speech.

Another ethical issue that many business journalists encounter is when they have obtained information during the writing of a story that they believe will move a company's stock up or down once it is published. Virtually all ethics codes prohibit reporters from acting on information that they obtain in the course of their jobs. However, the temptation can be great. Suppose someone within Microsoft told a reporter for the *Seattle Times* that the software maker would greatly miss analyst earnings projections for the quarter. Such information would likely send the company's stock crashing downward. A reporter could short a large amount of the company's shares and possibly make a profit. But the reporter and the newspaper would lose the trust of readers if the trade were disclosed. Rami Grunbaum, the business editor at the *Seattle Times,* would likely fire this reporter. The Dow Jones ethics code prevents its reporters and editors from trading in the stock of any company mentioned in one of its stories until the third trading day after the article has appeared.

Does stock trading still occur among business staff personnel? Probably. But the stock trading and ownership should be confined to companies and industries outside of the reporter's beat. In some cases, however, some media outlets have made exceptions. For example, professional investors and money managers have been allowed to write columns for online publications and other outlets. Media managers argue that these people provide an insight into stock ownership and trading that journalists cannot offer. In many cases, the stock ownership of the Wall Street pro is disclosed at the end of the column or article. In many cases, the writer will even disclose that he owns a stock in the article itself.

TIPS FROM THE PROS

Milwaukee Business Journal reporter Olivia Barrow on how she got started in business reporting:

Understand how your position impacts your company's bottom line. If you don't know where you fit in in your company's business model, you won't ever be able to innovate and find creative ways to improve your value. This doesn't mean finding out who the biggest advertiser is and buttering them up with fluff stories. This means finding out who the paper's readers are and developing new ways that you as a reporter can help them meet their goals, thereby increasing readership and/or subscriber counts and providing more value to advertisers.

Other ethical situations often arise when a journalist is reporting or writing business stories. For example, imagine you are a reporter interviewing the president of a local grocery store chain, and at the end of the interview, he gives you some loaves of bread, baked fresh from one of the locations, to take home. Do you take them? If you do not take them, do you think the executive would be upset or misunderstand why you are turning him down? Most business publications frown on their reporters and editors accepting anything of value, often defined as anything that is worth more than $25. In many cases, this is done to allow a public relations person or another source to buy a reporter lunch. But most media outlets would like their reporters to repay the favor the next time the staffer has lunch with the source.

Nothing should be accepted in return for coverage. A personal finance writer should not accept an offer to refinance her mortgage at a lower rate by a banker she is interviewing for a story. The situation can arise with even the most innocuous of stories. An executive at the advertising agency that handles the famous Aflac duck commercials once offered to let a reporter pick the next Aflac trivia question for a televised sporting event. Was the request just an honest, friendly gesture? Perhaps, but the reporter turned down the offer, not wanting anyone to think his coverage of the ad campaign had been tainted. In addition, companies will often send their products and promotional material to business desks along with news releases. In many cases, the material can be worth well more than $25. For example, when it announced its huge Pepsi Stuff promotion in which consumers could win everything from T-shirts to leather jackets several years ago, PepsiCo sent huge boxes of the material to dozens of newsrooms. Many reporters promptly shipped the goods back, while others donated the clothing to charity.

A journalist's interviewing and reporting tactics can often raise problems as well. In possibly the most famous case of an ethical transgression in business journalism, a reporter for the *Cincinnati Enquirer* was fired after spending a year reporting and writing a huge series of stories on Chiquita Brands International Inc. The reporter had illegally broken into the company's voice mail system.

Business publications should not allow their reporters and editors to break the law when trying to find news. Many of them do not allow their staff members to hide their identities or lie when obtaining news. "Our journalists' professional conduct is unassailable," states *BusinessWeek*'s code (2009), which its journalists are required to sign annually. "Our journalists' personal conduct, as it reflects on *BusinessWeek,* is beyond reproach."

Standard rules of journalism conduct apply to business reporting. Sources should not be made up. Quotes should not be faked. (The example of former *New York Times* reporter Jayson Blair, who fabricated dozens of interviews, should make this clear to everyone.) Reporters and writers should not use their position as members of the media for personal gain. Paid trips should not be accepted. Above all, it is the reporter's job to maintain integrity. If there is anything that might give even the appearance of impropriety, the reporter should not do it. As Bloomberg News' ethics code states, "When exposing the wrongdoing of others, we should be above reproach. The greater the story's impact, the greater our obligation to withstand the most exacting scrutiny" (Bloomberg, 2009, p. 57). Are there gray areas? Of course. Any reporter should discuss what he plans to do with his editor or a superior before taking action.

Appendix

Society of American Business Editors and Writers (SABEW) Code of Ethics

Statement of Purpose:

As business and financial journalists, we recognize we are guardians of the public trust and must do nothing to abuse this obligation.

It is not enough that we act with honest intent; as journalists, we must conduct our professional lives in a manner that avoids even the suggestion of personal gain, or any misuse of the power of the press.

It is with this acknowledgment that we offer these guidelines for those who work in business and financial journalism:

Personal Investments and Relationships

Avoid any practice that might compromise or appear to compromise objectivity or fairness.

Never let personal investments influence content. Disclose investment positions to your superior or directly to the public.

Disclose personal or family relationships that might pose conflicts of interest.

Avoid active trading and other short-term profit-seeking opportunities, as such activities are not compatible with the independent role of the business journalist.

Do not take advantage of inside information for personal gain.

Sources

Ensure confidentiality of information during the reporting process, and make every effort to keep information from finding its way to those who might use it for gain before it is disseminated to the public.

Do not alter information, delay or withhold publication or make concessions relating to news content to any government.

Gifts and Favors

In the course of professional activity, accept no gift or special treatment worth more than token value.

Accept no out-of-town travel paid for by outside sources.

Carefully examine offers of freelance work or speech honoraria to ensure such offers are not attempts to influence content.

Disclose to a supervisor any offer of future employment or outside income that springs from the journalist's professional activities or contacts.

Accept food or refreshments of ordinary value only if absolutely necessary, and only during the normal course of business.

Editorial Integrity

Publishers, owners and newsroom managers should establish policies and guidelines to protect the integrity of business news coverage.

Material produced by editorial staff should be used only in sections, programming or pages controlled by editorial departments.

Content, sections or programming controlled by advertising departments should be distinctly different from news sections in typeface, layout and design. Advertising content should be identified as such.

Promising a story in exchange for advertising or other considerations is unethical.

Using Outside Material

Using articles or columns from non-journalists is potentially deceptive and poses inherent conflicts of interest. This does not apply to content that is clearly labeled opinion or viewpoint, or to submissions identified as coming directly from the public, such as citizen blogs or letters to the editor.

Submissions should be accepted only from freelancers who abide by the same ethical policies as staff members.

Technology

Business journalists should take the lead in adapting professional standards to new forms of journalism as technologies emerge and change.

The business journalist should encourage fellow journalists to abide by these standards and principles.[4]

Notes

1. From "Hurricanes' owner says his company isn't for sale," by L. DeCock, May 9, 2003, *News & Observer,* p. C1. Copyright 2003 by (Raleigh) *News & Observer.* Reprinted with permission.
2. From "Companies make pitch for venture capital funds," by S. King, May 23, 2003, *Kansas City Star,* p. C3. Copyright 2003 by the Kansas City Star Company. Reprinted with permission.
3. From "Durham gets AAA credit rating from 3 agencies," by B. Evans, May 22, 2003, *Durham Herald-Sun,* p. B3. Copyright 2003 by the Durham Herald Company Inc. Reprinted with permission.
4. From SABEW Code of Ethics. Copyright by the Society of American Business Editors and Writers Inc. Reprinted with permission.

Key Terms

annual meeting
debt
private company
proxy statement

public company
Securities and Exchange
    Commission (SEC)
strategic alternatives

Suggested Exercises

1. Find 10 public companies and 10 private companies in your state. What information is available for each company? How does the information about the two groups compare?

2. Read the SABEW ethics code. Discuss what it says about stock ownership. Do you think that you can write objectively about a company in which you own stock? What about a company in which you've shorted stock?

3. You're writing a story about rising gasoline prices in your community. How would you go about finding consumers to interview for this story? What types of questions would you ask them?

4. Discuss what you would do if you were a reporter for a newspaper covering Walt Disney Co., and someone from its corporate communications department offered you and your family free passes to one of its theme parks for the weekend. Would you take them? If you would, why?

5. Write down 10 important pieces of information or facts that you think every business reporter and editor should know. Do you think that every person working on the business desk at your local newspaper knows this information? Why or why not?

Business Reporting Books

Clinton, P. (1997). *Guide to writing for the business press*. Lincolnwood, IL: American Business Press.

Fink, C. (2000). *Bottom line writing: Reporting the sense of dollars*. Ames, IA: Iowa State University Press.

Kurtz, H. (2000). *The fortune tellers: Inside Wall Street's game of money, media and manipulation*. New York: Simon & Schuster.

Leckey, A., & Sloan, A. (Eds.) (2003). *The best business stories of the year: 2003 Edition*. New York: Vintage Books.

Martin, P.R. (2002). *The Wall Street Journal guide to business style and usage*. New York: Wall Street Journal Books.

Surowiecki, J. (Ed.) (2002). *Best business crime writing of the year*. New York: Anchor Books.

References

Bloomberg. (2009). *The Bloomberg way: A guide for reporters and editors*. New York: Bloomberg L.P., pp. 57–78.

Blum, A. (1998, August–September). The long, hot summer: Chiquita, other retractions, firings shake newsroom ethics to the core. *The Business Journalist*, pp. 1, 12–14.

Business Week. (2009). Journalistic code of ethics. Retrieved December 24, 2015 from www.businessweek.com/ethics.htm.

CNNmoney.com. (2003). Disclaimer. Retrieved November 27, 2003 from http://money. cnn.com/services/disclaimer.html.

Coca-Cola Company. (2015 March 12). Form DEF14A. (SEC Publication No. 001-02217–15694880, pp. 84–85). Washington, DC: Securities and Exchange Commission.

DeCock, L. (2003, May 9). Hurricanes' owner says his company isn't for sale. *The News & Observer*, p. Cl.

Evans, B. (2003, May 22). Durham gets AAA credit rating from 3 agencies. *The Herald- Sun*, p. B3.

Fitzgerald, D. (2002, August 16). Nick's bows to bridge pressures. *Door County Advocate*, p. 1.

King, S. (2003, May 23). Companies make pitch for venture capital funds. *Kansas City Star*, p. C3.

Society of American Business Editors and Writers. (2009). Code of ethics. Retrieved October 3, 2009, from http://sabew.org/about/codes-of-ethics/sabews-code-of-ethics.

Tannenbaum, A. (1990, November). Ruminations: A self-inflicted scandal. *TJFR: Business News Reporter*, pp. 1, 4–5, 10–11.

3

BASIC BUSINESS JOURNALISM BEATS

We Got the Beat

Just like other news desks in any media operation, a business news outfit organizes its coverage by dividing its reporters into covering different beats. Unlike other news desks, however, where beats such as police, government, education and politics are staples no matter where the media organization is based, business news desks are like snowflakes—no two are exactly alike.

Here Are the Beats at the *Atlanta Business Chronicle* in Late 2015

1. Commercial real estate—Douglas Sams
2. Hospitality—Amy Wenk
3. Government—Dave Williams
4. Health care, movie industry—Ellie Hensley
5. Technology—Urvaksh Karkaria
6. Residential real estate, financial—Phil Hudson

If you're in Detroit working for the *News* or the *Free Press*, there are a couple of reporters on the auto beat at all times, but the *Denver Post* has no one on its business desk writing about cars. The *Los Angeles Times* has business reporters covering the business of movies and entertainment, but the only time movies get mentioned in the *St. Louis Post-Dispatch* is when they're reviewed in the features section. As a business reporter at the *Atlanta Journal-Constitution,* I spent most of my time writing about the beverage industry because the Coca-Cola Co. was headquartered two miles away from the newsroom. But there's rarely, if ever, a story about soft drinks on the business page of the *Houston Chronicle,* where covering the energy industry is a primary focus.

In other words, unless the business news organization is national in scope, like the *Wall Street Journal* or the *New York Times* business section, the coverage focuses on what's going on in the local economy that impacts the biggest number of readers. And even then, some business desks will have specialty beats that they share with other news departments. *The Sun-Sentinel* in Fort Lauderdale, for example, has historically had a sports business reporter whose stories have also appeared in the sports section.

Here's How the Competing *Atlanta Journal-Constitution* Broke Up Its Business News Beats in Late 2015

1. Airlines, airport, business of transportation, UPS—Kelly Yamanouchi
2. Retail (Home Depot, etc.), food and beverage (including Coke), some other news and trends tied to Fortune 500 companies—Leon Stafford
3. Housing and the economy—Michael Kanell
4. Economic development and commercial real estate—Scott Trubey
5. Finance, utilities and business general assignments—Russell Grantham
6. Business columnist—Matt Kempner
7. Statewide economic stories—Dan Chapman

There's also the understanding, particularly in these new times in journalism, that a business reporter can be called on to cover a variety of topics, whether they are his specialty or not. If the banking reporter goes on vacation and a big story breaks on his or her beat, someone else is going to have to step in and write that piece. And there may be so many different important industries to cover that a business reporter may be asked to juggle a few balls.

My first business news job, at the *Sarasota Herald-Tribune,* required coverage of the Port of Manatee, the boat builders in the region, orange juice maker Tropicana, and tourism as regular beats, with frequent trips to the U.S. Bankruptcy Court and attendance at downtown development authority meetings as well. There was no way to regulate when news broke either—in my office hangs a front page of a *Herald-Tribune* business section with one story about the port, two stories about Tropicana and another about the upcoming tourist season.

Working a beat requires a number of skills and strategies that can be used for virtually any type of coverage or story. Let's examine a few of those now.

Developing Sources

Good business journalists will want to develop sources on their beat. This requires getting out of the office and meeting people, having breakfast and lunch with strangers and exploring some unique and unusual ways of making contacts.

TIPS FROM THE PROS

BuzzFeed News retail reporter Sapna Maheshwari on covering the retail beat:

The retail landscape is sprawling, encompassing big-box stores, mall chains, ecommerce, small businesses and more. Work with your editor to figure out which topics and companies are worth focusing your efforts on and which matter most to your readers. Having a shortlist of topics and retailers you cover regularly will also help you develop relationships with sources and companies.

If your beat has some large companies, obviously it is important to know the people who work there. The public relations professionals can be, depending on the company's communications strategy, great sources. PR people strive to balance their job of presenting their company in the best possible way with giving a journalist the information he or she needs to tell a proper story. Some PR people give business reporters information about their companies that can be construed as negative, knowing that the reporter will come to respect them on future stories with less impact.

Developing a relationship with the company executives can also be key, but getting access to them is difficult without going through the PR staff. Some executives like to meet with new reporters on a beat to help them understand how the company works and its strategy. Ask if such a session might be available; it will likely be off-the-record, but it will help you understand what you're writing about. Some top business journalists develop closer relationships with the executives they cover. Fox Business Network's Charles Gasparino, for example, had dinner with former Bear Stearns CEO Jimmy Cayne. But such relationships can lead to questions about whether the journalist can cover the company impartially.

Other sources within a company can be even more important. Talking to lower-level employees can often give a business reporter a more accurate picture of what's going on at a company. These workers can often provide perspective on the effectiveness of the CEO's strategy and whether a new strategy has a chance of succeeding. They can also provide information that is widely disseminated within the company—such as internal newsletters or e-mail communications from executives—that could be newsworthy. While these employees will often only talk off-the-record for fear of retribution from the company, their closeness to the company can be invaluable.

Former employees and executives are often just as valuable when it comes to source development. While they can no longer tell a business reporter about what's going on at a company, they often remain in contact with current employees and can provide some perspective of what it was like to work at the business. Former board members are just as valuable. Look for press releases that name managers or executives at new companies and review their past work experience to see if they were once employed at a company you cover. The easiest way to do this is to search frequently via Google or LexisNexis.

Other sources can be developed that could be useful in covering a company. Competing businesses can often be invaluable sources. They will sometimes know as much about their competitor as they do about their own operations. Any profile or strategy story about a company should attempt to include a comment from or information about what a competitor is doing as well.

TIPS FROM THE PROS

BuzzFeed News retail reporter Sapna Maheshwari on covering the retail beat:

Stay on top of 10-Ks, 10-Qs and proxy statements. Monitor changes to how retailers describe themselves, risk factors, salaries and legal proceedings for potential stories—you can often find redlined versions of these reports online or on the Bloomberg terminal.

Suppliers are also good sources on any business beat. Suppliers can tell a business journalist whether a company is a good business partner. They can tell you if a company is demanding more product, asking for price breaks or resisting a price increase, or is slow to pay its bills. The latter could be an indication that a company is having some financial problems.

Wall Street analysts and investors are also good sources on any beat. Analysts who follow a company or a specific industry can often provide some perspective on whether a company's strategy is working and give opinions about its stock price. Investors will do the same. A word of caution for both, however: They have a vested interest in seeing the company prosper. Sell-side analysts who work for investment banks like to pump up a company so that investors will buy the stock through their firm, helping the analyst earn his or her salary with the commissions on those trades. And an investor profits by seeing the stock price go up. Of course, there are some investors, called short-sellers, who profit when a company's stock price falls, and they too can be valuable sources.

Let's not forget others, primarily professionals, who may come into contact with the companies or industries on your beat and can be good resources. Consultants often specialize in specific companies or industries and may have done work in the past for businesses that you cover. The same goes for university professors, particularly those at business schools. They may have worked in the industry before joining academia, and they, too, may have performed consulting work. There are also accountants and lawyers who may know a thing or two about the company. In many cities, there's typically an attorney who specializes in lawsuits against large companies.

Finally, read what other journalists are reporting about the industry or the companies on your beat. In many cases, there will be industry newsletters or publications that will write about the "inside baseball" of the business. While these stories may not be of interest to your readers, they do help you get up to speed on what's important, and they can give you story ideas.

How Things Work

Most of us became journalists because we didn't like taking math and science classes. Yet now that we're business journalists, we're forced to learn many of the math skills that we shunned, and, depending on the industry, we might be forced to learn some basics of science, medicine, chemistry, or another field. How is that going to happen soon enough for us to avoid looking like idiots in print?

TIPS FROM THE PROS

BuzzFeed News retail reporter Sapna Maheshwari on covering the retail beat:

Find the equity analysts who cover retailers on your beat and ask to receive their research notes. Chat with the friendly ones on a regular basis; they often know a lot of company gossip that they can't include in their reports.

Let's answer that question in a couple of ways. If you've never been a business reporter before, you're going to need a crash course in how to read company financial statements and decipher the numbers. Don't worry; all most business reporters need to do is some basic addition and subtraction, and maybe some percentages. That's all stuff each of us learned by the eighth grade, right? For more on how a business journalist should read financial statements, check out Chapter 5.

If you've already covered some business stories and are switching to a new beat, then the financial stuff should be somewhat familiar to you.

Let's plow ahead though to the industry-specific knowledge that you're going to need to write stories with enough knowledge and analysis to impress even the people who have worked at the companies you're covering.

When I started covering the Coca-Cola Co. in 1994, I thought that this would be an easy beat. I thought that there was nothing more basic than selling carbonated, colored sugar water. I couldn't have been more wrong. Any reporter who's going to infiltrate the soft drink industry with any success must understand the relationship that soft drink companies have with their bottlers, who are often the reason why a new beverage succeeds or fails.

They need to realize that these companies operate in dozens of countries around the world, and, in each, the company may have other products, so an understanding of the global economy is important. They have to come to grips with the fact that soft drink companies rely heavily on their advertising and the image that consumers have of them, so knowing the advertising and media world is key as well. And that reporter is going to need to know something about the fountain business, because when consumers purchase a soft drink at a restaurant or a convenience store, it's all about which soft drink company negotiated a better deal.

TIPS FROM THE PROS

 Bloomberg News tech reporter Sarah Frier on covering the tech beat:

To figure out what to write when you're starting out, read the news of the day and think about the unanswered questions and next steps. Fresh skepticism is hard to come by in the world of tech reporting, and yours is valuable.

In other words, after about two weeks on the job, I felt totally lost. It took me a good year to feel comfortable writing about all of these topics, as well as others on the beat—while I was also covering a non-beverage beat. Becoming comfortable with how an industry works and how a company in that industry makes or loses money takes time. But you've got to quickly learn the industry lingo to talk with the executives, consultants and hangers-on so that you'll understand what they're saying.

If possible, see if your news organization can send you to an industry conference or trade show. This will give you the opportunity to cram a couple of years of knowledge into a few days. The people and speakers attending such events have often been in the industry for decades. Don't be afraid to buttonhole them and ask as many questions as possible. Take notes and soak it all in. If there are people there from companies on your beat, follow them around and ask for some short tutorials if they're not busy.

TIPS FROM THE PROS

 BuzzFeed News retail reporter Sapna Maheshwari on covering the retail beat:

Follow the social media accounts of the brands you're covering and sign up for their emails so you can see what customers are seeing. Visit their Facebook, Instagram and Twitter accounts on a regular basis and read the comments—it's an easy way to get tipped off to problems.

See if there is a class available at a local community college related to your industry or even in basic accounting. Your news organization might even pay the tuition. Such courses are often offered at night, after you've spent the day in the newsroom, so they won't interfere with breaking news.

Again, read industry publications. If you're new to the banking beat, check out *American Banker*. My salvation on the Coke beat was *Beverage Digest*, a newsletter that came out every two weeks.

The learning curve on any business beat is steep, particularly if you're unfamiliar with the industry or the products. Don't get too worked up when you run across something that you don't understand, particularly during the early weeks on the beat. If someone is talking to you, ask him or her to explain what you don't understand. You'll essentially have to do the same for your readers or viewers later on, so it's better to get it explained now than to stare at a blank computer screen wondering how to write the gobbledygook that some executive told you.

Mining for Stories

One of the hardest things for a new business reporter to accomplish is to come up with new story ideas. A reporter who has been on the beat for several years knows what's been covered and what has been newsworthy in the past, but the new beat reporter has no context, particularly if he or she is new to the business desk.

One of the easiest steps for a new business beat reporter to take is to talk to the reporter who previously covered the beat. This person may still be at the paper, and their knowledge of the beat can be extremely valuable. Go over key sources on the beat and ask the previous reporter what kind of information these sources have been willing to part with in the past. Also ask the old beat reporter for strategies for dealing with companies.

TIPS FROM THE PROS

BuzzFeed News retail reporter Sapna Maheshwari on covering the retail beat:

Maintain a wide variety of sources: employees from the C-suite down to workers in stores, labor activists, trade group reps, lawyers, professors, headhunters, consultants, investors and analysts. Sometimes information from part-time store employees is just as newsworthy as what hedge fund managers know.

The new beat reporter should also look at the stories that the previous reporter wrote during his or her tenure. Some stories will repeat themselves, like earnings stories and stories about a public company's annual meeting, so reading these will let the new reporter know what angles have been covered in the past. Old stories could also spark new story ideas for the new beat reporter. Maybe a company on the beat made a major announcement several years ago about a new product. Readers and viewers might like to know how that new product is doing.

Don't be afraid to ask sources on the beat for story ideas as well. Ask an analyst who covers a company what information they'd like to know from a CEO before you interview that CEO. Talk to competitors to find out what they're most interested in knowing about the company. This type of information is typically interesting to business news readers as well. While a company's corporate communications staff will be more than willing to provide story ideas, make sure that they're legitimate and not just press releases that haven't been written. The best PR people will provide excellent story ideas, and they'll be good sounding boards to pitch story ideas off of.

Find out what the executives at the companies you write about read, and read those publications as well. Industry publications often cover esoteric material that only the hard-core industry people care about, but they also are often months ahead of the mainstream media in exposing topics or issues that are important.

Finally, talk to average, everyday people. Your friends, neighbors and acquaintances are prime sources to tap for story ideas, particularly if you're covering companies or industries that interact with consumers on a daily basis. They can tell you whether they're happy with the products they've purchased and the quality of the service. Plus, they often end up providing anecdotes to use in your stories to help explain what's going on.

Common Beats

TIPS FROM THE PROS

BuzzFeed News retail reporter Sapna Maheshwari on covering the retail beat:

Follow some good blogs for your beat—it could be zealots for a single brand, people who coupon for sport, parents who pen influential toy reviews. Bloggers often catch interesting developments at retailers before anyone else and can be good sources.

While it's true that no two business news desks are identical, there are some common beats that most business news organizations will cover. These include banking and/or financial services, manufacturing, technology, the economy, retail and health care. Some others might be investing/Wall Street and media/ advertising. Finally, most decent-sized business news operations have a regular columnist who provides opinions on trends and issues.

While beat reporters on a business desk might be covering different types of stories, how they report and write those stories is still basic journalism: They ask a lot of questions and try to get as much information as possible. A good business reporter is no different than a good crime reporter or a good government reporter. Each knows their turf, and they know where to look for good stories.

In fact, nonbusiness beats in a newsroom could stand to learn a few tricks from their business brethren. A business reporter commonly asks how money was spent and whether that money was spent wisely. A business reporter is also often interested in knowing the connections between two parties conducting business. Those aspects of business reporting—the money and the connections—are elements that all reporters would be wise to look for in their stories, even if they have little or nothing to do with business.

In the rest of the book, you'll learn about basic business stories that can be found on any beat—earnings, the naming of a new CEO, a merger or acquisition, etc. In this chapter, we'll take a look at some stories that are unique to the basic business beats.

TIPS FROM THE PROS

BuzzFeed News retail reporter Sapna Maheshwari on covering the retail beat:

Take time every day to search lawsuits filed by and against the retailers you cover. If you're willing to slog through a lot of slip-and-fall complaints and minor store employee disputes, there's a lot of fascinating, newsworthy information just waiting to be uncovered.

Remember one more thing about business beats: All businesses have competition. Think about what a competitor to the business that you're writing about would want to know in your story. You would do well to interview competitors on any beat for any story, even if it's about a local ice cream store that is giving away free ice cream one weekend. How does that impact sales of the closest ice cream store?

Let's take a look at how some reporters on these beats cover their territory and the stories they're writing.

Banking

A banking reporter writes stories about the financial institutions in a city. Given the economic conditions during the early part of the twenty-first century, with the federal government taking a closer look at banks and shutting some down, bank coverage has taken on a renewed interest in many communities. In cities where a major bank is headquartered, the bank might be the largest employer in the community as well.

TIPS FROM THE PROS

BuzzFeed News retail reporter Sapna Maheshwari on covering the retail beat:

Learn how to search the databases on the U.S. Patent and Trademark Office website. The site can be a great resource for figuring out what retailers are working on, whether it's new products they're developing or checkout systems they're looking to patent.

While many stories on the banking beat are similar to those of other beats, such as earnings and the opening and closing of new locations, there are other stories to tell. A savvy banking reporter checks a bank's market share data with the Federal Deposit Insurance Corporation (FDIC) to determine whether it's gaining or losing consumers' deposits in the community. A banking reporter is also looking at a bank to determine whether its lending strategy is successful or if it's making bad loans. This data can also be gathered from the federal government.

Rick Rothacker has covered banking for the *Charlotte Observer* for more than a decade, and in 2009, he received a Gerald Loeb Award, the Pulitzer Prize of business journalism, for his beat coverage of banking in Charlotte, where Wachovia and Bank of America are both based. Rothacker said that he's still learning on the beat. "It's good to do every interview you can, even when it's on a topic you're less excited about, because you never know when you may want to talk to that person again," said Rothacker. "People who used to work at the banks can be helpful sources. When you're the beat reporter, employees and others also know to contact you. You always can be doing more, though, to develop good sources."

Another important aspect of banking reporting—and for any business beat for that matter—is checking regulatory filings. Here's the lead to a Bank of America story that former *Charlotte Observer* business reporter Christina Rexrode, who now covers banking for the *Wall Street Journal,* wrote from an SEC filing:

> The shake-up in Bank of America Corp.'s boardroom, apparently orchestrated by the hand of government regulators, continued Friday evening, when the bank announced that three more of its directors have resigned.
>
> William Barnet, John Collins and Gary Countryman joined the board in 2004 after Bank of America bought FleetBoston Financial Corp., where they were serving as directors. The departure of Barnet, who is the mayor of Spartanburg, means there are no more directors with notable ties to the Carolinas except for bank chief executive Ken Lewis.
>
> The bank said in a regulatory filing, made after 5 p.m. on Friday, that each director's decision to resign "was not as a result of any disagreement

with the Corporation or its management," echoing the language of other recent board departures.[1]

Manufacturing

As the American economy becomes less reliant on industry and more reliant on services, the manufacturing beat has become less important for many news outlets. But it can still pack a punch in terms of importance and in driving local economies of some towns and cities.

TIPS FROM THE PROS

 BuzzFeed News retail reporter Sapna Maheshwari on covering the retail beat:

Everybody shops! Talk to your friends and family about where they're shopping and why and make it a point to visit the stores you're writing about in a variety of locations. (This is especially important if you live in a city—a suburban Target is different from the ones in San Francisco and Manhattan.)

In communities where there are large plants that make everything from steel to automobiles to frozen food, covering manufacturing can give a broader glimpse of the nation's economy. When things are going well for manufacturing locally, typically that means that the national economy is doing well. But when these manufacturers struggle and are forced to lay off workers, it's often a sign that the broader economy is struggling as well.

Manufacturing reporters don't necessarily write stories about the products that are being made at these plants, unless a factory's owner decides that a location is going to produce a new product and that might mean more jobs or that the current job force will be able to keep working. Instead, these beat reporters often focus on changes at the plant, such as whether a third shift has been added because of demand or whether the workers have been furloughed. These workers might also belong to a union, so any negotiations between the workers and the company over a new contract are also major stories.

TIPS FROM THE PROS

 BuzzFeed News retail reporter Sapna Maheshwari on covering the retail beat:

It's worth checking out some of the case studies about retailers from Harvard Business School, especially if you're new to the beat. They're dense with history and will help you understand how the industry works.

Manufacturing reporters may also spend some time on other types of stories as well, such as whether the plant is getting new equipment or whether the company has instituted a new flexible schedule that allows working moms the chance to return to the workforce. Unfortunately, because the employees of many manufacturing companies are working with heavy equipment, there's also the chance that some of these workers might get injured, or even die, while on the job. Writing about workplace safety or the specific injuries themselves commonly falls to the manufacturing beat.

Conflicts between manufacturers and their workers are bound to arise. Here's how Eric Connor, a reporter for the *Greenville News* in South Carolina, wrote a lead about one of these incidents:

> Ten former employees have sued the Columbia Farms chicken processing plant in Greenville, alleging the company refused to pay overtime that they worked and, in one case, fired a worker after accusing her of faking a workplace injury.
>
> The suit, moved into federal jurisdiction, comes as the company on Thursday appeared in federal court on separate, criminal charges alleging the willful hiring of illegal workers.[2]

Broader stories should also be written about manufacturers. The problems of the American automobile industry in recent years have been a story of how manufacturers have struggled to adapt to growing international competition. Many stories have examined where these manufacturers could have made changes in the past—or made different decisions—to prevent their current problems.

Retail

Because every community has stores that sell everything from clothing to car parts, retail is typically a beat that every business desk covers. Retail stories can include everything from a new company entering the market and opening stores, to a retailer closing its stores and exiting the market, to a retailer already in the market opening a new store, to a store that's opening a location different from its existing stores, to a new development such as a mall or strip center opening.

TIPS FROM THE PROS

Bloomberg News tech reporter Sarah Frier on covering the tech beat:

Set your own agenda. There's a constant stream of product releases, press events and embargoed announcements, but you can distinguish yourself from the competition by making your own decisions about what stories and themes are most important.

The best retail reporters are the ones who get out of the newsroom and spend most of their days talking to shoppers, store employees and others about what's happening. Through constant examination of the local retail scene, they're able to discern trends before others, like when a mall may be struggling because a new retail center opened up nearby.

A retail reporter needs to know how to gauge the health of a store or a chain. All retailers look at their same-store sales, or sales of stores that have been open for at least 12 months. An increase in same-store sales is a sign of a healthy retailer. The other measure for retailers is their sales per square foot. Compare the sales per square foot of retailers in the same line of business to determine which one is getting more business from their stores. Different types of retailers will have different levels of sales per square foot. Jewelers typically have the highest level.

Retailers are located across the country, so business reporters write stories about retailers even though the retailer may not be located in the media's market. In addition, reporters write stories about trends and issues in retailing, such as when big-box retailers began opening fast-food restaurants inside their stores or the rise of Internet shopping.

Retail reporters rarely, if ever, write about the trends or issues that retailers want them to write about, such as customer sales. Many retailers will attempt to pitch stories that are nothing more than an attempt to gain free publicity.

There is one notable exception, and that's the holiday shopping season that occurs between Thanksgiving and Christmas. Retail reporters earn their salaries based on how well they cover the holiday shopping season.

Sue Stock, the former retail reporter for the (Raleigh) *News & Observer,* has covered the retail beat for nearly a decade, and she has a number of recommendations for retail reporters when they're out talking to shoppers. She always wears comfortable shoes, and she leaves her coat in the car because she always ends up taking it off and doesn't want to have to juggle it while taking notes.

Stock's recommendation for interviews is to look for shoppers taking a break at the kid play area or at the food court. "This also allows you to sit for a minute and makes you less conspicuous," says Stock. "And people like to talk while they eat. They'll share more."

Retail stories on the day after Thanksgiving and throughout the holiday shopping season can be repetitive. It's best to try to find a new angle to tell this story. During the late 1990s and the early part of this century, the new angle was the rise of Internet shopping.

Here are some offbeat retail beat stories that I once did in an attempt to bring a somewhat different perspective to the typical Christmas retail shopping stories:

1. While at the *Tampa Tribune,* I spent the day after Christmas driving around on a garbage truck. Why? December 26 is the busiest garbage day of the year, just like the Saturday before Christmas is the busiest shopping day of the year. We saw presents that were thrown out— with the wrapping still on the packages.

2. When I was at the *Atlanta Journal-Constitution,* the first Christmas shopping season I covered, I spent the Friday after Thanksgiving shadowing a Target store manager, beginning at about 5 a.m. when she arrived at the store. You get a much different perspective of the first major shopping day when you look at it from the store manager's perspective.

3. Also in Atlanta, I spent one December 26 with two women who were shopping for next year's Christmas—only 364 days in advance. That was definitely a different perspective on the Christmas retail season.

4. Having worked at a Honey Baked Ham store during the Christmas holidays while I was in college, I knew how important the Christmas season was to ham stores. They get about 75 percent of their annual sales between Thanksgiving and Christmas. One year, the staff in the back worked 18 hours straight glazing hams, with the store managers bringing in pizzas for us. So I wrote a story one year about the "Ham Wars" between Honey Baked Ham, Hickory Ham and the other ham store locations.

5. I also went out one December 24 to find the stereotypical guys doing their last-minute shopping. That was a fun story, as I watched them frantically try to find presents for girlfriends, wives, kids, etc.

How did I find these people? For some of them, like the December 24 story, I just went to the mall and looked for guys who appeared to be playing hooky from work. For some of the other stories, the newspaper ran a small box on the front of the business section asking for readers who might fit the profile of someone who shops 364 days in advance for Christmas to contact us. For the garbage story, it simply took calling the local sanitation company. They were more than happy to oblige, although for me it meant getting to the dump at 4:30 a.m. the day after Christmas to begin writing the story.

TIPS FROM THE PROS

Bloomberg News tech reporter Sarah Frier on covering the tech beat:

Beware of jargon and hyperbole. Companies will be eager to tell you that their "innovative artificial intelligence solution" is "disruptive, best-in-class technology," but it's up to you to tell the reader what the startup actually does—and if they're actually good at it. Call outside sources.

The point is this: Don't just write the typical retail story that interviews store managers on the Friday after Thanksgiving. They're all going to say that sales are good. Don't just regurgitate the numbers that assess whether Christmas sales are up or down from the previous year. Have some fun writing Christmas retail stories and think outside the box.

Health Care

Health care is an important beat in nearly every media outlet for the sole reason that the local hospital is typically one of the largest employers. And while many news outlets cover health care by focusing on new illnesses, such as the H1N1 flu that swept the United States in 2009, or advances in treating illnesses and injuries, such as the coverage of drug testing company Theranos in 2015, an increasing number of them are also beginning to write stories about the business of health care in their communities.

And health care is big business. Most U.S. hospitals have more than $100 million in annual revenue, yet not all of them get covered as a business. Even though some of them are nonprofit, a business reporter should take a close look at their operations because they are run as businesses.

Let's say that one hospital in Tampa wants to add a neonatal intensive care unit, but there are three other hospitals in the city that already offer such a service. So, do regulators allow that hospital to expand and increase competition? That's a story to explore, as reporter Jill Cecil Wiersma did for the *Tennessean* newspaper in Nashville when she wrote this brief:

> Williamson Medical Center and Maury Regional Hospital filed a motion July 23 asking that media reports about the recession, General Motors' bankruptcy, unemployment rate predictions, and the local economy be allowed for the Aug. 19 date in Davidson County Chancery Court.
>
> That's when the court considers the next round of appeals in the 3-year-old case against HCA TriStar Health System's plans for a 56-bed hospital. The facility has twice earned a certificate of need from the state's Health Services Development Agency.[3]

A big story on the health care business beat is the rising cost of receiving medical care. While the costs of other products and services have stagnated, health care costs continue to rise. Some of it is because of new treatments and equipment that keep us alive longer. Some of the increase in cost is because consumers simply use more health care providers these days.

TIPS FROM THE PROS

Bloomberg News tech reporter Sarah Frier on covering the tech beat:

Regularly force yourself to leave your desk and have wide-ranging discussions with smart people in the industry, with whom you can gut check your tips and hunches. These informal background conversations lead to stories and scoops.

The health care beat also explores employment, because in many communities there's a dearth of qualified applicants for specific jobs, such as nursing.

When I taught at Washington and Lee University, one of my students wrote a great story about what the local drug stores were doing to recruit pharmacists to come work in rural Virginia.

The health care beat reporter often writes about insurance as well, and this can mean looking at topics such as whether basic health insurance policies cover new types of treatment, as well as contract negotiations between large health insurance companies and health care providers, such as a hospital group in your community or a chain of doctors' offices.

Writing about health care also means writing about the federal government, as the Medicare and Medicaid systems are large payers of health care. How much hospitals, doctors and other health care providers are reimbursed by these plans often means the difference between a profit and a loss for the year.

As with many other service-related beats, the health care beat can also result in writing about fraud—both by the consumer and by the provider. Look for lawsuits or state regulatory action to find these stories.

For more on health care as a personal finance story, please see Chapter 15. There's also information on how to cover nonprofit health care companies in Chapter 11.

Technology

The technology beat can seem like a fun one. With all of the new gadgets and software coming out each month, there's always something new to write about. Reporters such as Walt Mossberg of Re/code and David Pogue of Yahoo Finance are famous and appear on television because of their ability to critique these new products and tell consumers what's good and bad about them.

Most tech reporters look at their beat as a combination of providing advice to their readers about the products that the companies they cover are introducing and of providing more objective reporting about the financial aspects of the companies. Because many tech companies get started every year, a lot of tech coverage of smaller companies takes a look at whether these businesses have the funding, the business plan and the products to become successful.

The tech beat is a careful balancing act in that there are many large companies—such as Microsoft and Apple—that are trying to control how they are covered in the media, and there are many small companies that will take

TIPS FROM THE PROS

Bloomberg News tech reporter Sarah Frier on covering the tech beat:

After every great meeting, ask for introductions to other smart people to talk to. Cultivate those relationships by sometimes calling for general commentary and background before you need the person to trust you enough to confirm a tip.

just about any coverage they can get. The goal of any tech writer is to provide the coverage that he or she thinks will be most useful to readers. If you're not based in California or Seattle, then focus more on your local tech companies and save the national stories for the wire services. Your readers will want to know more about the local tech guys, and they can get news about Apple or Microsoft from a dozen other sources.

There are a number of blogs and websites that cover the tech area, including TechCrunch, Gizmodo, Engadget, Re/code and All Things Digital, as well as the traditional business media. In fact, a number of tech reporters have left print media and started blogs or sites. While some of these sites stretch the boundaries of traditional reporting in that they post rumors and information from off-the-record sources, they are valuable to read if you're a tech reporter.

A great place to look for tech stories is with the U.S. Patent and Trademark Office. This is where tech companies have to file patent and trademark applications for their inventions. In many cases, these patents will detail how and when the companies plan to launch new products.

Realize that many tech reporters now blog as well as write stories for their publication. These blogs are followed closely by the local tech community and represent a great way to make connections with potential sources.

Media/Advertising

Because most companies use the media to advertise their products and services, the local advertising industry is also a beat that many business news desks incorporate into their coverage.

Covering this beat means getting in touch with the local advertising and communication shops and finding out when they gain or lose business. If an ad agency obtains a new account for a national company, it likely means they'll be hiring employees to take care of that new work. The opposite is true, obviously, if the agency loses an account to another firm.

In the advertising and media business, a lot of work is based on relationships, so if one of these firms loses some of its key employees to a competitor, or employees leave to start their own firm, it could mean that business will follow those workers out the door as well. Track carefully the comings and goings of staff members. Sometimes a company will change ad agencies because a creative director has gone to a new shop.

TIPS FROM THE PROS

Bloomberg News tech reporter Sarah Frier on covering the tech beat:

 Balance access journalism with deep reporting. Your readers think they want to hear from the CEO—and they do—but you will only get a full read on what parts of the business are growing or slowing through background conversations with current and former employees, competitors, investors and partners.

Think about trend stories here as well. If one airline starts using more ads on Internet sites, then it could mean that competitors will follow. And look at how other news might affect a specific company's advertising. After an airplane crashes, it could mean a change in the tone of airline advertising, which might have been more flippant in the past.

An Associated Press story, which ran on the MSNBC.com site, looked at the new places where advertising was showing up on television in a strong trend story. Here is the lead:

> Coming soon to your TV: More advertising, in places you might not expect.
> The ads are showing up where people used to enjoy a break from advertising, such as video on demand and on-screen channel guides. Even TiVo, which became popular for its technology that lets people skip TV commercials, is developing new ways to show ads.[4]

One of the toughest stories on the media beat is covering your own employer, and many times that job falls to a business reporter. When the *New York Times* decided to offer the *Boston Globe* to potential buyers, business reporter Richard Perez-Pena garnered most of those bylines. It also means that the stories get close scrutiny from the business editor and potentially from editors higher up. It's a thankless job, but being accurate and fair in these types of stories should come as second nature.

Investing/Wall Street

Many larger business news desks will also assign a reporter to follow the markets for local readers. This means that the beat reporter needs to find a method to explain Wall Street in such a way that the locals can understand what's going on and how it impacts them.

Often, this results in the beat reporter writing a daily story about how local stocks performed and talking to local money managers to get their perspective on specific stocks or the overall market. And while these stories do perform a service for business news consumers, they're also shopworn, and the information can be found just about anywhere on the Web.

TIPS FROM THE PROS

Bloomberg News tech reporter Sarah Frier on covering the tech beat:

Find current and former employees through LinkedIn and Facebook, but also by asking your sources if they think their friends will talk to you. You'll be surprised how often people like to be helpful.

When looking at how newspapers and other media follow the markets, I'm impressed more with unique ways of telling the investing story. The *Cleveland*

Plain Dealer, for example, pits one of its reporters against a local stockbroker to see who's doing better. The *Atlanta Journal-Constitution* ran a column for years that looked at who inside companies was buying and selling the company's stock—often a sign that the price might be ready to jump or fall.

Look for interesting ways to tell your readers what's going on in the investment world if this is your beat. If gas prices are going up, write about the commodity market and how the price of a barrel of oil being traded there affects what we pay at the pump. Has a company's stock price failed to budge despite increasing quarterly profits for the past year? Compare its performance to that of other stocks in the industry; maybe it's actually outperforming its competitors in a down market.

Too often, a media outlet's investing coverage focuses on the stock market. Don't forget to look at bonds, commodities and currencies as well. These are all markets that affect local business news consumers, particularly if you live in a metropolitan area. Explain to people planning to travel abroad which currencies are doing better against the U.S. dollar. If a company has filed for bankruptcy-court protection, thus rendering its stock worthless, write about how the price of its bonds is holding up.

What is good about any business reporter new to a beat is that they have fresh ideas on how the topic should be covered. They aren't rewriting the same story they wrote five years ago when similar news comes up. Don't hesitate to try something new on your beat.

Other Beats

Of course, these aren't the only topics that a business desk covers. Depending on what's important to your readers and the local economy, you might find a few more beats. Real estate—both commercial and residential—is so important in every community that we're going to spend a later chapter talking about how it should be written about.

Business of Sports

The sports business beat is growing in importance as teams and leagues bring in more and more revenue each year. In fact, there's now a publication, the *Street & Smith's Sports Business Daily*, covering nothing but the business of sports. It's owned, not coincidentally, by the same company that owns 40 weekly business newspapers across the country.

Sports business stories can be on a number of different topics, from the financing of a new baseball stadium, to the raising or lowering of ticket prices, to the economic impact a hockey team brings to the local community by making a deep run into the Stanley Cup playoffs. Look for sports business stories in all kinds of sports, including those for kids. Soccer tournaments held around the country almost every weekend in the spring are big economic drivers.

Business Columnists

TIPS FROM THE PROS

Bloomberg News tech reporter Sarah Frier on covering the tech beat:

If you're working with other tech reporters on a team, be collaborative. Nobody has sources everywhere, and in a fast-moving industry it's best to work together to chase tips.

Many business desks have a business columnist. Some of the larger business news operations have several. The *New York Times,* for example, has a different business columnist for each day of the week. Each one writes a column about his specific area of interest. If you want a column on personal finance, then wait until Saturday with Ron Lieber. On Sunday, it's Gretchen Morgenson taking on Wall Street topics.

The business columnist's job is to provide some analysis and perspective—and, hopefully, his or her opinion—to what's going on in the business world. Some business columnists, like Matt Kempner of the *Atlanta Journal-Constitution,* will tackle national issues as well as those closer to home in Georgia. Others, like Tara Lachapelle of Bloomberg Gadfly, focus on a specific topic such as mergers and acquisitions.

Lachapelle, who had been a business reporter for Bloomberg before becoming a columnist, says she likes the freedom to move around and write about different deals with each column, as well as using graphics to accompany her columns. "This is one of the best parts of Gadfly," said Lachapelle.

> We are a treasure trove of charts displaying really interesting data that can often times make a point better than words can. Writers decide what data would be most useful in chart form, and we make them ourselves using a program that some really talented people here built. I have a passion for design and data visualization, so it's great to be able to do this on a daily basis. Journalists today should always be asking themselves: 'What's the best way to present this information to readers?' Readers are in a hurry, so you have to try to be as useful to them as possible.

The downside to column writing is that the columnist has to produce each day the column is scheduled to run, even if he or she has run out of ideas. And, if you become a columnist, be prepared to hear from readers who disagree with your point of view.

Agriculture

The ag beat dominates business news coverage in communities where farming is a vital part of society. The *Des Moines Register* in Iowa has had a farm editor who has covered the beat for decades.

Ag beat writers cover everything from the buying and selling of family farms by large conglomerates to the prices that farmers are receiving for their crops. At the *Bradenton Herald* and the *Sarasota Herald-Tribune* newspapers in Florida, for example, the price of frozen concentrated orange juice on the New York Board of Trade is an important story because the largest employer in the area is Tropicana, the biggest purchaser of the product.

Recently, the ag beat has expanded to include other issues, such as environmental business topics like ethanol. Some business news desks have even started a green business beat to examine how companies are adapting their operations to address issues such as global warming.

TIPS FROM THE PROS

Bloomberg News tech reporter Sarah Frier on covering the tech beat:

Escape the bubble and talk to regular people. Story ideas that really serve your readers might not come from the industry, but from your Luddite taxi driver who has trouble using Facebook, or your teen cousins who know what apps are taking off at school. There's also another set of people involved with the technology companies that your competition isn't talking to: customers, landlords, architects, security guards, contractors, event planners.

Transportation

The transportation beat is another common assignment on a business desk because virtually every consumer is affected in some way or another by transportation. This beat often shows up on the news side as well if a community has a major airport or port governed by a regulatory agency.

Business stories on the transportation beat can cover everything from United Airlines deciding to add six new flights at the local airport to Greyhound's decision to cut back on its bus stops within your state. If there are major trucking firms in your state, talk to them about whether they're seeing an increase or decrease in freight shipped from one place to another.

Ports provide major transportation stories, particularly with the increasing globalization of the economy. Products are shipped via major tankers from one side of the globe to another, and their first stop here in the United States is typically at a port. These ports keep statistics on what types of products are coming and going, and analyzing these numbers may result in an interesting find, such as a dramatic increase in the number of pineapples being shipped out of the Port of Miami.

Conclusion

As you learn more about your beat, you'll become more comfortable covering more complex stories. Please keep your reader or viewer in mind, however. The best business news beat reporters are ones who can talk to industry executives and understand difficult topics but who can turn around and write about those hard-to-understand issues in a way that the average person understands. The object of covering a business news beat is to inform, entertain and enliven the conversation.

Tips on Writing a Business Column

TIPS FROM THE PROS

From *New York Times* business columnist Andrew Ross Sorkin:

1. Make the reader think. That has to be the single goal of any column. Maybe you're introducing the reader to a new issue or person, maybe you're making an argument or offering a contrarian view. You may not always succeed in persuading the reader of your view or perspective, but you do, at minimum, have to have to get them to think. To say, hmmm, I hadn't thought about that. That's success.

2. The lede has to suck you in. Something provocative. I like short ledes. A couple of word sentences. Or a great quote. (Some people think quote ledes are cheap cop-outs; I disagree.)

3. The "nut" graf is the key. Within the first four paragraphs must be the thesis. It can't come too soon. The lede is not the place for the nut. But it can't come too late either.

4. The best nut graphs are a "turn" in the column. Maybe you've set up the conventional wisdom at the top or told a short anecdote. Then nail them with your new, fresh and unique perspective. I love to tell you one thing you think you know and then tell you why it is wrong.

5. A good column is reported. All too often, opinion writers just write their opinions, cribbing the news from earlier articles. But the best columns are supported by strong reporting of new material, or, at minimum, new context and analysis that only comes from meeting with sources and working the phones.

6. Tell the reader why you might be wrong. Even though it is a column, you should always tell the reader the other side—the other viewpoint. It makes your view more powerful by acknowledging the other side. And it will generate a certain level of respect from readers for being fair even when you're taking sides.

7. Use quotes. A great quote can really make a column. As a writer, it's also fun to play off of quotes. I often will use a quote I disagree with as a jumping off point.

8. Be straight with subject of column, especially if it's negative. This goes to the earlier point about fairness. It is critical to reach out to the subject and tell them your thesis. Don't hide it. They should know the column is going to be critical of them. I'll tell them: "I disagree with you and you're going to hate this column." It can make for an uncomfortable conversation, but, in the long run, there is huge value in being known as a straight-shooter.

9. Mix it up. Some very successful columnists have three or four themes that every column falls into. For me, there's more value in surprising the reader.

10. The last sentence is as important as the first, maybe more.

Notes

1. From "Turnover claims 3 more BofA directors: Government pressure is likely part of reason for resignations at the Charlotte-based bank," by C. Rexrode, August 1, 2009, *Charlotte Observer*, p. 1D. Copyright 2009 by *Charlotte Observer*. Reprinted with permission.

2. From "Columbia Farms workers sue company: Chicken processor enters not guilty plea to charges in hiring case," by E. Connor, July 31, 2009, *Greenville News*, p. 1A. Copyright 2009 by *Greenville News*.

3. From "Hospitals contend recession is factor against building new hospital," by J.C. Wiersma, July 31, 2009, *Tennessean*, p. 2. Copyright 2003 by *Tennessean*.

4. From "But wait! There's more! Ads on TV, that is," Associated Press, August 2, 2009. Retrieved August 2, 2009 from www.msnbc.msn.com/id/32259924/ns/businessmedia_biz.

Suggested Exercises

1. Other than the steps mentioned in this chapter, what would you consider doing to get up to speed on covering a specific business beat?

2. You have been assigned to cover the grocery store industry for your media outlet. Ask five friends what types of stories they'd like to see about grocery stores. Do you think any of them are valid story ideas?

3. Compare the beat breakdowns of the *Atlanta Business Chronicle* and the *Atlanta Journal-Constitution* listed earlier in the chapter. Which one do you think does a better job of covering the community based on its beat structure? What would you change about each paper's business news beats?

4. Think about what beat you would be most interested in covering if you were a business reporter. Find a media outlet somewhere in the United States that covers that topic from a business perspective. List three things you like and three things you dislike about its coverage.

5. List 10 types of people you would want to develop as sources if you were given the energy industry to cover, and list the type of information you'd

like to get from each one. These sources can be inside or outside the companies on the beat.

6. Compare the coverage on TechCrunch to the coverage of the tech industry in the *San Jose Mercury News*. Which one did a better job? How were they different in their coverage?

Books on Business Beats

Reed, R., & Lewin, G. (2005). *Covering business: A guide to aggressively reporting on commerce and developing a powerful business beat*. Oak Park, IL: Marion Street Press.

Thompson, T. (ed.) (2000). *Writing about business: The new Columbia Knight-Bagehot guide to economics and business journalism*. New York: Columbia University Press.

References

Associated Press. (2009, August 2). But wait! There's more! Ads on TV, that is. Retrieved August 2, 2009 from www.msnbc.msn.com/id/32259924/ns/business-media_biz/.

Connor, E. (2009, July 31). Columbia Farms workers sue company: Chicken processor enters not guilty plea to charges in hiring case. *Greenville News*, p. 1A.

Rexrode, C. (2009, August 1). Turnover claims 3 more BofA directors: Government pressure is likely part of reason for resignations at the Charlotte-based bank. *Charlotte Observer*, p. 1D.

Wiersma, J.C. (2009, July 31). Hospitals contend recession is factor against building new hospital. *The Tennessean*, p. 2.

4

COVERING ECONOMICS STORIES

What Drives the Economy

No story in the twenty-first century has been more important to every reader of business news than that of the economy. With housing prices down, the stock market fluctuating wildly, banks being taken over by the government, businesses closing and consumers saddled with debt, being able to report these issues clearly has become a necessity.

That's not an easy job. The economy of any town, city, county, state, or country can seem to be a nebulous concept for a reporter to grasp. What exactly makes an economy? An economy can be defined as the activities surrounding the production and distribution of goods and services for consumption in a region. Those activities include paying workers to manufacture products that are then sold. The money paid to those employees goes to work in the region as they purchase other goods and services to live. Economies can grow, and they can contract. If a country or region's economy is growing, jobs are being created. A business reporter interested in the economy could write a story about what kind of jobs are available, for what pay and in what industries. The converse is also true. When the economy starts to slow down or decline, there is not as much demand for a company's goods and services as there was in the past. When companies are faced with such an economic slowdown, they are often forced to lay off workers, as the U.S. economy saw in 2008 and 2009.

Companies—public and private, large and small—will increase or decrease their capital expenditures on the basis of where they believe the national or regional economies are headed. If the CEO and other executives at a company decide that the economy is going to keep growing and that consumers are going to spend more money in the future, they will likely increase capital expenditures. Capital expenditures can be defined as the money spent by a company to expand or build its business.

Companies will also decrease their spending when they think that there will not be as much demand for their products. Raleigh, North Carolina–based Martin Marietta Materials Incorporated makes products that help build roads and bridges, among other things. Company executives decreased its capital expenditures in 2009 after deciding that the economy, particularly the spending on new construction for neighborhood roads, was not going to grow as fast as it had in previous years. Thus, any business reporter looking for clues about the economy in his or her region will want to talk to business executives. Company managements watch the economy and economic indicators closely. They do not want to be caught with too much of their product sitting in warehouses when there is no demand, nor do they want to be caught with too little of their goods being manufactured when demand is great because they are likely to lose sales.

Others are interested in what companies are doing. If a company's executive team decides that the economy is about to grow stronger than it has in the past, it will increase its production, raising the possibility that it will sell more of its goods. If it sells more of its goods, it might have higher revenue and profits. This will attract the interest of investors on Wall Street, who might want to buy the company's stock.

On the national level, a key economic indicator is a report from the Department of Commerce's Bureau of the Census that measures manufacturers' shipments, new orders, inventories and unfilled orders. If new orders to manufacturers are rising, likely there will soon be more goods shipped. This is a positive indicator for the economy. Or, if manufacturers' inventory levels are going up, it means that they are not selling as many of their goods as they once were and their warehouses are filling up. This is a negative indicator for the economy.

TIPS FROM THE PROS

Bloomberg Businessweek economics editor Peter Coy on following the economics beat:

Economic imperialism. If you squint hard enough, every story becomes part of your beat. Sports. Sex. Innovation. Rutabaga cultivation.

The Federal Reserve Board looks at industrial production by industry—manufacturing, mining and utilities. And it also breaks its production report down by market group, such as consumer goods, business equipment and building materials. The information is typically released around the fifteenth of every month and is also closely watched by those interested in whether the economy is growing or contracting.

Plenty of other reports from a variety of groups also examine companies' production, inventory, orders and shipping levels. For example, the Institute for Supply Management, formerly the National Association of Purchasing Management, produces a monthly report on a national survey of manufacturing activity. The highlight of this report is a measurement called the Purchasing Managers' Index, or the PMI, which takes into account new orders, production, employment, deliveries and inventories. Big moves in the PMI can signal a change in the economy. The Reserve Bank in Philadelphia also issues a monthly report that looks at manufacturing activity in the region. The survey, based on a survey sent to about 250 manufacturers in the area, is more of an outlook on business activity. All of these reports on production by companies are closely watched. Although they often move in tandem, one moving in the opposite direction to the others may be the first sign that the economy is changing.

When writing about important economic barometers, understand that the millions of businesses in the country are the driving force of the economy. Businesses in any county or region may actually be increasing production or shipments while the rest of the state or country may be decreasing production and shipments. It always helps to keep close tabs on what local businesses are doing. When a report on industrial production comes out, the business reporter should be sure to check with a few local businesses. For example, some local economies try to entice businesses to move to their regions by offering tax incentives or zones where goods can be shipped tax-free. Others have economic development areas around downtown districts or other regions to stimulate growth. These, too, may have an impact on the local economy that does not show up in these reports.

 Federal Reserve Board: The governing body of the federal reserve system. They are appointed to the board of governors by the president, but they must be approved by the Senate.

Economics is not an exact science, and neither is writing about the economy. The economy can send mixed signals. It is important for writers trying to make sense of economic indicators or factors to understand what they are writing about. Otherwise their stories will also send mixed signals. Although the economic picture may be cloudy, writing about it should be clear.

What happened in the economy in 2008 and 2009 was one of the dominant stories covered by the media—and not just the business media. A recession caused by many factors, including a decline in the housing market, led many businesses and consumers to reconsider how much they were spending and what they were buying. Large amounts of debt have crippled many households, while businesses have closed their doors because they were unable to borrow the money they needed to continue operating.

One of the most important factors that led to the economic situation was the increasing role Wall Street played in the economy. More and more, Wall Street bundled together and sold the loans consumers bought to purchase items such as houses and cars. The increasing trend of securitization of selling loans to investors called collateralized debt obligations—without examining the creditworthiness of the loans and the consumers backing the investment—was an issue that few understood.

Yet, many of these trends, such as the increase in household ownership, the rising credit card debt levels and the push in sub-prime lending, which offered home loans to consumers who previously would not have been eligible for such borrowing, led to the economic troubles that economics reporters could have discerned if they had looked at numbers.

The rest of this chapter examines how a business reporter covers some basic economic stories.

The Federal Reserve

When Janet Yellen talks, people listen—especially reporters. The chair of the Federal Reserve Board is likely the most powerful person in the country, next to the president. And s/he is one of the few people who can determine the political fortunes of presidents by steering the economy. But, besides knowing the name of the first woman to leave the Federal Reserve, few Americans fully understand Yellen's job or the important role played by the Federal Reserve, or the Fed, as it is commonly known, in managing the country's economy.

TIPS FROM THE PROS

Bloomberg Businessweek economics editor Peter Coy on following the economics beat:

Be your own expert. There are many true things you can discover and report without a Ph.D. in economics. If you do your job right, the professors will be coming to you with questions.

The Federal Reserve, created in 1913, serves as the country's central bank. There are seven members on the board of governors, each of whom is appointed by the president and confirmed by Congress to serve a 14-year term. The primary responsibility of the board is to set the country's monetary policy, which may seem like a vague definition. Put simply, the Fed's monetary policies aim to stimulate economic growth without causing too much inflation. The Fed tries to make the economy grow when the board members believe it is slowing and slow down the growth when they believe it is growing too fast, which could cause prices of goods and services to rise faster than wages. The Fed accomplishes its goals by controlling the economy's money flow and available credit.

The seven board members make up a majority of the Federal Open Market Committee. There are five other members of the committee, who are presidents of regional Federal Reserve Banks, including the Federal Reserve Bank of New York, selected on a rotating basis. There are Federal Reserve Bank locations in major cities across the country, including Philadelphia, Chicago, Denver, Richmond, Atlanta, Kansas City and San Francisco.

 inflation: The rate at which the average price of all goods and services in the economy from one year to the next is rising, and therefore, purchasing power is falling.

This committee meets eight times each year to discuss the state of the country's economy and whether the group should take action on the basis of their assessment of various economic indicators. If the committee believes that economic growth is slowing, it might lower the federal funds rate to stimulate spending. Conversely, if, in the opinion of the committee, the economy is growing too fast, it might raise the federal funds rate to slow spending. The federal funds rate refers to the interest rate at which depository institutions lend balances at the Federal Reserve to other depository institutions overnight. It affects other economic factors, including the interest rate that banks and other lenders charge when a consumer purchases a home or a car. If banks and lenders start charging a higher interest rate, for example, consumers might hold off on purchasing an item using a loan. This could cause economic growth to slow.

Fed officials forecast where the economy is headed with their monetary policy. Because they are making a forecast, they are constantly looking at the trends in major economic barometers—many of which are discussed later in this chapter. Those include the unemployment rate, the Consumer Price Index (CPI), auto and home sales and consumer confidence. Unemployment and inflation are two of the Fed's biggest concerns.

After each committee meeting, the Fed issues a press release stating the action taken by the committee, even if no action was taken. This is always a story, particularly for major newspapers and other large media outlets. The release would read something like this:

> Information received since the Federal Open Market Committee met in October suggests that economic activity has been expanding at a moderate pace. Household spending and business fixed investment have been increasing at solid rates in recent months, and the housing sector has improved further; however, net exports have been soft. A range of recent labor market indicators, including ongoing job gains and declining unemployment, shows further improvement and confirms that underutilization

of labor resources has diminished appreciably since early this year. Inflation has continued to run below the Committee's 2 percent longer-run objective, partly reflecting declines in energy prices and in prices of non-energy imports. Market-based measures of inflation compensation remain low; some survey-based measures of longer-term inflation expectations have edged down.

Consistent with its statutory mandate, the Committee seeks to foster maximum employment and price stability. The Committee currently expects that, with gradual adjustments in the stance of monetary policy, economic activity will continue to expand at a moderate pace and labor market indicators will continue to strengthen. Overall, taking into account domestic and international developments, the Committee sees the risks to the outlook for both economic activity and the labor market as balanced. Inflation is expected to rise to 2 percent over the medium term as the transitory effects of declines in energy and import prices dissipate and the labor market strengthens further. The Committee continues to monitor inflation developments closely.

TIPS FROM THE PROS

Bloomberg Businessweek economics editor Peter Coy on following the economics beat:

An economics story is just a story. Every rule of journalism applies equally to economics journalism.

The Committee judges that there has been considerable improvement in labor market conditions this year, and it is reasonably confident that inflation will rise, over the medium term, to its 2 percent objective. Given the economic outlook, and recognizing the time it takes for policy actions to affect future economic outcomes, the Committee decided to raise the target range for the federal funds rate to 1/4 to 1/2 percent. The stance of monetary policy remains accommodative after this increase, thereby supporting further improvement in labor market conditions and a return to 2 percent inflation.

In determining the timing and size of future adjustments to the target range for the federal funds rate, the Committee will assess realized and expected economic conditions relative to its objectives of maximum employment and 2 percent inflation. This assessment will take into account a wide range of information, including measures of labor market conditions, indicators of inflation pressures and inflation expectations, and readings on financial and international developments. In light of the current shortfall of inflation from 2 percent, the Committee will carefully monitor actual and expected progress toward its inflation goal. The Committee expects that economic conditions will evolve in a manner that will warrant only gradual increases in the federal funds rate; the federal funds rate is likely to remain, for some time, below levels that are expected to prevail in the longer run. However, the actual path of the federal funds rate will depend on the economic outlook as informed by incoming data.

The Committee is maintaining its existing policy of reinvesting principal payments from its holdings of agency debt and agency mortgage-backed securities in agency mortgage-backed securities and of rolling over maturing Treasury securities at auction, and it anticipates doing so until normalization of the level of the federal funds rate is well under way. This policy, by keeping the Committee's holdings of longer-term securities at sizable levels, should help maintain accommodative financial conditions.

Voting for the FOMC monetary policy action were: Janet L. Yellen, Chair; William C. Dudley, Vice Chairman; Lael Brainard; Charles L. Evans; Stanley Fischer; Jeffrey M. Lacker; Dennis P. Lockhart; Jerome H. Powell; Daniel K. Tarullo; and John C. Williams.[1]

Reuters covered this five-paragraph release this way:

The Federal Reserve hiked interest rates for the first time in nearly a decade on Wednesday, signaling faith that the U.S. economy had largely overcome the wounds of the 2007–2009 financial crisis.

The U.S. central bank's policy-setting committee raised the range of its benchmark interest rate by a quarter of a percentage point to between 0.25 percent and 0.50 percent, ending a lengthy debate about whether the economy was strong enough to withstand higher borrowing costs.

"With the economy performing well and expected to continue to do so, the committee judges that a modest increase in the federal funds rate is appropriate," Fed Chair Janet Yellen said in a press conference after the rate decision was announced. "The economic recovery has clearly come a long way."

The Fed's policy statement noted the "considerable improvement" in the U.S. labor market, where the unemployment rate has fallen to 5 percent, and said policymakers are "reasonably confident" inflation will rise over the medium term to the Fed's 2 percent objective.

The central bank made clear the rate hike was a tentative beginning to a "gradual" tightening cycle, and that in deciding its next move it would put a premium on monitoring inflation, which remains mired below target.

"The process is likely to proceed gradually," Yellen said, a hint that further hikes will be slow in coming.

She added that policymakers were hoping for a slow rise in rates but one that will keep the Fed ahead of the curve as the economic recovery continues. "To keep the economy moving along the growth path it is on . . . we would like to avoid a situation where we have left so much (monetary) accommodation in place for so long we have to tighten abruptly."

New economic projections from Fed policymakers were largely unchanged from September, with unemployment anticipated to fall to 4.7 percent next year and economic growth hitting 2.4 percent.

The Fed statement and its promise of a gradual path represented a compromise between policymakers who have been ready to raise rates for months and those who feel the economy is still at risk from weak inflation and slow global growth.

"The Fed is going out of its way to assure markets that, by embarking on a 'gradual' path, this will not be your traditional interest rate cycle," said Mohamed El-Erian, chief economic advisor at Allianz.

Fed officials said they were confident the situation was ripe for them to make a historic turn in policy without much disruption to financial markets, which had expected the hike this week.

U.S. stocks rallied on the news, in part because the Fed made clear it would proceed slowly with further tightening. Yields on U.S. Treasuries rose, while the dollar was largely unchanged against a basket of currencies. Oil prices fell sharply before paring losses.[2]

The story quotes from the Fed's press release but also provides analyses from economists who have viewed the statement, giving insight into what the Fed's board may be thinking.

Later, the Federal Reserve releases minutes from the meetings. While the newsworthiness of what was discussed in these meetings is often muted as a result of the delay in the time between the meeting and the release of the minutes, they sometimes show disagreements among the members. The Fed also presents a report on the economy to Congress twice a year, and the chair is called to testify before Congress. As chair, Janet Yellen carries tremendous clout in influencing the economy. Yellen has been chair of the Fed since 2014, and she was a well-known economics professor at Cal-Berkeley. Because of that, her influence among the other board members is tremendous. They often vote based on what Yellen says and believes.

TIPS FROM THE PROS

Bloomberg Businessweek economics editor Peter Coy on following the economics beat:

Learn Excel. A stock rose from $25 in 2004 to $347 in 2015. What was its compound annual growth rate? Easy: =(347/25)^(1/11)−1. That's 27 percent.

Because of that influence, when Yellen talks, reporters carefully chronicle and analyze her words. Her speeches before Congress and others are considered major news. The Fed makes copies of Yellen's speeches and the speeches of other board members and bank presidents readily available to the media. Reporters who have spent years covering the Fed and monetary policy will look for clues as to what board members are thinking about the economy in these speeches.

Be forewarned, however. These speeches can be tedious to read unless you're a fan of academic writing. Many of the public comments are filled with long and complicated explanations of where the economy is going. The job for any reporter covering the Fed is to boil the speech down to its simplest form.

Investors also react to what the Fed chair says. Before Yellen and Ben Bernanke, the chair was Alan Greenspan. If Greenspan warned that the economy was growing faster than it should, investors sold stocks because that meant the Fed might raise interest rates to slow growth, causing profits for companies to ease. Or, if Greenspan believed that the economy needed a boost, some might have believed that interest rates would be lowered, leading investors to want to buy stocks because of the potential for higher profits. It has been common in the past for the Dow Jones Industrial Average and other stock indexes to jump or fall based on the Federal Reserve chair's comments or a decision by the Federal Open Market Committee.

Inflation

The best economics reporting, says Noam Neusner, who covered the economy for Bloomberg News and *U.S. News & World Report,* is all about spotting such important trends. So while it is important for any reporter to understand the content and nature of reports from the federal government that gauge different parts of the economy, the bigger focus needs to be on a few big ideas, says Neusner.

For example, inflation, or the price levels of goods and services, is an important economic barometer. If inflation is rising, the cost of goods and services for consumers is going up. But the business writer should not simply report that inflation is rising. In most cases, the story will be much more informative if the reporter finds consumers who are being affected by inflation at the grocery store or someplace else they shop. Consumers should be used in the story to let a reader see first-hand how a nebulous economic term such as inflation is changing everyone's lives.

TIPS FROM THE PROS

Bloomberg Businessweek economics editor Peter Coy on following the economics beat:

Round off. Eschew phony precision. Readers are turned off, and rightly so, when you write that home prices rose 2.93 percent over the past year.

The CPI measures inflation. It is one of the most widely recognized price measures for tracking the price of a basket of goods and services. The weight of each individual good or service is based on consumer spending patterns. For example, food and beverage make up 15 percent of the average person's budget, so a 1 percent increase in food prices would increase the CPI by 0.15 points.

The CPI is measured by the Bureau of Labor Statistics, and it is released monthly, typically three weeks after the end of the month. When reporting about inflation, a reporter typically looks at the increase from the previous month as well as the change in the past year. The reporter also looks at what goods and services increased or decreased dramatically in the past month. For example, gas prices declined by more than 30 percent in 2015, which allowed consumers to spend money elsewhere.

Note that while many inflation stories quote economists and not consumers, it's important to consider your audience. The typical MarketWatch.com audience is more investor focused. Wall Street investors, analysts and money managers looking to get economic and business news fast primarily read this website. They know how inflation affects consumers and do not need it explained to them. While this may also be the case for business magazines that cater to highly educated readers, it may not be true for the readers of most newspapers, who may have never actually thought about what inflation does to their own wallets. Explain to these readers that the CPI shows that they are paying more for goods and services by quoting consumers in how their spending is changed, and that is a concept they will understand.

A similar number is the Produce Price Index (PPI). It measures the prices received by producers when they sell the goods. The PPI is measured at three stages—finished goods, intermediate goods and crude goods. The index for finished goods is what reporters spend the most time reporting.

Unemployment

An economic topic most readers think they understand is the unemployment rate, but this can also be misinterpreted. The unemployment rate is the percentage of the labor force that does not have a job but is looking for work. It does not count the number of workers without a job who are not looking to become employed. So the unemployment rate may not always be an accurate barometer of how many people are without a job in any town or community.

Unemployment figures are collected for the country and for each state. If in one state the unemployment rate is lower than that of the rest of the country, a good story may be about why that is happening. Perhaps that state has more service-related jobs, and the bulk of job losses elsewhere in the country have occurred in manufacturing jobs.

The unemployment data is also collected by the Bureau of Labor Statistics, and it is released on the first Friday of the following month unless the first Friday is the first day of the year. It is collected in two ways—an establishment survey that assesses employment at companies, and a household survey that interviews consumers. The release also includes data on how much workers are being paid per hour, and how many hours per week they are working.

But in addition to the unemployment rate, this report also details the number of new jobs created each month. Job growth can indicate economic growth and is almost as important as the unemployment rate. Job gains can also signal the potential for inflation if there are a number of new workers willing to pay more for goods and services now that they are getting a regular paycheck.

Consumers are especially important when writing about employment or unemployment. Workers without a job can typically be found at the local unemployment office trying to find work. What are they doing to find a new job? Have they considered a job in a different field from their previous work experience? Will they need to be trained with new skills to make themselves more marketable to potential employers?

Sometimes, workers stop looking for jobs and are no longer counted in the unemployment rate; when they re-enter the job market, they are counted once again. Typically, out-of-work consumers start looking for jobs again when they believe the economy is getting better and work may have become available. Ironically, then, the first signal of a stronger economy may be a higher unemployment rate.

TIPS FROM THE PROS

Bloomberg Businessweek economics editor Peter Coy on following the economics beat:

Percent vs. percentage point. Use the terms right. If the top tax rate goes from 30 percent to 40 percent, you can call it either a 33 percent increase or a 10 percentage point increase.

The business reporter should not simply focus on the low-paying jobs. In many communities, the hardest hit in the unemployment line are those who were once making six-figure salaries and higher. They are often the workers who also have the toughest time finding a new job, and they may need to take a step down in pay to become employed again.

Thus, as Neusner suggested, it behooves the business reporter to look at the big picture. As mentioned earlier, business reporters should not simply write about the unemployment rate rising or falling without looking at what it means. One should take the national and state figures and apply them to the local community as well. Maybe what has been happening in the rest of the country is now occurring locally. It is easy to write about workers getting laid off or hired at one company. It is harder to write about the broader employment trends.

When companies hire workers, particularly a large number of workers, they are likely to announce this move with a news release heralding the event. "XYZ Products to expand local plant and add 200 workers," will likely be the headline on such a release. These stories can be informative to readers, particularly those who think they might be able to fill one of these jobs. Such stories provide a service to the readers if they give information on how to apply for the jobs or what types of jobs the company is looking to fill—manual labor, factory, administrative assistants, software development, etc.

The *Blackshear Times* in south Georgia began a front-page story on a business adding jobs to its community this way:

> A Jacksonville, Florida company that customizes vans and trucks for major Detroit automakers will build a $2.4 million plant in Waycross' industrial park.
>
> Sherrod Vans, a 23-year-old firm, will break ground Thursday at 9 a.m. on a 69,000 square-foot building located on 25 acres just across Industrial Boulevard from Clayton Homes. The company hopes to be in operation in approximately 10 months, employing at least 100 workers from this area with plans to expand to 150 soon after.
>
> Annual payroll for the company is expected to top $6 million.[3]

There are many sources for ideas about employment stories. An enterprising reporter can sometimes find out about a company's intent to hire local workers by scanning his newspaper's classified ads. Often, a business will advertise jobs in an area to see what kind of demand it will get from the local workforce before announcing the move. Also note that the Conference Board releases a monthly Help-Wanted Index that tracks the demand for workers by surveying advertising in major newspapers across the country.

In addition, individual company layoffs can also be important stories. Sometimes, they signal for the first time that a business may be in financial trouble. Layoffs can also be an indication that an industry is slumping or that a new competitor is taking away business. Many companies are not likely to want to discuss layoffs and rarely announce such decisions with a release, but disgruntled workers may call reporters to let them know. If an executive at the business writes a memo to employees explaining the decision, that memo often shows up anonymously on the newsroom fax machine, especially if reporters have cultivated relationships with workers.

There is another, more reliable method to find out about layoffs in a timely manner, however. A federal law known as the Worker Adjustment and Retraining Notification Act, or more commonly referred to as the WARN Act, requires businesses to notify their workers within 60 days of a plant closing or a layoff. These notifications are filed with state labor departments and local government officials and can be reviewed by the public. The WARN Act notices are also given to labor officials if the affected workers are represented by a union. If a reporter has never looked at a WARN Act filing, he or she should find out who in the area oversees these documents. They can be filled with stories of which the local media outlet was unaware. In general, businesses must file WARN Act notices if they have 100 or more workers, as long as the workers have been on the job for at least six months and work more than 20 hours per week. Plant closings are covered if the shutdown will result in the loss of work for at least 50 workers for more than 30 days. Layoffs are covered under the law if the company has more than 500 workers or more than 50 employees if the layoff will result in at least one-third of them losing their jobs.

TIPS FROM THE PROS

Bloomberg Businessweek economics editor Peter Coy on following the economics beat:

Data before anecdote. If the Bureau of Labor Statistics says food prices have fallen over the past year but the first five shoppers you buttonhole outside the supermarket say they've gone up, believe the BLS.

Finding workers who have changed jobs can lead to interesting employment stories that give a glimpse into the local economy. Is there a nursing shortage at the local hospital? If so, what are administrators doing to attract more nurses to the area? Drug store chains such as CVS often provide incentives for pharmacists to move to small towns for a certain time period. Another interesting employment trend may be that elderly workers who have already retired are rejoining the workforce. This may be for various reasons but could include the fact that they did not save enough for retirement or simply became bored with staying at home.

leading indicators: An economic measurement that begins to change before the economy moves in that direction.

Consumer Confidence

Gauging where the economy is headed is almost like being a psychologist for the country or a region. Many times, it is necessary to get inside the head of consumers to determine what they are thinking.

Economists, Wall Street investors and corporations widely watch consumer confidence reports because they are considered a leading indicator of where the economy is headed. If consumer confidence is on the rise, people are more likely to spend money in the future on goods and services; if consumer confidence falls, those purchases may be delayed. Many factors influence consumer confidence. The two most widely known consumer confidence reports come from the Conference Board and the University of Michigan.

TIPS FROM THE PROS

Bloomberg Businessweek economics editor Peter Coy on following the economics beat:

Read things you don't understand. Before you call professors with questions, struggle through their relevant research. You won't get everything but you'll conduct a smarter interview, and the professor will thank you for it.

The Conference Board, which polls 5,000 households every month, asks questions such as *How would you rate the present general business conditions in your area? Good, normal, or bad?* and *How would you guess your total family income to be six months from now? Higher, same, or lower?* The Michigan report asks questions such as *Would you say that you and your family living with you are better off or worse off financially than you were a year ago?* and *Now looking ahead, do you think that a year from now you and your family living with you will be better off financially, worse off, or just about the same as now?*

The Conference Board questions emphasize labor conditions, whereas the Michigan survey focuses on financial conditions. But each comes out with a number reflecting the change in consumer sentiment from the previous month based on an overall index. Consumer sentiment can be affected by other events, such as the 9/11 terrorist attacks, as well. After that, consumer confidence fell.

A Reuters reporter tied consumer confidence to other economic factors such as lower interest rates and incentives from car manufacturers when he filed a report that noted that consumer confidence increased. Despite their ability to refinance home mortgages at lower rates and buy new cars with little or no interest, consumers were still concerned about the economy. The report also noted that consumer confidence had hit its lowest level since the previous November but that the level of consumer confidence was higher than forecasted by economists.

Consumer Confidence Index: A measurement by the Conference Board on whether consumers are feeling optimistic or pessimistic about the economy.

Consumer confidence reports can be timely, issued within days of when consumers were questioned, so their findings are closely watched. Reporters interested in writing about the economy can follow up on the results of these studies on consumer confidence by interviewing local consumers and getting their feelings about the economy and spending.

Also note that another good picture of the economy comes from the Conference Board's Expectations Index, which projects consumer feelings about six months in the future. If that index falls below a rating of 80 for two months, then economists believe a recession is coming. Although the Conference Board and the Michigan reports are the two most widely cited in stories, other reports also gauge consumer sentiment, including one by ABC News and *Money* magazine.

Consumer Credit

A consumer's level of credit is also an economic factor that most readers can understand as long as it is explained to them properly. The Federal Reserve Board, which was discussed earlier in the chapter, tracks consumer credit in monthly reports. If consumers increasingly use credit cards to make purchases, they may have difficulty paying off those bills down the road, in turn hurting the economy. The *Charlotte Sun* in southwest Florida covered the rising problem of credit card debt on its front page in a package that explained the issue to any reader with a Visa or MasterCard in his or her wallet. The story began as follows:

> When you're overwhelmed with debt, every thought focuses on unpaid bills.
>
> Instead of sleeping nights, you spend them pacing the floor. Arguments at home take place more frequently. And the most dreaded sound is the phone ringing.
>
> "They hate the telephone," said Lennie Eisenberg, office manager of Consumer Budget Counseling Inc. in Southwest Florida, of his debt management clients. "People come in very stressed. Creditors are calling day and night and are very nasty. They're calling people at work. It gets to the point people don't even want to answer the phone—they feel haunted."
>
> Debt is a problem for one out of every 10 adults in the United States, according to Myvesta.org, a financial crisis treatment center in Gaithersburg, Md. And financial problems tend to trigger depression—more than death, family illness, work worries or marital problems—according to 88 percent of people surveyed for the National Depression Campaign.[4]

Does the above read like a business story? Not really. Yet it tackles a serious economic issue that faces millions of consumers across the country. That is the type of writing about economic topics that helps bring the reporting home to readers.

TIPS FROM THE PROS

Bloomberg Businessweek economics editor Peter Coy on following the economics beat:

Think micro. There's more to economics than predicting GDP, as the authors of *Freakonomics* can tell you. Bring supply-and-demand analysis to bear when writing about how local firms and families make decisions.

Readers understand how their household debt affects personal spending habits. The more debt they have, the more of their income must go to paying off that debt plus interest. The Federal Reserve releases a quarterly report on the household debt service burden, which during the first decade of the twenty-first century was at its highest level in the past two decades. If the reporter finds some readers with too much debt, then he or she will have a story that ties nicely into these statistics and backs up a national trend.

Business and economics reporters need to expand their ideas of what makes a good story about the economy. Too often, these stories simply report the numbers from a government report. This is too boring. Reporters need to take the extra step and explain what the numbers mean and put a face to the numbers by offering the reader personal examples and anecdotes based on interviews.

Simplicity and explanation are the most important elements of writing about the economy. Without those things, the reader will be lost.

Auto, Home and Retail Sales

When people spend money buying goods and services to live, economists and others wanting to get a feel for consumer spending trends watch and track their expenditures closely. Two of the biggest items tracked are sales of automobiles and sales of houses. Increases and decreases in both of these big-ticket items can give a good picture of where the economy is headed. Whereas employment information may tell readers whether a consumer has the ability to spend money, information about sales for specific items gives an even better picture because it shows how willing a consumer is to spend that money.

TIPS FROM THE PROS

Bloomberg Businessweek economics editor Peter Coy on following the economics beat:

Make friends with data. You should know your way around all of these websites: bls.gov, bea.gov, federalreserve.gov, census.gov, trade.gov, research.stlouisfed.org/fred2/, eia.gov, worldbank.org and imf.org. Know how to find the latest research on nber.org, ssrn.com and ideas.repec.org.

Individual automakers and the Bureau of Economic Analysis typically release sales statistics for cars and trucks right after the end of the month. Auto sales can be cyclical, depending on the economy, and are tied to interest rates as well. If interest rates are low, then there is an incentive for consumers to purchase cars. Car sales are about 5 percent of the country's gross domestic product (GDP), but since vehicle sales are considered "discretionary" purchases, they are often examined as a barometer for consumer behavior. An increase in car sales likely means that consumers are happy with their jobs and the economy and feel comfortable spending money on a new vehicle. If car sales slump, the decline could be an indication that consumers are worried about the economy.

Here is how the *Detroit News*, a paper that spends a lot of reporter resources and time covering the auto industry, typically covers car sales:

> Auto sales are on a record pace buoyed by strong consumer demand, low interest rates and fuel prices, as well as a strong array of new vehicles to entice them.
>
> U.S. sales were up 13.6% in October compared with a year ago with 1.46 million vehicles sold, according to Autodata. Importantly, the sales pace is a breakneck 18.24 million units, which is an impressive follow-up to September's 18.1 million pace. You have to go back to 2000 to find two consecutive months with an adjusted sales pace that tops 18 million.
>
> If this keeps up, 2015 auto sales will be one for the history books.
>
> "We've officially passed recovery mode and are now into record new-car sales," said Karl Brauer, senior analyst for Kelley Blue Book.
>
> Big winners: Detroit's automakers with their bevy of hot-selling trucks and SUVs. Underperformers: German brands including BMW which saw sales fall, as well as Mercedes-Benz and Volkswagen, which had single-digit increases. All lack a full truck lineup and VW is also starting to feel the effects of its admission it deceived consumers about the emissions coming from its diesel-powered vehicles.
>
> General Motors sales of its new cars and trucks rose 16% in October, Fiat Chrysler Automobiles climbed 15% and Ford posted a 13% increase.
>
> "Like 2005 all over again, truck sales are dominating the market, and driving not only growth but healthy profits throughout the industry," Bauer said.
>
> Toyota's sales rose 13%, selling more than 200,000 vehicles for its best October ever. Nissan was up 13% while Honda's sales were 9% higher than a year earlier.
>
> "October was a huge month for the industry, smashing expectations and continuing its hot streak," said Bill Fay, group vice president and general manager for the Toyota division.
>
> "Consumers blew the doors off new-vehicle sales in October with numbers echoing back to 2001, when the nation was recovering from September 11th and 'Keep America Rolling' was the industry battle cry, led by GM," said Rebecca Lindland, senior analyst for Kelley Blue Book.[5]

The story explains why car sales have increased and gives perspective as to when the last time sales increased for the industry. Although the story is numbers intensive, it also gives a broad overview of the industry and how it is affecting the economy. Missing, perhaps, are comments from consumers who either recently made a car purchase or are considering a car purchase.

Car sales data can sometimes fluctuate wildly, depending on manufacturers' incentives and dealer rebates. Sales may be strong one month but not the next. New model introductions also influence sales. For smaller media outlets, however, new car sales can be a vital story in explaining the local economy, particularly if there are just one or two new car dealers in the area. Getting information about new sales from those dealers can sometimes be hard, but they are likely the best gauge of a local economy's potential for growth—or decline.

Buying a home is the one purchase a consumer will make that will be worth more than a vehicle. Buying a home can be a stressful event, and many consumers go to great lengths to ensure that they are getting the right house for their needs. Nationally, the Bureau of the Census, which typically reports on a monthly basis, tracks new home sales. New home sales make up about 15 percent of total sales. The National Association of Realtors measures existing home sales, also issuing a report on a monthly basis.

Existing home sales make up about 85 percent of total home sales. Still, new home sales are important for the overall economy because they reflect new ownership, whereas existing home sales are typically current homeowners buying a new home and selling the old. Existing home sales numbers are based on contract closings, whereas new home sales data is based on the signing of a sales contract. In many communities, home sales data can be found by contacting a local realtors association. These local numbers are frequently more valuable to your readers than the national data, as this *Chicago Tribune* story suggests:

> Megan Keskitalo and her husband, Glenn Eckstein, were enthusiastic city dwellers until the suburbs began calling. First it was Chicago's crime, then it was worry about school districts, and in the end, it was money that pushed them past the city's edge.
>
> After a long search, the parents of two young daughters packed up their $1,300-a-month three-bedroom Lincoln Square apartment and in September paid $286,000 for a three-bedroom town house in River Forest.
>
> "We were looking (in the city), but we couldn't find anything in our price range, which was under $350,000," Keskitalo said.
>
> They aren't the only ones. While experts say Chicago's housing market is sizzling—home sales were up about 8.1 percent in Chicago through November of this year, says the Illinois Association of Realtors—not everyone can afford to buy in the city. That's because home prices are up too.
>
> For the first 11 months of the year, the median price of a home sold in Chicago was up 6.4 percent, according to data from the Realtor group.
>
> That means some potential homebuyers are finding that what they pay in rent in trendy neighborhoods like Lakeview, Lincoln Square and

Bucktown can afford them a home with lower monthly mortgage payment in the suburbs. The median home price for a detached single-family home in popular suburbs like Downers Grove, Elmhurst and Clarendon Hills can be two to three times less than those in hot city neighborhoods.[6]

Just like car sales, home sales are influenced by interest rates. When interest rates rise, home sales often decrease because potential buyers want to purchase at the lowest interest rate possible. When rates fall, buyers enter the market, as many may have been waiting to lock in a lower rate before signing a contract.

In addition, there are groups tracking other economic barometers that relate to home sales. For example, the Mortgage Bankers' Association publishes a weekly report that tracks the number of mortgage applications across the country and looks at the number of consumers refinancing a loan at a lower interest rate. This can be important to watch because when consumers are refinancing a loan, they are often freeing up more cash to spend on other goods and services.

The National Association of Home Builders also issues a monthly report based on three factors—current sales, expected sales during the next three months and potential buyer traffic at new home sites. Although this report is not as closely watched as other housing market data, it is more timely. The Census Bureau also issues a monthly report on housing construction starts and permits. The report tracks single-family home and apartment construction as well as permits authorized by local building authorities. The construction starts tend to get more attention than the permits, although it can be argued that the permit data is more reliable.

Another key indicator of consumer spending is retail sales. When consumers spend more at retailers, it is an indication that the economy is growing, whereas declining retail sales indicate that the economy is in trouble. The Census Bureau measures retail sales and also releases its reports on a monthly basis. Retail sales figures are broken down into sectors, which include furniture, electronics and appliances, food and beverage, clothing, gasoline, sporting goods and general merchandise.

Because retail sales are almost 30 percent of the GDP, the information can provide valuable insight into consumer spending trends and give readers and others an indication of where the economy is headed. Large retailers and some Wall Street investment banks also issue sales reports. Big retailers such as Wal-Mart and Target issue monthly sales reports based on the performance at their stores. Business reporters should watch these reports closely. They may provide the first signal that the economy is turning. They can also be used to show what consumers in small- and medium-sized towns are doing with their money.

International Trade

When retailers, automakers, homebuilders and other U.S. companies are not selling goods and services to consumers in this country, they are trying to sell their products in other countries. Likewise, foreign companies are interested in selling their products to American consumers.

When the U.S. economy exports more goods than it imports, there is a trade surplus. When it imports more goods than it exports, there is a trade deficit. An understanding of how our economy is interacting with economies of other countries can be an important factor in understanding business growth.

 trade deficit: When the buying and selling of goods and services between two economies results in fewer exports than imports.

In 2014 the U.S. economy imported approximately $505 billion more in goods and services than it exported. (The last time the U.S. had a trade surplus was 1975.) Most of the deficit resulted from goods such as automobiles, industrial supplies and materials, and consumer goods. The country is actually exporting more in services than it is importing.

Simply comparing the import and export figures, however, paints an incomplete picture of international trade. Foreign markets are much more open to U.S. goods and services than they were a decade ago, and the United States is also importing more goods than previously. Imports and exports were less than 10 percent of the GDP in 1960, but now they account for nearly a quarter of the GDP.

The Census Bureau at the Commerce Department measures international trade. Each month, the agency releases a report on imports and exports, broken down by industry. The most important number in the report is the change in the deficit from the previous month.

A typical story covering trade would begin like this one from MarketWatch. com:

> The U.S. trade deficit climbed 3.4% in October as exports of American-supplied goods and services fell to the lowest level in three years.
>
> The trade gap rose to a seasonally adjusted $43.9 billion from an upwardly revised $42.5 billion in September, the Commerce Department said Friday. Economists polled by MarketWatch had forecast the deficit would end up at $40.6 billion. The gloomier trade picture, the result of a strong dollar and weak global growth, is likely to weigh on the U.S. economy again in the fourth quarter. A higher deficit subtracts from gross domestic product.
>
> Exports dropped 1.4% to $184.1 billion, hitting the lowest level since October 2012. A strong dollar has made it more expensive for U.S. companies such as manufacturers to sell goods and services to foreign customers. A weak global economy has also made it harder for customers outside the U.S. to buy American goods.

U.S. imports also dipped, down 0.6%, though most of the decline stemmed from the cheaper oil. The value of U.S. oil imports was the lowest since 2003.

Similarly, the gap between how much petroleum the U.S. imports and how much it exports also slid to $4.5 billion, the lowest deficit since 1999. The falling petroleum gap largely reflects a surge in U.S. oil production owing to fracking.

The trade deficit with Mexico, meanwhile, rose to the highest level in three years.[7]

gross domestic product: The monetary value of all goods, services and products made by an economy during a certain time period. It includes purchases, investments and exports minus imports.

Why is international trade important? It lets businesses—and the workers who rely on jobs at those businesses—know how successful they have been in selling their goods to countries overseas. For many businesses, the more products they sell overseas, the more successful they are. Many U.S. companies make a large portion of their sales outside of the country. Coca-Cola is considered one of the many all-American companies, and yet this business sells approximately two-thirds of all of its drinks in international markets. Another U.S. company, Boeing, sells more than half of its airplanes to foreign markets.

But there is more to understanding international trade than sales. Many companies depend on strong international currencies for profits. When the currency in countries where businesses sell goods falls in comparison with the dollar, they receive less revenue and, thus, smaller profits when they convert that currency into U.S. cash. So many companies with large international operations or that sell their products to international markets actually want a weak dollar—a fact that can be surprising to some readers.

Because of wild fluctuations in the value of their currencies, many foreign economies are considered unstable, whereas the U.S. economy is viewed as relatively stable. Unstable economies often have huge ups and downs in inflation and hence in the value of their currencies, which can make doing business in a foreign economy a risky proposition. Business reporters should find out whether any companies they are writing about have business in foreign countries. Then they should research those countries to see whether their economies have had any upswings or downswings recently. That may be the cause of an increase or decrease in a company's profits.

The Bureau of Labor Statistics compiles import and export price indexes that measure prices of goods and services imported to or exported from the country. These monthly reports reflect changes in the prices paid by importers or the prices at which exporters sell their goods. Commodity products (such as oil) and agriculture products (such as wheat) often affect import price changes.

Knowing what is happening in foreign economies can be important to writing about the U.S. economy and to writing about specific American companies. It is also vital to have an understanding of foreign corporations that may have local or regional operations. These foreign businesses may be affected by economic events back home, whereas the U.S. subsidiary is operating smoothly. Although information about foreign companies is limited, documents and other filings on foreign companies can be obtained from U.S. regulatory agencies that help explain trade with other countries.

Notes

1. From Federal Open Market Committee news release, December 16, 2015, Federal Reserve Board.
2. From "Fed raises interest rates, citing ongoing U.S. recovery," by H. Schneider and J. Lange, December 17, 2015, Reuters. Copyright 2015 by Reuters. Reprinted with permission.
3. From "Customizing van facility means 100+ jobs for area," by R. Williams, September 25, 2002, *Blackshear* (Georgia) *Times,* p. 1. Copyright 2002 by *Blackshear Times.* Reprinted with permission.
4. From "Anguish, bills go hand in hand," by R. LePere, April 7, 2002, *Charlotte* (Florida) *Sun,* p. 1-A. Copyright 2002 by *Charlotte Sun.* Reprinted with permission.
5. From "U.S. auto sales on record pace; Detroit three lead the way," by A. Priddle, November 3, 2015, *Detroit News,* p. 1A. Copyright 2015 by *Detroit News.* Reprinted with permission.
6. From "Chicago's home prices drive some buyers to the suburbs," by C. Shropshire, December 22, 2015, *Chicago Tribune,* p. B-5. Copyright 2015 by *Chicago Tribune.* Reprinted with permission.
7. "U.S. exports fall to lowest levels in three years," by J. Bartash, December 4, 2015, MarketWatch.com. Copyright 2015 by MarketWatch.com. Reprinted with permission.

Key Terms

Consumer Confidence Index	inflation
Federal Reserve Board	leading indicators
gross domestic product	trade deficit

Suggested Exercises

1. Pick one stock or a set number of stocks at the beginning of the semester. Track the prices of the stocks you picked throughout the semester. At the end of the semester, compare the performance of your stocks with that of others in the class. What economic factors do you think influenced the rise or fall of your stocks?
2. Pick a day of the week and look at a dozen stocks in your community or in your state. Did they rise or fall for the day? How did they do compared to the rest of the stock market? Was there something that happened during the day that caused stocks of companies in one industry to rise or fall while the rest of the stock market moved in the opposite direction?

3. Go around the class asking your fellow students what type of jobs they've had during summer vacations or other times in their lives. How did they get these jobs? What was it like to be in the workforce? Were any of them ever afraid of losing their job? How hard was it to find a job?

4. Conduct a consumer confidence survey of 30 students on campus using some of the questions used by the Conference Board and the University of Michigan and report your findings in class. Do your results differ from those of other students who asked the same questions? If so, why do you think there's a difference in opinion?

Books on the Economy

Cleaver, T. (2006). *Understanding the world economy* (3rd ed.). New York: Routledge.

Foster, J.B. (2009). *The great financial crisis: Causes and consequences*. New York: Monthly Review Press.

Harris, E.S. (2008). *Ben Bernanke's Fed: The Federal Reserve after Greenspan*. Boston: Harvard Business School Press.

Kansas, D. (2009). *The Wall Street Journal guide to the end of Wall Street as we know it: What you need to know about the greatest financial crisis of our time—and how to survive it*. New York: Harper.

Tuccille, J. (2002). *Alan shrugged: Alan Greenspan, the world's most powerful banker*. New York: Wiley.

Woodward, B. (2002). *Maestro: Greenspan's Fed and the American boom*. New York: Simon & Schuster.

References

Bartash, J. (2015, December 4). U.S. exports fall to lowest levels in three years. MarketWatch.com. Retrieved December 27, 2015 at www.marketwatch.com.

Federal Reserve Board. (2015, December 16). Federal Open Market Committee news release. Retrieved December 27, 2015 from www.federalreserve.gov.

LePere, R. (2002, April 7). Anguish, bills go hand in hand. *The Charlotte (Florida) Sun*, pp. 1A–2A.

McCartney, M.S. (2000, April 18). Teaching' economics to the masses. Poynter.org. Retrieved December 10, 2002 from www.poynter.org.

Priddle, A. (2015, November 3). U.S. auto sales on record pace: Detroit three lead the way. *The Detroit News*, p. 1A. Retrieved December 27, 2015 from www.detroitnews.com.

Schneider, H., & Lange, J. (2015, December 17). Fed raises interest rates, citing ongoing U.S. recovery. Reuters. Retrieved December 27, 2015 from www.reuters.com.

Shropshire, C. (2015, December 22). Chicago's home prices drive some buyers to the suburbs. *The Chicago Tribune*, p. B-5. Retrieved December 27, 2015 from www.chicagotribune.com.

Williams, R. (2002, September 25). Customizing van facility means 100+ jobs for area. *The Blackshear Times*, p. 1.

5

EVALUATING A COMPANY'S FINANCIAL PERFORMANCE

Income Statements and Balance Sheets

A company is in operation to make money. If it is not making money, it needs to change its business in a way that enables it to be profitable. But how does one determine whether a company is making money? Public and private companies provide charts of financial numbers to the SEC and state regulatory agencies that are important to read and analyze. One is called the income statement, and the other is called the balance sheet. Both are equally valuable in the information they contain and the story they convey about a company's performance. Yet, too often, business writers focus on the income statement and ignore the balance sheet, as well as the cash-flow statement.

An income statement is a chart that records a company's financial performance. To the experienced reader, the income statement tells dozens of stories and gives plenty of clues about a company's financial performance. It details a company's sales, its expenses and its profits. A company typically provides its income statement for a three-month period, known as a fiscal quarter, and compares the performance in that time with the same three months of the previous year. Analysts should not compare one quarter with the previous quarter. The comparison may not be valid, particularly if a company's business is seasonal. For example, Coca-Cola sells more soft drinks in the second and third quarters of the year than it does in the first and fourth quarters. Why? It is hotter in the second and third quarters, so people purchase more soft drinks.

An income statement is an important barometer of a company's success and health. A business reporter should review the performance in the income statement and compare the growth rates of revenues, expenses and profits with each other. If revenues are growing faster than profits, one interpretation of those two numbers could be that a company is cutting the cost of its products. If profits are increasing faster than revenue, then a company could be cutting expenses. If expenses are rising faster than revenues or profits, then a business might have begun an advertising campaign that has yet to boost sales. There are three possible story ideas right in the income statement.

Table 5.1 shows what a typical financial statement for a fiscal quarter might look like.

The income statement of a company such as Coca-Cola is basic enough for anyone to understand if they know what they are looking at. The top line in this statement is called "Net operating revenues." What this means for a company such as Coca-Cola is that during the months of July, August and September of 2015, it sold $11.4 billion worth of Coke Classic, Diet Coke, Fanta, Mr. Pibb and other drinks. That is a decrease of 5 percent from the $11.9 billion worth of soft drinks it sold during the same three months of 2014.

Table 5.1 Condensed Consolidated Statements of Income

The Coca-Cola Company and Subsidiaries (Unaudited)

Three Months Ended (in million dollars except per share data)	October 2, 2015	September 26, 2014
Net operating revenues	11,427	11,976
Cost of goods sold	4,577	4,630
Gross profit	6,850	7,346
Selling, general and administrative expenses	4,207	4,507
Operating income	2,379	2,711
Interest income	155	169
Interest expense	138	113
Equity income (loss)—net	200	205
Other income (loss)—net	(871)	(312)
Income before income taxes	1,725	2,660
Income taxes	272	538
Net income	$1,453	$2,122
Less net income attributable to noncontrolling interests	4	8
Net income attributable to shareowners	$1,449	$2,114
Diluted net income per share	$ .33	$ .48
Average shares outstanding	4,399	4,445

Note: From Coca-Cola Company, Form 10-Q, filed with the SEC on October 28, 2015.

income statement: An accounting of sales, expenses and net profit for a given period.

The next line is called "Cost of goods sold." This line includes how much money it cost Coca-Cola to make the concentrates and syrups used to make the soft drinks. For this quarter, it cost the company nearly $4.6 billion, down 1 percent from the $4.6 billion it cost in the same quarter of 2014. Note that the cost to make the soft drinks for the company did not decline at nearly the same rate as sales. Maybe the decline in the costs was because Coca-Cola was charged less by its suppliers for the cost of the ingredients, such as artificial sweeteners, used to make its drinks. Understanding that a change in growth rates always has an underlying reason enables the business writer to ask the right questions of executives and Wall Street experts.

Next is "Gross profit." This figure is essentially sales minus the cost to produce the product. It excludes company expenses for running the business, which appear in the next line, called "Selling, general and administrative expenses." This line is also commonly called SG&A. These expenses include everything from advertising to executive and employee salaries to the cost of heating corporate headquarters and the company's telephone bill. At Coca-Cola, during this quarter, the SG&A costs were $4.2 billion, down 7 percent from the same quarter the previous year.

For a quick comparison of the numbers on an income statement, the back of the 10-Q—a document filed with the SEC by a company after the first three fiscal quarters—contains a section called "Results of Operations." Here, a company will review its performance for the time period, typically explaining the increase or decrease in each number listed in the income statement.

To review, we have a company for which revenue, or sales, decreased by 5 percent, the cost of making its product fell 1 percent and its SG&A expenses dropped 7 percent. By comparing the growth rates of these three figures, the business reporter should begin to understand what happened at the company that quarter. In the case of Coca-Cola, revenue declined slower than its SG&A expenses. That is an indication that the company decreased its expenses faster than it decreased sales. Ideally, when sales decline, investors would like to see a decline in expenses that the company can control, such as travel and pay. Somewhere, spending fell faster than sales.

By taking the revenue, or sales figure, and subtracting the cost of the goods and the SG&A expenses, a company arrives at its operating income, or the amount of money it made or lost before paying taxes and before other accounting effects. The operating income figure gives a business reporter an indication of how the company's core business is performing. In this case, Coca-Cola's operating income fell 12 percent when compared to the same quarter of last year. This decline is more than its revenue decline because of an operating charge of $264 million in the third quarter of 2015 that is not shown in the chart here. In the third quarter of 2014, that charge was less than half that amount, or $128 million.

TIPS FROM THE PROS

Southern Investigative Reporting Foundation founder Roddy Boyd on how to investigate a company:

A Sense of Rational Skepticism: Please don't leave the newsroom without it.

Most journalists, or rather, most *good* ones would try to cover even the most modest political rally or campaign with a sense of considered skepticism. Many business reporters don't apply that rule to press releases from companies, however.

The next few lines in the income statement reflect the money the company made or lost from its investments and from money it holds in bank accounts. This information typically does not heavily influence most companies' earnings. However, in some industries, it can have an impact. For example, insurance companies typically take premiums from consumers and invest that money in stocks and bonds. They then record income or losses from those investments here. Note that the losses reflected here are in parentheses instead of having a minus sign before a number. Don't report that a number from a company's earnings was positive when it has parentheses around it. A number inside parentheses means that it's a negative number. In the case of Coca-Cola, it reported an $871 million loss in the third quarter of 2015 on its investments in other companies, primarily bottlers around the world. But in the same three months of 2014, the company reported a loss of $312 million on those investments.

After adding and subtracting interest income and expenses, as well as income and losses from investments, the company arrives at an earnings figure before paying taxes. It then subtracts the amount of taxes paid in the quarter to arrive at a net income amount. This is the number that is arguably most important for the business reporter to assess because it reflects how much money a company made or lost during the quarter. Coca-Cola reported net income of $1.4 billion, a decline of 31 percent from the net income figure it reported in the same quarter the previous year.

Public companies such as Coca-Cola break down their net income figures to show how much money was made for each share of outstanding stock. This is called "Diluted net income per share" in Table 5.1, but it is typically known simply as earnings per share, or EPS. This number is calculated by dividing the net income by the total number of shares outstanding. The math for Coca-Cola is $1.4 billion in net income divided by the 4.4 billion shares outstanding, or 33 cents per share figure.

EPS is a barometer for Wall Street to measure a company's earnings. Many Wall Street analysts estimate a company's EPS on the basis of projections and computer models before a company actually reports the figure. If the company's actual EPS beats Wall Street analysts' estimates, then the company's stock could rise. If its EPS is lower than the estimate, the stock price could fall.

The following fictional excerpt explains how the above numbers could have been used to help explain Coca-Cola's earnings to readers:

> The Coca-Cola Co. reported third-quarter earnings that fell 31 percent due to lower sales of its carbonated beverages and a weak dollar.
>
> The Atlanta-based company reported net income of $1.4 billion, or 33 cents a share, compared with $2.1 billion, or 51 cents a share, in the quarter in 2014. The results were in line with Wall Street analyst expectations. Revenue fell 5%, to $11.4 billion from $11.9 billion, due to the weak currency exchange rates.
>
> The company's stock fell 1.3%, at $50.35 a share as investors worried about the lower revenue number, which missed projections, analysts said.

Note that the emphasis in the lead is on the growth in earnings, or net income. The actual net income numbers are not included until the second paragraph, in which the reporter also assesses where the EPS was in relation to estimates. For a more in-depth treatment of writing earnings stories and earnings estimates, see the "Writing the Earnings Story" section of this chapter.

TIPS FROM THE PROS

Southern Investigative Reporting Foundation founder Roddy Boyd on how to investigate a company:

Common Sense: Basic articles that wondered how a mortgage issuer can be highly profitable over time (and market cycles) issuing mortgages to a population subset that defaults with increasing frequency or, alternately, how they set increasing revenues or profit targets in a business dependent on interest-rates would have done much early on to expose two of the absurdities of what became the credit crisis.

Balance sheets are also important barometers of a company's financial status, but rarely do you see reporters writing stories about the company's balance sheet. They should, because the balance sheet shows the company's assets and debts. Though a company reports net income, it could have more liabilities than assets—possibly a truer reflection of that company's health. You can find out important information about a company by assessing the balance sheet.

 assets: Anything owned that has economic value. An asset is also a balance sheet item showing what a company owns. Assets are bought to increase the value of a firm or benefit the firm's operations. They can be anything from real estate to products.

The balance sheet is just what its name implies. The assets of a company on its balance sheet should be equal to the sum of its liabilities and the shareholders' equity in the company. Assets are typically divided into three areas: current; property, plant and equipment; and intangible assets. These will be explained in more detail after we look at a sample balance sheet. Since we discussed Coca-Cola earlier, let's look at its balance sheet at the end of the same quarter.

 shareholders' equity: A firm's total assets minus total liabilities. It is the amount of the company that is financed through common and preferred shares. Also known as capital.

Table 5.2 reflects the listing of the company's total assets as of October 2, 2015. The worth of these assets can change every day, particularly for items such as cash and cash equivalents, so it is important to view these numbers as a snapshot of a company's assets on just that day.

The top section lists how much cash Coca-Cola has in its bank accounts as of October 2. It also details the value of the inventory of soft drink ingredients and other materials the company had at the end of the quarter. This is called "Inventories." Another large item in this section is "Prepaid expenses and other assets." This line could include items such as money Coca-Cola has paid for advertising on television but has not yet used.

The next section of the list of assets is called "Investments and other assets." These columns list investments Coca-Cola has made in other companies around the world, either by purchasing stock or by adding money into the company. The investments listed by Coca-Cola are in companies that bottle and ship its soft drinks to retailers. Coca-Cola Enterprises, for example, is the largest soft drink bottler in the United States. Coca-Cola Amatil is a large bottler in Australia.

 balance sheet: A company's financial statement. It reports assets, liabilities and net worth at a specific time, typically the end of a quarter.

Table 5.2 Condensed Consolidated Balance Sheets

The Coca-Cola Company and Subsidiaries (Unaudited)

Three Months Ended (in million dollars except par value)	October 2, 2015	December 31, 2014
Current		
Cash and cash equivalents	9,983	8,958
Short-term investments	9,177	9,052
Total cash, cash equivalents and short-term investments	19,160	18,010
Marketable securities	3,614	3,665
Inventories	2,910	3,100
Assets held for sale	3,853	679
Total current assets	36,594	32,986
Equity method investments	12,504	9,947
Other investments	2,430	3,678
Other assets	4,446	4,407
Property, plant and equipment	12,615	14,633
Trademarks with indefinite lives	6,032	6,533
Goodwill	11,357	12,100
Other intangible assets	897	1,050
Total Assets	**$93,008**	**$92,023**

Note: From Coca-Cola Company, Form 10-Q, filed with the SEC on October 28, 2015.

Why does Coca-Cola invest in these companies? Maybe it is because company executives know that the success of these businesses is intertwined with Coca-Cola's own success. Such investments can be very important for a company—which is why it is vital for a business reporter to evaluate this section of the balance sheet. If a company is making investments in other companies that have nothing to do with its business, maybe those assets need closer examination. (Why would a beverage company invest in a software developer, for example? There should be some valid business reason for the investment.) A business reporter also wants to see whether these investments are increasing in value for the company. If they are not increasing, maybe the company's strategy of investing in other companies needs to be assessed. That review could turn into a story.

Following its investments, Coca-Cola lists the value of its property, plant and equipment. This is the land its headquarters is on, its other buildings, its computers, company cars, trucks and other items, such as vending machines. The value of these items decreases regularly as a result of an accounting measure called depreciation. Depreciation can be thought of this way: When a consumer buys a car, the worth of that car immediately declines as it is driven off the lot. That is the depreciation of the value of the car. If it is a Mercedes, its value may not decrease as fast as a Chevrolet's. The same depreciation in value happens with other items, such as computers and vending machines.

Last, the company lists the value of its trademarks and other intangible assets. Here, Coca-Cola assesses the value of the franchise rights it grants to bottlers. A breakdown of these assets can also be found in the filing.

All of these assets, minus depreciation, totaled $93 billion as of October 2. That is an increase of nearly $1 billion in assets for the company in the first nine months of 2015. And although this number may seem impressive, it is always smart to find out why assets are rising or falling. Typically, a company will explain this somewhere in the financial filing. In the case of Coca-Cola, the increase in assets is partly attributed to an increase in its property, plant and equipment.

Now, let's look at the other side of the balance sheet: the liabilities and shareowners' equity (Table 5.3). This side of the balance sheet should equal the company's assets.

The "Accounts payable and accrued expenses" section of the liabilities side of the balance sheet lists the money that the company owes various suppliers

Table 5.3 Condensed Consolidated Balance Sheets

The Coca-Cola Company and Subsidiaries (Unaudited)

Liabilities and Shareowners' Equity (in million dollars except share data)	*October 2, 2015*	*December 31, 2014*
Current		
Accounts payable and accrued expenses	9,877	9,234
Loans and notes payable	17,545	19,130
Current maturities of long-term debt	2,692	3,552
Accrued income taxes	383	400
Total current liabilities	31,545	32,374
Long-term debt	25,949	19,063
Other liabilities	4,194	4,389
Deferred income taxes	5,053	5,636
Shareowners' equity		
Common stock, 25 cents par value Authorized	1,760	1,760
11,200 shares issued: 7,040 and 7,040 shares, respectively		
Capital surplus	13,715	13,154
Reinvested earnings	65,209	63,408
Accumulated other comprehensive income	(10,813)	(5,777)
Treasury stock, at cost—2,698 and 2,674 shares, respectively	(43,822)	(42,225)
Equity Attributable to Shareowners	26,049	30,320
Equity Attributable to Noncontrolling Interests	218	241
Total Equity	26,267	30,561
Total Liabilities and Equity	$93,008	$92,023

Note: From Coca-Cola Company, Form 10-Q, filed with the SEC on October 28, 2015.

and vendors for the ingredients to make its soft drinks and other items. "Loans and notes payable" details the money that the company owes banks and other lenders. These are both included in current liabilities, or short-term debts, which are generally obligations that a company must pay within a year. Under this section, Coca-Cola lists how much long-term debt it owes. Long-term debt is typically payable in more than a year. Note that the long-term debt for the company more than doubled during the six-month time frame. Whenever you see a number increase by a significant amount, you should look into the reasons. In the case of Coca-Cola, part of the reason for the increase in long-term debt was its issuing of bonds to replace short-term debt.

TIPS FROM THE PROS

Southern Investigative Reporting Foundation founder Roddy Boyd on how to investigate a company:

Who Owns the Business? Probably the most basic component in understanding a company: who is taking the economic risk—and reaping the benefit—from starting a for-profit enterprise? The U.S. generally has quite thorough disclosure laws for businesses, although matters often get more complicated when it is a function of privately held businesses, as opposed to those companies where ownership interests (shares) are traded on an exchange. Still it is the rare business indeed that can't be made to reveal even the basics of its life, such as locale and ownership.

Finally, the company lists the value of the shareowners' equity, which is also commonly referred to as the book value of the company. This is essentially how much money shareholders would receive if the company sold everything in its possession, went out of business and paid its investors the money. Again, most companies discuss the increase or decrease in each of these numbers later in their financial disclosures. But it is important to compare the "Total current assets" side of the balance sheet with the "Total current liabilities" side primarily because companies typically pay the liabilities with the assets. If liabilities are exceeding assets, then a company may have to borrow money to pay some of those liabilities. Obviously, it is important to look at these balance sheet numbers for any large increases or decreases that might be a signal of something else going on at the company that could result in a story.

---

off-balance sheet financing: The way a company raises money that does not appear on the balance sheet, unlike loans, debt or equity that does appear on the balance sheet. Examples are joint ventures, research and development partnerships, and leases (rather than purchases of capital equipment).

Because of the failure of Enron Corporation, many casual readers of the business page may have heard of an "Off-balance sheet transaction." These are deals that a company enters into that are not included on a balance sheet. They may be the creation of a joint venture with another company, or they may be a loan to another company to help it get started. For example, oil companies create off-balance sheet subsidiaries to explore for new oil wells. Generally accepted accounting rules allow for these to be excluded from a company's balance sheet, but most of them must be detailed in the footnotes. These footnotes can be difficult to read and even harder to understand because they are written by accountants and reviewed by attorneys. If you encounter footnotes for an off-balance sheet transaction, it would be wise to take the information to an accountant, lawyer or another expert who understands what the disclosure is stating. In the case of Enron, the company was using the off-balance sheet transactions to pump up its earnings and mask enormous losses in many businesses.

Financial Statements for Private Companies

The first part of this chapter assessed the financial performance of a public company. Shares of Coca-Cola are traded on the New York Stock Exchange (NYSE). Because anyone can purchase its stock, it is considered a public company. Yet, Coca-Cola's financial statements are constructed very similarly to financial statements for a private company. That is why understanding how a company derives the numbers in its income statement and balance sheet can be important for any type of business reporting—whether the company is public or private.

Many beginning business reporters operate under the assumption that a private company is just that—private. They think that because investors do not own its stock, it is not required to divulge its financial performance. Nothing could be further from the truth. Many business reporters are surprised to learn that thousands of private companies, such as banks and insurance companies, are required to file documents disclosing their financial performance with state and federal regulators.

For example, when Publix Super Markets Incorporated, one of the country's largest grocery store chains, began expanding its operations out of Florida northward into Georgia, Alabama and South Carolina in the 1990s, smart newspaper reporters in those states delved into the company's financial performance as disclosed to the SEC, even though the Lakeland, Florida-based company is considered to be private. Why did Publix provide this information? Because companies with more than $10 million in assets with securities that are held by more than 500 owners must file annual and other periodic reports. Publix fits this description. Its stock is held by hundreds of store employees and by the Jenkins family. When Publix files financial information, it is news. The company's competitors want to know how it is performing, and so do its thousands of employees. Yet few reporters bother to look for this information. Here is a story from Bloomberg News that provided the results:

> Publix Super Markets Inc., a closely held supermarket company, said its profit last year was unchanged at $530.4 million.
>
> Per-share earnings rose to $2.62 from $2.52 a year earlier, as the company had fewer shares outstanding. Sales rose 4.8 percent to $15.3 billion from $14.6 billion in 2000, which had an extra week in the period, Publix said in a statement.
>
> Same-store sales rose 3.2 percent. Sales in stores open at least a year are a key indicator of a retailer's business because they exclude new and closed locations.
>
> Shares of Lakeland, Florida-based Publix, with 691 stores in Florida, Georgia, South Carolina and Alabama, are owned by family members and Publix employees and directors. The shares are valued at $41.[1]

The information in this story about a private company is the same as it would be for a public company. The lead emphasizes the company's profit, similarly to the lead in the story on Coca-Cola's earnings. Sales, or revenue, are just as important a barometer for private companies as for public ones. All companies, whether they are public or private, strive to keep increasing the amount of money they make. A company, public or private, is considered healthy if it continues to increase its sales and profits.

Similar financial information can be obtained from other regulatory agencies for private companies in other industries. For example, state commissioners regulate the insurance industry. Insurance companies that do business in a state are required to file financial information with the commissioner. (For more information about what is available from regulatory agencies, see Chapter 14.)

Although public and private companies report similar financial information, reporters should interpret the numbers differently. Public companies are in the business of increasing the stock price for their shareholders. To do that, many of them engage in practices such as cutting SG&A expenses to increase their profits. A private company, however, may not be as interested in improving profits. Management at private companies, often run by owners that have no interest in making the company public, may actually lower earnings for a year or two and use that money to build a new plant or add a new corporate headquarters building. Many private companies, particularly private businesses that have few shareholders, do not worry about EPS. And for very small private companies, there may be only one owner.

Why Companies Disclose Financial Information

Imagine for a minute that no company, public or private, ever divulged how much money it was making, how much money it was losing, or how its sales rose or fell from quarter to quarter or from year to year. How would potential investors assess whether to purchase stock in such companies? Would they just have to believe what the company told them? What about consumers deciding whether to buy a product from Company A or Company B? Obviously, there are some companies whose word is not to be trusted. Company executives know that by releasing financial information about their company's performance, they build confidence among their customers that it is not going to go out of business, and they may convince investors to buy stock if they can demonstrate an ability to increase revenue and profits.

TIPS FROM THE PROS

 Southern Investigative Reporting Foundation founder Roddy Boyd on how to investigate a company:

What Do They Do? A question that is incredibly basic but oddly, many reporters trip on it, hurting credibility and closing off profitable areas of investigation. For example, Pershing Square Holdings, Vanguard Group and T. Rowe Price manage investment capital for individuals, but their approach to making investments and their targeted customer base could not be more different. Then there's what we *think* we know: if you are about 50 years old IBM may still be a giant computer manufacturer but to a 25 year old it is more likely to be a technology consulting operation. In other words, things change.

The business world is set up in a way that requires companies to release detailed information about their financial performance to a multitude of audiences. Companies with stock that is traded on an exchange regularly file documents with the SEC that disclose their profits, losses, sales and many other financial measures. Private companies also disclose financial information, although it may be tougher to obtain. Many of them provide results to the SEC, which surprises many reporters. Other private companies disclose their financial performance to lenders, rating agencies and state regulators. In short, all companies keep close tabs on where they are spending and where they are making their money. The business reporter can find this kind of information for thousands of companies by carefully reading the financial statements filed with the SEC and with state regulatory agencies.

Being able to read and assess a company's financial statement is the cornerstone of a business reporter's job. The writer needs to be able to analyze how a company is performing and how its performance compares with that of its competitors. It can be argued that assessing a company's financial numbers is the root of everything else important in a business reporter's job. Without a proper understanding of profits, sales, revenue, and other measures, a business reporter cannot (a) interview a CEO about his or her company's performance, (b) begin to properly understand why a company might want to acquire a competitor or (c) comprehend a board member's opinion that management needs to be changed.

As mentioned above, the SEC regulates all companies that regularly trade stocks or bonds. Because the SEC is there to protect the investor, it requires a lot of information to be filed for public dissemination. This can be a treasure trove for business reporters—if they know what they are looking for and where to find it.

Why does the SEC require these filings? If the SEC requires companies to file information about their operations on a regular basis, investors and potential investors will be able to assess for themselves whether the company's performance is improving or waning. If bad information is disclosed, usually in an SEC filing and not in a news release, a company's stock price will likely fall. Good information, likely disclosed in a release with horns blaring and whistles blowing, will send the stock price up.

Professional investors on Wall Street review these filings every day for this type of information. That is why good business reporters also read the SEC filings. If a reporter can find this information before anyone else and write a story about it, he has a scoop. It is not always that easy, however. Business reporters need to be able to understand what they are reading, and they need to be able to analyze its importance. Lastly and most importantly, business reporters need to be able to then take that newsworthy information and write a story that makes sense to a reader who may not have the time to go looking through the SEC filings.

Evaluating a Company's Financial Health

This chapter and the previous chapters outline the basics of how and where to look to assess whether a company is making or losing money. Essentially, a company that reports increasing profits and rising revenues is generally considered to be healthy, whether it is public or private. This section discusses some of the financial information a company discloses that can be manipulated to determine barometers of health or sickness.

The cash-flow statement is another table of financial information that every company discloses in its SEC filings, along with its income statement and its balance sheet (Table 5.4). This statement helps a business reporter analyze where a company is getting its money and how that money is being used.

As the first section of this chapter shows, assessing the income statement and balance sheet requires only simple addition, subtraction and division. There is no need to know complicated formulas or to understand algorithms to assess how a company is performing. The same holds true for a cash-flow statement. It is a simple table that shows how much money a company is getting from its operations, investments and financing. The basic test of health is whether a company is generating positive cash flow. That is, is more money coming into the company than flowing out? If the company is generating more money than it is spending, this is the sign of a healthy company.

Table 5.4 Condensed Consolidated Statements of Cash Flows

The Coca-Cola Company and Subsidiaries (Unaudited)

(in million dollars)	*Nine Months Ended*	
	October 2, 2015	*September 26, 2014*
Operating activities		
Consolidated net income	6,130	6,353
Depreciation and amortization	1,443	1,477
Stock-based compensation expense	171	143
Deferred income taxes	212	(179)
Equity income or loss, net of dividends	(150)	(259)
Foreign currency adjustments	(76)	305
Gain on sales of assets, including bottling interests	(550)	410
Other operating charges	697	192
Other items	859	38
Net change in operating assets and liabilities	(346)	(501)
Net cash provided by operating activities	8,390	7,979
Investing activities		
Purchases of investments	(12,006)	(14,098)
Proceeds from disposals of investments	10,403	9,558
Acquisitions of businesses, equity method investments and nonmarketable securities	(2,489)	(343)
Proceeds from disposals of business, equity method investments and nonmarketable securities	416	73
Purchases of property, plant and equipment	(1,670)	(1,618)
Proceeds from disposal of property, plant and equipment	50	150
Net cash used in investing activities	(5,413)	(6,558)
Financing activities		
Issuances of debt	34,298	33,292
Payments of debt	(30,159)	(28,494)
Issuances of stock	732	1,058
Purchases of stock for treasury	(1,966)	(2,963)
Dividends	(4,313)	(2,680)
Net cash used in financing activities	(1,178)	(196)
Effect of exchange rate changes on cash and cash equivalents	(774)	(555)
Cash and cash equivalents		
Net increase during the period	1,025	670
Balance at beginning of period	8,958	10,414
Balance at end of period	$9,983	$11,084

Note: From the Coca-Cola Company, Form 10-Q, filed with the SEC on October 28, 2015.

cash flow: The amount of cash a company generates and uses during a period, calculated by adding non-cash charges (such as depreciation) to the net income after taxes. Cash flow can be used as an indication of a company's financial strength.

The cash flow from operations is an indication of the money the company is receiving from selling its product or services. If the cash flow from operations is increasing, that is a sign of a healthy company. If it is decreasing, the company may be having some problems selling its goods or services. That could be a sign to a business reporter to check into the company further.

The cash flow from investing activities explains how the company is investing its excess money and how it is trying to use that money to expand its operations. In the case of Coca-Cola, there is spending to purchase bottling companies and property, plant and equipment (represented by values in parentheses). Business reporters should be wary of the money a company spends on investing activities. If this money has increased dramatically, why has the company determined that it needs to spend even more to expand its operations? What is the new business opportunity that was not available at the same time last year?

TIPS FROM THE PROS

 Southern Investigative Reporting Foundation founder Roddy Boyd on how to investigate a company:

What's Core? (What They Really Do): Then again, many companies benefit mightily from reportorial misunderstanding of what they really do. GE, to a generation of people, is a light bulb and appliances company. In reality, circa 2006, 38% of its corporate revenues came from GE Capital, the world's largest credit card issuer. Every time someone used that Home Depot or Target card, GE got exposure to the increasingly leveraged American consumer. In 2014, J.P. Morgan Chase had over 35% of its revenue come from Wall Street related activities. While it's still a global consumer and corporate bank, Wall Street is where its profit margin and growth possibilities lie. (As 2008 and other scandals show, it is also where economic misfortune and reputational risks reside.) Frankly, any company that offers financing (i.e., the ability to purchase its goods on credit) can easily become what amounts to a troubled bank during a weak consumer credit cycle as all those loans begin to pile up in arrears.

The last section of the cash-flow statement shows cash spent on financing. This reveals how companies get extra money to grow their businesses and whether they are paying off their debts. It is vital for a company to pay its debts, or interest keeps adding to the total, making the debt higher and higher. The higher the debt gets, the more difficult it becomes to pay off. Companies that keep borrowing money by issuing debt will eventually have to pay it off. Some companies wind up in bankruptcy court if they cannot pay off their debt.

Healthy companies have an overall positive cash flow. If the overall cash-flow number is negative, the company is spending more money to operate the business than is coming in through the sale of products and services. In healthy companies, cash flow continues to increase from time period to time period. In the case of Coca-Cola, its cash flow in the first nine months of 2015 was $9.9 billion, down from the $11.1 billion in the first nine months of 2014.

profit margin: Net earnings after taxes divided by revenues. This is a number that is usually displayed as a percentage.

Wall Street investors and business reporters also measure a public company's financial performance in other ways. One of these measures is an analysis of a company's profit margin. Profit margins can be high for some industries and low for others. The profit margin for grocery retailers is low, sometimes as low as 2 percent. However, whether high or low, a profit margin is the net income divided by the revenue. If we look back at Coca-Cola's profit margin, the net income of $1.4 billion can be divided by its revenue of nearly $11.4 billion to show a profit margin of a little more than 12.7 percent. With this information, investors and reporters can see how Coca-Cola's profit margin compared with that of its rival PepsiCo, for example. One must simply find the same numbers for PepsiCo and do the math. In this example, investors and reporters will find that Coca-Cola has a higher profit margin (12.7%) than its competitor (3.3%). A similar measure of a company's health is its operating margin, which is another case of simple division, where operating costs are divided by sales. Again, this number for a specific company should be compared with those of competitors and of the overall industry.

Another measure of comparison within an industry is return on equity (ROE). This measure divides net income by shareholders' equity. ROE assesses how well a company uses the money shareholders put into it. Many well-run companies have ROEs above 20 percent. In simple terms, this means that every $1 invested in the company creates 20 cents in profits.

price-to-earnings (P/E) ratio: A stock analysis statistic in which the current price of a stock is divided by the company's earnings per share (EPS).

A similar measure of a company's performance is called return on assets (ROA), or return on investment. This is another division problem in which a company's net income, plus its interest expense, is divided by its total assets. All three of these numbers can be found on the income statement and the balance sheet. A company looks at its ROA to determine whether to take on new projects. If its ROA is 5 percent, for example, the company may decide not to borrow money to build a new plant if it is going to have to pay its lender 7 percent interest.

One of the most basic measures investors use to examine a company is a P/E ratio. This is a simple relationship in which the stock price of a company is divided by the EPS. For example, if a company has a stock that is trading at $60, and it has earned $2.50 per share in earnings, then it has a P/E ratio of 24. This number is then compared with competitors' P/E ratios and the overall stock market.

If the company with the P/E ratio of 24 has a competitor with a P/E ratio of 30, there may be something about the competitor that causes its stock price to be higher. Maybe its management team is considered more valuable. Or maybe the company with the lower P/E has had some financial problems in the past, and investors are not willing to give it the benefit of a higher ratio just yet. Such a comparison can be useful to a business reporter evaluating a company's strategy and where it stands in relation to its peers. Companies with higher P/E ratios are generally considered to be businesses with greater growth potential than those with lower P/Es. In addition, some industries generally have higher P/E ratios than other sectors of the economy—always evaluate this number within an industry.

Another important barometer of a company used by both Wall Street and business journalists is the price-to-book (P/B) ratio. This equation divides the price of the company's stock by the company's book value. A company's book value per share is often provided in SEC filings and is arrived at by dividing its assets by the number of shares outstanding. If a company has a stock price of $60 per share, but its book value is $50 per share, then it is said that the stock is trading above book value. Put another way, the stock price is 1.2 times the book value.

TIPS FROM THE PROS

Southern Investigative Reporting Foundation founder Roddy Boyd on how to investigate a company:

The People Running the Business: A proper investigation of a company should include an awareness of who runs it. Public companies have prospectuses (SEC forms S-1 and 424B2) and most importantly, DEF 14A, which is better known as the proxy. For a larger public company, this gives what should be a broad career outline of the so-called C suite, or chief executive, operating and financial officers, the general counsel and maybe the heads of a division or two. Nothing dramatic will arise, but you can start plugging those names into search engines and legal libraries and see what you come up with.

Again, the P/B ratio is a measure that can be valuable to business reporters assessing a company's performance in the stock market relative to competitors. Companies with stock that trades below book value may be considered cheap by investors. But there may also be a reason why the stock is trading below book value. Maybe the company has been reporting losses or revenue has been falling. Investors, scared that the company could be in trouble, may be selling the stock, depressing its value. Overall, the stock market trades slightly above book value. The stock of some companies may trade at three or four times the book value. Microsoft is a good example of a company that is valued by investors for always reporting solid earnings and is therefore rewarded by being traded at higher values.

Writing the Earnings Story

This chapter discussed the information contained in a Form 10-Q and Form 10-K before reviewing the information companies provide in quarterly earnings news releases. That is because the information and analysis in the filings are more detailed than they are in releases. The filings expose a complete, often unfettered, picture of a company's financial health, whereas the releases provide the company's interpretation of its performance. The two may not always correlate.

Unfortunately for business writers, a company rarely, if ever, files its quarterly 10-Q or annual 10-K with the SEC before it discloses its earnings in a press release. As a result, most stories about a company's earnings are written on the basis of information that is disclosed in the release, not in the filing. By the time a company gets around to filing a 10-Q or 10-K with the SEC, most reporters forget to look at it and, consequently, may miss a story. This chapter has emphasized these filings because they often contain important nuggets of information.

Many companies like to put out earnings releases before the stock market opens at 9:30 a.m. or after the stock market closes for trading at 4 p.m. For many reporters, particularly those that work at wire services such as the Associated Press, Reuters, Dow Jones or Bloomberg News, this means that the morning and afternoon can be busy times during earnings season. It is important to note again that a company can use its earnings releases to put a spin on its performance. Sometimes a company will emphasize strong growth in revenue to mask the fact that it spent a lot of money that quarter on advertising or something else, making earnings lower than expected. Other times, companies will trumpet strong earnings growth despite weak sales. That is why the business reporter needs to look at the complete picture in an earnings release. Although Wall Street analysts and investors primarily focus on whether the company "made" its earnings projections, a better story may be told by looking at the overall performance of the company.

Let's look a typical earnings release from a company:

The Home Depot, the world's largest home improvement retailer, today reported record net earnings of $940 million, or $0.40 per diluted share, for the third quarter of fiscal 2002, an increase of 21 percent compared with net earnings of $778 million, or $0.33 per diluted share, in fiscal 2001. Sales for the quarter increased 9 percent to $14.5 billion and comparable store sales decreased 2 percent.

"The Home Depot delivered strong earnings in the third quarter as we continue to reinvest in our facilities and associates. The operational initiatives we launched a year ago are delivering results, thanks to our dedicated associates, loyal customers and vendor partners," said Bob Nardelli, Chairman, President & CEO of The Home Depot. "The current retail environment, coupled with merchandising changes and resets within our stores, affected customer traffic. Throughout the quarter, however, we saw customers respond to great values in areas like appliances, flooring, and power tools, supporting growth in our average ticket."

"Looking forward, our customers can be assured of everyday low prices, broader assortments and excellent service at the heart of our activities through the fourth quarter and into the next fiscal year," Nardelli said. "While we remain cautious on the outlook for the economy into next year, the strength of our balance sheet and our operating performance allows us to stay on strategy."

"This year we will open 200 new stores and add 40,000 associates. Our financial condition remains unsurpassed in retail, with $4.0 billion in cash and more than $20 billion in equity at the end of the quarter," Nardelli said.

During the quarter, The Home Depot added 34 stores, including two stores in Mexico. At the end of the quarter, the company operated a total of 1,471 stores.

The Home Depot reconfirmed that it expects to earn $0.31 diluted earnings per share for the fourth quarter of fiscal 2002, an increase of 15 percent over the fourth quarter of 2001 on a 13-week basis. The company also indicated that it is comfortable with $1.57 diluted earnings per share for the fiscal year, a 25 percent increase over fiscal 2001 on a 52-week basis.[2]

This earnings release begins with the numbers that everyone will care about: the net income and net income per share. At Home Depot, the profit increased by 21 percent from the same quarter in the previous year. Note that the comparison is not made with the prior quarter in the same year but with the same quarter a year ago to provide a more accurate picture of how the company is performing.

TIPS FROM THE PROS

Southern Investigative Reporting Foundation founder Roddy Boyd on how to investigate a company:

Resume gaps. It's likely not a big deal when a 45 year old chief operating officer at a company doesn't have her 15-week stint at a stillborn Dot Com company from 1997 on a resume—especially if everything else checks out. But if the same executive didn't list her time running a unit in the center of a big lawsuit or there's a two-year gap between jobs, you'd want to know about it. Using a search engine to try and flesh out who corporate executives are away from the job is useful. If they sit on a series of trophy corporate and or philanthropic boards, a great question is, "How do you have the time to manage your professional and personal lives?" Similarly, otherwise minor legal entanglements, a DUI, litigation in small claims court, perhaps a failure to pay tradesmen or local businesses in a dispute, certainly does happen, but what you are looking for is a pattern. A multi-millionaire CEO, for instance, who is repeatedly sued by landscapers or household help at their vacation house over a failure to pay them is definitely something you should be aware of.

The business reporter should be leery of any company that tries to compare earnings from two sequential quarters. That is not how Wall Street assesses earnings, and that is not how reporters should, either. It is also smart to check the company's math. For example, a reporter should look at the 21 percent growth in earnings figure that is given by Home Depot. Does that number apply to the growth in net income or the growth in net income per share? If one does the math, the actual figure is 20.8 percent growth in net income and 21.2 percent in net income per share, so the 21 percent growth reported by the company could reflect either the growth in net income or net income per share.

For other companies, however, the percentage increase in earnings may not be uniform. The lead paragraph of an Intel Corporation earnings release (2002) began with the statement that third-quarter revenue was up 3 percent from the previous quarter and from the same quarter a year ago before mentioning in the second paragraph that net income rose. The net income figure was up 547 percent from the same quarter of the previous year but net income per share was up 400 percent. Why does this happen? Intel had more shares outstanding in the recent quarter. Because a company often issues more stock or repurchases stock to make its net income per share figure grow at a faster rate than its net income, a better barometer of a company's earnings growth is the percentage gain in net income, not the percentage gain in net income per share. A business reporter should not fall into this trap but should focus on the growth or decline in the dollar amount noted in net income.

Intel mentioned its revenue before its earnings, whereas Home Depot mentioned its earnings before its revenue, or sales. In some industries, revenue and sales can be more important than profits as barometers of how a company is performing. This is often the case in the computer industry, for example. However, the success of most companies is still measured by their profits.

Other industry barometers are also important in earnings releases. For retailers such as Home Depot and Wal-Mart, many experts like to measure their success by comparable, or same-store, sales, a figure mentioned in the first paragraph of the Home Depot release. This figure tells how sales have done at stores that have been open for at least a year. In the case of Home Depot, these sales fell by 2 percent, but the company was still able to increase its overall sales by 9 percent. The company achieved this by opening new stores during the quarter, thereby boosting total sales.

Other industries have similar measures of performance that a business reporter will want to look for in the earnings statement. Beverage companies such as Coca-Cola and PepsiCo report increases or decreases in the number of cases of soft drinks sold during a quarter. Anheuser-Busch and Coors report gains or losses in the number of barrels of beer sold during a quarter. In the table that accompanied Home Depot's earnings release, the company also disclosed information such as the average purchase at one of its stores.

Business writers typically receive the earnings release from a company by facsimile or, increasingly nowadays, by e-mail. Here is how a reporter in Bloomberg's Atlanta bureau took the information from the Home Depot release and explained what was important. This story was sent out on Bloomberg's wire at 9:50 a.m., less than two hours after the earnings were released. The conference call mentioned in the story began at 9 a.m.:

> Home Depot Inc., the world's largest home-improvement retailer, said third-quarter earnings rose 21 percent as the company controlled expenses. Sales at stores open at least a year declined.
>
> Net income increased to $940 million, or 40 cents a share, from $778 million, or 33 cents, a year earlier. Sales in the three months ended Nov. 3 rose 8.9 percent to $14.5 billion, Home Depot said in a statement. The company's shares dropped as much as 12 percent.
>
> Home Depot's sales at stores open at least a year fell 2 percent, the second-biggest decline in Robert Nardelli's two years as chief executive. The company had forecast a gain of as much as 4 percent. Home Depot is grappling with slower growth after saturating the U.S. market. Smaller rival Lowe's Cos. is also entering Home Depot's turf in bigger cities such as Boston.
>
> "I'm disappointed with my sales performance," Nardelli told investors on a conference call. "The operational programs set in place a year ago are (helping) to expand gross margins. They are not all perfect, but it's better than doing nothing."
>
> Nardelli said the company won't meet its revenue-growth forecast of 15 percent to 20 percent this year. Same-store sales are expected to fall 3 percent to 5 percent in the fourth quarter, Chief Financial Officer Carol Tome said on the call.

Home Depot has enlarged the appliance and home-decor departments in its stores to attract customers. The moves hurt sales, spokesman Bob Burton said. The changes reduced same-store sales by 2 percent to 3 percent in the second quarter, according to a regulatory filing.

"They've been running so far behind Lowe's. It's a company that's trying to get its footing," said Arnhold & S. Bleichroeder Inc. analyst Barbara Allen, who rates Home Depot a "neutral" and doesn't own the shares. "I don't have a good sense whether Nardelli understands what Home Depot really needs."

Falling lumber prices trimmed same-store sales by 1 percent, while new Home Depot stores pulling business from older ones hurt sales by 4 percent, Tome said.

Shares of Atlanta-based Home Depot fell $2.72 to $25.88 at 9:45 a.m. in New York Stock Exchange composite trading, after dropping to $25.05. The stock had tumbled 44 percent this year, making it the biggest decliner in the 30-member Dow Jones Industrial Average.

Home Depot, in a statement, reiterated a fourth-quarter profit forecast of 31 cents a share, one cent less than the average analyst estimate from Thomson First Call. Third-quarter earnings met the analysts' average forecast.

Same-store sales fell 3 percent in the first quarter of 2001, the biggest decline under Nardelli.[3]

The story shows that the reporter understands what is important to Home Depot's results and conveys her knowledge of the retail industry. Her lead paragraph explains why profits rose faster than sales—the company cut its expenses for running its stores. The story explains why sales fell at Home Depot stores open for more than one year, and the reporter adds comments from the conference call that she knows her readers will want to know about, such as sales estimates for the next quarter.

In addition, the story includes people's reactions to the results, with a comment from an analyst and a description of how the stock price fell after the earnings were released. Also note that in the next-to-last paragraph of the story, this reporter tells readers that the earnings reported by Home Depot were in line with analyst estimates. This is an important barometer when writing about a company's

earnings guidance: A report by a company that its earnings may vary considerably, either positively or negatively, from expectations, or that earnings will still be in line with expectations.

earnings performance. If the earnings had come in below or above Wall Street estimates, the reporter likely would have mentioned it earlier. Last, she reports the earnings Home Depot expects to report in the next quarter—31 cents per share—and points out that this guidance from the company is a penny lower than what analysts were expecting at the time of the release. Maybe that is why the stock price fell.

Earnings guidance like this is important for business writers to track because the stock prices of companies can rise and fall dramatically on the basis of the release of this information. Any time a company issues a statement forecasting what it expects to report in earnings for a quarter or a for year, a business reporter should compare those numbers against both Wall Street expectations and earlier guidance given by the company.

The reasoning for this is simple but important. If a company issues earnings guidance that is higher than it previously stated or higher than Wall Street thought it would be, its stock price is likely to rise that day. Many investors decide how much they are willing to pay for a stock on the basis of how much a company is expected to report in earnings that year. If the company expects to report higher earnings, investors will be willing to pay a higher price for the stock. The reverse is also true. If a company discloses that it expects to report earnings lower than it previously stated or than Wall Street estimated, the stock price is likely to fall. A business reporter's story on the release of new guidance should emphasize why the earnings estimate has changed, for better or worse. In most cases, the reason is that the company's business is performing better or worse than expected.

The following is how a company will typically release such information:

> UnitedHealth Group anticipates a continuation of its strong growth and operating performance in 2003, expecting that its operating margins will increase in the aggregate, with every business segment showing stable or expanded margins next year.
>
> At its annual Investor Conference last week, management provided the following key data points for 2003:
>
> > Revenues of approximately $29 billion, supported by 13 percent organic revenue growth across the aggregate of the company's businesses.
> >
> > Operating earnings at or above $2.57 billion.
> >
> > Margins expanding from an estimated 8.7 percent in 2002 to 8.9 percent or more in 2003.
> >
> > Earnings per share increasing to at least $5.05 per share, representing the high side of the company's guidance range, 20 percent above $4.20 in earnings per share currently expected in 2002.
> >
> > Cash flows from operations exceeding $2.6 billion in 2003, up from $2.3 billion in 2002.
> >
> > Return on equity at or above 34 percent.[4]

The fourth bullet point in this release is the earnings guidance, and it indicates that UnitedHealth, a managed care company, believed that its earnings for 2003 would be higher than it had expected. This news release was issued shortly after 6 a.m. Though it's doubtful that many reporters were in their newsrooms at that time, many companies like to issue releases early in the morning because executives know that editors will assign the story to reporters before the day gets busy.

A Reuters reporter took the UnitedHealth information and explained why the company released the information—to counteract the previous day's drop in stock price based on an analyst's concerns and the stock market's reaction. The reporter noted that the earnings outlook came a day after a Wall Street analyst downgraded UnitedHealth, which caused its stock to fall by nearly 10 percent. After the company released its earnings projection, the stock rose about 3.5 percent. The story also noted that the company's earnings projections for 2003 were slightly higher than analyst estimates and that its revenue projections were in line with previous expectations. This comparison should be in every earnings-related story.

Company releases explaining earnings for the previous quarter or projections for the next quarter contain some of the most important news of a business. These releases can be a barometer of the company's performance, letting the rest of the world know whether the business is healthy or sick. That is why it is important for a business writer to know how to read these releases and turn the information into a story that will explain what is going on.

Other News in a Financial Report

Reporters can find information in addition to earnings in the SEC filings—Forms 10-Q and 10-K—that detail a company's financial performance. There is a lot of good, useful information in these filings that at first glance may not seem to be telling anyone a story.

TIPS FROM THE PROS

 No blog does a better job of digging up fascinating factoids and newsworthy nuggets in 10-Q and 10-K filings than www.footnoted.org, which is run by business journalist Michelle Leder.

Leder, a former business journalist at the *Tampa Tribune* and the *Bradenton* (Florida) *Herald,* launched her site in August 2003. Since then, it's gained a following from investors, analysts and business reporters from around the country. Reporters have credited her site in their stories. And during the 2009 proxy season, Leder's site contributed content to the *New York Times'* Dealbook blog.

In October 2009, Leder had a post about a disclosure in Microsoft Corporation's proxy statement regarding its political campaign contributions. A late September posting about First Marblehead notes the huge severance packages given to former executives, who oversaw a large drop in the company's stock price.

While most of Leder's site is free, she recently launched a site called FootnotedPro for which subscribers who pay $2,500 a year can get even more information and data from the SEC filings that Leder and her team review each day.

The best-known SEC filing is a Form 10-Q. This is the quarterly financial statement for each company that falls under the SEC's regulations. This form must be filed with the SEC within 40 days following the end of the quarter. Because the fiscal year of most companies is the same as the calendar year, May 10, August 10 and November 10 are busy reading days for most business reporters. Quarters typically end on March 31, June 30, September 30 and December 31. Companies that do not file within this time frame typically ask for extensions and usually are having some sort of financial problem.

Form 10-Q filings have a section that discusses the financial performance during the previous quarter, explaining the ups and downs of revenues and profits. In addition, these filings tell the business reporter whether the company is buying its own stock. This is an interesting disclosure and one that could turn into a potential story because it tells investors whether the company's executives believe the stock is cheap or expensive. If a company has been repurchasing a large amount of its stock in the recent quarter, the CFO or CEO probably thinks the company is a good investment. If they have not purchased a significant amount of the company's stock, maybe they think the stock price is high. That is information a business reporter would want to tell his or her readers because those readers often buy and sell stocks on the basis of this information.

The following excerpt shows how this information is disclosed in a 10-Q:

> The Company may repurchase as much as $120 million of its outstanding Class A common stock through December 31, 2002. During the second quarter of 2001, 25,500 shares were repurchased at a total cost of $734,295 or an average price of $28.80. The Company repurchased 149,957 shares at a total cost of $4,300,216 during the second quarter of 2000.
>
> (Form 10-Q, Erie Indemnity, 2001, p. 20)

What does this tell the business reporter? This statement implies that whoever is in charge of this company's stock buyback plan may have thought the stock was a lot cheaper in the second three months of 2000, during which time $4.3 million was spent to buy stock, than in the second quarter of 2001, during which time only $734,000 was spent to buy stock. Again, companies tend to buy their own stock when it is cheap and they believe it is going to go up.

The 10-K is a company's annual filing with the SEC, and it must be filed within 60 days of the end of the fiscal year, which typically makes the last week of February and the first week of March a busy time for business writers who read these filings. The 10-K provides a history and an overview of the company's business that is informative reading for a reporter just beginning to cover the company. It also details the number of employees a company has and the property it owns.

If a reporter knows how to compare the growth rate of two numbers provided in a filing, that information might make a story. As Bill Barnhart, financial markets columnist for the *Chicago Tribune*, wrote, it is important to determine whether there is a variance in the numbers. "Identify these variances before you read management's discussion of results," said Barnhart. "Often an interesting trend or anomaly will appear in the financial statements that the company fails to address in the report text. You may have a story. This is particularly true during sluggish economic times, when a company may grow profits by tweaking seemingly incidental line items" (Barnhart, 2001, p. 1).

For example, Barnhart reviewed a filing from McDonald's Corporation that showed the company issued $2.4 billion in long-term debt, boosting the company's debt-to-equity ratio to its highest level since 1991. Barnhart noted that the company used nearly all of that money to repurchase its shares, causing its net income per share to increase, even as cash flow from its business declined during a tough year. In other words, McDonald's did not have a great year. But it looked like it did to the unsophisticated business reporter who could not connect the stock repurchase to the increase in net income per share.

Another important disclosure that is often found in these filings is an estimate of a company's future spending to improve its infrastructure or other operations. This may involve building a new factory or adding new computers. Not every company reports this in a 10-Q or 10-K filing, but when it does, it can estimate the financial impact on future earnings—something that investors will look for. If a business writer can write a story about this information before anyone else finds it, his story may move the company's stock price.

Disclosures like this can read something like the following:

> In 2001, the Company began the development of several eCommerce initiatives in support of the Erie Insurance Group's business model of distributing insurance products exclusively through independent agents. The eCommerce program includes initiatives to replace property/casualty policy administration systems as well as customer interaction systems. The eCommerce program also includes significant information technology infrastructure expenditures. The program is intended to improve service and efficiency, as well as result in increased sales. Total five-year expenditures for the program are estimated at $150 to $175 million. The cost of these initiatives will be shared among several companies of the Erie Insurance Group, including the Company. Based on preliminary estimates, which will be further refined in the second half of 2001, the after-tax effect on net income of the Company is estimated to reduce earnings per share between $0.08 and $0.12 for 2001 and between $0.05 and $0.07 per share for each of the next four years of the program.
> (Form 10-Q, Erie Indemnity Group, 2001, p. 21)

A business writer who discovers information like this in a 10-Q or 10-K should immediately try to find out if Wall Street has factored this expenditure and lower earnings guidance into the stock price. It is also important to assess what the company's competitors are doing. If they are not building new plants or adding new product lines when the company you are writing about is, there could be a good reason to add that information to your story.

Litigation is also frequently discussed in 10-Q and 10-K filings. Business lawsuits are discussed in depth in Chapter 12, but suffice it to say for now that these filings can give the business writer clues as to where to look for this information. Business lawsuits can be quite nasty and can affect stock prices. Companies will often set aside money to pay for potential settlements or adverse rulings resulting from lawsuits. This information can be even more important to readers if the litigation involves two companies.

In Coca-Cola's 10-K filed in February 2009, the company disclosed that it and some of its executives were sued in the U.S. District Court for the Northern District of Georgia on October 27, 2000. The lawsuit alleges that the executives misrepresented the company's financial performance. A similar lawsuit was filed on November 9, 2000. The filing notes that a judge consolidated these two lawsuits in 2001 and that the company filed a motion to dismiss in September 2001. The company noted in the filing that it finally settled the litigation in May 2008 for $138 million and that a court approved the settlement in October 2008.

A review of the litigation sections for competitors of the company a reporter is writing about may also have value. For example, a reporter for the *Richmond Times-Dispatch,* whose beat includes writing stories about Markel Corporation—a local company that provides insurance for everything from horse farms to day care centers—would want to read the litigation sections of 10-Q filings of other insurance companies.

A Markel 10-Q filing disclosed the following litigation:

> On January 31, 2001, the Company received notice of a lawsuit filed in the United States District Court for the Southern District of New York against Terra Nova Insurance Company Limited by Palladium Insurance Limited and Bank of America, N.A. seeking approximately $27 million plus exemplary damages in connection with alleged reinsurance agreements. The Company believes it has numerous defenses to these claims, including the defense that the alleged reinsurance agreements were not valid. The Company intends to vigorously defend this matter; however, it cannot predict the outcome at this time.
>
> On May 29, 2001, Reliance Insurance Company was placed in rehabilitation by the Pennsylvania Insurance Department. At June 30, 2001 and December 31, 2000, Reliance Insurance Company and its affiliates owed the Company approximately $33.4 million in reinsurance recoverables for paid and unpaid losses. These balances were considered in the normal course of assessing the collectability of reinsurance recoverables.
>
> (Form 10-Q, Markel Corporation, 2001, p. 13)

However, the filing did not disclose other litigation that involved Markel. If the reporter covering the company had spent some time reading the litigation sections of 10-Q filings by other insurers, they would have discovered this entry from PXRE Group:

> PXRE entered into weather option agreements in May 1999 with two counter-parties. In April 2000, these counter-parties submitted invoices to PXRE Delaware in the aggregate sum of $8,252,500 seeking payment under the weather option agreements, which invoices have been paid. PXRE Delaware insured its obligations under these weather option agreements through two Commercial Inland Marine Weather Insurance Policies issued by Terra Nova Insurance Company Limited ("Terra Nova"). PXRE Delaware submitted claims under these policies to Terra Nova in April 2000. Terra Nova has denied coverage, contending that its Managing General Agent had no authority to issue these policies. PXRE Delaware disagrees with Terra Nova's denial and has filed suit against Terra Nova in the United States District Court for the District of New Jersey. Both parties have submitted motions for summary judgment to the court and the trial of this matter has been postponed pending the court's ruling on the pending summary judgment motions. The aggregate sum of $8,252,500 is included in Other Assets; management has concluded that it is realizable and no valuation allowance is necessary.
>
> (Form 10-Q, PXRE Group Limited, 2001, p. 15)

The reporter who writes stories about Markel has just found himself a story. Because the reporter has been covering the company for several years, he knows that Markel recently acquired another insurance company called Terra Nova, which is having a dispute with PXRE that appears to have the potential to cost the company some money. If Markel is forced to pay that money to PXRE, its profits could be less than investors expect.

Quite often, a company will disclose the sale price, or purchase price, of a recent deal in a 10-Q or 10-K. Or it may use the 10-Q as a way to update investors on the progress of a recent acquisition. Business reporters are always interested in these nuggets of information because likely the price has not been disclosed elsewhere or it contains numbers that have not been seen before. Here are some examples from property and casualty insurers St. Paul and MetLife.

St. Paul's update on an acquisition read:

> In connection with the MMI purchase, we established a reserve of $28 million, including $4 million in employee-related costs and $24 million in occupancy-related costs. The employee-related costs represent severance and related benefits such as outplacement counseling to be paid to, or incurred on behalf of, terminated employees. We estimated that approximately 130 employee positions would be eliminated, at all levels throughout MMI. Through June 30, 2001, 118 employees had been

terminated, with payments totaling $4 million. Our remaining obligations for employee-related costs at MMI are expected to be less than $1 million.
(Form 10-Q, St. Paul Companies, 2001, p. 23)

In this case, the reserve charge had been previously reported, but not how much had been paid. Also, St. Paul appears to be saying that it is spending more to fire MMI employees than it originally estimated.

The following is another entry from a 10-Q filed by MetLife, the large life insurer and money manager based in New York:

On July 2, 2001, the Company completed its sale of Conning Corporation ("Conning"), an affiliate acquired in the acquisition of GenAmerica Financial Corporation. Conning specializes in asset management for insurance company investment portfolios and investment research. The Company received $108 million in the transaction and will report a gain of approximately $17 million, net of income taxes of $11 million, in the third quarter. The sale price is subject to adjustment under certain provisions of the sale contract.
(Form 10-Q, MetLife Incorporated, 2001, p. 20)

In this filing, MetLife discloses for the first time how much money it will receive for the sale of a subsidiary and how the sale is going to affect its earnings in the upcoming quarter. These numbers, particularly because they have not been disclosed before, should be the basis of a story.

Companies also disclose important information about other business transactions in their filings. For example, in the back of a 10-Q for Coca-Cola is a section called "Recent Developments." At the bottom of this section is a paragraph detailing two business contracts designed to promote the company's drinks:

In July 2002, our Company announced long-term agreements with the National Collegiate Athletic Association (NCAA) and CBS, and with the Houston Astros Baseball Club with a combined value of approximately $650 million to $800 million. Our Company, CBS and the NCAA will participate in an integrated marketing and media program that includes, for our Company, beverage marketing and media rights to 87 NCAA championships in 22 sports. Additionally, The Minute Maid Company, an operating unit of our Company, and the Houston Astros Baseball Club will participate in a long-term marketing and community partnership, including naming rights for Astros Field, which will be renamed "Minute Maid Park."
(Form 10-Q, Coca-Cola Company, 2015, p. 27)

Now, these deals may not be news, particularly because the company issued releases about both of them, but what is news is the value of the agreements. Even for a company such as Coca-Cola, more than $650 million is a lot.

However, as can be gleaned from the following item in another company's Form 10-Q, these disclosures may not always be good news.

In late July, the [Commerce Insurance] Company received notice from the Massachusetts Teachers Association (MTA) that the MTA is terminating its agency relationship with the Company and has withdrawn their endorsement, effective January 1, 2002, of the personal automobile group-marketing plan made available to members of the MTA by The Commerce Insurance Company. Commerce expects that approximately $16.7 million of premiums written will not be renewed as a result of this.

(Form 10-Q, Commerce Group, 2001, p. 14)

Commerce Group lost nearly $17 million when MTA terminated its contract with the insurer. For a mid-size business like Commerce, the loss of that money hurts. This information is not always contained in the same place for every 10-Q or 10-K. The lawsuit information is commonly under a header called "Contingency," whereas the information about rate increases and business decisions can sometimes be found under "Management's Discussion." In other 10-Qs, this information is located in a footnote. Sometimes it pays to read the entire filing.

With a good understanding of how to read and analyze a company's financial statements and the related information that many businesses disclose, a business reporter has begun taking the steps to a better understanding of how he can use these numbers to tell better stories about a company.

Notes

1. From "Publix Super Markets annual profit unchanged at $530.4 million," by S. Elam, March 1, 2002, Bloomberg News. Copyright 2002 by Bloomberg News. All rights reserved. Reprinted with permission.
2. From "Third quarter 2002 earnings release," by Home Depot Incorporated, November 19, 2002. Copyright 2002 by Home Depot. Reprinted with permission.
3. From "Home Depot 3rd-qtr earnings rise 21% on cost controls," by M. Clayton, November 19, 2002, Bloomberg News. Copyright 2002 by Bloomberg L.P. All rights reserved. Reprinted with permission.
4. UnitedHealth Group Inc. news release, November 26, 2002. Copyright 2002 by UnitedHealth Group Inc. Reprinted with permission.

Key Terms

assets	income statement
balance sheet	off-balance sheet financing
cash flow	price-to-earnings (P/E) ratio
earnings guidance	profit margin
Form 10-K	shareholders' equity
Form 10-Q	

Suggested Exercises

1. Find a local public company. If your area doesn't have public companies based locally, it may have a location of a public company such as McDonald's or Wal-Mart that would suffice. Read the 10-Q filing for the company and write a 400-word analysis of its income statement and balance sheet. Then review this analysis in class together.
2. Review a cash-flow statement from the same company. Take turns explaining what a line in the cash-flow statement means. Then vote as to whether the cash-flow statement is from a company whose health is improving or declining.
3. Find the earnings press release and a Form 10-Q for the same company on its website. Compare the financial information disclosed in both. If possible, find a press release that does not include a balance sheet or cash-flow statement.
4. Compare and contrast a company's analysis of its performance in an earnings news release and in the Form 10-Q for the same time period. Are there issues in the filing that aren't discussed in the news release?
5. Calculate the profit margin, operating margin, P/B ratio and P/E ratio for a company. Take 10 minutes, and then compare the numbers with a competitor.
6. Read the 10-Q and 10-K filings for a company. List three potential news stories from the narrative information provided in the filing.

Books on Company Finances

Apostolou, N., & Crumbley, D.L. (1994). *Keys to understanding the financial news* (2nd ed.). Hauppauge, NY: Barren's Educational Series.

Handler, J. (1994). *How to use financial statements: A guide to understanding the numbers.* New York: McGraw-Hill.

Kline, B. (2007). *How to read and understand financial statements when you don't know what you are looking at.* Ocala, FL: Atlantic Publishing Co.

Leder, M. (2003). *Financial fine print: Uncovering a company's true value.* New York: Wiley.

Schilit, H. (2002). *Financial shenanigans; How to detect accounting gimmicks & fraud in financial reports* (2nd ed.). New York: McGraw-Hill.

Tracy, P. (1999). *How to read a financial report.* New York: Wiley.

Warfield, G. (1994). *How to read and understand the financial news* (2nd ed.). New York: HarperCollins.

References

Barnhart, B. (2001, August/September). Financials tell tales, not analysts. *The Business Journalist*, p. 1.

Borden, W. (2002, November 26). UnitedHealth: Profit at high end of view. Reuters.

Clayton, M. (2002, November 19). Home Depot 3rd-qtr earnings rise 21% on cost controls. Bloomberg News.

Coca-Cola Company. Form 10-Q. (2015, October 28). (SEC Publication No. 0000021344–15–000041, pp. 2–5). Washington, DC: Securities and Exchange Commission.

Commerce Group Incorporated. Form 10-Q. (2001, August 13). (SEC Publication No. 0000811612–01–500048, pp. 14–15). Washington, DC: Securities and Exchange Commission.

Elam, S. (2002, March 1). Publix Super Markets annual profit unchanged at $530.4 million. Bloomberg News.

Erie Indemnity Company. Form 10-Q. (2001, July 19). (SEC Publication No. 0000922–621–01–500002, pp. 20–21). Washington, DC: Securities and Exchange Commission.

Home Depot. (2002, November 19). Third-quarter 2002 earnings release.

Intel Corporation. (2002, October 15). Third-quarter 2002 earnings release.

Markel Corporation. Form 10-Q. (2001, August 8). (SEC Publication No. 0000916641–01–500824, pp. 13–14). Washington, DC: Securities and Exchange Commission.

MetLife Incorporated. Form 10-Q. (2001, August 14). (SEC Publication No. 0000950123–01–505612, pp. 20–22). Washington, DC: Securities and Exchange Commission.

PXRE Group Limited. Form 10-Q. (2001, August 20). (SEC Publication No. 0000950117–01–501018, pp. 15–16). Washington, DC: Securities and Exchange Commission.

St. Paul Companies. Form 10-Q. (2001, August 14). (SEC Publication No. 0000086312–01–50012, pp. 23–25). Washington, DC: Securities and Exchange Commission.

UnitedHealth Group. (2002, November 26). Corporate news release.

6

BASIC COMPANY NEWS STORIES

SEC Filings Are a Reporter's Best Friend

Before the Internet, it was tough to convince some publicly traded companies to provide copies of their SEC filings to reporters. Many companies knew that if reporters were not in Washington, DC, or New York, it was often hard for them to get their hands on these documents. Services that would make copies of filings and mail them to newsrooms typically charged $25 a pop. For many penny-pinching newspapers, that was a lot of money for a boring regulatory filing that might not have contained news that would end up in the paper.

Never, however, did a business editor object to spending money on a Form 8-K filing. That is because Form 8-Ks contain more actual news than any other form companies file with the SEC. In legal lingo, a Form 8-K is a "current event report" for a "materially important" occurrence in the life of a corporation. This means that the 8-K may disclose just about anything. The SEC has determined that 16 events require disclosure in an 8-K. They are as follows:

1. Change in control;
2. Acquisition or disposition of assets;
3. Bankruptcy-court filing or regulatory action;
4. Change in accounting firm;
5. Resignation of directors;
6. Financial statements and exhibits;
7. Change in fiscal year;
8. Entering or terminating a material definitive agreement;
9. An off-balance sheet financial arrangement;
10. Costs related to the disposal or exiting of a business;

11. Any event that accelerates or increases a financial obligation;
12. Material impairments;
13. Notice of delisting of the stock;
14. Unregistered sale of stock;
15. Operational or financial results; or
16. Any other event deemed important to the company.

Quite often, the 8-K filed is simply a copy of the news release issued by a company. However, sometimes the 8-K will contain extra information not provided in the release. And at other times, the 8-K will be filed without a release being issued. Those are, quite often, the best for news. As a general rule of thumb, when a company files an 8-K but does not issue a news release, the company must—but may not want to—disclose the information therein.

Many 8-Ks are filed on Friday afternoons, particularly if the news is bad. Companies hope that the business reporter will forget to look for the filing and is instead thinking about the weekend. With more and more reporters becoming aware of these filings, however, such moves typically fail. In addition, services that alert reporters whenever a company on their beat files a document with the SEC help prevent news from flying below the radar.

Companies must file dozens of documents with the SEC that disclose information vital to reporters. Chapter 5 explained the valuable information that a 10-Q and a 10-K can provide. This chapter discusses the important information that gets disclosed in proxy statements, as well as forms filed by executives whenever they purchase or sell company stock.

Form 8-K: A report of unscheduled material events or corporate changes that could be of importance to the shareholders or the SEC. Examples include an acquisition, bankruptcy or a change in fiscal year.

Simply put, SEC documents can be a reporter's best friend. These pieces of paper—although most of these forms are now filed electronically—disclose news and information that can provide valuable insight into how public companies and some private companies operate. Although many of these documents are written in legalese that can be hard to understand, they often disclose the key details of the inner workings and important decisions made in a business, as long as the reporter understands what is being explained.

Here's how MarketWatch.com technology editor Jeremy Owens used an 8-K to explain how an acquisition would result in a loss of jobs:

> EMC Corp. which has *agreed to be acquired by Dell in one of the largest tech mergers of all time,* said late Thursday that it will cut jobs as part of an $850 million restructuring plan. In *a filing with the Securities and*

Exchange Commission, the Hopkington, Mass., storage firm said it would reduce its workforce, with most of the layoffs happening in the first quarter of 2016 and all completed by the end of the year. The company did not give any details on scope besides saying that it faces charges of about $250 million resulting from the job cuts.[1]

In stark contrast to 20 years ago, SEC documents for companies can now be obtained in a variety of ways. Many companies make their most recent SEC filings, such as the 10-Q, 10-K and proxy statement, available on their websites. But they often do not provide insider trading filings made by executives or filings made by investors.

The easiest way to review all of a company's SEC filings is by going to the agency's website at www.sec.gov and clicking on "Search for Company Filings." From there, reviewing filings is as easy as typing in the name of the company and clicking on the "Find Companies" link. Another site that many reporters use to read SEC filings is http://secfilings.com. This site requires the user to register. The company also runs subscription-based sites that use

---

TIPS FROM THE PROS

The Associated Press business desk's recommendations for finding news in SEC filings:

Set alerts for companies you're following to get immediate word of an SEC filing.

---

information and data from SEC filings. A third site some advanced business reporters use is Sqoop.com. Many reporters use this service because it allows a journalist to search a specific company's filings for certain words and phrases. For example, if a reporter wants to review all Coca-Cola filings to see if they mention Pepsi, a search on this website could tell him or her where the competitor is discussed. (The SEC's website has a similar function that allows reporters to search for specific words and phrases, such as "material impairment.")

Reading SEC filings can be a valuable tool for reporters, particularly those new to their beats, because new journalists need to learn about and understand the companies on which they are going to be writing stories. Reading an SEC filing may not result in a story every time. In fact, it is unlikely that reading SEC filings will result in a story even half of the time. But it is good practice for reporters to read the filings of companies on their beats. Such diligence pays off when a story does appear buried in the back of a filing. And reading all of the filings will help paint a picture of the company that will give the reporter the understanding needed to produce stories that show the writer knows his or her stuff.

Required Disclosures

In the past few years, public companies have dramatically increased the number of times they file 8-Ks. First, it is important to know the various reasons that a company must file a Form 8-K and when it must be filed. According to current SEC regulations, companies are required to file 8-Ks within four business days. If the filing is to satisfy compliance with Regulation FD, then the document must be filed even earlier. Sometimes, companies file 8-Ks on the day the event occurs. But many times, companies wait a few days or even a week. This is important to note, especially if the company issues a news release: A follow-up story may be waiting in the filing.

Certain events in a company's operations require that an 8-K be filed. Many of these events are important changes in a company that regulators have determined investors have a right to know about. Business writers should take their cues from the regulators—these disclosures are often important news that should be reported by media outlets. One of these events is when the company names a new leader. Because a new CEO or president is almost always announced by a news release, the filing of an 8-K with this information rarely becomes a newsworthy event. However, sometimes an 8-K about an executive change discusses important information. For example, note the details filed in this 8-K by TheStreet.com on December 22, 2015, about its executives:

1. The chief business officer of the company was leaving;
2. He will work as a consultant the first three months of 2016 and be paid $18,333 each month;
3. The new board chairman will receive $20,000 in cash and $40,000 in stock;
4. The CEO, should she depart the company, will receive two years' salary after leaving instead of the one year's salary previously agreed upon.

These changes are important for the business reporter to write about because this disclosure can help investors and employees determine whether a company is spending money wisely. In addition, whenever a company acquires or disposes of assets—buys or sells a business—it is required to file an 8-K detailing the transaction. Quite often, the 8-K about a transaction discloses financial details of the deal not included in the release. Other items may include the merger agreement, including the stock option agreement if there is one, any amendments or modifications to the merger, the closing of the deal, financial statements of the company being acquired and financial statements of the combined operations.

Sometimes an 8-K may even disclose an acquisition. For example, note the details from this story in the *Charlotte Observer* when investor Warren Buffett bought $5 billion worth of Bank of America stock:

In Thursday's deal, Bank of America is selling 50,000 shares of preferred stock with a value of $100,000 per share to Berkshire Hathaway in a private offering. The stock has a dividend of 6 percent per year and can be redeemed by Bank of America at any time at a 5 percent premium.

In addition, Berkshire Hathaway will also receive warrants that allow for the purchase of 700 million shares of Bank of America common stock at a price of $7.14 per share. The warrants may be used at any time during a 10-year period following the closing of the transaction. Bank of America receives $5 billion in cash for issuing the preferred shares and warrants. The transaction is expected to close early next month.

If Buffett were to trigger the warrants it would cause Bank of America to issue new shares, diluting the holdings of existing stockholders. After issuing new stock to absorb losses and fortify its balance sheet in recent years, the bank's share count has increased to 10.1 billion from 4.5 billion at the beginning of 2008. That means earnings are spread over more than twice as many shares.

Buffett told CNBC that it's "very likely" Berkshire Hathaway will exercise all of the warrants over the 10 years. If Buffett does so, Berkshire would own about 6.5 percent of Bank of America's common stock. Buffet made a profit on paper Thursday of $355 million from the warrants.

The deal prohibits Buffett from raising his total stake in the bank above 14.9 percent, according to an **8-K** form the bank filed Thursday.[2]

Without the filing of the 8-K, it is unlikely that the details of Buffett's investment would have been disclosed in the media until a news release was issued.

When a company files for bankruptcy-court protection or is the recipient of regulatory action, it must file an 8-K. These filings often contain valuable information for reporters covering companies with operations in other states or companies incorporated in states other than the one in which their headquarters are located. For example, thousands of companies are incorporated in

---

TIPS FROM THE PROS

The Associated Press business desk's recommendations for finding news in SEC filings:

Find out about lawsuits against the company in the Legal Proceedings section.

Delaware because of its friendly corporation laws, so a large number of bankruptcies (and lawsuits, for that matter) are filed in that state. Thus, a reporter in Portland, for example, probably will not know what has been filed in Delaware courts by companies or by regulators across the country.

Writing stories from these types of filings should be basic reporting, because the disclosures spell out what is going on at a company. For instance, when

CyNet Incorporated, a provider of Internet, voice and fax messaging software, filed for Chapter 11 bankruptcy protection, reporters covered the event, detailed in its 8-K filing. Other 8-K filings might include documents such as letters from regulators to companies detailing limits placed on their future operations or restraining orders preventing companies from continuing to do business. In many of these cases, the companies do not issue news releases, which makes it vitally important for reporters to read 8-K filings.

Companies also file an 8-K when they change their accounting firm. Their accountants may have resigned, or they could have been fired. In either case, this event leads to a filing, even if the parting is amicable. It should be noted that an accounting firm often ends its relationship with a client when there is a disagreement about or a discrepancy in the company's financial statements. Given what happened between Enron and Arthur Andersen, Enron's former accounting firm, reporters should expect more companies to take a closer look at their relationships with their auditors. In addition, look for more accounting firms to re-assess relationships with clients with whom there has been friction.

auditor's report: Recorded in the annual report, it tests to see that a corporation's financial statements comply with generally accepted accounting practices, or GAAP. This is sometimes referred to as the "clean opinion."

Writing a story about a company changing its auditors may not seem like an exciting day in the newsroom. But a change such as this may hint at further problems within the company, particularly if the business is struggling. Accounting firms used by companies are approved each year at the company's annual meeting. If an accounting firm declines to put itself up for re-election at the annual meeting, that decision could be a sign that there has been a disagreement. A small story in the newspaper about a change in auditors could lead to a call from a source—either at the company or at the accounting firm—who wants to tell the reporter more about what happened. Check the company's proxy statement, or DEF 14A, to see if there are new accountants up for election at the annual meeting.

An 8-K must also be filed when a member of the board of directors resigns. This is not typically a front-page story for a business section either, unless the board member was well known and carried some clout on the board. Typically such resignations are simply a brief, no more than two or three sentences. But again, the sudden resignation of a board member may signal growing discord between the board and the executive team at the company. Several board members resigning at the same time may also indicate conflict between the board and company management. The resignation of a Hewlett-Packard board member in 2006 led to the disclosure that the company was spying on business journalists to determine who on the board was leaking information.

The board member resigned because he disagreed with the tactic, and the chairwoman of the board ended up resigning as well.

TIPS FROM THE PROS

The Associated Press business desk's recommendations for finding news in SEC filings:

Check auditor's statements in the 10-Q or 10-K to make sure no red flags were raised.

A company also files an 8-K for its financial statements and exhibits and when it changes its fiscal year. Rarely do these disclosures result in a story, but they could. For example, an exhibit could be something such as an employment agreement with a new executive, and if the details have not been disclosed before, a reporter could write a story. The financial statements are typically from the most recent quarter, and if they were not included in the company's earnings release, they should be reviewed.

The SEC also requires that other events material to a company's business be disclosed in an 8-K filing. Whether an event is "material" enough to be disclosed is up for interpretation by company executives. But, as a result of recent events such as the economic crisis that occurred in the United States in 2008 and 2009, many companies have been criticized for not disclosing information, which, in turn, has caused a number of businesses to file 8-Ks just to be on the safe side of federal regulation. For example, Nathan's Famous Incorporated, a New York–based hot dog restaurant chain, filed an 8-K noting that Home Depot terminated eight restaurant license agreements at stores in which Nathan's operated, accounting for about 15 percent of the company's total sales. This information was valuable enough to be picked up by a reporter covering Home Depot for the *Atlanta Journal-Constitution*.

Other times, companies file 8-Ks projecting earnings for the next quarter or for the next year. Many times, these projections are given to analysts and investors at conferences or presentations. Thus, in these instances, 8-Ks are filed so that the information is given to everyone at the same time.

When MONY Group Incorporated, New York–based life insurer and asset manager, filed an 8-K on January 16, 2003, it provided the SEC with the slides from a presentation that it was giving to investors and analysts later that day. Wire service reporters and others immediately reviewed the filing to determine whether there was news in the slide show.

This is how Michael Crittenden, who followed MONY for the online news site SNL Financial, led his story that day:

Life insurer MONY Group Inc. suggested in a Jan. 16 regulatory filing that its fourth quarter operating earnings could easily beat Wall Street expectations.

In the Form 8-K, the New York-based company said that its preliminary fourth quarter results yielded pretax operating earnings in a range of $8 million to $13 million, or 11 cents to 18 cents per share. That range is well ahead of the Thomson First Call consensus estimate of 3 cents per share, with a high estimate of 11 cents and a low estimate of breakeven.

MONY Group said preliminary net income for the fourth quarter should be between $9 million and $14 million, or 12 cents to 19 cents per share.[3]

Interestingly, that same day, Dan Lowrey, a reporter for Dow Jones, chose to focus on other disclosures in the filing. His lead noted the company's earnings estimates for 2003—30 cents to 35 cents per share—compared with the average earnings estimate by Wall Street analysts, which was 33 cents per share. Both reporters reviewed the entire filing, which, in this case, was more than 30 pages. And in both cases, the reporters found news important to their readers.

Other times, the 8-K may disclose financial results that can be important in assessing how a company is performing. For example, the Associated Press reported that computer networking equipment maker Cisco Systems Incorporated noted in an 8-K filing that 5 percent of its $275 million quarterly loss provision was related to customer accounts. The company set aside $14 million for losses on doubtful accounts, up from $5 million in the same quarter the previous year. In writing about this disclosure, the reporter nicely compared Cisco's first-quarter loss provision with the loss provision for the first quarter of the previous year. That comparison shows the reader that the company is setting aside nearly three times as much money to pay for overdue payments than it had previously, an indication that maybe its customers are having trouble paying their bills.

A brief in the *Pittsburgh Post-Gazette* used information from an 8-K filed by Adelphia Communications Corporation to show that the cable company was losing subscribers and thus projecting lower earnings.

TIPS FROM THE PROS

The Associated Press business desk's recommendations for finding news in SEC filings:

Read the footnotes and exhibits for every filing.

The brief story took the earnings projections for Adelphia and showed why the company was lowering its estimates. It is important for any business reporter writing a story based on an 8-K to explain why the news is happening to give it context.

Also note that all of the stories used as examples cite the documents from which the information was obtained. Doing so lends credence to the report and to the reporter by showing readers that he or she is tracking the company closely. Often, a reporter must read through numerous pages in the filing to find snippets of news and then combine that information into a compelling story. A reporter has to condense thousands of words and numbers into a story that often is no longer than 300 to 400 words.

An individual investor may not be able to assess this kind of information. But a business journalist, with the help of experts and a proper understanding of what he or she is writing about, can properly assess the information and write a story telling the investor why the disclosure is important.

Resignations of Board Members and Executives

The previous section mentioned that an 8-K must be filed on numerous occasions, including when a company changes its executives and when a board member resigns. These are, arguably, the most important disclosures under the SEC rule because the executive team and the board are the people in charge of running the company and ensuring that the business is making money. However, if one or more of them leaves, you should not automatically assume that something is wrong.

Many times, company executives change for reasons that have nothing to do with the company's performance. A CEO or board member may reach retirement age. In some cases, a CEO will leave a company for health reasons or decide that it is simply time to let someone younger have a chance to run the shop. A board member may take on a new commitment with another business opportunity and feel that he or she does not have the proper time to devote to the board.

These are all good reasons for a changing of the guard at a company. But in an increasing number of cases, a CEO or a board member moving on may be an indication that there is unrest.

The first time business journalists might have thought there was trouble at Enron was when its CEO, Jeffrey Skilling, abruptly resigned shortly before its accounting problems were disclosed. At the time, Skilling said in a statement that he was leaving the company for personal reasons that had nothing to do with the company. Although "personal reasons" may be a valid explanation in a number of cases, it is also the terminology, unfortunately, that many companies use to mask tense situations ranging from a board becoming dissatisfied with the CEO's performance to an outright coup forcing executives into retirement.

In many cases, boardroom intrigue is one of the most fascinating stories for a business reporter. Executives and directors are only human, and they have personalities that can clash. These personalities often drive a company, which takes on the personal styles and mannerisms of its executives. Writing a story about a resignation from a news release or a filing may just be the beginning of a bigger story that delves into a number of other issues, such as who will replace the deposed executive or why the board member left.

An enterprising reporter reading the 8-K explanation of a CEO's departure should become curious enough to want to find out more about the executive's performance. In fact, the following story from the *Tampa Tribune* about the resignation of a CEO implies that more than meets the eye was going on behind the scenes:

> The recently announced resignation of Tropical Sportswear International Corp. Chief Executive Officer William Compton raises the question of how much publicly traded companies are required to disclose to regulators and shareholders.
>
> Although they don't have to disclose everything that goes on within the business, companies must notify the Securities and Exchange Commission of "material events," corporate governance experts said.
>
> That means disclosing information "a reasonable investor would deem important in making an investment decision," said Charles Elson, director of the University of Delaware's Center for Corporate Governance and a former professor at Stetson University College of Law in Gulfport. In the case of a material event, the filing, on a document known as Form 8-K, must be made within 10 days after the close of the month in which the event occurred. A similar filing must also be made with the stock exchange on which the company's shares are traded.
>
> In Tropical Sportswear's case, the company filed a Form 8-K on Nov. 19, the day after Compton's resignation.
>
> It disclosed Compton's resignation and included his severance agreement and a company press release announcing that Compton had agreed to resign "following a review by a committee of the board of directors of recent management issues related to Mr. Compton."

TIPS FROM THE PROS

The Associated Press business desk's recommendations for finding news in SEC filings:

The "Related Party Transactions" section in each proxy (DEF14A) will provide details on executive perks and interesting business deals.

> The release did not elaborate on the management issues leading to Compton's departure other than to say they were "not systemic to the company and will not result in any adjustments to or restatements of the company's financial statements."
>
> The definition of what is material, and required to be disclosed, has been refined by the courts over the years on a case-by-case basis.
>
> It "leaves a lot of latitude in the judgment of the company" about what it must report, said Willis Riccio, a securities law partner with

Adler Pollock & Sheehan in Providence, R.I., and a former New England regional administrator for the SEC.

"They can make a good-faith judgment about whether what has occurred is material, in terms of disclosure," Riccio said.

Reforms in Congress, including the recently enacted Sarbanes-Oxley Act, are likely to shorten the amount of time companies have to make disclosures, Riccio noted.

Companies also have a continuing duty to supplement their filings if they obtain important new information about a material event.

"What is clear, is that when they say something, it has to be correct in all material respects," Elson said.[4]

In addition to explaining what must be disclosed, this story raises the question of why Compton left Tropical Sportswear. It is a question that many investors would obviously like to have answered; thus, it is a good question for reporters to be asking. Other times, the filing may show the specific reasons why board members want to get rid of executives, as was the case with this Colorado-based company in the following story from the *Denver Post*:

Three directors of an Arapahoe County technology company recommended that the company's top managers resign as a result of long-term accounting problems in the firm, according to the directors' letters of resignation, filed with the Securities and Exchange Commission this week.

Laser Technology Inc.'s chief executive officer, David Williams, who spoke to *The Denver Post* on Wednesday, said everyone's overreacting to a problem caused when a sale was logged as having occurred in the 1993 fiscal year but possibly should have been recorded in fiscal 1994. He wouldn't give details,

Richard B. Sayford, R. James Lynch and William R. Carr quit the board of Laser Technology after the company's full board of directors rejected the recommendations, the Jan. 11 letters said. The company, which makes laser speed- and distance-measuring devices, filed the letters this week as an amendment to its form 8-K. The three directors' proposals came out of their investigation, begun in October, into the company's accounting practices.

The recommendations, according to the letters, called for the resignations of Williams, Chief Financial Officer Pamela Sevy, Director H. DeWorth Williams and Secretary and Director Dan N. Grothe.

They also stated that David Williams "pay all amounts, if any, that are due from him to the company," that the company hire a new CEO and CFO from outside the company, and that Laser immediately retain a reputable accounting firm that's independent from any of the company's officers and directors.

Asked if he planned eventually to resign, Williams said: "Not today."[5]

Clashes between board members and executives can occur for several reasons. The company may not be making as much money as the board expects. Or the CEO and president may be running the company with a style that upsets other employees, lowering morale and hurting the company's performance because the workers have no incentive to better the business. Executives may also have reasons to be upset with board members. Coca-Cola CEO Doug Ivester left the top spot at the company in 1999 after only two years on the job because he felt board members interfered with his ability to run the company. Because executives run the company on a day-to-day basis, they may have a better feel than the board for what the company needs.

TIPS FROM THE PROS

The Associated Press business desk's recommendations for finding news in SEC filings:

See compensation trends and details for executives and directors in the proxy.

In either case, it is wise to watch for such disagreements between the executive suite and the boardroom, even if they are not events disclosed in an 8-K. Infighting, no matter what size the company, can turn into a gripping story about the control of a business that often becomes the best-read story in the business section. The clues can be found in 8-K filings as long as the reporter knows what to look for.

Many investors—and therefore readers—want to know the price of getting rid of an executive. In some cases, the 8-K provides the details. If not, the proxy statement, discussed in more detail in Chapter 9, could provide the information.

The following excerpt shows how a story in the *Sun-Sentinel* in Fort Lauderdale handled the price of a company getting rid of its chief operating officer:

> Fort Lauderdale-based staffing and recruitment giant Spherion Corp. said Tuesday it will write off an additional $250 million to $300 million for the value of goodwill in acquisitions—on top of the $692 million it wrote off earlier in the fiscal year.
>
> In the same announcement, Spherion said Chief Operating Officer Robert Livonius has left the company, a departure that will cause the company to take an additional $3.5 million charge in the fourth quarter.
>
> Spherion filed an 8-K report with the Securities Exchange Commission disclosing both events before the market's opening. Its stock closed down 42 cents at $6.21.
>
> Company spokeswoman Patricia Johnson said Livonius' position was eliminated in an effort to reduce layers of management and to flatten the

organization. Livonius had been with the company since 1991 and was appointed executive vice president and COO in 1997 under former CEO Raymond Marcy.

Livonius, with an annual salary of $495,000 plus options, was the second highest paid executive in the organization, after the chief executive. The company will give him a $3.5 million severance agreement.

CEO and President Cinda A. Hallman said in a statement on Livonius' departure that she will assume direct responsibility for business operations.

"We sincerely appreciate Bob's many contributions to the company and wish him well in the future," she added.[6]

The charge mentioned in the second paragraph of the example above essentially states that the executive received $3.5 million to leave the company. Exorbitant pay to leave a company is often criticized by investors and executive pay experts. Disclosures like this should be reported because investors and employees of the company want to know if the company is spending money wisely. Thus, business reporters covering events such as these should find out whether the company will receive benefits totaling more than the severance package as a result of getting rid of the executive.

When Companies and Accountants Collide

The relationship between a company and its accounting firm has come under increasing scrutiny in recent years. Before the collapses of Enron, WorldCom and other companies, a company and its auditor were closely tied. A company would pay its accounting firm millions of dollars to audit its financial records and to provide a statement in its SEC filings giving it a clean bill of health. The accounting industry's role was to provide some sense of comfort to investors and others who did business with the company.

What actually happened, it turns out, was that accounting firms went along with what company executives wanted as far as reporting revenues, sales and other financial numbers because they feared losing their income if they said no. In other cases, companies hid the actual financial performance of their operations from their auditors, making it nearly impossible for the accountants to properly do their job.

TIPS FROM THE PROS

The Associated Press business desk's recommendations for finding news in SEC filings:

The term "going concern," used by the company or its auditors in filings, indicates serious financial trouble and perhaps even a looming bankruptcy filing.

Still, the auditors must take some blame. According to a study by Weiss Ratings, a Florida-based firm, accounting firms gave a clean bill of health to more than 90 percent of companies that later had accounting irregularities uncovered. The Weiss research also disclosed that few companies that announced accounting problems had a statement from their auditors expressing concern. These companies had a market capitalization of more than $1.9 trillion on Wall Street before their accounting irregularities were uncovered. Afterward, their value on Wall Street fell by more than $1.2 trillion. That is a huge story for business journalists and shows how important it is to understand the relationship between companies and accountants.

In these circumstances, business reporters are also put in a difficult position. How can a business journalist trust a company's numbers or uncover a wrongdoing if the company's own auditors are not being told the truth? There are still a number of documents that a journalist should examine to determine whether the relationship between a company and its accountants is legitimate. Most importantly, the reporter should review the accountant's statement in a company's 10-Q and 10-K filings. Sometimes the auditor's statement discusses concerns about a company's continuing ability to operate, in which case the writer has not only a story for tomorrow's newspaper or evening newscast but also a clear indication that the relationship between the company and its accountants is legitimate. The following excerpt from the *San Jose Mercury News* illustrates how an auditor's statement expressing concern about the future of a company is a story:

At Home, the nation's largest provider of high-speed Internet access, is at risk of being buried under its heavy debt and operating losses, the company said in an updated annual report filed Monday with the Securities and Exchange Commission.

The Redwood City company, once a high-flying player in the Internet economy, said auditors Ernst & Young have expressed "substantial doubt" about its ability to continue as a "going concern."

Shares of At Home lost nearly half their value Monday, falling 46 cents to 47 cents a share.

The company, which does business as Excite@Home, faces a possible delisting from the NASDAQ stock market, which would trigger a $100 million payment to its convertible bondholders. With only $183.4 million in cash as of June 30, At Home would soon run out of money and be forced to declare bankruptcy if it had to make the payment, analysts said.

In June, At Home obtained through a convertible bond a crucial $100 million injection from two investment firms that specialize in financing struggling companies. That deal included a requirement that the company stay listed on one of the major stock exchanges.

At Home currently fails to meet NASDAQ's minimum requirements for continued listing. Its stock price has dropped below $3, the lowest bid price allowed under one of NASDAQ's standards. Alison Bowman, an At Home spokeswoman, said the company has not received a delisting notice from NASDAQ.[7]

It is always important to read the auditor's statement, particularly if the company has been losing money for the last few years. Most companies receive a clean bill of health from their accountants, so it is a major development when the statement raises questions about the company. Other companies receive qualified opinions, which typically mean the company's financial books are

qualified opinion: Suggests that the information provided was limited in scope or the company being audited did not maintain GAAP accounting principles. Contrary to its connotation, a qualified opinion is not a good thing. Auditors that deem audits as qualified opinions are advising that the audit is not complete or that the accounting methods used by the company do not follow GAAP.

not up to par. In addition, if its accountants question a company's future viability, reporters should check the statements in the 10-K or 10-Q to see if the language in the statement has changed. If it has—for better or worse—then a story updating the company's condition is likely warranted. When the going concern statement is made, it may be filed in an 8-K, as in the case of Boston Chicken, disclosed in the following *Denver Post* story:

> Boston Chicken Inc.'s auditor has filed a statement with the federal Securities and Exchange Commission saying there is "substantial doubt" that the restaurant chain can stay in business.
>
> In the SEC document, dated May 19 and filed Wednesday, auditor Arthur Andersen LLP gives a detailed account of Boston Chicken's financial woes.
>
> The auditor describes how Boston Chicken's money problems could trigger default on hundreds of millions of dollars in debt. There can be "no assurance," the document says, that the company will be able to "meet its financial obligations." On the 8-K form, Arthur Andersen says it has included a paragraph in its 1997 audit report that "there is substantial doubt about (Boston Chicken's) ability to continue as a going concern."
>
> The same statement is included in Arthur Andersen's assessment of Boston Chicken's franchisees—called area developers. Andersen, the company that also audited each of the franchisees, questions each franchisee's ability to continue "as a going concern."
>
> An 8-K is a form a publicly held company files with the SEC to report on any events that might affect its financial situation or the value of its shares of stock.

An auditor's inclusion of the "going concern" statement in a financial audit is "serious," according to a partner at KPMG Peat Marwick, a national auditing firm.[8]

It is also wise for a business reporter to check with the suppliers, competitors and government agencies who know a company's operations. Competitors often know

Form 8-K going concern: A statement made by independent auditors that raises doubts about the company's ability to function in the future.

if another company is experiencing difficulty or losing market share. Suppliers are particularly important sources because they can tell you if the company pays its bills on time. If a company pays late, that may be an indication that there are financial problems that the accountants have not uncovered or mentioned in the filings. One should also look for lawsuits to see if a company is being sued for nonpayment.

TIPS FROM THE PROS

The Associated Press business desk's recommendations for finding news in SEC filings:

Form 4s will offer information about which "insiders" are selling or buying shares.

Sometimes, the SEC initiates investigations or actions against companies that it believes may have improperly stated financial problems. The results of SEC actions can be disclosed in 8-Ks or filings such as the 10-K or 10-Q.

The following is an example of how Bloomberg News reported the disclosure of a look into a company's books:

Alpharma Inc. said the Securities and Exchange Commission has begun a formal investigation of the company's methods for recognizing revenue. Alpharma shares declined 13 percent, falling $2.75 to $17.90.

The Fort Lee, New Jersey, manufacturer of generic drugs and animal health products last November restated its earnings. The investigation, reported in a filing with the Securities and Exchange Commission, involves two revenue recognition practices connected with the restatement.

Shareholders had alleged in a class action lawsuit that the company used improper revenue recognition policies in regard to its animal health business in Brazil. The U.S. District Court for the District of New Jersey dismissed the class action suit, the company reported today.

Alpharma in October said it would revise its earnings statements because some sales of animal products were billed when the orders were recognized, not when they were actually shipped. The problem was corrected by the third quarter of last year, the company had said.

Alpharma in November restated earnings to report 59 percent more net income, or $35.7 million, for the first half of 2001, and lower earnings than reported for the previous three years.

Net income in 2000 was $55.5 million, Alpharma said, not $61.1 million as it had reported. In 1999, the company earned $29.9 million, $7 million less than reported, and in 1998, it earned $22.8 million. It had reported $24.2 million for that year. Once the commission approves the opening of a formal examination, staff members have the authority to subpoena information.

Alpharma anticipates cooperating with the SEC investigation, according to the filing.[9]

An investigation like this can lead a company to restate its financial results, lowering its revenue or its earnings. When this happens, a company is essentially admitting that its accountants goofed. However, investors are not humored by the event. They will usually dump the stock, sending its price downward. That is why a business reporter should always be on the lookout for any hint of impropriety in a company's financial statements. The writer who is first to report an investigation or a problem does his or her readers a great service.

Earlier, the "Required Disclosures" section mentioned that companies must file an 8-K when they part ways with auditors. It cannot be emphasized enough that a company firing an auditor or an auditor declining to work with a company is one of the best indicators that there may be some future problems. (An exception to this is when an accounting firm such as Arthur Andersen goes out of business, forcing all of its former clients to find a new auditor to review its books.) Often, the 8-K discloses that there was a disagreement between the company and its accountants that led to the parting. Other times, a reason is not given. It is still an important event—one that a reporter should watch closely. He or she should perhaps even call sources to determine the real reason for the switch.

A story from the *Tampa Tribune* below details how a company in bankruptcy court picked a new auditor. The story implies that the new auditor was selected to provide a fresh look at the company's financial situation:

Anchor Glass Container Corp. has dismissed Andersen as its independent public accountant but said the decision has nothing to do with Andersen's recent troubles.

The loss deprives Andersen of a Tampa Bay client that paid $503,000 in fees in 2001, Securities and Exchange Commission records show.

Anchor retained PricewaterhouseCoopers for 2002, according to an SEC 8-K filing April 15.

"It has nothing to do with Andersen; we would have done this regardless," said Dale Buckwalter, chief financial officer for Anchor Glass. "It reflects we have a new owner and a new law firm," Carlton Fields in Tampa.

The SEC filing states Anchor's board made the decision April 11.

"There were no disagreements with Arthur Andersen on any matter of accounting principle or practice, financial statement disclosure or auditing scope or procedure," the SEC filing states.

Anchor was forced to file for protection from bankruptcy April 15 because its parent company, Toronto-based Consumers Packing Inc., filed for bankruptcy protection, company officials said.

Business at the Tampa-based subsidiary is the best it's been in two decades, Anchor Chief Operating Officer Richard M. Deneau said last week. PricewaterhouseCoopers, which gains Anchor's business, is the largest accounting firm in Tampa Bay.

"Obviously, Anchor Glass is a large and important client for us," said Andrew McAdams, office managing partner for PricewaterhouseCoopers' Central Florida practice.

In an indictment March 14, a federal grand jury accused Andersen of destroying "tons of paper" and deleting computer files in the financial collapse of Enron Corp.[10]

TIPS FROM THE PROS

The Associated Press business desk's recommendations for finding news in SEC filings:

When a company hires a new top executive, it will often file the employment contract with the SEC soon after, providing interesting compensation details.

With the increasing scrutiny of the relationships between companies and accountants, many hope that auditors will become more vigilant in reviewing the financial statements of their clients. Such a development could lead to more auditors making disclosures about problems at companies.

The SEC appears to be taking a more aggressive stance in (a) reviewing business dealings between auditors and companies and (b) fining and censuring accountants whose dealings call into question their independence as auditors. Another important step that could prove valuable for business reporters is a measure designed to increase the clout of the auditing committee on a company's board of directors. The auditing committee reviews the relationship between a company and its outside accountants. Many companies hire

CFOs from accounting firms with which they do business. Some reviewing corporate governance have criticized that relationship.

One more interesting development in the relationship between companies and auditors is that executives at the largest companies are now required to certify that their financial statements are as correct and accurate as possible. Though this certification applies to the 900 largest companies, or those with more than $1.2 billion in assets, other smaller companies have also had executives attest to their results. This means that the onus is now on company executives to provide accurate financial statements that reflect the true picture of the company to auditors and the general public.

Most companies give as accurate a picture of their financial results as possible. But there will always be a few businesses that stretch the limits of accounting rules in a bid to make themselves appear better than they actually are. The relationship between a company and its outside accountants is important to understand, particularly for the business journalist, so he or she can assess whether the business is being truthful or if it needs closer examination.

Regulation FD and Conference Calls

Remember the example earlier in this chapter where MONY Group disclosed its projected earnings in an 8-K filing? Why did the company disclose such information?

A news release issued two days before the filing provides a clue. It mentioned that the company was going to hold its annual meeting with investors and analysts and that its management team would provide an "overview and outlook for the company and its business units" (MONY Group, 2003). The release also mentioned that the meeting could be heard via the Internet from its website. So, at the same time the 8-K was filed, the company held a meeting to discuss the information in the filing. The meeting, the release and the 8-K filing by MONY Group were done to comply with a set of SEC rules called Regulation FD that went into effect in 2000 and profoundly changed how Wall Street and the business media obtained information from companies.

Regulation Fair Disclosure (FD): A rule passed by the Securities and Exchange Commission (SEC) in an effort to prevent selective disclosure by public companies to market professionals and certain shareholders.

Amid opposition from companies and Wall Street firms, Regulation FD was enacted to bring a level playing field to the investment community. Regulators saw companies providing information about their financial performance and their business operations to favored analysts and investors, allowing them to trade in the company's stock before the information was shared with others. Regulation FD now prevents companies from providing information to a select few on Wall Street. A company or executive must now provide the information to everyone at the same time.

TIPS FROM THE PROS

The Associated Press business desk's recommendations for finding news in SEC filings:

You can ask for older SEC filings through a public records request. This can allow you to track interesting details, such as number of stores and store closings throughout the years. Example here:
www.usatoday.com/story/money/business/2015/06/18/mcdonalds-shrinking-in-us/28920223/

Companies have chosen to comply with Regulation FD in a number of ways. One of these ways has been through filing information in an 8-K. Another way has been to open conference calls discussing quarterly earnings or other important developments to anybody who wants to listen via the Internet or a toll-free telephone number. This includes the media and small-time investors. In the past, companies limited who could listen to these conference calls to analysts and investors. Although some companies allowed reporters to listen to these calls, others, such as Anheuser-Busch, did not. If a reporter noticed a company's stock rising or falling while a conference call was ongoing, he or she would have to wait until the call was over to call analysts and investors he or she knew were listening to find out what had caused the stock to move.

conference call: An event in which investors can call into via a special phone number and hear the management of their company comment on the financial results of the recently completed quarter, or another important corporate event.

The business journalism community rallied strongly behind Regulation FD. Bloomberg News wrote countless stories about companies that did not allow broad access to their conference calls. The SABEW wrote letters in support of the legislation. The reasoning was simple: In addition to helping investors, Regulation FD gave reporters more information as well. Reporters can now listen to the calls that were previously just the territory of Wall Street insiders. Though business journalists cannot always ask questions during the calls, they can use the conversations among executives, analysts and investors to improve the content of their stories, explaining why people on Wall Street are angry or happy with a company's performance. The result has been more detailed stories, making listening to the conference call an important part of the business journalist's daily routine. Some reporters often have several conference calls to listen to in a single day, particularly during earnings season. And most companies provide information about how to access their conference calls directly to journalists in the form of releases.

The increase in conference calls as a result of Regulation FD, some argue, has not had the intended effect of providing more information. The executives now read from carefully worded scripts and do not provide any out-of-the-ordinary information when discussing their companies. And the major analysts and investors who follow that company still ask the bulk of the questions on the call. Many companies limit the number of questions that a single person can ask during the call, and with prepared remarks sometimes lasting as long as 30 minutes, there is little time to answer all questions on a call that is usually limited to an hour.

Conference calls about quarterly earnings results, in particular, can be extremely boring, especially if the company reported earnings in line with Wall Street estimates and is not expected to reveal any surprises on the call. It takes a savvy reporter who has followed a company for years to listen to such a call and determine whether there has been any news disclosed. Many times, the only news on such calls comes during the question-and-answer period. But increasingly, analysts and investors do not want to ask probing questions for their competitors to hear. Then, the news is typically if a company provides any sort of earnings guidance during its call. If that happens, the company has usually provided the news in a release and in an 8-K filing. Often, if a company executive, in answering a question on the call, provides information that the company determines is material to its performance, the company will later file an 8-K.

Still, listening to conference calls can be a valuable experience for business reporters, even if the time spent on the call does not result in a story. The journalist can assess how the CEO or CFO interacts with analysts and investors by noting whether the questions are hostile or friendly. The tone of the questions and the responses can tell the reporter whether Wall Street is happy or upset with the company. How an executive responds to a question can also be an indicator of how he or she thinks the business is performing or what he or she thinks about the company's future prospects.

Anyone who went back and listened to the first-quarter 2001 earnings conference call for now-bankrupt energy giant Enron would have run across this exchange between Highfields Capital Corporation analyst Richard Grubman and CEO Jeff Skilling on why the company had not released a balance sheet along with its earnings statement:

Grubman: Yes, good morning. Can you tell us what the assets and liabilities from price/risk management were at quarter-end, what those balances were?

Skilling: We don't have the balance sheet completed. We'll have that done shortly.

Grubman: But you're the only financial institution that can't produce a balance sheet or a cash flow statement with their earnings.

Skilling: You—thank you very much. We appreciate it.

Grubman: Appreciate it.[11]

Skilling then muttered an expletive. Less than six months later, he resigned from the company, which then restated its earnings and filed for bankruptcy-court protection. The tense conversation between Skilling and Grubman could have been an indicator to anyone listening that maybe someone needed to take a closer look at Enron's performance.

Sometimes, the conference call can provide unintended results. The following Bloomberg News story illustrates a case in which shareholders disclosed information on a conference call about a relationship between the company and its CEO:

Insignia Financial Group Inc. Chief Executive Andrew Farkas' compensation was criticized by two of the property broker's biggest investors, who said he is profiting from company partnerships at shareholder expense.

An arrangement giving Farkas a 22 percent share of profits from a company managed investment fund after a certain return is met isn't in the best interests of shareholders, Daniel Loeb of Third Point Partners LP said on a conference call.

Insignia also shouldn't have paid Farkas $950,000 for company use of a personal plane and boat he owns, Loeb said. The compensation arrangements put Insignia, whose Insignia/ESG unit is New York's biggest broker, at risk of "a major backlash" from shareholders at a time when the company's shares are down 24 cents for the year, said Loeb, whose firm had a 4.9 percent stake in Insignia at the end of March.

"Right now you're in a position to make a lot of money while your stock is languishing," Loeb told Farkas on the call.

Company officials declined immediate comment. On the call, which was held to discuss Insignia's second-quarter results, Farkas said Loeb's analysis wasn't "entirely accurate."

I "believe that the interests of shareholders and the interests of management, including all those who participate in promote programs, are in fact very much aligned," he said.

Insignia's counsel and compensation committee, which consists of Related Cos. Chairman Stephen Ross and H. Strauss Zelnick, former head of Bertelsmann AG's BMG Entertainment music unit, reevaluate its "programs on a regular basis," Farkas said.

Insignia yesterday said it had second-quarter net income of $3.18 million, or 12 cents a share, compared with a loss from continuing operations of $1.75 million, or 9 cents, a year earlier. Losses on Internet-related ventures reduced results for the latest quarter by $2.6 million, Insignia said.

The company's shares fell 30 cents to $8.20 on the New York Stock Exchange. Another shareholder, hedge fund manager David Einhorn of Greenlight Capital LLC, joined Loeb in his criticism on the call. Greenlight owned a 7.4 percent stake in Insignia at the end of March, making it the company's third-largest shareholder.

"We feel similarly to him," Einhorn said. "And we think the company should come back promptly with how to fix its corporate governance issues before this turns into some sort of media circus."

Before taking personal benefits from new ventures, Farkas should first make sure Insignia recoups its losses, Loeb said. Insignia has taken $34.7 million of charges for failed Internet ventures spearheaded by Farkas, including EdificeRex.com, which sought to provide services to apartment renters.

"It seems like you can keep setting up these partnerships one after another and if one doesn't work well, so be it," Loeb said. "You go on to the next one. What I'd rather see is us all sitting at the same table and eating from the same trough, if you will."[12]

A month later, Insignia Financial filed an 8-K disclosing that it would no longer reimburse its CEO for the company's use of his personal boat and would stop paying for the plane he co-owns. (That resulted in another story for the Bloomberg reporter covering the company.) This is a case in which the investors in a company, not the executives, used the conference call to make news.

For most business reporters, accessing these calls is as simple as finding the company's website. Most companies include a link to the conference call via the Internet. Others provide the phone number that can be called at the end of a news release. But there are also websites that specialize in providing access to company conference calls. One of the best free sites is http://seekingalpha.com. Another good site—although it is a subscription-based site—is www.bestcalls.com because it also provides transcripts of calls.

It has now been more than a decade since the SEC imposed Regulation FD. It took regulators more than two years to crack down on companies suspected of violating the rules. Even then, the companies received little more than slaps on the wrist, as the following *San Jose Mercury News* story explains:

Siebel Systems agreed to settle a federal charge that it had violated a Securities and Exchange Commission regulation prohibiting companies from selectively disclosing information to favored Wall Street analysts before releasing the news to ordinary investors.

The agreement with the San Mateo software company marked the first litigation brought to enforce Regulation FD (for Fair Disclosure), which was adopted in August 2000 in order to ensure the public equal access to important investment information.

The SEC also announced Monday the settlement of administrative proceedings against Secure Computing, a San Jose security-software maker, and Raytheon, a Lexington, Mass., defense contractor.

All three companies agreed to cease and desist from any future violations of Regulation FD without admitting or denying any wrongdoing. Siebel Systems also agreed to pay a civil penalty of $250,000.

"They are trying to send a message that SEC is serious about enforcing the Regulation FD," said Gordy Davidson, chairman of Fenwick & West, a Silicon Valley law firm that emphasizes its technology practice.

The three cases illustrate how broadly Regulation FD has affected the way companies communicate with investors. Before it was adopted, analysts generally relied on private conversations with executives to form an opinion about a company's financial prospects. Analysts at larger, more prestigious firms often received special guidance.

"These cases, and Raytheon in particular, describe the kind of conduct that Regulation FD was supposed to prevent," said Mark Schonfeld, associate regional director of the SEC's Northeast Regional Office.

According to SEC documents, Raytheon Chief Financial Officer Franklyn Caine called individual analysts following a February 2001 earnings call to let them know their estimates for first-quarter earnings were "too high" or "very aggressive."[13]

Regulation FD did give companies some guidance about the "what and how" of information they are supposed to provide to the public. As the corporate world has moved forward and begun to understand these regulations better, companies have moved back to pre–Regulation FD days and become more comfortable and forthcoming in providing information during conference calls.

Understanding how companies make and disseminate news can help business reporters cover that news competently. Nothing hurts a business journalist more than botching an explanation of what it means for a board member to resign or for an auditor to express doubt about a company's future.

Notes

1. From "EMC plans to cut jobs amid Dell Deal," by Jeremy C. Owens, December 31, 2015, MarketWatch.com. Copyright 2015 by MarketWatch.com. All Rights Reserved.
2. From "Buffett investing $5B in BofA—Deal brings the ailing bank a much-needed endorsement; billionaire to get big dividends and right to buy bigger stake," by R. Rothacker and K. Pittman, August 26, 2011, *Charlotte Observer*, p. A-1. Copyright 2011 by *Charlotte Observer*. Reprinted with permission.
3. From "MONY sees fourth-quarter results ahead of estimates, in line 2003," by M. Crittenden, January 16, 2003, Insurance Investor Interactive. Copyright 2003 by SNL Financial. Reprinted with permission.
4. From "Firms base disclosure on relevance to investors," by G. Haber, December 10, 2002, *Tampa Tribune*, p. 4. Copyright 2002 by *Tampa Tribune*. Reprinted with permission.

5. From "Laser Technology execs' exit urged," by L. Kokmen and E. Hubler, January 21, 1999, *Denver Post*, p. C1. Copyright 1999 by *Denver Post*. Reprinted with permission.

6. From "Spherion taking $250 m goodwill charge; COO post eliminated to cut costs," by J. Fleischer Tamen, January 8, 2003, *South Florida Sun-Sentinel*, p. 10. Copyright 2003 by *South Florida Sun-Sentinel*. Reprinted with permission.

7. From "At Home warns it may run out of cash," by J. Kwan, August 21, 2001, *San Jose Mercury News*, p. 1C. Copyright 2001 by *San Jose Mercury News*. All rights reserved. Reprinted with permission.

8. From "Boston Chicken woes mount," by P. Parker, May 29, 1998, *Denver Post*, p. A1. Copyright 1998 by *Denver Post*. Reprinted with permission.

9. From "Alpharma says SEC investigating its revenue methods," by M. Weiss, June 3, 2002, Bloomberg News. Copyright 2002 by Bloomberg L.P. All rights reserved. Reprinted with permission.

10. From "Anchor Glass drops Anderson, retains PricewaterhouseCoopers," by T. Jackovics, April 23, 2002, *Tampa Tribune*, p. 5. Copyright 2002 by *Tampa Tribune*. Reprinted with permission.

11. From "Any more questions? Company conference calls still leave investors out," by M. Marbaro, October 6, 2002, *Washington Post*, p. H1. Copyright 2002 by *Washington Post*. Reprinted with permission.

12. From "Insignia Financial CEO's pay package criticized by shareholders," by D. Levitt, July 25, 2002, Bloomberg News. Copyright 2002 by Bloomberg L.P. All rights reserved. Reprinted with permission.

13. From "Siebel to pay fine to SEC; $250,000 settles charge of disclosure violation," by E. Ackerman, November 26, 2002, *San Jose Mercury News*, p. 1. Copyright 2002 by *San Jose Mercury News*. All rights reserved. Reprinted with permission.

Key Terms

auditor's report	Form 8-K going concern
conference call	qualified opinion
Form 8-K	Regulation Fair Disclosure (FD)

Suggested Exercises

1. Find examples of 10 of the reasons an 8-K is filed, along with stories that were written from those filings. This could be a project that is spread out across an entire semester.

2. Write a 500-word essay explaining the increase in 8-K filings due to Regulation FD. Explain Regulation FD and give examples of the types of 8-Ks being filed as a result and why they're stories.

3. Find a company where a top-ranking executive has recently left or been replaced. Compare the information disclosed in the company's news release to the information disclosed in the Form 8-K.

4. Listen to a company's conference call and write a story based on what news you thought was disclosed during the call. After you turn the story in, compare the prepared remarks at the beginning of the call to the Q&A session at the end of the call.

References

Ackerman, E. (2002, November 26). Siebel to pay fine to SEC; $250,000 settles charge of disclosure violation. *San Jose Mercury News*, p. 1.

Associated Press. (2000, December 5). Cisco prepares for delinquent accounts.

Associated Press. (2002, December 27). CyNet files for chapter 11 bankruptcy protection. *San Jose Mercury News*, p. 2.

Barbara, M. (2002, October 6). Any more questions? Company conference calls still leave investors out. *Washington Post*, p. H1.

Chubb Corporation. Form 8-K. (2003, January 21). (SEC Publication No. 0000950123–03–000485, pp. 1–22).

Crittenden, M. (2003, January 16). MONY sees fourth-quarter results ahead of estimates, in line 2003. *Insurance Investor Interactive*. Retrieved January 30, 2003 from www.snl.com.

Haber, G. (2002, December 10). Firms base disclosure on relevance to investors. *Tampa Tribune*, p. 4.

Home Depot ends 8 Nathan's licenses. (2002, September 21). *Atlanta Journal-Constitution*, p. 2R.

Jackovics, T. (2002, April 23). Anchor glass drops Andersen, retains PriceWaterhouse Coopers. *Tampa Tribune*, p. 5.

Kokmen, L., & Hubler, E. (1999, January 21). Laser technology execs' exit urged. *Denver Post*, p. C1.

Kwan, J.L. (2001, August 21). At home warns it may run out of cash. *San Jose Mercury News*, p. 1C.

Levitt, D.M. (2002, July 25). Insignia Financial CEO's pay package criticized by shareholders. Bloomberg News.

Lowrey, D. (2003, January 16). MONY Group 2003 earnings outlook tracks estimates. Dow Jones Newswires.

MONY Group. (2003, January 14). Corporate news release.

Owens, J. (2015, December 31). EMC plans to cut jobs amid Dell Deal. MarketWatch.com. Retrieved January 11, 2016 from www.marketwatch.com/story/emc-plans-job-cuts-amid-dell-deal-2015–12–31.

Parker, P. (1998, May 29). Boston chicken woes mount. *Denver Post*, p. Al.

Rothacker, R., & Pittman, K. (2011, August 26). Buffett investing $5B in BofA—Deal brings the ailing bank a much-needed endorsement; billionaire to get big dividends and right to buy bigger stake. *Charlotte Observer*, p. A-1.

Subscriber loss hurts Adelphia. (2002, November 6). *Pittsburgh Post-Gazette*, p. D-4.

Tamen, J. Fleischer. (2003, January 8). Spherion taking $250M goodwill charge; COO post eliminated to cut costs. Fort Lauderdale, FL: *Sun-Sentinel*, p. 1D.

Weiss, M. (2002, June 3). Alpharma says SEC investigating its revenue methods. Bloomberg News.

7

MERGERS AND ACQUISITIONS

Why Companies Buy Each Other

At some point in time, virtually every business reporter will write a story about one company buying another. It is like a police reporter writing a story about a murder. Both of these news events happen with regularity. In the first half of 2015, there were $1.7 trillion worth of mergers and acquisitions, according to Mergermarket, an 11 percent increase from the same time period in 2014 and the highest level for a six-month time period since the first half of 2007. In addition, large deals—those worth more than $10 billion—hit a record high in the first half of 2015.

Simply put, mergers and acquisitions occur with such regularity that they have become a staple of business reporting. Because of their frequency, it is important for journalists to understand how and why mergers and acquisitions occur and what information is important for readers and viewers to receive. Virtually every huge company, and plenty of small ones, too, were created by one or more mergers or acquisitions. Citigroup is the combination of the former Citibank and Travelers; AOL Time Warner was created by the merger of America Online with Time Warner, itself the creation of a deal between Time and Warner Brothers; and Disney bought television network ABC, which brought ESPN into the new company.

The economic crisis forced some companies to sell themselves to remain in business. The federal government has played a part in mergers and acquisitions as well, sometimes finding suitable acquirers to purchase companies in trouble. In September 2008, the government backed Citigroup Incorporated's purchase of Wachovia Corporation but later backed Wells Fargo & Company's acquisition of Wachovia because Wells Fargo & Company offered a higher price. In the same month, the federal government seized Washington Mutual Incorporated and sold the bulk of its assets to J.P. Morgan Chase & Company.

TIPS FROM THE PROS

 Bloomberg Gadfly columnists Tara Lachapelle, Brooke Sutherland and Gillian Tan on covering mergers and acquisitions:

Bloomberg Gadfly

Know the deal landscape inside and out so that when you speak to sources, you're as informed—or maybe more informed—than them in terms of recent or potential deals, comments made about acquisitions, activists taking stakes, what's been written by the competition, etc. The less it feels like they need to educate you, and that you're sometimes reminding them of angles that could turn into dealmaking for them, the more fruitful conversations will be. Similarly, the more you know, the less you'll be spun by sources when you're interviewing them and the more you'll be able to dig deeper in your reporting.

Most companies, whether they are public or private, like to get bigger. Many of them make acquisitions under the belief that a larger company can spread its expenses around more efficiently. For instance, why have two CEOs and two CFOs when two companies can be combined to only have one of each? Why operate two headquarters when one would suffice? That is what most companies hope for. But, in reality, mergers and acquisitions do not always work out that way.

First, the terms should be defined. Although the terms merger and acquisition are sometimes used interchangeably, there is a big difference. Merger refers to when two companies agree to combine their operations into one company. In a true merger, the past owners of the two companies will each own 50 percent of the new company. In a merger, the combined company's board of directors is also typically split among the board members of the two old businesses. In many cases, the management teams of the old companies also combine to form one new executive team. That is how it is supposed to work.

However, despite how hard companies try to make mergers equal, one company typically has the upper hand. For example, its headquarters becomes the new headquarters for the combined operation, its CEO takes over running the new company, or its shareholders may end up owning 55 percent of the new company.

Acquisition refers to when one company buys a controlling interest in another company. An acquisition does not always mean that one company purchases 100 percent of another company. Sometimes, a company will just purchase 51 percent because if one company becomes the majority owner, it can control how the entire company is operated.

acquisition: When one company purchases a majority interest in another company.

Companies buy other companies for various reasons, one of which may be because the CEO wants to see the company grow. Sometimes, the easiest way to grow a company is to acquire another company. But sometimes an acquisition is not a smart move. The acquired company may not fit in with the business, either operationally or culturally. In most cases, however, mergers or acquisitions take place for specific reasons. An acquisition may be part of a company's expansion strategy. For example, in the mid-1990s, Coca-Cola wanted to round out its portfolio of beverages. One of the biggest holes in its product line was in root beer. The company sold a brand called Ramblin' Root Beer in a handful of locations, but its competitors all had better-known brands, such as Mug, Dad's and A&W. So Coca-Cola looked around until it found a root beer company it could buy. In 1995, it purchased Barq's, a New Orleans–based company.

Other times, companies make acquisitions to expand into new geographic territories. Maybe the company's operations are primarily in the Midwest and the West, but it would like to expand into the Mid-Atlantic. The following is a story from the *Washington Post* written about one company's acquisition that helped it move into new markets:

Trigon Healthcare Inc., the largest health insurance company in Virginia, agreed yesterday to be acquired by Anthem Inc., the fifth-largest publicly traded U.S. health insurer, for $3.8 billion in cash and stock.

Both Blue Cross Blue Shield companies formerly operated on a not-for-profit basis but converted to stockholder-owned enterprises. In recent years, many regional Blue Cross plans have announced plans to merge with larger "Blues" to better compete with big insurers such as Aetna Inc. and UnitedHealth Group Inc.

Indianapolis-based Anthem serves 8 million customers in eight states. If approved, the merger would give Anthem 2.2 million members in Virginia and the District and a foothold in the Southeast and Mid-Atlantic, where it does not have a presence. Under terms of the deal, Trigon stockholders would receive $30 in cash and 1.062 Anthem shares for each Trigon share they own. Based on Friday's closing prices, the package is worth $105.08

a share to holders of Trigon. Trigon stock surged $14.62 a share, or 17.4 percent, to $98.87 yesterday on the New York Stock Exchange. Anthem shares fell $4.05, or 5.7 percent, to $66.65.

Trigon chief executive Thomas G. Snead Jr. said the deal would have no immediate impact on premiums the company's customers pay. He said he expected double-digit premium increases "for at least the next couple of years."

"Premiums are set as a result of the underlying medical costs and administrative costs that are required to service the product," he said.

But over time, he said, the merger would create a stronger health insurer with greater financial resources and technological capabilities.

"This is a strategic alliance," Snead said. "Both parties sat down and figured out what we could look like together versus separate and, I got to tell you . . . this makes an awful lot of sense."

The merger agreement is subject to approval by Virginia insurance regulators.[1]

premium: The difference between the actual cost for acquiring a target firm versus its value before the acquisition.

Note that the lead paragraph of this story first mentions the company being acquired, Trigon, not the company making the acquisition, Anthem. That is because the reporter knows what his readers will care about the most. With a large contingent of readers in Virginia, the *Post* focuses its coverage of this acquisition on the Virginia-based company. The lead paragraph also details how much money is being paid for the acquired company. The price is the most important detail in any merger and acquisition story. The money being paid places a value on the transaction. If a company does not disclose how much it is paying for another company, the reporter should ask. For mergers and acquisitions involving public companies, regulators require the company to disclose the price. Private companies conducting transactions are not required to disclose the price, but they may choose to release that information.

TIPS FROM THE PROS

Bloomberg Gadfly columnists Tara Lachapelle, Brooke Sutherland and Gillian Tan on covering mergers and acquisitions:

Build a wide network of trusted relationships. The information you're dealing with can be highly sensitive/market-moving but obviously needs to be corroborated. It should only be shared with sources who are likely to be involved rather than dealmakers that have no track record working with the companies in question.

The story also explains that the company is being purchased with a combination of cash and stock. This is another important detail that should be disclosed in most merger and acquisition stories. It lets the reader know where the money to fund the acquisition is coming from. Public companies often use their stock to help pay for a deal.

The exchange ratio is also detailed in this story. For mergers and acquisitions in which stock is being used, this is vital information. It informs the shareholders of the company being acquired how many shares they will receive in the combined company. In the case of the Trigon/Anthem deal, it was slightly more than one share in Anthem for every share of Trigon stock owned, in addition to cash. With mergers, this exchange ratio is often one share for one share, or a ratio close to 1:1.

exchange ratio: The number of shares of the acquiring company that a shareholder will receive for one share of the acquired company.

This story also informs readers how the deal values the acquired company on a per share basis. For readers of the *Post* who also owned Trigon stock, this is important information. This tells them how much money they will receive for each share of stock they own, and it enables them to assess whether the deal is a good one. In this case, most investors in Trigon likely were happy with the price Anthem paid. Trigon stock was trading for about $84 before the deal was announced, yet Anthem paid $105 per share for the company, a 25 percent gain for investors. This 25 percent is considered the premium paid by Anthem for Trigon. A premium is how much more the acquirer is willing to pay for a company than the company's current value.

Companies pay premiums to acquire other companies for various reasons, but many are tied into their overall merger and acquisition strategies. Maybe the management of the acquiring company thinks it can do a better job of running the acquired company, increasing its sales and profits. If the acquiring company is right, the company being acquired is probably worth more than it is currently valued. Or maybe the executives at the purchaser think that they can cut costs at the acquired company by combining the two operations, thus lowering the expenses related to running the company. This is called synergy.

TIPS FROM THE PROS

Bloomberg Gadfly columnists Tara Lachapelle, Brooke Sutherland and Gillian Tan on covering mergers and acquisitions:

Do your homework and be as sure as you can about tips before seeking wider corroboration: reputation is everything, and it's best to be a reporter that has solid information rather than one who tests various theories/rumors on sources.

The acquisitions that have been referenced so far are what are typically called friendly takeovers, which means the acquiring company negotiates with the board of the company being sold, and they come to an agreement on the purchase price before the acquisition is announced. But this does not always happen. Sometimes a company will want to acquire another company that does not want to sell. Or sometimes, a company will negotiate to acquire another company, but those talks will end without an agreement. When that happens, sometimes the company wanting to make the acquisition launches what is called a hostile takeover.

 takeover: Change in controlling interest of a corporation. A takeover may be a friendly acquisition or an unfriendly bid that the target company may fight. If the company is publicly traded, then the acquiring company will make an offer for the outstanding shares.

A hostile takeover attempt can even occur when companies have reached an agreement. A third company may enter the fray, offering more money or a different structure than the original offer. Such an event occurred in the Southeast when Wachovia and First Union agreed to merge and create one bank. However, another bank, SunTrust, became upset with the transaction and made a separate offer for First Union. In the end, Wachovia won the battle. Such hostile takeovers are great news stories for business reporters because they typically involve competitors and angry CEOs who want to talk to the media to get their side of the takeover out for discussion. In many cases, CEOs, in the hopes of convincing people their bid is better, use the media to speak directly to the shareholders of the company up for sale.

This is just one of the many types of stories that can be written about mergers and acquisitions. Large acquisitions typically are announced on late Sunday or early Monday after negotiations are finalized during the weekend. This often happens because the companies involved in the deal want as much coverage from the media as possible. Because little business news occurs during a weekend, the companies know that they are likely to get stories written about their deal. They also realize that the *Wall Street Journal* reporters who specifically cover mergers and acquisitions could give the deal good play. The *Journal* does not publish on Sunday, so its editors look for the latest news for its sections on Monday.

The following *New York Times* story helps explain why companies sometimes use publicity to make their case in a hostile takeover attempt:

> The big hostile takeover is coming back, but it is warmer and fuzzier this time. They even call it the bear hug.
> So far this year, unsolicited offers account for 19.5 percent of the value of all deals, compared with only 2.9 percent during the corresponding

period a year ago, according to Thomson Financial Securities Data. In past years, many of these offers came in the form of tender offers, in which the bidder went straight to the shareholders of a company. But recently, many of the most publicized bids have been made not to shareholders but to the companies' managements, in some cases because they could not go directly to shareholders. But unlike quiet, behind-the-scenes takeover talks, these "bear hugs" are made in a very public way.

EchoStar Communications' unsolicited $30 billion offer this week for Hughes Electronics, is one example. Comcast's takeover bid for AT&T's cable-television business is another. A third is the toolmaker Danaher Corporation's unsolicited $5.5 billion bid for a rival, Cooper Industries, which rejected it yesterday.

In each of these cases, the bidders knew they stood little chance of winning. They also knew that even if they lost, in many ways they would still win.

Take EchoStar's bid. The chairman, Charles Ergen, took his proposal public partly to get the attention of the board of General Motors, parent of Hughes. He had held discussions with executives at Hughes, but said he was worried that G.M.'s board had not reviewed the proposal.

TIPS FROM THE PROS

Bloomberg Gadfly columnists Tara Lachapelle, Brooke Sutherland and Gillian Tan on covering mergers and acquisitions:

Don't be intimidated by finance-speak. Bankers, investors, CEOs and even PR people may try to steer you off a story by using numbers and terms that initially go over your head. When they do that, ask them to walk you through the numbers very slowly and specifically so that you fully understand. Complex financial stuff should never be a reason to drop a story (in fact, it's reason to pursue it harder). And often it's not as complex as it's made out to be.

Yesterday, Mr. Ergen said he was "encouraged that G.M. is taking our proposal very seriously," after a decision by G.M.'s board on Tuesday to review the offer. The publicity of a bear hug is also meant to stir shareholders to apply pressure to the company's board. Since EchoStar made its bear hug, four lawsuits have been filed against G.M. by shareholders effectively pushing the company to consider EchoStar's offer. Comcast's public offer for AT&T Broadband forced AT&T to postpone spinning off the unit, putting the business in play. And while Cooper Industries may have rejected Danaher's offer, Cooper did say it will consider a variety of alternatives to increase shareholder value, effectively putting the company up for sale. Cooper also postponed a vote to move the company to Bermuda, where a takeover would be much more difficult.

The biggest problem with making such a public offer is that it reduces a suitor's chance of being able to negotiate for the target without competition. Since Comcast made its offer for AT&T Broadband, half a dozen suitors have begun circling the business, some discussing forming consortiums to buy the business simply in an effort to keep it from Comcast.

In another situation, the Shell Oil Company, the United States arm of the Royal Dutch/Shell Group, made an offer for the Barrett Resources Corporation. Barrett rejected Shell's offer, but decided there was enough pressure from shareholders to put itself up for sale. In the end, the Williams Companies, an energy trader and pipeline operator, won control of Barrett.

Companies also like the bear hug because it is easier and cheaper than a tender offer, which can involve a costly, lengthy appeal to thousands of shareholders. All it requires is a press release and a postage stamp to send the proposal to the company's board.

Some companies are also more comfortable about going public with their offers because they aren't worried about losing. "The old rule of thumb that you don't start something publicly you can't finish doesn't seem to hold anymore," said Donald Meltzer, global head of mergers and acquisitions at Credit Suisse First Boston. "More acquirers are prepared to go public with an offer and take the risk of losing, demonstrating they are disciplined about the price they are willing to pay."

When SunTrust lost its fight against First Union for control of Wachovia, SunTrust's chairman, L. Phillip Humann, said the loss was acceptable.

"Clearly we would have preferred a different outcome to this contest, but not if it meant abandoning our business discipline to pursue an acquisition at a price that did not make sense for our shareholders," he said. "Now we'll do just what we said we would in this situation—close the book."[2]

Like snowflakes, every transaction is different. But stories about mergers and acquisitions should answer these questions:

1. What is the total price and per share price of a deal?
2. Is the acquisition being paid for with cash, stock, debt or a combination?
3. If it's a stock transaction, what is the exchange ratio?
4. What is the price compared to that of similar transactions in the industry?
5. When will the deal be completed and who must approve the transaction?
6. What is the reason for this deal? Does it make the company the largest in its industry or business line?
7. How did investors react to the acquisition announcement?
8. Will the merger or acquisition affect specific competitors?

9. Did the trading activity of the stocks of the companies involved in the transaction increase shortly before the deal was announced?
10. Will the deal be accretive or dilutive to the acquiring company?

Any time a deal is announced, the reporter should ask him or herself why the transaction makes sense for both the acquiring company and the selling company. Many times, executives at the companies will hold a conference call to explain to Wall Street and others why they think the move is a good one. Always listen to these calls. If the analysts and investors are skeptical about the deal, there's probably a good reason you should be also.

Funding the Deal

Companies use various ways to fund the purchase of another business. The three most common methods of payment are cash, stock and debt. A company can also use a combination of two or more of these methods to raise the cash needed to buy another company.

TIPS FROM THE PROS

Bloomberg Gadfly columnists Tara Lachapelle, Brooke Sutherland and Gillian Tan on covering mergers and acquisitions:

Don't believe everything you hear. In the world of M&A [mergers and acquistions], there is far more speculation and rumors than actual deals. And everyone has an angle, so know what side of the table that source is on when you're talking with them.

Cash is the easiest method of payment to understand. Basically, if a company has enough cash sitting in its banks to make an acquisition, it has enough money to pay for the acquisition. Business writers can look at the company's cash-flow statement filed with its quarterly or annual financial statements to determine whether a company has the cash to do a proposed deal. Sometimes companies announce that they will use cash to pay for an acquisition, even though they do not actually have that cash in their accounts. The money can come from bonds, debts or offerings, as discussed in Chapter 8. This is similar to borrowing the money from a bank.

At other times, a company will pay for an acquisition using its stock. This means that the company will give the owners of the company it is acquiring shares of stock. To do so, the acquirer will often have to file documents with the SEC to sell the additional shares. These filings disclose lots of information about the transaction. Companies often like to use stock to pay for acquisitions when their stock price is high compared to its historical valuation. The rationale behind such transactions is this: The higher the stock price, the fewer shares a company has to issue to fund an acquisition. If Company A agrees to buy Company B for $100 million, it would have to issue 10 million shares at $10 each. But if its stock is trading at $20, then it would only have to issue 5 million shares to fund the deal. That is an important consideration for many companies and their existing shareholders, who do not like to see their holdings diluted by the company issuing more stock.

Companies can also factor in debt as part of the purchase price. If the company being acquired owes money to banks or other lenders on its books, it may want the acquiring company to assume the debt and pay off those loans as part of the acquisition. If the acquirer is not assuming the debt from the seller and there are debts on the seller's books, it is important for a reporter covering the story to find out how this debt will be repaid, particularly if the coverage is focused more on the seller than the buyer. Assumed debt is often considered part of the purchase price of a company. If a company buys another company for $150 million in cash plus the assumption of $50 million in debt, the total purchase price is often considered to be $200 million. That is the total amount of money the acquiring company will eventually have to pay for the deal.

Not all acquisition prices are this cut-and-dried. In the Anthem/Trigon acquisition, Anthem agreed to purchase Trigon for a combination of cash and stock. Other times, an acquisition will be for cash and assumed debt, or stock and assumed debt. Other deals could be a mix of all three. Obviously, what the buying company wants to do is structure how it pays for an acquisition in the most advantageous way. If the company's stock price is low, it may want to avoid using stock, particularly if it thinks that the stock price is going to go up soon. Stock may also be used to entice the management of the selling company to remain with the operation. If the management of the selling company are shareholders and they receive stock in the acquired company as part of the deal, then they have an incentive to remain with the company to try to drive the stock price higher by improving the results. Shareholders of the selling company, in turn, may negotiate to receive more cash from the acquirer if they believe that the stock price of the buyer is not going to get any higher. Or they may ask for more stock if they believe that the stock price could rise soon.

TIPS FROM THE PROS

Bloomberg Gadfly columnists Tara Lachapelle, Brooke Sutherland and Gillian Tan on covering mergers and acquisitions:

Don't be afraid of cold calls. There are a range of sources—from investors to bankers, lawyers, executives and buyout experts—who may be more willing to offer insights on M&A than you'd think. You never know until you reach out.

The balance between cash, stock and debt is part of the negotiating process between the buyer and the seller. In addition, taxes may play a part in whether a transaction uses cash, stock or debt. Many owners of small companies sell for cash, which is taxed as a capital gain. Despite this, owners of private companies may look for strictly cash deals because they do not want to remain stockholders in the purchasing company. If they do receive stock, many times the owners will sell their holdings within a year or two of the deal.

Often, a company determines what it is willing to pay to buy another company with the help of an investment banker. An investment banker reviews the performance of the business being acquired compared to other companies in the same industry. The bankers also review the target's future prospects and other acquisitions in the industry and give the potential acquirer a range of prices to pay. Typically, the board of the acquiring company, on the basis of the information from its investment banker, makes an offer to the board of the company it wants to buy. This can often be in the form of a letter, often later released in SEC filings if the companies are public. Occasionally, in the letter, a buyer will offer what is known as a collar. A collar is often offered to guarantee a minimum payment to the seller and can be used as an incentive for management/owners to stay on board rather than to leave to perhaps start a competing business.

The target can choose to accept the offer or to reject it and hold out for a higher price. When the two companies finally agree on a price, a news release is typically issued with glowing praise about how the combined operations will be a success for many years to come. But, as any skeptical business writer knows, the proof is in the results a year or two later.

Good Deals and Bad Deals

As mentioned earlier, not every merger or acquisition works for both the acquiring and selling company. And with just a basic knowledge of how mergers and acquisitions work, a business reporter can determine if the deal is good or bad.

accretive: An acquisition that will increase the acquiring company's EPS. As a general rule, an accretive merger or acquisition occurs when the P/E ratio of the acquiring firm is greater than that of the target firm.

dilutive: An acquisition that will decrease the acquiring company's EPS. As a general rule, a dilutive merger or acquisition occurs when the P/E ratio of the acquiring firm is less than that of the target firm.

The first indicator of whether a transaction is going to be successful or unsuccessful for the acquirer is if it is immediately accretive or dilutive to the acquiring company's earnings. An acquisition that is accretive immediately adds to the acquiring company's EPS. This happens when the P/E ratio is higher at the acquiring firm than at the business being purchased. If the acquiring company has a P/E ratio of 18, but the company being acquired has a P/E ratio of 14, then it is an accretive acquisition. (For a review of P/E ratio, see Chapter 5.) A dilutive acquisition is one in which the acquiring company's EPS decrease as a result of the deal. This happens when the P/E is lower at the company making the purchase than at the company being sold. Typically, a company will state in the release announcing the acquisition whether the acquisition is accretive or dilutive. If this information is not in the release, an analyst or an investor will likely ask this question on a conference call discussing the transaction.

TIPS FROM THE PROS

Bloomberg Gadfly columnists Tara Lachapelle, Brooke Sutherland and Gillian Tan on covering mergers and acquisitions:

It's best to wait to call companies for comment until you are comfortable that you have enough sourcing on a story. Sometimes, beat reporters will know if companies are going to provide any sort of guidance or a response beyond a "no comment," but it's good for companies to know you have enough to go with the story, even without their blessing. That too, may encourage them to give you a nod, albeit on background.

Investors typically want mergers and acquisitions to be accretive, or at least neutral, to earnings. After all, these are the people who buy a company's stock believing that earnings will rise. A dilutive acquisition makes earnings go down. To appease its investors, a company making a dilutive acquisition will often state that the deal will begin to add to earnings in the next year or the year after that. It can turn a dilutive acquisition into an accretive acquisition by improving the results of the acquired company.

After the acquisition is complete, a reporter should follow the company's progress in integrating the purchased business into its own operations. Watch its quarterly earnings for any indication of whether the acquisition actually was accretive to earnings. Often, companies trumpet the success of their deal-making in earnings releases. If that information is not in a release, an analyst or investor will typically ask for updates on an acquisition's progress during an earnings conference call. If that does not happen, a reporter can always ask the company. If a deal that was supposed to be accretive has not been, that is a potential story and warrants further investigation.

Deals also go bad because they are a bad strategic fit. Companies acquire other companies believing that they need to expand their operations to continue to be successful. But that is not always true. Just because a company has been successful in one business does not mean it can translate that success into another operation.

Consider what happened to First Union, the Charlotte-based bank, before it merged with Wachovia, as was noted earlier in this chapter. In 1998, First Union decided it wanted to expand its lending operations and become a major player in that business, so it purchased the Money Store. Two years later, however, First Union shuttered its lending business, effectively saying that the acquisition of the Money Store was a colossal flop. Heather Timmons (2000) of *BusinessWeek* explained why this deal failed in a story soon after the announcement. She noted that First Union took a $2.6 billion charge to earnings to shut the consumer lender, and her reporting disclosed that First Union's $34-a-share offer for the company was 25 percent more than what the company would have accepted. In addition, First Union paid about 20 times the Money Store's earnings, whereas rival Bank of America paid about eight times earnings for a similar company. This deal failed because First Union paid much more for the Money Store than competitors were paying for similar operations. Timmons used P/E ratios to compare what First Union paid to what others paid. She also noted that First Union underestimated the business of lending to low-income consumers.

TIPS FROM THE PROS

Bloomberg Gadfly columnists Tara Lachapelle, Brooke Sutherland and Gillian Tan on covering mergers and acquisitions:

After breaking news about a company, personally send links on to sources you know will be interested so they can hear it directly from you and potentially sooner than they would otherwise. It also keeps them in the flow and they may be able to reach out to clients that may want to react to the news sooner than their rivals. If it's feature-based, they may also circulate it, which could result in interesting feedback or other story ideas from co-workers you may not have met yet.

In a story, it is always important to compare what a company is paying in acquisition to what other companies have paid to acquire similar businesses. Such a comparison of P/E multiples, or other barometers, gives the reader an indication of whether a company is overpaying. Another example of this is illustrated by the Anthem acquisition of Trigon. In the managed care business, companies base their acquisitions on the price per member in the managed care plans. Anthem paid more per member for Trigon's operations than competitors had paid for similar companies. Reporters who knew the importance of such a comparison dutifully reported the high price for their readers.

---

writedown: Reducing the book value of an asset because it is overvalued compared to market values.

The *BusinessWeek* story mentions a writedown, or a charge to earnings, which is an important factor for any business writer looking to determine whether a merger or acquisition was successful. A deal that worked for the buyer will not have any writedowns, which are exactly what they sound like. A writedown is when a company reduces the value of an asset on its financial statement because that asset is overvalued compared to market values for similar assets. This typically shows up on the income statement as an expense, thereby lowering net income.

In the case of acquisitions, the assets that get written down are often the assets of the business that was purchased. When the assets are written down, what a company is essentially saying is that it paid too much for the business and is now being forced to lower the value of the assets it purchased. In other words, the deal was a flop. Business reporters should look at any company writing down its assets as a sign that an acquisition it made in the recent past failed. Conversely, if a company is not writing down its assets, that means it probably made an acquisition that fit nicely into its operations. Writedowns are commonly called goodwill impairment charges because what is being written down is the value of the goodwill purchased. Goodwill arises when more was paid for the business than would be expected from just looking at the value of its assets and liabilities. Goodwill can be considered to be the loyalty of a company's customers or the locations of its stores.

TIPS FROM THE PROS

 Bloomberg Gadfly columnists Tara Lachapelle, Brooke Sutherland and Gillian Tan on covering mergers and acquisitions:

Always think about what's next. What does a deal mean for a company's peers? Or for another industry? One acquisition can often set off a domino effect.

The following article in the *San Francisco Chronicle* does an excellent job explaining why companies take goodwill charges to earnings and how this affects a company's performance:

"Goodwill impairment" sounds like a good topic to bring up if you want to shoo off somebody at a cocktail party.

It's one of those subjects stock investors would rather not think about, right up there with margin calls and capital gains taxes.

But as one company after another writes off billions of dollars' worth of impaired goodwill, you have to ask yourself what the heck is going on here, and should I care?

JDS Uniphase last week announced a record-breaking goodwill writedown of $44.8 billion, which is less than a billion shy of the amount California will spend on K-12 education in the next year.

Other companies taking large goodwill charges in the latest quarter include Nortel Networks ($12.4 billion) Corning ($4.8 billion) and VeriSign ($9.9 billion). But the write-downs we've seen so far might be the tip of the iceberg.

"In the first quarter of next year—wow, you won't believe it. There will be hundreds of billions of dollars" in goodwill write-downs," says Robert Willens, a tax and accounting analyst with Lehman Bros.

Here's why:

Goodwill is created when a company buys another firm for more than the value of its identifiable assets minus its debts. Goodwill supposedly represents a company's unidentified intangible assets, such as its reputation, customer base and workforce.

"It's what makes the whole worth more than the sum of the parts," says Kim Petrone, a project manager with the Financial Accounting Standards Board. The FASB recently changed the way companies must account for goodwill.

Under the old rules, a company has to "amortize" or write off a fixed portion of goodwill over time. This write-down reduces a company's operating earnings. The hope is that the merger will create enough earnings to exceed the added charge.

Companies are supposed to take an additional write-down any time they discover their goodwill has become "impaired," which means the purchased company isn't worth as much as they originally thought.

Because goodwill charges don't represent cash outlays such as salaries or Super Bowl ads, analysts often ignore them when valuing a company's performance and prospects. But that doesn't mean you should.

PURCHASE VS. POOLING: Goodwill is only created when a company treats an acquisition, for accounting purposes, as a "purchase" transaction.

Under accounting rules, acquisitions treated as "pooling of interests" do not generate goodwill. Although pooling deals have drawbacks, many companies have preferred them because they could avoid goodwill charges.

To create a more level playing field, the FASB recently adopted a new rule—Statement 141—that outlaws pooling. All acquisitions announced after June 30 must be accounted for under the purchase method, which means all mergers will potentially create goodwill.

The FASB's other new rule—Statement 142—says companies will no longer have to amortize goodwill on a fixed schedule.

Instead, they will only have to take write-downs when they determine goodwill has become impaired under a new method spelled out in Statement 142. The new method replaces several different methods companies use now.

Companies whose acquisitions haven't gone sour will benefit from the new rule because they won't have to take quarterly goodwill charges.

Genentech, Marriott and other companies have already estimated how much the accounting change will add to earnings next year.[3]

There are a couple of other things for business reporters to consider, in addition to bad strategic fits, accretion/dilution and writedowns, when assessing acquisitions. Sometimes, how the acquisition is structured can be vitally important to its future success.

leveraged buyout (LBO): A strategy involving the acquisition of another company using borrowed money, i.e., bonds or loans. The acquiring company uses its assets as collateral for the loan in hopes that the future cash flows will cover the loan payments.

In the 1980s, many companies were acquired in what is called a leveraged buyout, or an LBO. An LBO typically occurs when the company is sold to its management and other investors, who put up part of the cost to buy the company but fund the rest of the acquisition by borrowing money, or issuing debt such as bonds. The management then hopes that it can raise enough cash by managing the company to repay the debt or bonds.

Often, the management sells parts of the company to help raise the cash. Some of these LBOs of the 1980s failed when the company was not able to generate the cash to repay the debt. This can happen if a company cuts expenses, such as advertising and store employees, in a bid to control costs, but the result is lower sales in its stores. If a reporter is writing about an acquisition, particularly one in which the management has been involved in buying the business, he or she should always look at how the transaction is structured. Not all LBOs fail. But many have resulted in companies that ended up in bankruptcy court or were forced to sell operations to raise money.

golden parachute: Lucrative benefits given to top executives in the event a company is taken over by another firm, resulting in the loss of the job. Benefits include items such as stock options, bonuses, severance pay, etc.

LBOs became popular because management teams could run the companies for several years and then offer stock in the company in an IPO—essentially selling the company to the public. In doing so, many executives became rich by selling their stock. Although LBOs do not occur with as much regularity as they used to, some acquisitions are still structured in ways that allow management to gain financially. Some companies add so-called "golden parachute" language into their corporate bylaws that allows management to receive millions of dollars should the business be sold. A company often implements a golden parachute to fend off an unwanted takeover, such as a hostile takeover. But should a company decide to sell itself and its bylaws contain this language, its executives would receive stock options, bonuses or lump-sum payments if they lost their jobs as part of the transaction. In some cases, executives have received tens of millions of dollars. Business reporters should look for golden parachute language in the SEC filings. If reporters find such agreements in the filings, they have got a story.

TIPS FROM THE PROS

Bloomberg Gadfly columnists Tara Lachapelle, Brooke Sutherland and Gillian Tan on covering mergers and acquisitions:

If a story about a deal or M&A trend seems to be hitting a wall, don't drop it all together. There might be something to it, so keep chipping away at it and the right opportunity to publish it may come along later. Keep in touch with those sources during that time as well.

Transactions also have what are called break-up fees built into them. A break-up fee is money that a company involved in an acquisition must pay to the other company should the transaction fall through for some reason. In some cases, the break-up fee is set high to discourage a company from breaking the deal. Like golden parachutes, these break-up fees are often disclosed in the SEC filings related to a deal. The existence of a break-up fee, or of a golden parachute for that matter, does not mean that a deal is bad or good. But they are important potential payments of large sums of money that could result in stories.

break-up fee: A fee paid by a target company to bidders during an acquisition if the pending deal is terminated for any reason. Some companies being acquired may also require a break-up fee clause from the company acquiring it as part of the deal.

Another important factor to consider is whether a company has adopted a poison pill statement. This allows a company to fend off an acquisition from another company if it does not want to sell. The poison pill allows a company's shareholders, other than the potential acquirer, to purchase additional shares in the company at a lower price. This forces the potential acquirer to have to pay much more than it would typically want to.

Sometimes deals fall apart before they are completed. Another buyer may step in and offer more money, and the original buyer may bow out of the agreement. Or a company making an acquisition may run into financial difficulty and be forced to back away from a transaction. In other instances, government regulators may scuttle a deal. In some cases, the purchase price may be renegotiated if the performance of the company being sold changes dramatically. These are also details that reporters can find in a company's filings.

 poison pill: A strategy used by a corporation to discourage a hostile takeover by another company by making its stock less attractive. Sometimes, a poison pill will allow existing shareholders to purchase more shares of company stock if an offer is made for the company.

How the Deal Was Negotiated

A story in the *San Francisco Chronicle* about the acquisition of Compaq by Hewlett-Packard leads with an anecdote of a financial analyst asking Hewlett-Packard president Michael Capellas if he could dance, a reference to the fancy footwork done by the executive to ensure his company's acquisition of Compaq. "I have been known to do whatever it takes," replied Capellas before breaking into a dance. This anecdote came from a private meeting between company executives, analysts and investors. These meetings between analysts, shareholders, portfolio managers and company executives are not typically open to the public or to reporters. But there is a way for a savvy business reporter to find out what was said during those meetings, particularly if they involve a merger or acquisition. The *Chronicle* reporter makes a brief mention of where this information can be found at the end of his second paragraph (Pimental, 2001, p. E1).

Many business reporters and editors ignore S-4s when they are filed with the SEC, but they should pay attention to them. These documents are important because they do the best job of any SEC filing at telling a story. An S-4 is filed when a company wants to sell more shares of its stock and needs shareholder approval to do so. The most common reason a company would want to sell more stock is that it wants to make an acquisition. For example, Illinois-based Arthur J. Gallagher & Company filed an S-4 in 2008 to sell an additional 10 million shares of its stock. Gallagher, which operates insurance agencies across the country, has been an active acquirer of smaller agencies in the past few years. In 2007, it made or announced 20 deals. The year before, it made or announced nine deals. After this filing, Gallagher completed deals to buy 10 agencies before the end of 2008. So it should come as no surprise that Gallagher's S-4 filing contains the following language:

> We expect to offer and sell the shares covered by this prospectus in connection with future acquisitions within the next two years. We anticipate that our future acquisitions will consist principally of additional insurance brokerage and related businesses. The consideration for such

acquisitions may include cash, including installment payments, shares of common stock, other securities including securities which may be converted into common stock, guarantees, assumptions of liabilities, or any two or more of the foregoing, as determined from time to time by negotiations between us and the owners or controlling persons of the businesses or properties to be acquired. In addition, we may enter into employment contracts and non-competition agreements with former owners and key executive personnel of acquired businesses. At this time we are engaged in preliminary discussions with a number of candidates for possible future acquisitions.

In general, the terms of each future acquisition will be determined by negotiations between our representatives and the owners or controlling persons of the businesses or properties to be acquired. The factors taken into account in determining the terms of an acquisition may include the established quality and reputation of the business to be acquired and its management, its gross commission revenues, earning power, cash flow, growth potential, the location of the business and properties to be acquired and the geographical and service diversification we anticipate as a result of the acquisition. We anticipate that shares of our common stock issued in any future acquisition will be valued at a price reasonably related to the then current market value of our common stock as reported on the New York Stock Exchange at or about the time or times of delivery of the shares. We do not expect to receive any cash proceeds, other than cash balances of acquired companies, in connection with any such issuances.

(Form S-4, Arthur J. Gallagher & Co., p. 11)

True, this is not Hemingway. And it is probably not enough by itself to warrant a story in virtually any publication. But it does give some insight into Gallagher's acquisition strategy and how it goes about negotiating deals with potential acquirees. It also tells readers that it is likely to announce more deals in the near future. A business reporter can use that information whenever he or she talks to Gallagher's CEO about its acquisition strategy.

Other S-4 filings can be juicier. Consider the S-4 filed by Pulte Homes Incorporated regarding the stock it was issuing as part of its acquisition of fellow homebuilder Centex Corporation. It gave the reader a lot of background about the deal that had not been previously disclosed. The result was a nice story written by Sarah Yaussi, a reporter for *Big Builder News,* an online site that tracks the home building industry.

Yaussi's story covered Centex and Pulte's negotiations, as well as the fact that there were two other interested bidders. The following excerpt from her story reads as follows:

On March 11, Eller presented to Company B's CEO in an in-person meeting a so-called "merger of equals." However, the proposed deal would give Centex shareholders 51% ownership of the combined company and

Company B stockholders the remaining 49%. In addition, the combined company board would be an even split between Centex and Company B picks, Eller would be the new company's chief executive, and the combined company's headquarters would be in Dallas.

A little less than a week later, Company B came back with a counteroffer that made the so-called merger of equals actually equal, with ownership split down the middle between Centex and Company B shareholders. Moreover, Eller would assume the combined company's chief executive role but that corporate headquarters would shift to Company B's corporate offices.[4]

Note that the S-4 filing can often be the only source of information detailing the negotiations between acquirer and acquiree. Many times, company executives are not willing to talk about these negotiations. Sometimes, they will give the excuse that the transaction has not yet closed.

For the reporter trying to write a story about how an acquisition came about, the S-4 is the best place to look for background information and details about the negotiations. If executives are not willing to talk, they should be politely reminded that the information will come out when the S-4 is filed. It is surprising how many executives suddenly want to talk. Sometimes the level of detail about the negotiations and the background in an S-4 can reveal stories that should have been reported months earlier.

The S-4 filed by American International Group Incorporated to sell shares as part of its acquisition of HSB Group Incorporated did not engender stories from many business reporters, but maybe it should have. The filing included previously undisclosed details, such as the fact that HSB CEO Richard Booth was basically installed as the company's CEO just to sell the company. However, Booth neglected to reveal this to reporters when he was interviewed after being named to the position a year earlier. The following S-4 goes into detail about when and where Booth and AIG CEO Hank Greenberg met and what they talked about:

As part of the process Mr. Booth undertook, he met with a number of entities with which HSB then currently had or might form strategic relationships, joint ventures or other alliances. One such meeting occurred on April 13, 2000, between Mr. Booth and Mr. Maurice R. Greenberg, Chairman and Chief Executive Officer of AIG, at AIG's headquarters in New York. They discussed industry conditions, strategies being pursued by AIG and HSB and the competencies of each company in their respective marketplace. Both prior and subsequent to this meeting, Mr. Booth met with other industry senior executives to discuss potential relationships which could provide a strategic breakthrough for HSB.

At a June 5, 2000 meeting, Mr. Booth discussed with the HSB Board the results of his review to date, the various strategic options available to HSB and an evaluation of the various operating risks facing HSB. Representatives of Goldman Sachs discussed various shareholder value issues with the HSB Board. After a thorough discussion, the HSB Board instructed and authorized Mr. Booth to explore all strategic options, including the possible sale of HSB. On June 14, 2000, HSB engaged Goldman Sachs as its financial advisor in connection with possible strategic transactions, including a possible sale of HSB. Goldman Sachs contacted nine entities regarding potential interest in a strategic transaction with HSB. At a July 24, 2000 meeting, Mr. Booth updated the HSB Board on strategic options and Goldman Sachs reviewed shareholder valuation issues with the HSB Board. After considerable discussion, an indication of interest from AIG was judged to be superior, based on price and currency, to indications of interest from other potential bidders. The HSB Board authorized Mr. Booth to proceed with discussions with AIG.

On July 26, 2000, Mr. Booth, Mr. Saul L. Basch, Senior Vice President, Treasurer and Chief Financial Officer of HSB, and Mr. Normand Mercier, Senior Vice President and Chief Global Insurance Officer of HSB, met with Mr. Greenberg and other members of AIG senior management in New York to discuss corporate strategies and the potential benefits of a business combination. Thereafter, AIG and HSB conducted due diligence. AIG was provided with a form of proposed merger agreement by HSB. Following several days of intensive negotiations, commencing early in the week of August 13, 2000, the principal elements of a transaction and related documentation were agreed upon.[5]

Nowhere else can a business reporter get a first-hand account about with whom a CEO of Hank Greenberg's stature met and what was discussed, except if the CEO lets the reporter sit in on the meetings. Unfortunately, this filing does not detail the haggling about the purchase price, as some S-4s do. Sometimes that information is in the filing, and sometimes it is not.

In this case, it was not there. It is vital that the reporter writing about a merger or acquisition be on the lookout for the filing of the S-4. Often the filing contains many more details about the transaction than the companies will have released in their announcements of the deal. Likely, the filing will divulge who the other bidders for the company were and whether the purchase price was negotiated higher or lower during the process. In addition, the reporter can likely get an important glimpse into the process of how the merger or acquisition was structured. However, reporters who do not know to look for them often ignore S-4s. Those that do know what they are and the information they contain will likely make their editors happy.

All company filings related to an acquisition should be reviewed, not just the S-4. An acquisition could upset some shareholders, who could make it known through filings that they intend to fight the deal. Such a case occurred with Hewlett-Packard's acquisition of Compaq, when a relative of one of the company's founders decided the deal was bad for the company. His filings with the SEC led to stories like the following Bloomberg News report:

> Hewlett-Packard Co. director Walter Hewlett, the son of company co-founder William Hewlett, will lobby shareholders to fight the planned acquisition of Compaq Computer Corp., according to a regulatory filing.
>
> Edwin van Bronkhorst, a shareholder and Hewlett-Packard's former chief financial officer, two sisters of Hewlett and the William R. Hewlett Revocable Trust also will participate in the proxy fight, the Securities & Exchange Commission filing said.
>
> Hewlett and David Packard, the son of the company's other cofounder, have criticized the $23.3 billion purchase, saying it would make Hewlett-Packard more reliant on personal-computer sales and require too many layoffs. A shareholder vote is expected early next year.
>
> "Hewlett coming out against the deal definitely raised a number of questions," said David Katz, chief investment officer at Matrix Asset Advisors Inc., which owns Hewlett-Packard shares and opposes the purchase. "Clearly, he is going to try to stop the deal."
>
> Last week, Hewlett hired proxy-solicitation firm MacKenzie Partners Inc., which started speculation that Hewlett would go on the offensive to try to lure other shareholders to his side.
>
> Hewlett may decide not to pursue a proxy fight, said Hewlett spokesman Todd Glass. The filing was meant to keep Hewlett's options open, Glass said, adding that "Mr. Hewlett has not decided on a course of action."
>
> Van Bronkhorst is a former trustee of the David and Lucile Packard Foundation, which owns 10.4 percent of Hewlett-Packard's shares and hasn't said how it will vote on the deal. The two Hewlett sisters are Eleanor Hewlett Gimon and Mary Hewlett Jaffe.[6]

When a company is involved in an acquisition, it is extremely important that business writers review anything that might seem remotely involved with the deal. They may be surprised at what they find.

Regulatory Oversight of Deals

Just because the board of directors of both the buying and selling companies have agreed on an acquisition does not mean that the transaction is complete. In virtually every case, other participants in the deal must also approve the transaction. For example, shareholders vote whether to approve or turn down a deal before it goes through. Often, a company's management will line up agreements from large shareholders to get them to vote for a deal. When Hewlett-Packard announced its acquisition of Compaq, its management then spent a lot of time wooing shareholders to vote for the deal.

But there is another important player that has the final say on many mergers and acquisitions, particularly those that involve the two biggest companies in a certain industry or business. State and federal regulators review many acquisitions each year to determine whether the deal will hinder competition in a certain field or whether consumers will be hurt by a transaction through unfair or deceptive acts or practices, such as higher prices because of the elimination of a competitor.

The FTC must review all mergers and acquisitions, no matter what industry the companies are involved in. When a deal is announced, the FTC and the Department of Justice have 30 days to review the transaction. They can request an additional 30-day review period if the deal is complicated. That is why it is typical to see the statement "The transaction is subject to shareholder and regulatory approvals" in many news releases announcing transactions. A review by the FTC involves the filing of a Hart-Scott-Rodino report, which is confidential and almost always a formality.

Still, the FTC plays an important part in reviewing deals. In 2012, the latest data available, the FTC reviewed 1,420 mergers and acquisitions. If the FTC reviews an acquisition and decides to oppose a deal, it can seek a preliminary injunction against the companies in federal court. In 2012, it did so 44 times. The court can then grant a temporary restraining order preventing the deal from being completed until the FTC files an administrative complaint or begins an administrative proceeding. In December 2015, the FTC filed a complaint halting the merger between office retailers Staples and Office Depot. Sometimes, the FTC can simply imply to the companies involved in a transaction that the deal is unlikely to be approved. That nudge can scuttle a deal—and create a story for a business writer tracking the progress of a merger or acquisition. For example, in January 2015, the FTC required grocery store chains Albertsons and Safeway to sell 168 locations as part of an agreement allowing the two to merge.

The following shows a case reported in the (Raleigh) *News & Observer* in June 2009 in which questions about a deal by the federal agency ended a transaction:

> The top executive at Talecris Biotherapeutics vowed to continue expanding the company's business, after its $3.1 billion buyout by an Australian company was scrapped Monday.
>
> The proposed deal with CSL Ltd., announced last August, would have been one of the Triangle's largest corporate marriages. Talecris is based in Research Triangle Park and has a large drug manufacturing plant in Clayton.
>
> But the deal raised red flags at the U.S. Federal Trade Commission, which worried that the combination would hurt competition and raise prices for medicines made from blood plasma. Last month the FTC asked a federal judge to block the buyout.

CSL and Talecris officials said that they planned to fight the FTC in court but announced on Monday that they were throwing in the towel. Analysts who follow CSL had predicted the company didn't want to wage a long, costly legal battle with the FTC.

The move likely saves local jobs. Analysts had expected the combined company would eliminate some positions as it reduced costs, especially at Talecris' RTP headquarters. Talecris employs about 4,750 worldwide, including more than 2,000 in the Triangle.

"We simply felt it was in the best interest of all our stakeholders to move on," Talecris CEO Lawrence Stern said. "We can take some time and evaluate what our next best step is."

Talecris is in solid financial shape and "we don't need to take any specific action," he added. The company reported revenue of $1.4 billion last year, up more than 15 percent from 2007.

The company continues to research new medicines, expand its chain of 66 blood-plasma centers across the United States and hire new workers. Since the beginning of the year, Talecris has added 222 jobs in North Carolina.

Over the next several years, the company is also planning to shift production of a drug to treat a rare blood-clotting disease from Berkeley, Calif., to its Clayton plant, Stern said. That move will add an undetermined number of workers in Clayton.

"Over the past 10 months, we've continued to invest in the business and we feel we're very well-positioned for the future," he added.

Still, Talecris' owners will likely seek another buyer or revive plans for an initial public offering of stock. Talecris was formed in 2005 after two investment firms bought Bayer's blood-plasma business for $303.5 million. Those firms, Cerberus Capital Management of New York and Ampersand Ventures of Wellesley, Mass., could decide to simply hold Talecris for now, but will want to cash out their investment at some point.

"Only our equity owners can determine what they want to do," Stern said. Calls to Cerberus weren't returned on Monday.

Stern said he notified Talecris employees about the canceled CSL deal on Monday with a mass voice mail message and a letter. "People worked very hard to consummate this transaction," he said. "Our team has already moved on."

The failed deal has a bright spot for Talecris. As part of their agreement, CSL will pay Talecris a $75 million break-up fee. CSL will also continue to supply plasma to Talecris.

The FTC objected to the deal because of worries that the combined companies would control too much of the market for blood-plasma medicines. The merger would have reduced the number of companies that make medicine for blood plasma from five to four, the FTC wrote in a court filing.[7]

The Department of Justice also reviews large mergers and acquisitions and may challenge them by seeking an injunction in federal court. When a deal has been completed, the Department of Justice may require a company to divest, or sell, some of its operations. The Justice Department often works with the FTC in reviewing mergers and acquisitions, and quite often it does require changes in a deal before it can be completed. When Exxon and Mobil combined operations, federal regulators forced them to sell more than 2,400 gas stations in the Northeast, Mid-Atlantic, California and Texas because it was determined that the resulting company would have too much of the gasoline business in those markets. BP and Amoco were also required to sell some of their gas stations when they merged.

There are other regulatory agencies that look at mergers and acquisitions. The Federal Communications Commission (FCC), for example, reviews deals that involve radio and television stations. The Federal Reserve Board has a say in transactions involving banks and thrifts, as does the Office of the Comptroller of the Currency. Regulators in Europe also review transactions that involve a U.S. company buying another company with large operations there. In general, American mergers and acquisitions that would result in a company with more than $225 million in annual revenue from Europe fall under the domain of the European competition commissioner. That is how General Electric's proposed $45 billion acquisition of Honeywell International was scuttled, even though U.S. regulators had approved the deal.

State regulators also often have a say in whether a transaction goes through. State insurance commissioners still largely regulate the insurance industry. Banks also must receive state regulatory approval for mergers and acquisitions.

Business reporters should know the regulators that must approve any deal and should find out if these regulators plan to hold a public hearing on a merger or acquisition. Such hearings often occur at the state, not federal, level. Before the Anthem/Trigon deal was completed, the State Corporation Commission—a regulatory agency in Virginia, where Trigon was based—held a public hearing in which a number of doctors spoke out against the deal. A reporter attending the hearing would have ended up with a nice story.

If there are no public hearings, reporters should find out what documents about the transactions are available. The FTC and the Department of Justice often ask for comments from other companies when an acquisition occurs in their industry. When Coca-Cola announced its agreement to purchase Barq's, the head of the company that owns A&W opposed the deal in a statement to the FTC. For the reporter at the *Atlanta Journal-Constitution* covering Coca-Cola, the comments made by John Brock, president of the U.S. soft drinks business of Cadbury Schweppes, turned into a story.

If the public comments on a transaction are unavailable, the reporter can simply call the biggest competitors. A company spokesman will likely be able to divulge whether it has opposed the deal with federal regulators and, if so, on what grounds.

As with any other business story, reporters should think about who might be affected by a merger or acquisition. In many cases, it is the other companies in that business. If a reporter can think about the effects of a deal, he or she is one step ahead of competitors at another newspaper.

Notes

1. From "Indiana company to buy Trigon: Insurers agree to $3.8 billion deal," by B. Brubaker, April 30, 2002, *Washington Post*, p. E1. Copyright 2002 by *Washington Post*. Reprinted with permission.
2. From "The warm and fuzzy version of the hostile takeover bid," by A.R. Sorkin, August 9, 2001, *New York Times*, p. C1. Copyright 2001 by *New York Times*. Reprinted with permission.
3. From "Large goodwill write-downs a sign company made bad buyouts; JDS uniphase leads list of firms posting charges," by K. Pender, August 2, 2001, *San Francisco Chronicle*, p. B1. Copyright 2001 by *San Francisco Chronicle*. Reprinted with permission.
4. From "Pulte S-4: Centex discussed possible acquisition with two other bidders," by Sarah Yaussi, May 11, 2009, *Big Builder News*. Retrieved October 11, 2009 from www.bigbuilderonline.com/industry-news.asp?sectionID=363&articleID=963768. Copyright 2009 by Hanley Wood LLC. Reprinted with permission.
5. From Form S-4, by American International Group Incorporated, September 15, 2000, SEC Publication No. 0000950123–00–008562, pp. 26–30. Washington, DC: Securities and Exchange Commission.
6. From "Hewlett-Packard director to wage merger proxy fight," by P. Horvitz, November 16, 2001, Bloomberg News. Copyright 2001 by Bloomberg News. All rights reserved. Reprinted with permission.
7. From "Talecris and CSL Ltd. halt buyout attempt," by A. Wolf, June 9, 2009, (Raleigh) *News & Observer*, p. E6. Copyright 2009 by (Raleigh) *News & Observer*. Reprinted with permission.

 ## Key Terms

accretive	leveraged buyout (LBO)
acquisition	poison pill
break-up fee	premium
dilutive	takeover
exchange ratio	writedown
golden parachute	

 ## Suggested Exercises

1. Find a news release for a recent merger or acquisition in your area. Answer the following questions: What information did the company disclose about the sale price? What information was released about how the acquired company will be integrated into the purchasing company? Why do you think the purchasing company decided to buy the acquired company?
2. Find a Form S-4 for an acquisition involving stock. Review the section of the S-4 that discusses how the negotiations for the acquisition occurred. Write a 500-word analysis of the negotiations, including whether there

were any other potential suitors and whether the acquired company was able to negotiate a higher stock price.

3. Discuss the differences between accretive acquisitions and dilutive acquisitions with another student. List reasons why a company would make a dilutive acquisition.

4. Assess the recent rise or decline in the stock price of a company making an acquisition. Do they attribute the rise or fall to the acquisition? What details about the acquisition are making investors nervous or happy?

5. Find an acquisition where the acquiring company used all stock or all cash to pay for the acquired company. If the company used all cash, assess the company's stock price at the time of the acquisition to historical levels. If the stock is down from its all-time high, discuss whether the stock price played a part in how the acquisition was funded. If the company used stock, do the same assessment and ask why cash was not used. This exercise might require reviewing the acquiring company's cash-flow statement.

Books on Mergers and Acquisitions

Foster Reed, S., Reed Lajoux, A., & Nesveld, P. (2007). *The art of M&A: A merger acquisition buyout guide* (4th ed.). New York: McGraw-Hill.

Gaughan, R. (2001). *Mergers, acquisitions, and corporate restructurings* (3rd ed.). New York: John Wiley & Sons.

Paulson, E. (1999). *The complete idiot's guide to buying and selling a business.* New York: Macmillan.

Rickertson, R., Gunther, R., & Lewis, M. (2001). *Buyout: The insider's guide to buying your own company.* New York: AMACOM.

Sherman, A., & Hart, M. (2006). *Mergers and acquisitions from A to Z: Strategic and practical guidance for small- and middle-market buyers and sellers.* (2nd ed.) New York: AMACOM.

References

American International Group Inc. Form S-4. (2000, September 15). (SEC Publication No. 0000950123–00–008562, pp. 26–30). Washington, DC: Securities and Exchange Commission.

Arthur J. Gallagher & Co. Form S-4. (2008, August 1). (SEC Publication No. 0001193125–08–163735, p. 11). Washington, DC: Securities and Exchange Commission.

Brubaker, B. (2002, April 30). Indiana company to buy Trigon; Insurers agree to $3.8 billion deal, *Washington Post*, p. E1.

Horvitz, P. (2001, November 16). Hewlett-Packard director to wage merger proxy fight. Bloomberg News.

Pender, K. (2001, August 2). Large goodwill write-downs a sign company made bad buyouts; JDS Uniphase leads list of firms posting charges. *San Francisco Chronicle*, p. B1.

Pimental, B. (2001, November 4). Selling the deal; HP-Compaq road show fails to convince many analysts that merger is the solution. *San Francisco Chronicle*, p. E1.

Radian Group Inc. Form S-4. (2000, December 27). (SEC Publication No. 0000950123–00–011830, pp. 23–29). Washington, DC: Securities and Exchange Commission.

Sorkin, A.R. (2001, August 9). The warm and fuzzy version of the hostile takeover bid. *New York Times*, p. C1.

Timmons, H. (2000, June 10). How the Money Store became a money pit. *Business-Week*, p. 62.

Uchitelle, L. (2000, February 13). As mergers get bigger, so does the danger. *New York Times*, p. C4.

Wolf, A. (2009, June 9). Talecris and CSL Ltd. halt buyout attempt. *The (Raleigh) News & Observer*. Retrieved October 11, 2009 from www.newsobserver.com/business/technology/story/79566.html.

Yaussi, S. (2009, May 11). Pulte S-4: Centex discussed possible acquisition with two other bidders. *Big Builder News*. Retrieved October 10, 2009 from www.bigbuilderonline.com/industrynews.asp?sectionID=363&articleID=963768.

8

COVERING WALL STREET

A Walk Up and Down the Street

Nothing dominates business coverage in mass communication like Wall Street. During the day, viewers of CNBC, Fox Business Network and Bloomberg TV are bombarded with live reports from the trading floor of the New York Stock Exchange, along with a rolling tape of stock prices on the bottom of the screen. Yet few experienced journalists, let alone beginning business reporters, understand enough about what is happening to be able to write a cohesive and clear story about how the stock market performed in a single day or why the stock prices of particular companies might have risen or fallen.

In actuality, the basic principle behind Wall Street is not that complicated. Reporters should think of Wall Street as a huge marketplace, where investors from all over the world gather each day to buy and sell stocks, bonds and other investments. Although there is an actual Wall Street, a lot of the trading occurs via computers from offices around the globe. And though the U.S. exchanges— New York Stock Exchange, American Stock Exchange and NASDAQ—are open Monday through Friday from 9:30 a.m. to 4 p.m. for trading, trading in stocks of American companies now occurs virtually 24 hours a day in overseas exchanges and after-hours markets using computers.

 American Stock Exchange: The third-largest stock exchange in the United States. The AMEX is located in New York and handles approximately 10 percent of all securities traded in the States. The exchange is primarily for smaller companies and derivatives.

Investors buy and sell stocks on the basis of how well they believe a company will perform in the future. If an investor believes that Vanilla Coke is going to boost Coca-Cola's sales and profits, he or she might be willing to buy the company's stock at $60, even if it began trading in the morning at $58. The higher the earnings in the future, the higher the stock price might rise. If another investor samples Vanilla Coke and does not like the taste, he or she may believe the product could be a failure and might sell some stock. (For a refresher on how a company's performance affects its stock price, see Chapter 5.)

The old adage "buy low and sell high" was created on Wall Street because every investor buys and sells stocks and other investments to make money. The investor who purchased Coca-Cola stock at $40 per share may be willing to sell some of it at $60. In doing so, he or she will have realized a 50 percent return on his investment. But the investor who bought Coca-Cola stock at $58 per share may want to hold onto it a little bit longer, hoping that it will rise above $60. At that price, he or she will have realized a return of only 3.4 percent.

The trick for investors, of course, is that not all stock prices rise. Many investors who entered Wall Street in the late 1980s and rode the spectacular gains throughout the 1990s and into the 2000s came to expect double-digit gains in their stock portfolios every year. But the performance of the stock market at the end of 2008 shows that Wall Street will not always go up, and only the experienced and smart investor can continue to find and invest in stocks that will rise. Since that time, the stock market has gone up and down. In 2015, the Dow Jones Industrial Average fell slightly, while the Standard & Poor's 500 Index rose slightly.

The exchanges where stocks are bought and sold are like huge grocery stores that offer every possible food and drink available. The only difference is that the consumers, or investors, are determining how much they are willing to pay. Each day, investors come to the exchange, wanting to buy and sell stocks. But many of them have a set price for those stocks. If they want to buy Microsoft stock but think that the company's shares are worth only $50 per share, then they will not purchase any stock if the price is above $50. There must be a buyer for every seller of stock. Thus, the stock market operates under the economic idea of supply and demand. If there is a demand for stock in a company, then the supply of stock available to purchase at a low price might be minimal. But if the supply of stock in a company is large because many investors want to sell the stock for one reason or another, they may have to sell it at a lower price than they had hoped.

Stock gives an investor a piece of ownership in the company that is selling the stock. Businesses sell shares to raise money so that they can expand by building a new plant or buying another company. The stock is sold to investors with the idea that the money given to the company will be put to good use, resulting in higher profits and more sales that will, in turn, make the stock price go up because other investors will see the company's success and want to buy the stock, too.

TIPS FROM THE PROS

Yahoo Finance reporter Julia LaRoche on covering Wall Street:

Establish a base knowledge of Wall Street by reading. This might seem really obvious, but it's incredibly important to know the history and have context. Make it a daily habit to read in the morning and in the evenings or on the subway. Make sure you read the news, the blogs, and research reports. There are tons of great books that can be an excellent resource for developing background/context. For example, I love *More Money Than God* for hedge funds because it dedicates a chapter to each of the legendary fund managers (George Soros, Julian Robertson, Paul Tudor Jones, Stan Druckenmiller, etc.). It's a great reference when trying to understand how to explain someone's investing style/personality. You'll want to read *Barbarians at the Gate, Predator's Ball, When Genius Failed, Too Big to Fail, Inside the House of Money,* and Michael Lewis' books are great too. (I download them from iTunes and listen when I'm walking to work or on the stairmaster in the gym.)

This is not always the case, however. Some companies fail in their strategies to expand their business. And when that happens, stock prices begin to fall as well. For example, a widget company sells 1 million shares of stock at a price of $20 per share to a number of investors. At that price, the company has raised $20 million to expand its business. Imagine that one of those investors bought 100,000 shares, spending $2 million. That investor now owns 10 percent of the company, which would require him to file certain disclosures with the SEC (which are discussed in Chapter 9). As the owner of 10 percent of the stock, the investor would be entitled to 10 percent of the company's assets should it be liquidated.

The prices of stocks rise and fall on the basis of a number of factors that all boil down to one overriding reason: investor sentiment. If investors believe that a stock is going to go up for whatever reason, they are willing to pay more for that stock. The opposite also holds true. Investors may believe a stock will fall because the company is unlikely to report higher profits than in the past or because the CEO is leaving to run another company.

Investors look at a number of factors in determining whether a stock is worth buying. Some of these factors are fundamental numbers, such as the P/E ratio and the P/B value discussed in Chapter 5. Others may look at quarterly earnings results or earnings projections from analysts for future quarters or years. Still others use qualitative reasons for buying and selling stocks, such as whether they like the CEO or how often they purchase the company's products.

TIPS FROM THE PROS

 Yahoo Finance reporter Julia LaRoche on covering Wall Street:

 Ask questions and take notes: When I first started out, I would keep a Word doc with different terms I encountered and definitions/examples as I learned about them. For example, when I was at CNBC.com as an intern there was an M&A story that broke in the afternoon. My editor mentioned something about a "white knight." I didn't understand so I looked it up. She also explained it to me later. It's OK to ask questions.

A business reporter asked to write a story about the stock market's performance during a day, week, month, quarter or year will want to look at the factors that caused stocks to rise or fall. Many newspapers ask their markets reporters to focus their stories on how local stocks performed. But even in those cases, stocks could go up or down on the basis of a number of factors, many of which may not be directly related to the company. Maybe investors have become skittish about the economy or fear the war with Iraq may cut off oil supplies from the Middle East, raising the cost of doing business for many companies. Maybe the government has released a report on spending or consumer confidence that came in below projections. Or maybe the president urged the passage of a tax cut designed to put more money into the pockets of consumers, hoping that they will go out and spend it on goods and services.

Understanding why the broader stock market rises or falls on a given day is not as easy as assessing the performance of a single stock or the stocks of companies in a specific industry. But often, a single stock or a few stocks in a sector may cause the overall market to fall. For example, the Dow Jones Industrial Average is perhaps the best-known barometer of stock performance on Wall Street. Every day, hundreds of reporters detail how the Dow moved up or down. But the Dow includes just 30 stocks, albeit 30 stocks of well-known companies, such as Coca-Cola and Walt Disney. If one of the stocks in the Dow happens to fall dramatically one day, the overall index could drop.

Other indexes may not fluctuate as much on the basis of the performance of a single stock. The Standard & Poor's 500 Index is made up of 500 stocks, while the Russell 2000 Index includes the stocks of 2,000 small companies. Other indexes exist for certain industries and for specific markets.

The following excerpt is an example of a Bloomberg News story that explains why some of these indexes declined:

> U.S. stocks fell as a drop in orders for durable goods and disappointing retail sales during the holiday season gave investors new reasons to avoid equities. Financial shares including Citigroup Inc. led the decline.
>
> As the Standard & Poor's 500 Index and Dow Jones Industrial Average complete their first three-year losing streak since 1941, mounting tensions

in Iraq, North Korea and Venezuela are adding to concern that growth in companies' earnings is slowing.

"It's all going to add up in the negative column for the moment," said Erick Maronak, director of research at NewBridge Partners, which manages $3.5 billion. "Does it mean that we're going to get thrown back in a recessionary environment? That's tough to say."

The S&P 500 fell 4.91, or 0.6 percent, to 892.47. Financial stocks counted for one-third of the drop. The Dow Average shed 45.18, or 0.5 percent, to 8448.11, its fifth loss in six days. The Nasdaq Composite Index slid 9.22, or 0.7 percent, to 1372.47.

Today was the slowest session since Christmas Eve last year as trading on the New York Stock Exchange totaled 461 million shares. U.S. markets shut at 1 p.m. in New York and will remain closed tomorrow for Christmas, About eight shares fell for every seven that rose on the exchange.

All three indexes have declined so far this month after gaining in October and November. For the year, the Dow has lost 16 percent, the S&P 500 22 percent and the NASDAQ 30 percent.

"Everyone wanted to get excited as we finished the third down year of the market," said Crit Thomas, who helps oversee about $26 billion at National City Investment Management Co. "The market really wanted to rally, but it's having a hard time in the face of more negative news."[1]

Later in the story, the writer explains that stocks of retailers such as Best Buy, Lowe's and Target declined during the day as investors became worried about slow sales at their stores during the Christmas shopping season.

Bloomberg's handbook for reporters, called *The Bloomberg Way*, lists four questions that should be answered early in a story about the market. Those questions are the following:

What happened to my investments today?
Why did it happen? (theme of the day)
How does today's move compare with the past?
Who said what? (key quote)

(Bloomberg, 1995, p. 100)

Each of these questions is answered early in the story. It is not until the fourth paragraph that the reader is given the specific numbers indicating how the broad indexes fell on the day. *The Bloomberg Way* later advises reporters in answering the third question to consider the following comparisons:

Biggest advance/decline since when?
How many days in a row up/down/little changed?
How much have prices/yields changed in that time?
Highest/lowest level since when?
Narrowest/widest range since when?

(Bloomberg, 1995, p. 101)

Bloomberg News does one of the best jobs in writing about the market because its primary audience is the traders and investors buying and selling stocks every day. Its reporters and editors know they have demanding readers who want to know what is happening and why in a clear and concise manner. Too many stories about the stock market dance around the "why" without fully explaining the market's movement.

Twenty or thirty years ago, reporting about the stock market was not considered important to many media outlets. But as more people across the country poured their retirement savings into 401(k) plans and variable annuities that invested in Wall Street, more readers wanted to know how the stock market was performing. Now, writing about Wall Street is one of the most important stories in mass communication today.

Bonds

Investors do not just buy stocks in companies. They can also purchase another investment called bonds. A bond is considered a loan given to a company by an investor. An investor purchases the bond, and the money goes to the company. In return, the company pays the investor interest on the bond, and at the end of the bond's term, the company pays the balance of the bond. To illustrate, a company sells $100 million in bonds at an interest rate of 6.75 percent over a 30-year period. Each year, the company pays the interest to investors, and at the end of 30 years, it pays the $100 million back.

TIPS FROM THE PROS

Yahoo Finance reporter Julia LaRoche on covering Wall Street:

Meet people in the business: Since this is a relationship business, you'll have to develop sources. How do you do that? Sure, you can always go to bars where the finance crowd tends to populate though that can get exhausting after a while. Make email introductions or pick up the phone and let people know what you're interested in covering. Introduce yourself to the firm's PR. A lot of the banks will have background meetings with various executives.

A company hopes to recoup the $100 million and the interest paid by using the money during that time period to expand its operations into new businesses that will bring in much more than the cost of the interest. The longer the time period for the bond, the higher the interest rate the company will pay. For example, a one-year bond may only give an investor a 3 percent yield. But the 30-year bond would pay 6.75 percent a year. So-called junk bonds are issued by companies that have low credit ratings from companies such as

Standard & Poor's or Moody's. Because of their low ratings, these companies must offer higher yields to attract investors. Some bonds issued by these companies may offer returns of more than 10 percent.

Bonds are traded every day in the market, just like stocks. But what usually trips up business reporters is that when the price of a bond goes up, the yield declines, and vice versa. For example, if one investor buys a $1,000 bond from a company with a 7 percent return, he would receive $70 a year from the company until the bond matures, when he would receive his $1,000 back. But if the investor sells that bond for $999, the yield goes up slightly because the new bondholder would get the $1,000 back when the bond expired—more than what he originally paid—in addition to the interest payments.

bond: A bond is considered a debt investment—you are loaning money to an entity (company or government) that needs funds for a defined period of time at a specified interest rate. In exchange for your money, the entity will issue you a certificate, or bond, that states the interest rate you are to be paid and when your loaned funds are to be returned, otherwise known as the maturity date.

One important distinction between bonds and stocks occurs when a company files for bankruptcy-court protection. When this happens, a bondholder is usually first in line to be repaid what he is owed. But a stockholder rarely, if ever, gets anything in a bankruptcy proceeding. (For more on bankruptcy court, see Chapter 12.)

Bonds and stocks are alike in a fundamental manner: They are both sold by large Wall Street firms known as brokerage houses or investment banks. Many of these firms have long-standing relationships with the companies whose stocks and bonds they are selling to investors. And they have offices across the country where their stockbrokers try to get investors to purchase shares in these companies. When investors want to purchase stock, they place orders with their stockbrokers. The orders are typically for a set number of shares (e.g., 1,000) at a specific dollar amount (e.g., $20 per share). The broker then goes out to find a buyer willing to sell those shares at that price.

institutional investor: A non-bank person or organization that trades securities in large enough share quantities or dollar amounts that they qualify for preferential treatment and lower commissions. Institutional investors face fewer protective regulations because it is assumed that they are more knowledgeable and better able to protect themselves.

These firms do not buy stocks and bonds; they only sell and receive commission fees on the shares they sell. The more shares they sell, the more money they make. That is why these companies have stockbrokers and people called sell-side analysts who peddle these stocks to investors. Whereas local stockbrokers primarily spend their time selling stocks to local, small-time investors, analysts focus on selling these stocks to large investors known as institutional investors. An institutional investor is someone who buys and sells stocks for a living. He or she may work for an insurance company or a mutual fund operation. Their job is to find stocks before they go up in price and sell them before they fall. Sometimes institutional investors are successful in accomplishing that task, but other times they are not.

TIPS FROM THE PROS

Yahoo Finance reporter Julia LaRoche on covering Wall Street:

Attend charity events: This is perhaps the best place to meet people. I like to find events that are hosted by hedge fund managers or anything honoring a big name in finance. If you contact the organizers and say you're a reporter, you usually won't have to pay. When you go, talk to people and exchange business cards. I like to take my camera and try to attend various charity events whether it's a playground cleanup or a poker tournament with billionaires. While I'm there, I snap some photos of Wall Streeters doing something good. Who doesn't love seeing their photograph in the society pages? It's also a great way to get people to recognize you for future stories.

In the past two decades, another type of investment, called a collateralized debt obligation, has also entered the market. These investments, also known as asset-backed securities, have been blamed for the market's fall in 2008. A collateralized debt obligation is an investment security backed by a pool of bonds or loans. For example, a collateralized mortgage obligation is backed by mortgages. By 2006, more than $500 billion worth of these investments alone had been issued. Problems arose when the property owners began defaulting on their loans when the real estate market declined in value in 2008 and 2009. There was no money to pay the investors who had purchased these securities. The investors in the book *The Big Short* made billions by betting that these securities would decline in price.

The analysts at a stock brokerage house or a rating agency will research the companies in which their firm is selling securities and determine which ones are the best investments. Recent investigations into this practice, however, discovered the secret that most professional investors on Wall Street already knew—that analysts were influenced by their firms to push stocks of companies with which they already did business, such as helping them find potential acquisitions or sell more stock and bonds. This occurred with the collateralized debt obligations. Many were sold with investment-grade ratings. A closer inspection when real estate prices started falling revealed that the mortgages were highly speculative and had been sold to consumers with a high potential of defaulting on the loans.

As a result, the credibility of Wall Street has suffered in the eyes of many consumers, as well as business reporters. Some media outlets now closely examine the assets backing an investment. Others now require their reporters to divulge the potential conflicts of interest between a rating agency or an investment banking firm's analysts and its other businesses when quoting the analyst. Stories now typically read something like the following:

> "Widget Co.'s earnings were much stronger than its competitors' because it's built a better widget," said Fred J. Muggs, an analyst at Salomon Smith Barney who owns shares in the company. However, his firm has not done investment-banking business for the company.

A business reporter needs to know the relationship between an analyst and the investments—whether they're stocks, bonds, commodities or something else—he or she is following to help determine whether the analyst is as objective as possible. See the "Sell-Side and Buy-Side Analysts" section later in this chapter for a closer look at sell-side analysts and the role they play in business reporting.

Buying and Selling

Demand for a stock can rise and fall from one day to the next. But over months and years, there are some stocks that are constantly in demand by investors. All stocks are not created equal, and how the companies that issue these stocks perform typically determines which investors are willing to buy them and what price they are willing to pay.

Investors come in all shapes and sizes, and with all kinds of preconceived ideas about which stocks perform better than others. It is important for a business reporter to understand the connections among a company's business strategy, its size, its management team, its past history and its investors' willingness to purchase its stock. Some investors may want to acquire stocks in companies where there is great potential for future growth.

TIPS FROM THE PROS

Yahoo Finance reporter Julia LaRoche on covering Wall Street:

Develop a handful of go-to sources: You'll want to cultivate a handful of repeat sources that you can speak with regularly on your beat. It's important that you stay in touch. Meet up for lunch, coffee or drinks. Pick up the phone when necessary. Don't waste their time though.

In the mid-1990s, a grocery store chain in Atlanta called Harry's Farmers Market Incorporated went public, selling shares to investors with the promise that it was going to revolutionize the grocery industry in much the same way that Home Depot Incorporated had changed the do-it-yourself business. Early investors in Home Depot, after it went public in 1981, became millionaires many times over as a result of the company's rapid growth, which made it one of the top ten retailers in the world. But Harry's was not able to follow up on its promise. It never expanded outside of the Atlanta market, and many of its investors lost money.

For every 10 Harry's, however, there is a Home Depot or a Microsoft Corporation. Investors who like to buy stocks in companies in which there is a lot of growth potential look for what are called growth stocks. Investors in growth stocks are looking for the price of the stock to rise because of the increase in the company's revenue profits as a result of an expansion plan. Most growth stocks do not pay dividends to their investors. Growth companies are businesses in which revenues or profits are typically increasing at multiples of the rest of the company. Revenues may be rising by 30 percent every quarter, and profits may be increasing by 25 percent or more.

dividend: A cash payment using profits that's announced by a company's board of directors to be distributed among stockholders. Dividends may be in the form of cash, stock or property. All dividends are declared by the board of directors.

The opposite of a growth-oriented investment strategy is one that focuses on buying stocks in companies on the basis of their value. So-called value investing looks at the worth of the stock price compared to quantitative barometers. For example, a value investor may look to purchase stocks that appear cheap on the basis of the P/B value.

If a company's P/B value is below that of its competitors or the overall market, then an investor may consider it to be cheap. A value investor may also look at a stock on the basis of its P/E ratio. If a stock price of a company is trading at around 10 times its earnings but the rest of the stock market is trading at around 15 times earnings, that stock may be considered to have value.

The opposite is also true. If the P/B or P/E of a company gets to be higher than that of competitors or the rest of the market, an investor may consider selling his holdings. It is wise for reporters to track these values of the companies on their beats to look for potential stories about why the stock price is rising or falling.

Other value investors prefer to purchase stocks in companies that pay dividends to their investors. A dividend is a payout to investors, often done on a quarterly basis, that serves as an incentive to own the stock. For example, Atlanta-based Southern Company, a power company, currently pays the people who own its stock about 44 cents as a quarterly dividend for every share they own. Many investors purchase stocks just to receive the quarterly dividend check from a company. That is why it is always a story when a company decides to cut its dividend and use that money elsewhere. Cutting a dividend will cause investors to sell the stock, leading to a drop in the stock's price.

TIPS FROM THE PROS

 Yahoo Finance reporter Julia LaRoche on covering Wall Street:

It's a two-way street. In order to get something, you're probably going to have to share. For instance, let's say you're covering hedge funds and you get the investor letters from sources. One source might want to trade one letter for another. (Pro tip: Make sure the letter does not have a watermark. You don't want to give away who's leaking them).

For the most part, investors who take a growth-oriented strategy to investing are taking a greater risk than value investors. Growth means that a company is expanding, and growing means that there is always the chance of something going wrong. Maybe a retailer is putting its stores in the wrong place. There is less risk with value investing, in general, because these are companies looking to entice investors with their slow, methodical growth. However, a growth-investing strategy may also pay greater rewards for the investor if the company is successful in growing itself at a fast rate.

The reputation and reliability of a stock are important to many investors. For most of the 1990s, General Electric Company and Coca-Cola Company were attractive stocks to own for many investors because they routinely reported earnings that met or beat Wall Street expectations. Although these companies were criticized for sometimes using accounting changes to control their earnings growth, investors appreciated their ability to match what Wall Street predicted. Investors do not like negative surprises, and if a company can report earnings that are in line with estimates, then the stock price is unlikely to fall.

Investors and business reporters can measure this reliability simply by comparing the numbers. If Company X reports second-quarter earnings of 25 cents per share but was expected to report earnings of 27 cents per share, investors may be scared off. But if the company was expected to report earnings of 24 cents per share, then investors are more likely to be happy. This last point is an important one for business reporters to consider, particularly when they are writing stories about a company's earnings performance. A strong earnings performance could cause a company's stock price to rise, but weak results could lead to a drop in the stock price. If either one of these is the case, it is good to call an investor and talk to him or her about the stock's movement.

The size of a company can also be a determining factor in whether an investor purchases its stock. Some investors refuse to even look at the stock of any company that has a market capitalization of less than $1 billion. The market capitalization is the value of the company on Wall Street and is computed by multiplying the current stock price by the number of shares outstanding. Other investors like to purchase stock in companies that have small market capitalizations. Some mutual funds, for example, specialize in investing in companies with market caps, as they are called, of less than $500 million.

Other investors may be looking solely at the company's strategy or structure. There are a number of investors whose strategy is simply to purchase stock of thrifts that convert from being owned by the depositors into having the thrift's shares sold on the market and being owned by stockholders. These investors have made money in the past on these conversions, and they are willing to bet that others will also make them money.

Many investors also look at the company's business strategy with regard to how it sells its products or services. Investors are often more willing to purchase a stock in a company if they use that company's product. Many investors look at how a product is sold or at a company's local store. For example, an investor may go into a Gap store and see many customers, but if he or she notices that a number of those shoppers walk out without buying clothes, the investor may think about selling some of his or her stock. Another investor may want to buy stock in Starbucks because he or she has to wait in long lines every day for a cup of coffee.

TIPS FROM THE PROS

Yahoo Finance reporter Julia LaRoche on covering Wall Street:

Getting people to talk can be a challenge: People aren't going to want to talk, especially if the story is negative. You're probably going to have to persuade people to talk to you. Come to them with a piece of information. If you call up someone and you say, "Can you tell me what happened?," chances are they're going to hang up. If you have information already and they feel you might know more they're more likely to talk. For example, there was a hedge fund manager whose fund blew up. One of his investors had told me that a number of key traders had left the fund in the previous months but they were not made aware of that fact. I went to the fund manager with that information and he agreed to talk.

Another qualitative measure that many investors consider is the strength of a company's management. Like business reporters, investors like to meet and talk with the CEO and CFO of a company. How an investor perceives management's ability to run the company and espouse a coherent strategy can go a long way in determining whether he purchases stock. If an investor comes away from a meeting with a CEO thinking that the company leader does not have a firm grasp on its operations, he is unlikely to buy the stock. Conversely, if the CEO can explain his vision for the company in a way that makes sense, investors will be more likely to purchase the stock.

There are other investors who simply look for companies that might be acquired by other companies. Because acquiring companies often pay more than the value at which a selling company's stock is currently trading, a savvy investor who can find companies that are for sale or could be bought if the right buyer came along can make a lot of money. After Congress passed the Gramm-Leach-Bliley Act in 1999, many investors looked to purchase stock in insurance companies and financial services companies because the new law allowed banks to own these companies for the first time. A reporter who recognizes the significance of such an event can find a nice story that will inform readers by interviewing investors who will make decisions on buying and selling stocks on the basis of new developments.

Some investors in company stock are called "activist" investors because they purchase the shares in an attempt to change how the company operates. By owning a large number of shares, they can express their opinion to the CEO and the board about changes that they think may increase the stock price of the company. These changes may be selling off parts of the company or forcing the company to increase its dividend. Activist investors have become such a big part of covering companies that the *Wall Street Journal* named a reporter, David Benoit, to cover the activist beat in 2013, and his reporting led him to be named Talking Biz News' Business Journalist of the Year in 2015.

The biggest investors are those who manage mutual funds and hedge funds. These investors often oversee billions of dollars, and their influence in the market can sometimes be tremendous. A mutual fund is an investment tool where consumers pool their money, giving it to the fund's manager with the understanding that he or she will then invest the money in a way that will provide them a return. The fund may have a specific investment strategy, such as those mentioned earlier in this section. For example, a fund may focus solely on stocks with a low P/E multiple or stocks of companies in the retail industry. Started in the 1920s, mutual funds now total more than 8,000, and they had nearly $16 trillion in investments to be managed at the end of 2015.

Hedge funds are similar to mutual funds in that they pool money together from investors. Otherwise, they operate differently. The manager of a hedge fund, unlike a mutual fund manager, typically has money invested in the fund, and he or she takes a cut of the profits from the fund. In addition, hedge funds invest in securities other than stocks, such as bonds and commodities. Lastly, hedge funds sometimes bet that some investments will fall in price, and they use strategies to make money when that occurs as well. Hedge funds were managing $2.7 trillion in assets in 2014, the latest figures available from the Managed Funds Association.

Investors who look for companies whose stock price they believe is actually going to fall are called short-sellers. They are not actually purchasing the stock of the company. Instead, they are borrowing stock from a stockbroker, betting that the price is going to fall. This investment strategy can be extremely risky, because if the stock price rises, the short-seller continues to lose money until he stops borrowing the stock. Many such investors spend intense weeks and months examining a company's financial statements to find a business that may be having problems and could see its stock price drop.

TIPS FROM THE PROS

Understanding short selling:

The investment strategy of short selling is one of the most misunderstood by business journalists because it runs counter to how the rest of the market works. An investor is betting that he or she will make money if the price of an investment goes down.

Here's how it works:

Let's say I am a money manager opening a hedge fund operation. I have researched a company's financial statement and cash-flow statement, and I believe this company is about to run into trouble.

So, I go to my broker, and I borrow 1 million shares of the stock that the broker is holding for another investor. The broker will let me do this because I regularly direct my trading through his firm, which receives commissions on my trading. I turn around and sell those 1 million shares to another investor at a price of $12 a share, which means I collect $12 million and put it in my bank account.

If the problems that I discovered in the company's financial statement become known to other investors, causing the stock price to fall to $8 a share, I can then go back into the market and repurchase those 1 million shares for $8 million, returning the shares to the brokerage firm. That results in a $4 million profit for my operation.

However, if the stock price rises to $15 a share, my broker may call me and ask for the shares back. If that's the case, my agreement with the broker may require me to go back into the market and buy back the 1 million shares at the higher price. At $15 a share, I would have to spend $15 million, resulting in a $3 million loss.

By now, it should be evident that it is important for a business reporter to understand the different reasons why an investor becomes attracted to buying stock in a company. If a business reporter can develop sources among investors that only buy stocks in companies that might be sold, he or she is likely to be able to write a story about that company being sold days and even weeks before an official announcement is made.

Take the case of Bethany McLean, the *Fortune* writer credited with detailing the potential problems at Enron less than nine months before it reported huge losses and filed for bankruptcy-court protection. McLean was initially tipped off that Enron might need closer examination by an investor, Jim Chanos of Kynikos Associates, who was shorting the company's stock. Chanos suggested that McLean review the company's Form 10-K.

McLean said she found "strange transactions," "erratic cash flow," and huge debt. "It made you wonder, if their business was so phenomenally profitable, why they had to be adding debt at such a rapid rate," said McLean in a *Washington Post* article about how she wrote her story (Kurtz, 2002, p. C1).

Now, the motive behind Chanos' discussion with McLean is obvious. He was interested in seeing a story in print that was critical of the company in the hopes that it would cause the stock to fall. As long as a business reporter understands that an investor always has a motive, these people can be valuable sources of information. For instance, when working on any type of story that involves a public company, a reporter should consider calling investors. They often know more about the company than the business reporter, as they have researched the company's strategy, management, past performance and operations.

To be sure, all investors have a vested interest in what a reporter is writing. Many of them want to see the stock price of the company go up, whereas others want to see the stock price fall. But an investor may also have more access to company management than a reporter and thus may be able to provide more insight into what is going on at a business, particularly if the company is not talking. A large investor in a company typically gets his phone calls returned quickly from a CEO or a CFO.

In addition, just because an investor has a vested stake in the performance of a company does not mean he is going to gush about its performance. Many investors, particularly those who believe management is not doing enough to increase the stock price, will be honest in talking to reporters assessing a company. Many large investors freely and openly criticize companies in which they are investors. They may be upset that the stock price is falling. Notice how the following story from the *San Jose Mercury News* uses an investor to explain why other investors should be upset. The story also explains why the investor was interested in buying the stock in the first place:

When Internet software company Unify Corp., of San Jose, admitted Monday that it had overstated its revenue for its last fiscal year and possibly the previous fiscal year as well, it looked like other cases in which ambitious executives at high-tech companies may have engaged in creative accounting.

But over the last few days, upset investors in the company have focused on another unsettling fact: At the same time the company was overstating its revenue—and thus boosting the market's valuation of the company—the company's CEO Reza Mikailli was busy selling, or otherwise disposing of, many of his 1.4 million shares.

In fact, according to his filing with the Securities and Exchange Commission and confirmed by the company, Mikailli had sold all of his shares in the company by June 20—about six weeks before the company announced its revenue problems and NASDAQ halted trading in the company's shares this Monday. All told, since June 1999, he has sold shares valued at $7.34 million. "Can this be normal?" said Mark Gardy, a partner at Abbey, Gardy & Squitieri, a law firm that has also filed a class action lawsuit on behalf of Unify's investors. "I don't believe in coincidence when you reduce your holdings to zero just before bad news comes out."

TIPS FROM THE PROS

Yahoo Finance reporter Julia LaRoche on covering Wall Street:

Listening is crucial: Sometimes it can be intimidating speaking with a hedge fund manager or bank executive when you first start out because you might feel this urge to prove you can hold your own and talk shop with them. You should definitely learn about their business, but let them talk after you ask a question. Once you think they've finished, pause for a moment. I find that some of the best stuff can happen in periods of silence before jumping to the next question.

On Monday, the company put Mikailli and the company's chief financial officer, Gary Pado, on leave and announced it had engaged in "improper accounting practices." This meant the company had "improperly recognized" revenues during the last fiscal year, and perhaps the one before that.

The company's board said the company's audit committee is investigating the matter, and that it has retained Gray Gary Ware & Freidenrich as counsel. Gray Gary, in turn, has asked PricewaterhouseCoopers to assist with the investigation as independent auditors.

Unify's outside auditors, Deloitte & Touche, are also participating.

The company has provided no other information on why it chose to put the two executives on leave, or why Deloitte & Touche had not discovered the revenue misstating problem earlier. Mikailli did not return a phone call to his Saratoga residence, and his lawyer could not be reached for comment.

Eleven law firms representing shareholders have already filed lawsuits against the company, most of them alleging that the executives sought to profit by wrongfully boosted revenue.

"As a result of Unify's alleged misrepresentations and omissions, the price of Unify's stock was artificially inflated," alleges a class-action suit by Kirby McInerney & Squire, in New York, "allowing insiders to receive artificially high prices for selling their stock and forcing investors to pay artificially high prices to buy the stock."

A number of questions are hanging over the stock sales of Mikailli and other company's insiders. Mikailli suffered a heart attack June 5, and the company announced he was taking medical leave June 6, though the company says he is currently at home.

On Friday, company spokeswoman Deb Micciche said many of Mikailli's sales came to light only three weeks ago, when he was apparently "catching up" on some of his filings to the Securities and Exchange Commission of stock sales. Only then, during the week of July 17, did his disposal of between 700,000 and 900,000 shares suddenly show up in public documents, she said.

At least 163,000 shares were categorized by Mikailli in his filings as "disposed via transfer," though Micciche says the company still has no idea to whom or where the shares were transferred. Normally, such a category refers to a transfer to a relative or to a personal trust.

Pado, the CFO, sold 14,595 shares in May, or about a fourth of his total holding of 53,115 shares, according to the Web site insiderwatch.com. Vice President Frank Verardi sold 50,000 shares in May, about two-thirds of his holdings of 77,850 shares.

Investors, meanwhile, were broadsided. David Kupler, a Hayward investor in Unify, said he was tracking insider sales at Unify on insiderwatch.com and saw that Mikailli still appeared to have about half of his position left in May. He went to the company's annual reports, checked its debt and cash levels, and concluded that the company's shares looked like a good buy.

"I bought the stock," said Kupler, "but I based my analysis on public documents. If the company cooks the books, how can I make the right decision?" Kupler spent $12,000 to buy the shares at about $6 each. They slid to $3.94 on Monday when NASDAQ stopped their trading.

"This is extraordinarily suspicious," Kupler says. "Insiders sell their shares in their own company all the time, but they usually hold on to a few."[2]

This story has plenty of skepticism about the stock trading. That's a sign of a good reporter.

Sell-Side and Buy-Side Analysts

For decades, sell-side analysts who track stocks and bonds have been the business reporter's best friends. Analysts regularly take phone calls from reporters wanting to talk about everything from a company's CEO to the new potato chip it is rolling out next month. Become friendly with analysts and quote them fairly, and they will return phone calls and give tips about potential news at a company. In return, the media made analysts such as Henry Blodget, Mary Meeker and Jack Grubman stars, trumpeting their bold prognostications that a stock was going to double in the next year. As the stock market rose higher and higher, so did the public stature of the sell-side analyst.

Analysts, however, have come under increasing scrutiny as to whether they can be objective in discussing the companies and stocks they cover. Some of the analysts who made bold predictions about the future of technology or telecommunications companies came under fire when those businesses failed or filed for bankruptcy-court protection. Many of them privately thought the companies they covered were feeble, and expressed those opinions in e-mail correspondence to friends and co-workers but maintained bullish recommendations of "strong buy" or "buy" because of financial relationships their firms had with the companies.

TIPS FROM THE PROS

 Yahoo Finance reporter Julia LaRoche on covering Wall Street:

 Ask them to explain it again: When someone's talking they might say something interesting. Just a tiny little nugget. Ask them to expand or clarify. I've had interviews that I've transcribed and I'm like, "Why didn't I ask so and so about that meeting they casually mentioned?" Don't be afraid to ask.

Any business reporter who covers a public company followed by sell-side analysts should now be well aware of the inherent conflicts of interest. It is the job of the analyst to sell investors stock of the companies they cover. However, the analyst's firm may have other business relationships with the companies they cover. The firm may be the company's investment bankers, which means it receives fees anytime the company decides to sell more stock, issue additional debt or make an acquisition. As such, many analysts in the past have been pressured to paint a rosy picture about a company's future.

With hundreds of millions of dollars in fines now levied against Wall Street firms for these unethical practices, sell-side analyst research operations have overhauled how they do business. More of them are now grading stocks as "sell" or "neutral," which means that the shares of the company are not worth buying, at least in the mind of the analyst. Other firms created stricter separations between their research departments and their investment banking outfits.

A business reporter should still value the sell-side analyst as a source of information. In a way, both the reporter and the analyst are in the same job. They both inform people about companies, and they both go about their jobs by asking questions and examining a company's operations. The only difference is that a reporter does his or her job to better inform readers, whereas the analyst does his or her job to better inform investors. Good analysts for the business reporter are those that know inside and out the companies they follow. They are willing to criticize a company when it is warranted and praise it when laudatory remarks are deserved. Like a business reporter, an analyst should call a spade a spade.

In addition, analysts are like reporters in that they write about the companies they track. The analyst's report can be a revealing insight into what a Wall Street pro thinks about a company's future. Any reporter writing regularly about a public company should be reading research reports about the operation to get a feel for what the investment community thinks. Some reports are short, no more than a page. They sing with their simplicity. Other reports, particularly reports in which an analyst is initiating coverage on a company, can be long documents, often 30 pages or more, filled with charts and data.

Some analysts are excellent writers and do a great job explaining the rationale behind their feelings about a company. Others have subordinates write the reports. A company often lists the analysts who follow its stock and issue research reports on its website under the "Investor" section. The number of analysts following a company can range from one or two to nearly three dozen for a large company such as General Electric.

Virtually all analysts issue recommendations for the stocks they cover. At most Wall Street firms, the top recommendations are "strong buy" or "buy." This means that the analyst believes that the company's stock will outperform a broader market index, such as the Standard & Poor's 500 or the Dow Jones, during the next 12 months. These are the stocks that the analysts are pushing their clients to acquire. Many times, an analyst will own the stock in his personal investment portfolio, though some Wall Street firms now require analysts to disclose what stocks they own.

Lower ratings from analysts for stocks could be "outperform" or "accumulate." These rankings are not as strong as the "strong buy" or the "buy" ratings, but they still indicate the analyst believes the stock is likely to beat the performance of the overall market. Lower ratings are "neutral" or "hold." In previous years, these ratings often meant that an investor should sell the stock. But as many Wall Street brokerage houses attempt to overhaul their rating system, these ratings may begin to mean what they actually state, that the stock has become fully priced in relation to the rest of the market and is unlikely to rise soon. The lowest rating from an analyst is a "sell" rating. Studies showed that only about 1 to 2 percent of all analysts' ratings were the equivalent of a "sell" shortly before the market fell in 2000. Although the number of these ratings has increased in recent years, stocks with "sell" ratings only accounted for about 8 percent of the total 24,000 stock recommendations made by analysts in late 2002, according to a *Los Angeles Times* article on the subject (Peltz, 2002, p. 4). And many of those lower ratings were put on companies only after their stock prices fell by 50 percent or more. (The percentage of analyst "sell" ratings had risen only to about 7 percent in 2015.)

TIPS FROM THE PROS

Yahoo Finance reporter Julia LaRoche on covering Wall Street:

Aim big and get over being afraid: Ask that banker or hedge fund manager for an interview. The worst thing they can say is "no." That's not so bad. Besides "no" now might not be "no" forever. Sometimes I get nervous when I am considering approaching someone. I just suck it up and get over it. I find that if you treat these people like normal human beings they'll respond well.

It is important for a business reporter to know how an analyst rates a company's stock if the reporter plans to quote that person in a story. If an analyst is making positive comments about a company during an interview but has a "hold" rating on its stock, the reporter should question whether the analyst is accurately portraying his or her feelings, either in the interview or in the report. The same questions should arise if an analyst makes negative statements about a company but gives it a "strong buy" rating. If the reporter does not know what the analyst's rating is on a company, he or she should always ask during the interview. Many analysts provide copies of their research reports to reporters via mail or e-mail. A reporter should ask to get on the analyst's e-mail distribution list. Reporters should read analyst reports thoroughly and look for clues about changes in an analyst's thinking about a stock. The most obvious change would be if the analyst downgrades his rating on a company from a "buy" to a "hold," for example. Upgrades from the analyst should also garner some attention. If the change in the rating is based on newsworthy information about the company, the reporter should write a story like the following one written by a *Baltimore Sun* reporter about a shopping mall developer:

A financial analyst accused Rouse Co. yesterday of improperly accounting for $25 million in expenses, a move that allowed the shopping mall giant to report record quarterly earnings to the public.

David Pick, an analyst at Legg Mason Wood Walker Inc., said investors were being misled by the company and recommended they sell the stock.

Rouse executives said the company did nothing wrong but acknowledged that they did not follow industry guidelines by excluding such expenses as bonuses and retirement costs from funds from operations, a benchmark of performance used by most real estate investment trusts.

"We felt what we were doing was providing the best measure of recurring income," said David Tripp, a Rouse vice president and director of investor relations. "We were upfront in how we were calculating our results. We don't think it would have given you a very good big picture to have added those charges." The sell order did not appear to affect Rouse stock, which closed yesterday at $29.40, down 20 cents.

Pick made his recommendation a day after Rouse released its third-quarter earnings. The company reported Monday that in the quarter that ended Sept. 30, its funds from operations were $96.8 million, or $1.03 a share, compared with $69.9 million, or 92 cents a share, in last year's third quarter.

Pick said the company was able to report record results only because it excluded the $25 million it planned to spend by the end of year on a signing bonus for a new executive and costs related to buyouts, retirements and layoffs.

Rouse took an $8.6 million third-quarter charge and said it would take a $16.4 million charge this quarter. Had Rouse included the expenses in funds from operations, Pick said, the costs would have reduced per-share earnings by 12 cents, or 19 percent, in the third quarter.

"They should not be allowed to get away with this kind of misleading financial report," Pick said. "We ultimately believe that they reported their earnings incorrectly."[3]

This story explained why the analyst downgraded the stock and added comments from another analyst who did not lower his rating. That is the type of information from an analyst report that leads to a story. In addition, many analyst firms have simplified their rating systems after many technology stocks fell precipitously in the early 2000s. Many stock ratings are not as hard to decipher as they were before.

Another potential story in an analyst report could be written when the analyst changes his earnings estimates for a company. The best reports that change quarterly or annual EPS estimates come out before the company issues an earnings advisory stating that it will be unable to meet the consensus analyst estimate—the average earnings estimate for a company on the basis of the predictions of all of the analysts covering the company. Research reports that change estimates after the company issues its guidance are merely following the herd and are not likely worth a story unless the new estimate from the analyst is dramatically lower than the number given by the company.

Also, a reporter should be wary of an analyst's report that changes a company's earnings estimates downward after a company has issued an earnings warning but does not downgrade the rating, especially if that rating is a "strong buy" or "buy." An earnings warning is a company's way of telling Wall Street that the fundamentals of its operations are not clicking on all cylinders.

Most analyst reports also have a price target noted on them. This is the price that the analyst thinks the stock will hit sometime in the next 12 months. If a report does not have a price target, it will often be because of an overall "neutral" or "avoid" rating on the stock. Beware of analyst reports that do not have a price target but also have a "strong buy" or "buy" rating. If it were really such a strong buy, the analyst would tell investors and business reporters how strong he or she thinks it will be. Reporters should always look at the company's current stock price in relation to the price target. If the current stock price is near the analyst's price target, the reporter should expect the analyst to raise the price target if he or she thinks the stock can go even higher or to downgrade the stock because he or she now believes the stock is fully valued.

 buy-side analyst: A term used to describe the analysts at investing institutions like mutual funds, pension funds and insurance firms, who tend to buy large portions of securities. These analysts provide research for the firm's money managers.

Most analysts estimate revenue, income, EPS and other numbers for a company for the next year or two in their reports. These numbers are quite often better barometers of how well the analyst thinks the company is going to perform going forward. If the analyst has a "strong buy" rating on a company but is only projecting 5 percent earnings growth, something is wrong.

There are other analysts who follow the stocks of public companies. These analysts are called buy-side analysts and credit analysts. A buy-side analyst is someone who works for an investment firm such as a mutual fund company or even a local university's investment operations. These analysts can also be valuable sources for business reporters, but few of them issue reports on the stocks that they follow for the outside world. Buy-side analysts provide their research on companies to investors within their company.

A credit analyst is someone who tracks the debt offerings for a company. These analysts often work for the same Wall Street firms as the buy-side analysts, but they are analyzing the debt, not the stock, issued by a company. They may also work for a credit rating agency. Analysts for rating agencies did a much better job of raising concerns about Enron and other companies that recently encountered problems.

Going Public

When a private company wants to convert and become a public company, it makes a large filing with the SEC. A Form S-1 filing can be the most important filing for a business reporter because it gives the first glimpse of a company that has previously been private and has not disclosed any financial information or analyses of its performance. The S-1 is the statement filed with the SEC that tells the world: "We want to sell stock in our company to the public, and we think there are enough people out there willing to take a chance on our future." The Wall Street community then reviews the filing and determines whether it wants to invest money in the company. Often, a company will amend these filings, adding more information.

Form S-1: A document filed with the Securities and Exchange Commission (SEC) by a company desiring to go public. This is also known as the registration statement, and it is often amended frequently.

For a business reporter, the S-1 can provide some valuable information. Business journalists can find out how much money a private company has made or lost in the past. Reviewing the financial performance disclosed in this filing is the first step any business reporter should take. A reporter always wants to read this over very carefully and compare (a) how the company did in its most recent quarter with how it did during the same quarter a year ago, and (b) how it did in its most recent full fiscal year with how it did the previous year. That will give the reporter a good indication as to whether the company's earnings are increasing. For example, the initial S-1 statement for Hartford-based Phoenix Companies, which went public during the summer of 2001, did not disclose its first-quarter 2001 financial performance, but an amended statement filed in May 2001 did disclose those numbers. The company reported a loss in the first quarter, compared with a profit in the same quarter during 2000.

How does a business reporter take this information and write a story about it? The *Hartford Courant*'s Diane Levick wrote a story on the day the filing occurred, leading with the fact that the company reported a net loss of $157.5 million in the first quarter because of losses in its venture capital investments (Levick, 2001).

The second paragraph of Levick's story mentions that the company had reported a profit in the same quarter the previous year—another fact disclosed in the filing—and then the story mentions that the company faces two lawsuits challenging its IPO.

Levick read the entire filing and compared what was in the filing with information disclosed in an earlier filing. By taking the time to read and analyze the filing, she was able to write a story that was helpful to readers in explaining the company's performance.

It is also good to note dramatic shifts for the positive. London-based Willis Group Holdings' F-1 statement (similar to an S-1, but filed by foreign companies) disclosed that the company reported net income of $9 million, or 7 cents per share, in 2000. In 1999, the broker lost $132.0 million, or $1.11 per share. Willis' profits are still below the range of competitors, so it is also good to compare profits and profit margins with comparable companies. The filing often details the company's plans for future growth, as well as potential pitfalls in its strategy.

 initial public offering (IPO): The first sale of stock by a private company to the public. IPOs are often smaller, younger companies seeking capital to expand their business.

The initial S-1 statement may not always include the specific amount of money the company wants to raise by going public. And it may not initially include the stock price range at which the company believes it can sell its stock or the total number of shares it plans to sell. But these are the most important numbers and the numbers that every investor wants to know because the number of shares that a company hopes to sell in its IPO can give investors an indication of how popular this offering might be. The more shares a company sells, in general, the more interest the underwriters are having in getting their clients to buy the stock.

The stock price range is also important because it can be an indication of the demand for the offering. In Levick's story (2001), she noted that Phoenix initially filed its S-1 and gave a stock price range of $9 to $16 per share. Later, it increased the range of the offering to $14.50 to $17 per share in an amended S-1 filing. That shows people who track these things that the underwriters are getting a lot of interest from investors in the stock. And that is the kind of information that business reporters should be tracking and writing stories about.

It is not that simplistic. Note that the changes in the stock price range should be looked at in conjunction with the number of shares being offered. At the same time Phoenix increased the stock price range of its offering, it also decreased the amount of shares in the IPO, from 73.8 million to 48.8 million. It upped the price but lowered the amount of shares it is going to sell. This is a case of basic supply-and-demand economics. The fewer shares, the greater the demand from investors; thus, in all likelihood, Phoenix will up the price. It is important to always check for amended S-1 filings to see if the stock price range or the number of shares being offered has changed. And the total amount of money that the company hopes to raise in the IPO may also change.

Normally included on the bottom of the first page of the S-1 statement is a list of the underwriters of the stock offering. The underwriters are the Wall Street firms that will sell chunks of the company's stock to investors. This is important information for a business journalist to assess because the listing of the underwriters will indicate how successful the company could be in selling the stock. If big Wall Street firms like Goldman Sachs, J.P. Morgan, and Morgan Stanley are listed as underwriters, the disclosure should be a sign that these firms will be selling as much of the offering to their institutional clients as possible. That increases the chances of the IPO rising shortly after the stock begins trading. It is important to note, however, the relationships between the underwriters and the company going public detailed in the S-1 filing. Sometimes that tells a better story. Consider this MarketWatch.com story about J.P. Morgan, which was one of the underwriters for Square Incorporated's IPO:

> Square Inc.'s initial public offering may have priced much lower than expected, but one of its underwriters may have benefited.
>
> J.P. Morgan was one of the underwriters on Square's IPO, while its investment banking arm was an investor in the company's series E funding

round. As part of that investment, the bank had an anti-dilution provision, called a ratchet, in place that protected it if the share issue price came in below $18.56.

The IPO priced Wednesday at $9 a share, and Square had to issue 10.3 million additional shares at a value of $93 million to J.P. Morgan and Rizvi Traverse, an investor that also had a ratchet in the series E round, according to *The Wall Street Journal*.

As an investor in Square's series E round, J.P. Morgan paid $15.46 per share. So although it "lost" money on the initial investment, it made money on the additional shares issued. The stock closed at $13.07 Thursday, 45% above the $9 issue price.

J.P. Morgan declined a request to comment.

Goldman Sachs, the lead underwriter of Square's IPO, was also an investor in Square, but did not have the anti-dilution protection, according to the prospectus. J.P. Morgan & Co. Strategic Investments was an investor in Square before the series E round, and with all affiliates beneficially owned 5.5% of shares before the IPO.

J.P. Morgan's position was disclosed in the S-1 filing as a conflict of interest under rules set by the Financial Industry Regulatory Authority. The prospectus said Square followed FINRA's conflict of interest provisions and had Morgan Stanley act as a "qualified independent underwriter."

Square declined a request for comment.

Richard Blake, head of the public offerings group at Gunderson Dettmer, said having J.P. Morgan as both an underwriter and an investor with anti-dilution protection is "a little unusual" but that Morgan Stanley's role would "make sure that J.P. Morgan's role in the offering doesn't overcome reason or the conflict of interest doesn't win the day," Blake said.

J.P. Morgan was listed as third on Square's prospectus, after Goldman Sachs and Morgan Stanley.[4]

In today's business world, regulators commonly scrutinize such relationships. And if regulators are interested in such information, it is obvious that a business reporter should also care about these disclosures and likely should be writing stories about them.

One of the most important disclosures a company makes in an S-1 is its tangible book value. This is what every investor wants to know, and this information will tell people buying the stock whether the shares are worth more or less than the company's actual value.

An investor would like to buy stock at a price near the tangible book value. But that is not what happened with the Willis Group Holdings' IPO. Its F-1 filing noted that it had a negative net tangible book value (note the numbers in parentheses) before it went public. The following is what the filing said:

After giving effect to 20,000,000 shares of common stock which we are selling under this prospectus at an assumed initial public offering price of

$ 11.00 per share, the midpoint of the range indicated on the cover page of this prospectus, and after deducting an assumed underwriting discount and estimated offering expenses and giving effect to the intended use of proceeds assuming that we used all the net proceeds to purchase preference shares of TA II Limited, our adjusted net tangible book value as of March 31, 2001 would have been approximately $(838) million, or $(5.82) per share. This represents an immediate increase in net tangible book value of $2.55 per share equivalent to existing shareholders. This also represents an immediate dilution of $(16.82) per share to new investors purchasing shares under this prospectus.[5]

In other words, investors who bought the Willis stock during its IPO did so at a price much higher than the value of the company. This is something that a business reporter would want to write a story about.

Reporters also need to let readers know if control of the company will change after the IPO. Shareholders who buy stock in a company going public may not always have any say as to what is going to happen with the operation going forward. In some cases, other companies will maintain majority control. This means that, as in the case of a New York company called Odyssey Re, its former parent—in this case, Fairfax Financial—is still pulling the strings after the IPO. According to Odyssey's S-1 statement, a unit of Fairfax Financial Holdings Limited retained a majority stake in the company after its offering. TIG Insurance Company controls more than 70 percent of the stock. And investors should not expect Fairfax to cede control of the company any time soon. In Odyssey's filings, Fairfax states that it "cannot foresee any circumstances under which it would sell a sufficient number of shares of our common stock to cause it not to retain such control" (Form S-1, Odyssey Re Holdings, 2001, p. 14). In addition, the filing states the following:

In order to retain control, Fairfax may decide not to enter into a transaction in which our stockholders would receive consideration for their shares that is much higher than the cost of their investment in our common stock or the then current market price of our common stock.[6]

This is the type of disclosure to which business reporters should pay attention. With this information, they can write stories explaining to their readers that investors may not be interested in buying stock in this company for these reasons.

Another good section to read in S-1 statements is the "Risk Factors" section, in which every company going public has to list anything and everything that could possibly go wrong that would result in its stock price going down. Some of these risk factors are basic and are included in virtually every S-1. They talk about how a downturn in the overall market would hurt a company's business, how higher rates being charged would increase profits, and what the company's competition looks like. In addition, a company's proverbial dirty laundry is also aired here. So, what a reporter should look for are risk factors that are unique to the company. Understanding what risk factors are unique is a skill that takes some time to develop, but after reading a few of these filings, the reporter will begin to pick up on what is normal and what is not.

The following excerpt from an S-1 statement notes a company's high debt levels, which may limit its ability to finance growth and make acquisitions.

> Our debt level reduces our flexibility in responding to changing business and economic conditions, including increased competition in the insurance brokerage industry. And our debt level limits our ability to pursue other business opportunities, borrow more money for operations or capital in the future and implement our business strategies.[7]

It is also important to find the company's dividend policy, which is another important disclosure in the S-1. This will disclose the company's plans on offering a dividend after it becomes public. A dividend is often a quarterly payment to investors to entice them to purchase and hold the stock.

There are plenty of other sections within an S-1 that can also provide valuable information. Most S-1 statements include the first disclosures about executive compensation, stock options, loans to corporate executives and other juicy tidbits. When reporting on an S-1 statement, it is important to read the entire document because some information might be included in sections other than one would expect. For example, an amended S-1 statement filed by Phoenix included a paragraph in the "Underwriting" section about how the company asked the IPO syndicate to set aside 5 million shares of stock for one buyer—State Farm. This is information that most frequent S-1 readers would have wanted to read in the summary that begins each S-1 because it is significant news that one company, particularly one as large as State Farm, wants to invest in another. That is the type of story the business reporter should be writing.

The number of IPOs has increased in the past few years as the market has risen. There were 364 IPOs—the highest number in the past decade—in 2014 and 239 in 2015, meaning that a reporter covering the IPO market had plenty to write about. In contrast, there were slightly more than 100 IPOs in both 2008 and 2009.

Covering Debt

This chapter evaluates how the stock market works and how and why investors, analysts and company executives pay a lot of attention to stocks. But another important investment vehicle that many companies use to raise money and that is often ignored by the business media is debt.

A debt, or bond, offering often comes from a company. But local or state governments can also issue them as a way to fund building projects such as new hospitals or new roads. Although writing stories about issuing bonds to finance construction projects may seem like drab reporting, some of the best business journalists learned the craft while working at the *Bond Buyer*, a newspaper dedicated solely to reporting, writing and editing stories about all kinds of debt issues.

Watching the debt market can be very similar to analyzing the stock market. In both cases, companies—or government entities, in the case of bonds—are reliant on finding enough buyers to purchase shares or bonds to allow them to do what they want with the incoming money. And in both cases, investors expect to receive a return on their investment. The nature of the return, however, is where stocks and bonds differ. Historically, stocks have given investors a larger return than bonds. However, bonds are considered the safer investment. Rarely does a government entity, be it city, county, state or federal, fail and become forced to file for bankruptcy-court protection. To be sure, businesses that issue debt do sometimes go into bankruptcy court, but even in such cases, bondholders are more likely to be repaid than owners of the company stock.

Understanding how the bond market works is also important for another reason that differs from the stock market: Private companies frequently issue debt to fund projects. And when a private company issues debt, it must often disclose information about its past performance.

A bond is like a mortgage, similar to one people take out to purchase a home, or a loan one may use to buy a first car. The company or government body that issues the bond needs money for some reason, so they sell bonds, typically worth $1,000 each, to investors. In return, the company or government promises to pay the investor

coupon: The interest rate stated on a bond when it's issued. The coupon is typically paid semiannually.

a certain amount of money each year. This payment is known as a coupon. On a $1,000 bond with a 7 percent annual interest rate, the coupon is $70 each year. At the end of the time period of the bond, known as the maturity date, the company or government repays the bondholder the $1,000 plus the coupon.

Companies and governments issue bonds because it can sometimes be difficult for them to go to a bank and ask the bank to loan them $500 million to build a new bubble gum factory. Most banks are not large enough to loan a single company that much money. Banks do not want to make such a large loan to one company because they fear that if the business is unable to pay the loan back, the bank itself will be stuck. So, instead, companies and governments issue bonds and spread the risk around to hundreds and sometimes even thousands of investors.

maturity date: The date the borrower has to pay back the money it has borrowed through a bond issue.

The following excerpt from an Associated Press story about the building of the Florida Aquarium in Tampa explains how bonds work, why they were issued in this case and how the bonds were expected to be repaid:

> Most of the money for the glass-domed structure was raised through the sale of $84 million in revenue bonds that are partly backed by the city, a package that Racanelli said he wouldn't have recommended if he had been on board at the time.
>
> The public financing package means the aquarium essentially borrowed money from the bond-buyers—individuals and corporations—and must pay it back with money it takes in from visitors.
>
> That seemed easy before the aquarium was built. Studies showed that it would draw 1.8 million visitors a year. By charging $13.95 for each adult admission, the aquarium would raise enough money to cover its $7.2 million annual bond payments.
>
> But in hindsight, the figures seem questionable. The attendance figure was dependent on state tourism increasing 4 percent. Also, the admission price at Florida Aquarium is the highest in the country.[8]

This story provides an example of a bond issued by a state or local government. Two other types of bonds are also widely issued and written about. These two types are bonds issued by corporations and bonds issued by the U.S. government, sometimes known as treasury bills.

Corporate bonds fall into two main categories—investment grade and junk bonds. When a company issues a bond, the bond is given a rating by an agency such as Standard & Poor's or Moody's. The rating determines whether the offering is investment grade or junk. To be considered investment grade, the bonds must be rated BBB or higher. Higher ratings include AAA, AA and A. Lower ratings are BB, B, C and D. When bonds are given these lower ratings, they are considered junk.

yield: In general, a return on an investor's capital investment. For bonds, the coupon rate of interest divided by the purchase price, called current yield. Also, the rate of return on a bond, taking into account the total of annual interest payments, the purchase price, the redemption value and the amount of time remaining until maturity.

The higher the rating, the lower the yield. When companies have high ratings, they can offer bonds at a lower interest rate. Companies with junk bond ratings are typically newer companies or companies that have had recent financial trouble. To entice investors into purchasing these higher-risk bonds, the companies offer higher yields.

The ratings that companies receive are often important stories, and business reporters should watch for them. When a rating agency lowers a company's credit rating, the company will have to spend more money paying interest the next time it wants to borrow money. If a company's credit rating rises, then its cost of borrowing money will go down. That could be a good story, too, particularly if the company can tell you what it plans to do with the extra money.

In addition, the ratings analysts at the agencies that issue the ratings are good sources because they have looked at the company issuing the bonds and know its performance. These analysts are similar to sell-side analysts in some respects, but they are not pushing investors to purchase the bonds, so they may be more objective. However, their firms do receive money from the companies issuing the bonds in exchange for the ratings.

Investors in these bonds are good sources as well. Just like investors in stocks, bondholders have typically done extensive research into the companies from which they are purchasing bonds. Sometimes, these investors purchase bonds that can later be converted into company stock, so they are looking for the company to perform well and have its stock price go up. These bonds are called convertible bonds.

The prices of corporate bonds do not fluctuate as much as the price of stocks. A bond that sells above its face value is considered to be selling "at a premium." But there are many instances when the price of corporate bonds rarely moves despite large fluctuations in the company's stock price. And a corporate bond can sell close to its face value even when the stock price of the company falls dramatically.

The municipal bond market is smaller than the corporate bond market but still provides plenty of good stories. Because reporters writing for the news section typically cover state and local governments, these reporters too need to know how bond offerings work and how the money is being spent. Investors often favor municipal bonds over corporate bonds because municipal bonds are tax exempt. This means that the interest paid to investors is exempt from federal taxes. However, municipal bonds typically offer lower rates than corporate bonds. Just like corporate bonds, agencies issuing municipal bonds have to repay their investors. Sometimes state and local governments must find other ways to raise cash to repay their bondholders.

The following Bloomberg News story explains how a state water agency in Massachusetts issued bonds and now wants to raise its rates and cut its expenses to help it repay its bonds:

> The Massachusetts Water Resources Authority, Boston's water and sewer utility, plans to raise rates, fire 50 employees and spend more of a $135 million reserve fund to meet a $48 million budget deficit.

The authority's board voted to fill the deficit with $16 million in spending cuts, including the firings, $16 million by increasing rates 4 percent, and by using $16 million from a reserve fund, according to authority spokesman Jonathan Yeo.

Earlier this year, acting Governor Jane Swift and the state legislature eliminated the authority's $48 million subsidy.

The authority, which supplies sewer and water to 61 municipalities, spends about 60 percent of its operating budget to repay its $5.1 billion of outstanding debt. The authority's senior debt is rated AA by Standard & Poor's, Aa3 by Moody's Investors Service and AA- by Fitch Ratings.

"We're very keen on maintaining our strong bond rating, and I think that was shown in the board's judicious use of reserves," said Yeo, who also noted that the authority has about $350 million in reserves that are required by bond covenants.

U.S. states are cutting subsidies and programs as they deal with budget deficits brought on by a loss of tax revenue from the decline of the economy and stock market. Massachusetts has a budget deficit of at least $300 million this fiscal year, and is projecting a deficit that could exceed $2 billion next year.

Yeo said the board now plans to spend its $135 million reserve fund, which was created for rate relief, over four years rather than five as it had planned.

The rate increase, which could go into effect by February, comes midyear and will be on top of the 2.9 percent increase passed before the fiscal year began July 1. So rates from February through June will be 6.9 percent higher than the previous year.

The authority's 5.25 percent coupon note maturing in 2012 rose 0.3 cent on the dollar to 111.5, yielding 3.767 percent, according to Bloomberg data.[9]

This story provides the reader with the bond rating and the yield. By detailing the ratings and the price information, the reporter helps the reader understand the soundness of investing in these bonds.

The last type of bond is a U.S. Treasury bond. These come in different denominations with different maturity dates and are issued by the federal government to help fund U.S. government projects. Treasury bills are issued with a maturity date of a year or less and have a price of $10,000. Treasury notes are issued with a maturity date ranging from one year to 10 years and have a value of $1,000. Treasury bonds have a maturity date ranging from 10 years to 30 years and can be purchased in $1,000 denominations. The later the maturity date, the bigger the yield. These bonds are considered some of the safest investments in the world because the U.S. federal government has never defaulted on a payment.

It is important to assess economic factors with all types of bonds. If interest rates are rising, corporations and governments may issue fewer bonds because their cost will increase.

There is also a connection between corporate bonds and Treasuries, as the following story explains:

> U.S. Treasuries headed toward their biggest weekly decline in more than two months on increasing signs the economy is gaining strength.
>
> Demand for Treasuries fell today after the Commerce Department said construction spending rose for a third month in November. The benchmark 10-year note had its largest drop in more than a year yesterday, ending a four-week rally, after an industry report showed the biggest increase in a manufacturing index in 11 years and as stocks surged.
>
> "The tone for the first six weeks of this year could be positive for the economy, which is good for corporate bonds and not so positive for Treasuries," said Dan Shackelford, who helps invest $6 billion of bonds at T. Rowe Price Group Inc. in Baltimore. He said the firm has added higher-yielding corporate and asset-backed debt at the expense of Treasuries.
>
> The benchmark 4 percent 2012 note this week lost $1\frac{3}{4}$, or $17.50 per $1,000 face amount, to at 3:15 p.m. in New York, its biggest slump since the week ended Oct. 18. The note's yield rose 22 basis points to 4.03 percent. The $1\frac{3}{4}$ percent 2004 note fell about 3/8 as its yield grew 18 basis points to 1.77 percent. A basis point is 0.01 percentage point. On the day, prices were little changed. The 10-year note rose 1/32 while the two-year note was unchanged.
>
> The interest-rate differential between the two securities grew 5 basis points this week to 2.26 percentage points, the widest in two weeks. A wider gap suggests traders see the Federal Reserve's target overnight lending rate, at a 41-year low of 1.25 percent, underpinning an economic recovery.
>
> Some investors sold Treasuries this week to make room in their portfolios for an expected increase in the supply of corporate debt, analysts said. Trump Hotels & Casino Resorts Inc. and Kreditanstalt für Wiederaufbau, Europe's fourth-largest seller of debt, are among companies slated to sell about $4 billion of bonds in coming days. The average investment-grade corporate bond yields 1.81 percentage points more than Treasuries, according to a Merrill Lynch & Co. bond index.[10]

Treasury bonds provide a lower yield than corporate bonds, so when corporate bonds are sold, some investors dump Treasuries to purchase them. This is a trend in the bond market that business reporters should watch because it might affect the bond issue of companies they cover.

Although the majority of Wall Street coverage focuses on the rise and fall of stocks, it is still vitally important for any business reporter to understand the bond market as well. Bonds can often tell a broader and clearer story about a company or government body. If a company is issuing a large amount of bonds, it may be gearing up for a large expansion, or it may be getting ready to make an acquisition. For one reason or another, it needs money. It is the business reporter's job to find out why.

Conclusion

This chapter explains why and how companies raise money through the stock market and the bond market and how this process is important to the success of the business. Companies that perform well by increasing profits and sales will likely see their stock price rise, allowing them to sell additional stock and use the stock to compensate their employees.

But where does this money that's raised in the stock and bond markets go once it gets into the bank accounts of the companies? Companies are sometimes not specific in telling their shareholders what they plan to do with the money. Typically, the money goes to one of four uses: to pay off past loans and debt; to acquire another company or business; to build something, such as a new plant or headquarters; or simply to sit in the company bank account and be used to fund expenses when necessary.

As mentioned earlier, by going public, companies sell shares of ownership to investors. Often, the S-1 will explain what the company intends to do with that money. For example, when New York–based Cosi Incorporated, a casual restaurant chain, went public, it explained how it intended to use the money from the sale of its stock in broad terms:

> Our management has broad discretion as to the use of the net proceeds that we will receive from this offering. We cannot assure you that our management will apply these funds effectively, nor can we assure you that the net proceeds from this offering will be invested in a manner yielding a favorable return.[11]

This statement is about as nebulous as it can get. But elsewhere in the filing, the company provided more detail that explained how the money was going to be spent—that is, opening new restaurants:

> The addition of new restaurants has been our primary source of growth historically and we anticipate that it will be the primary source of growth in the near term. We believe that we have adopted a manageable growth strategy and intend to develop many of our new restaurants in our existing markets, and selectively enter new markets, to gain operational efficiencies, enhance convenience for our customers and increase brand awareness. We do not utilize a commissary system and thus our expansion is not restricted by geographic proximity to commissary kitchens. Our site selection criteria is flexible and allows us to adapt to a wide variety of real estate paradigms including central business districts, urban and suburban residential locations and suburban shopping centers. We plan to open approximately 25 new restaurants during fiscal 2002, and approximately 53 to 59 new restaurants in fiscal 2003. We expect the majority of our restaurants to be opened in the future will be in the Cosi all-day format.[12]

The bottom line is that many companies raise money because they can. Often, they do not have a specific usage for the money, but they want to have the money available when they need it.

Anytime a company announces a major initiative that will cost money— everything from a new national advertising campaign to the construction of a new factory to the acquisition of another company—a business reporter should ask where the money is coming from. If the company does not say how much the new initiative is going to cost, the reporters should ask for an estimate. If it does not give you an estimate, find an expert in that business to provide a ballpark figure. Then look at the company's financial statements to see if it has enough money to fund the project. If it does not, then the company could borrow the money from a bank or sell stock or bonds.

The money for businesses to expand has to come from somewhere. Most often, it comes from investors buying and selling stocks and bonds on Wall Street. A business reporter who can follow the money trail from how the cash was raised to how it will be spent can provide a valuable service to readers and listeners by writing stories that help explain if the money is being spent wisely.

The money trail is the most important aspect of being a business journalist. This chapter explains how money flows from investors into companies and why companies sometimes need money. Later chapters discuss other ways companies spend their money.

Notes

1. From "U.S. Stocks fall as durable, retail data lag: Citigroup drops," by S. Fu, December 24, 2002, Bloomberg News. Copyright 2002 by Bloomberg L.P. All rights reserved. Reprinted with permission.
2. From "Stock sale jolts Unify investors," by M. Marshall, August 5, 2000, *San Jose Mercury News*, p. 1C. Copyright 2000 by *San Jose Mercury News*. Reprinted with permission. All rights reserved.
3. From "Legg analyst accuses Rouse of a misleading 3Q report," by M. Cohn, October 30, 2002, *Baltimore Sun*, p. 1C. Copyright 2002 by *Baltimore Sun*. Reprinted with permission.
4. "J.P. Morgan did well with Square's IPO," by C. Huston, November 20, 2015, MarketWatch.com. Copyright 2015 by MarketWatch.com. Reprinted with permission.
5. From Form F-l, Willis Group Holdings, May 15, 2001, SEC Publication No. 0000912057–01–516288, p. 25. Washington, DC: Securities and Exchange Commission.
6. From Form S-1, Odyssey Re Holdings, March 26, 2001, SEC Publication No. 0000947871–01–000156, p. 16. Washington, DC: Securities and Exchange Commission.
7. From Form F-l, Willis Group Holdings, May 15, 2001, SEC Publication No. 0000912057–01–516288, p. 11. Washington, DC: Securities and Exchange Commission.
8. From "Flagging crowds make aquarium a Florida flop," by Lisa Holewa, March 17, 1996, Associated Press. Copyright 1996 by Associated Press. Reprinted with permission.

9. From "Massachusetts water taps reserves, raises rates and fires 50," by E. Baeb, December 27, 2002, Bloomberg News. Copyright 2002 by Bloomberg L.P. All rights reserved. Reprinted with permission.

10. From "Treasuries fall in week on expectations economy growing faster," by H. Bandur, January 3, 2003, Bloomberg News. Copyright 2003 by Bloomberg L.P. All rights reserved. Reprinted with permission.

11. From Form S-1, Cosi Incorporated, April 17, 2002, SEC Publication No. 0000950123–02–003869, p. 12. Washington, DC: Securities and Exchange Commission.

12. From Form S-1, Cosi Incorporated, April 17, 2002, SEC Publication No. 0000950123–02–003869, p. 3. Washington, DC: Securities and Exchange Commission.

Key Terms

American Stock Exchange	Form S-1
bond	initial public offering (IPO)
buy-side analyst	institutional investor
coupon	maturity date
dividend	yield

Suggested Exercises

1. Compile a list of local stocks and monitor their performance throughout the day. Write a story based on the gains and losses in the individual stocks and the indexes. Then compare your story to the stock market story in the local newspaper.

2. Review a research report for a local company issued by a sell-side analyst. Write a 250-word analysis of the analyst's rating for the company, discussing whether you believe the rating is justified.

3. Discuss the differences between sell-side analysts and buy-side analysts. Compile a list of five ways a sell-side analyst can help a business reporter and five ways a buy-side analyst can help a business reporter. Think of ways both analysts might try to use reporters to their advantage.

4. Review the S-1 registration statement for a company that has recently gone public. Assess the size of the offering and the initial stock price. List five items in the filing that are newsworthy and should be included in a story about the stock offering.

5. You are the editor of a magazine that follows bank stocks. You arrange a Q&A interview with the manager of a mutual fund that invests in bank stocks. The mutual fund is part of the magazine's 401(k) retirement plan, and the editor is part of the plan. Should you conduct the interview, or should you find a staff member who has not invested in the retirement plan to conduct the interview? If you find a staff member to conduct the interview, should you be involved in editing the transcript?

Books on Wall Street

Apostolou, N.G., & Crumbley, D.L. (1994). *Keys to understanding the financial news* (2nd ed.). Hauppauge, NY: Barron's Educational Series.

Faber, D. (2009). *And then the roof caved in: How Wall Street's greed and stupidity brought capitalism to its knees*. New York: John Wiley & Sons.

Gasparino, C. (2009). *The sellout: How three decades of Wall Street greed and government mismanagement destroyed the global financial system*. New York: Harper Collins.

Kansas, D. (2009). *The Wall Street Journal guide to the end of Wall Street as we know it: What you need to know about the greatest financial crisis of our time—and how to survive it*. New York: Harper Collins.

Sorkin, A.R. (2009). *Too big to fail: The inside story of how Wall Street and Washington fought to save the financial system—and themselves*. New York: Viking.

Warfield, G. (1994). *How to read and understand the financial news* (2nd ed.). New York: Harper Collins.

Wurman, R.S., Siegel, A., & Morris, K.M. (1989). *The Wall Street Journal guide to understanding money & markets*. New York: Access Press.

References

Baeb, E. (2002, December 27). Massachusetts water taps reserves, raises rates and fires 50. Bloomberg News.

Bandur, H. (2003, January 3). Treasuries fall in week on expectations economy growing faster. Bloomberg News.

Bloomberg. (1995). *The Bloomberg Way*. New York: Bloomberg Business News, pp. 100–101.

Cohn, M. (2002, October 30). Legg analyst accuses Rouse of a misleading 3Q report. *Baltimore Sun*, p. 1C.

Cosi Incorporated. Form S-1. (2002, April 17). (SEC Publication No. 0000950123–02–003869, pp. 1–45). Washington, DC: Securities and Exchange Commission.

Fu, S. (2002, December 24). U.S. stocks fall as durable, retail data lag; Citigroup drops. Bloomberg News.

Holewa, L. (1996, March 17). Flagging crowds make aquarium a Florida flop. Associated Press.

Huston, C. (2015, November 20). J.P. Morgan did well with Square's IPO. Market Watch.com. Retrieved December 29, 2015 from www.marketwatch.com/story/jp-morgan-did-well-with-squares-ipo-2015–11–20.

Kurtz, H. (2002, January 18). The Enron story that waited to be told. *Washington Post*, p. C1.

Levick, D. (2001, May 12). Phoenix lists a loss of $157 million for quarter. *Hartford Courant*, p. E1.

Marshall, M. (2000, August 5). Stock sale jolts Unify investors. *San Jose Mercury News*, p. 1C.

Max Re Capital. Form S-1. (2001, May 31). (SEC Publication No. 0000950130–01–502080, pp. 1–83). Washington, DC: Securities and Exchange Commission.

Odyssey Re Holdings. Form S-1. (2001, March 26). (SEC Publication No. 0000947871–01–000156, pp. 1–37). Washington, DC: Securities and Exchange Commission.

Peltz, J.F. (2002, October 14). Analysts' tougher ratings take toll on Wall Street. *Los Angeles Times*, p. 4.

9

EXECUTIVES AS A NEWS STORY

Story CEO as Rock Star

During the 1990s, it became popular to write profiles about the CEOs of major corporations, treating them like movie stars or rock icons. The business media lauded the exploits of Microsoft's Bill Gates, GE's Jack Welch and Coca-Cola's Roberto Goizueta, to name a few. Many CEOs received the credit for the companies' successes, even though they oversaw operations with thousands of employees who contributed to the companies' positions as industry leaders. The coverage was perhaps a bit over the top. Certainly, it was not nearly as critical as it should have been. We now see business reporters taking a harder look at the successes and failures of CEOs in running their companies.

Tyco International's Dennis Kozlowski was considered one of these rock stars in the 1990s. His face adorned the cover of many business publications, and his strategy of building a conglomerate was praised. Now, Kozlowski no longer leads Tyco. The disgraced executive resigned from the company shortly before he was indicted for tax evasion in 2002 and now sits in prison. In addition, he stands charged with looting the company of $600 million to sustain an extravagant lifestyle that included a $15,000 umbrella stand and a $6,000 shower curtain. Ozzy Osbourne likely lives with such amenities, but when a corporate executive uses money from a public corporation to buy them, he is playing with fire and should draw the scrutiny of the business media.

Kozlowski's business reputation, once excellent, is now in tatters. Under Kozlowski's direction, to raise cash, Tyco sold operations at less than half of what it paid a few years earlier. The business media was not critical enough. Just months before his arrest, Kozlowski was named one of the country's best managers by *BusinessWeek*.

Kozlowski is not alone, unfortunately. Former Enron CEO Kenneth Lay apparently used the corporate jet to transport his daughter's furniture. Ex-Adelphia Communications head John Rigas took $13 million from the cable company to build a golf course. Even former icons such as Welch and Goizueta are facing re-evaluations of their performances. Welch retired from GE, but the company has since struggled to maintain the growth rate it had under his reign, even before the start of the recession in 2008. This is primarily because it can no longer make acquisitions big enough to fuel higher earnings, and also because it can only squeeze so much excess spending out of its existing businesses—strategies that Welch used to grow the company. And Welch had his excesses, too. His divorce negotiations disclosed that GE had given him a generous retirement package, including paying for items such as a Manhattan apartment and country club fees.

The performance of Goizueta, who died as Coca-Cola's CEO in 1997, now is also being examined in a new light. A man who easily obtained meetings with presidents of countries around the world, Goizueta led Coca-Cola in an overhaul that was supposed to ensure its success for decades to come. Just more than two years after taking over from Goizueta, however, Doug Ivester resigned as Coca-Cola's CEO. The job was too much for the Georgia-born accountant, Goizueta's hand-picked successor. He was unable to withstand the spotlight brought on by a racial discrimination lawsuit, a tampering scare in Europe and sluggish sales, as suggested in a December 1999 story in the *Atlanta Journal-Constitution,* which called Ivester's resignation a "surprise" and noted that his tenure as leader of the company was "tumultuous" (Unger, 1999, p. 1A). The story also noted that Ivester resisted pressure from the board of directors to name a No.2 executive. Coke has since been through four more CEOs in the past 15 years and had other problems.

TIPS FROM THE PROS

Crain's New York Business senior reporter Aaron Elstein on covering executive compensation:

Remember that the key to a great exec pay story is generally not just the sheer amount of money involved, but how the money compares to the company's performance. When Bob Nardelli got paid a huge amount at Home Depot, what gave the story real bite—and drove so many shareholders nuts that he got pushed out—was that he'd driven a very successful company astray.

In many of these cases, business reporters appear to have been all too willing to give CEOs the benefit of the doubt when documenting their companies' performances. Powerful CEOs and their public relations staffs often coddle reporters with grand visions of future corporate glory that will ultimately result in shareholders becoming unbelievably rich. Their promises are seldom realized, however. Few companies have been able to sustain the kind of repeated growth over a long period of time that makes their shareholders wildly rich. In recent years, former blue-chip companies such as Merrill Lynch and Citigroup have forced out their CEOs amid problems. Virtually every CEO on Wall Street has come under criticism in the wake of the problem with derivatives and mortgage-backed investments.

Talkative and quirky CEOs also get a fair amount of attention. But is it warranted? In many cases, it may not be. A senior writer for TheStreet.com, an online business news service, Dagen McDowell, wrote on the site:

> A company also will get a lot more attention from the media if it's run by a colorful personality who could serve as an engaging character in an otherwise dry financial story. . . . A corporate executive who is blunt, outspoken, opinionated and maybe even a little nuts will get a lot more media time than someone who is, well, boring. Unfortunately for investors, an outsize personality doesn't always mean a great corporate leader.
>
> (McDowell, 2002)

Every rock star has his or her critics. The same should hold true in the corporate world. Business journalists should learn from the recent disclosures of excess and hold executives accountable for their actions. To be sure, some CEOs and other executives act in the best interests of their shareholders and their employees. But there are enough who do not to merit more scrutiny by reporters.

Reporters can dig into the world of corporations and write stories that expose what is going on inside the executive suite and the boardroom. Laws require public companies to disclose the salaries and bonuses, as well as stock options and other perks, of their top executives every year. In the case of some private companies, salaries, bonuses and other compensation are disclosed to state regulators, and that information can be obtained if a reporter knows where to look or whom to ask.

The question is: Why have boards allowed their CEOs to get away with spending corporate money on personal items? The answer is that many boards, including members of the Tyco board, have professed ignorance as to what their CEOs have done. Many boards now aggressively look at such spending, which can be good news for business reporters looking to find such information. A friendly board member might provide the documents for a story.

Another question might be: Why do boards agree to pay executives such large sums of money? In many cases, successful executives receive seven-figure salaries and bonuses to keep them at the company. But executive compensation has become an increasingly controversial topic that business reporters now cover with more diligence. Later chapters detailing real estate records and court filings explain how to uncover an executive's financial holdings as they relate to his company. But before any reporter begins to interview executives and write stories about what they are doing, it is important to understand how a company is structured.

Who Does What?

The CEO is the most important person in any business, no matter the size. The CEO is the executive who sets the strategy for the company, and everyone on the organizational chart must eventually answer to the CEO.

TIPS FROM THE PROS

Crain's New York Business senior reporter Aaron Elstein on covering executive compensation:

It's worth remembering, too, that sometimes the definition of overpaid is anyone who gets paid more than you. As you approach these stories, try to be at least open to the idea that there are people worth a lot of money. If you go in ready to hang 'em all, you risk missing the nuances that make these stories sing.

In many companies, the CEO can hold other titles. A lot of times, the CEO is also the chairman of the board of directors. Many companies have boards, which are set up to provide guidance to the executive team.

At some companies, when a CEO is also chairman, that person can seem to have absolute power. But not always. Consider the story of one of Coca-Cola's CEOs, Doug Daft. Daft also held the title of chairman of the board, as did his predecessors. But the Coca-Cola board at the time included Warren Buffett, one of the richest men in the world, who owns 8 percent of the company's stock. Many believe that Buffett's stature gave him more power in making important decisions for Coca-Cola than Daft, who owns much less of the company. There were reports that Buffett and other board members turned down Daft's request to buy Quaker Oats, which included Gatorade, in 2001 (Valdmanis and Howard, 2000). Instead, rival Pepsi bought the company.

A board of directors is typically made up of other CEOs and executives at other companies, friends of the company CEO, or people who have business relationships with the company and executives. Many boards, spurred by regulators and investors seeking more independent boards who are willing to speak up and hold CEOs accountable for excessive spending and other decisions that may affect the company's future, are adding members from outside the company who have no ties to the CEO. Others are adding minority and female board members to add different perspectives.

board of directors: People selected to sit on an authoritative standing committee, or governing body, taking responsibility for the management of an organization. Board members are chosen by shareholders, but in practice they are usually selected by the current board's recommendations. The board usually includes major shareholders.

If the CEO is not the chairman of the board, it is important for these two people to have a good working relationship. The chairman is essentially the CEO's boss, and if the chairman does not have confidence that the CEO is doing the job well, he or she may ask the other board members to help find a new CEO.

Another interesting relationship between CEOs and boards sometimes occurs when a CEO retires from that position but maintains the title of chairman of the board. Many former CEOs-turned-chairmen have been unable to let go of the reins and allow their successors a chance to run the company without interference. When reviewing a board's composition, it is important for a journalist to see if there are former company executives lingering.

Board meetings for companies, even public companies, are not open to reporters. Depending on the company, boards get together on average about once a month or every other month and often meet for an entire day. They hear reports on the performance of the company's operations and discuss managerial changes. Boards vote to approve major company moves, such as building a new plant or hiring a new CFO. Boards also vote on matters such as whether to split a company's stock or to raise the dividend paid to investors. Companies will typically disclose newsworthy events decided at board meetings via a news release.

It is smart for business reporters to know the board members of the companies they are writing about. Most companies provide a list of board members on their websites and at the back of their annual reports. Board members may often speak to reporters about the CEO's job performance, and they often can give insights into boardroom discussions related to acquisitions. This chapter details how to find more information about board members.

chairman of the board: The most senior executive in an organization. The chair is responsible for running the annual meeting and meetings of the board of directors. He or she may be a figurehead, appointed for prestige or power, and may have no role in the day-to-day running of the organization. Sometimes the roles of chair and chief executive are combined, and the chair then has more control over daily operations. Sometimes the chair is a retired chief executive.

The CEO, the top executive of a company, may also hold the title of president. The president of a company typically is the person in charge of the day-to-day operations, overseeing major divisions and manufacturing. If the two jobs are split, the president typically reports to the CEO. The major difference in these two jobs—if held by separate people—is that the CEO is often more focused on a company's plans, whereas a president oversees the current, running business.

Figure 9.1 is a typical organizational chart for a manufacturing company. The chairman in this company is also the CEO.

If a company does not have a president, it may have a chief operating officer, or COO. These jobs are similar, and often one person may hold both titles. It is not significant if a company has a COO but not a president. However, a company with a COO and a president may have a power struggle near the top. Or it could be setting up those two executives in a horse race to replace the current CEO. That is something that bears watching and could lead to a story.

Corporate Organizational Chart

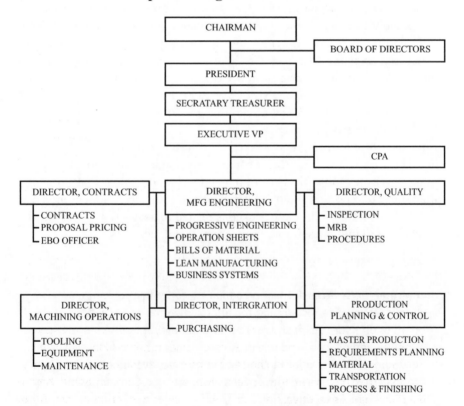

Figure 9.1 Typical Organizational Chart for a Manufacturing Company

TIPS FROM THE PROS

Crain's New York Business senior reporter Aaron Elstein on covering executive compensation:

Now, as you get into the nitty-gritty of reading the proxy materials and crunching numbers, start by reading the annual report from the compensation committee contained in the company's annual proxy statement. This is where the company's board of directors rationalizes how they paid the CEO and other top exec what they gave them. Read it carefully. If the company says it pays the CEO based on profit growth or some other criteria, how does it define profits? Is it a complicated definition or a simple one? Has the definition changed over the years? (The only way to know, sorry, is to read reports from previous years' proxies.) For example, Rupert Murdoch gets paid based on "adjusted earnings per share." By "adjusted," the News Corp. board means earnings before such ordinary business expenses as restructuring costs (i.e., severance to fired employees), depreciation of assets, write-downs and other such things. You will find that companies devise all sorts of creative ways to gloss over bad news and justify lavish pay.

president or chief operating officer: The officer responsible for the day-to-day management of a company who usually reports to the chief executive officer.

The relationship between the president/COO and the CEO of a company is important. A CEO will often pick someone as his right hand for the slot, knowing that he needs a No. 2 executive who can execute orders effectively and quickly. CEOs and presidents often meet regularly to discuss corporate strategy and a company's operations. At Coca-Cola in the 1990s, the CEO and president got together weekly with other executives at lunch to discuss business.

Typically at the same level as the president and COO is the CFO, who is in charge of keeping the company's books together. The CFO typically has a better handle on the financial performance of the company than most other executives. The CFO is involved in preparing a company's quarterly earnings statement and will quite often discuss those results when the company holds a conference call for analysts and investors.

Below the president and COO can be a number of positions, depending on how the company is structured. A company like Coca-Cola that is heavily focused on marketing and geographic operations might have executives in charge of its North American, European, Middle Eastern, South American, African and Asian operations, as well as a chief marketing officer. All of these executives report to the president. Another company may be structured differently and have executives in charge of manufacturing or specific products reporting directly to the president.

A reporter should understand the relationships among these executives. A chief marketing officer and the head of an operating unit at a company may need to spend a lot of time together. When a company unveils a new product, it wants to sell as much as it can. So the operating executive will need to discuss the selling points for the new product with the chief marketing officer.

Other important relationships exist in a company. An operating executive may need money to expand a plant or to develop a new product. To get that money, he will have to go to the president or the CEO. At a company like Wal-Mart, the head of the Sam's Club division may want to install new computers in the stores to track the sales of various products. To get those new computers, he will need to ask the head of information systems, also sometimes called the chief information officer.

Or, if Wal-Mart is opening a new location, it will need to hire new employees. A vice president of human resources will need to know from the head of the retail division where the store is located, when it is expected to open, and how many full-time and part-time employees will be needed.

TIPS FROM THE PROS

 Crain's New York Business senior reporter Aaron Elstein on covering executive compensation:

After you examine the compensation committee's report, check out things like the "peer group" of companies that the board used to help it determine the CEO's pay. This is important because boards always point to the pay practices of others to justify their actions. Is the peer group realistic? Does it include companies that are much larger or even in different businesses? Small companies have a tendency to compare their pay practices to larger ones, because big companies generally pay more than smaller ones do. (I've found the correlation between pay and performance to be much less important than the correlation between pay and company size.)

It is important to know the responsibilities of each executive. For a reporter writing a story about Microsoft's business in Brazil, it is probably better to interview the head of the company's South American operations than to talk to Satya Nadella, the current CEO. Most companies have other executives who can also be important to a business reporter. A reporter covering a drug company such as GlaxoSmithKline may want to cultivate a relationship with the head of research, a person who might be willing to talk about drugs being developed for future sale. A reporter writing a story about how the automated teller machines failed at a bank may want to interview its chief information officer or vice president of information systems.

Larger companies have corporate communications staffs that handle media requests. The better corporate PR staffs work to put the business reporter and executives together, rather than talking themselves. They realize that it is the executives who know what is going on at the company better than anyone else and can give better answers. In most cases, these executives are trained to answer questions in a specific manner.

Reporters should be diligent in their interviews to ensure that questions are answered satisfactorily. Sometimes executives can be like politicians: They try to answer a question that was not asked, not the one that was. It is important for reporters to listen to the answers during the interview and return to questions that go unanswered. Often, just asking the question again will get an answer; sometimes it takes two or three times.

Executives are busy people. In many cases, they have multibillion-dollar corporations to manage. They tend to get impatient with poorly framed questions. A reporter should prepare for interviews by conducting background research on the executive so that time is not wasted on basic questions. A reporter should ask about the executive's strategy for the company, not how long he or she has been CEO. The reporter who shows that he or she is prepared and knows the business will be more likely to get an interview the next time.

Figure 9.2 is another typical organizational chart for a company. (The CEO in some countries is called the executive director.) Note that the head

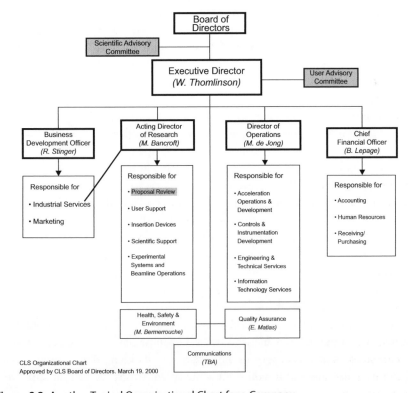

Figure 9.2 Another Typical Organizational Chart for a Company

of communications for this company reports directly to the company leader but is at a lower level of power than the director of operations or the CFO. Often, a vice president of corporate communications will work directly with a president or CEO in setting the company's strategy toward handling media requests.

Salaries, Bonuses and Stock Options

Companies are in the business of making money. So are their executives. A company CEO knows that the more successful he makes his company, the more likely he is to get a pay raise or a higher bonus. A CEO will take on projects or business ventures for a company that have the best possibility of succeeding and being profitable, knowing that his wallet stands to benefit as well.

bonus: A financial incentive given to employees in addition to their base pay in the form of a one-time payment.

The SEC requires every public company and some private companies to disclose information about their operations to investors. This disclosure of information includes the compensation packages of top executives. Increasingly, the disclosure of this information is becoming a major business story because of some of the examples of excess described at the beginning of this chapter. The Obama administration also moved in 2009 to limit executive compensation at companies that accepted bailout money during the economic crisis.

A business reporter can find this salary information in several places. Every year, public companies send a filing called a proxy, or a DEF 14A filing, to every registered shareholder of that company about six weeks before the annual meeting. A separate voter card asks shareholders to vote on various items detailed in the proxy. This mailing typically happens in late February or early March for companies whose fiscal year coincides with the calendar year. A business reporter should check with the companies that he or she tracks to see when they expect to release the proxy. Often, the proxy contains news that the reporter's newspaper will want in the next day's business section.

Typically, several members of the board of directors are up for election. Board members are often elected in staggered terms, so the majority of a board rarely changes in a year. Often, companies will ask shareholders to approve executive option plans. Typically, companies also ask shareholders to vote against proxy proposals presented by dissident shareholders—such as unions—that they think could limit executive control over the company's affairs. A common dissident shareholder proposal is to ask a company to

TIPS FROM THE PROS

Crain's New York Business senior reporter Aaron Elstein on covering executive compensation:

Read the compensation table to get a list of the company's five best-paid people. Does this list include anyone who you wouldn't expect to get paid as much (or more) than the CEO? However, the table that reads "total compensation" is not the true number for the executives' total pay. To get that figure, you must go further into the proxy and look up the value of the stock and options that were granted to the executive during the year and add that figure to the "total compensation." The easiest solution is to ask a service like Equilar or Salary.com, which are research firms that crunch pay data for a living, to tell you what their reading is of the numbers.

increase the number of outside directors on the board and decrease the number of company executives on the board. This information can often result in good stories for business reporters.

The following story shows how Larry Thomas of *Furniture Today* looked at how a dissident shareholder tried to take over the board of furniture maker Ethan Allen Incorporated:

Final vote totals from the proxy battle at Ethan Allen show that four of the company's seven existing directors each received about 59% of the shareholder vote, while one of dissident shareholder Sandell Asset Management's six nominees captured nearly 39%.

In a filing with the Securities and Exchange Commission, the company confirmed that all seven current directors were re-elected, and said board member John Dooner Jr. received the most shareholder votes at 15,859,730.

proxy statement: A document sent to shareholders of public companies to invite owners of the company's stock to its annual meeting. The proxy statement will include information about proposals to be voted on at the annual meeting and executive salaries.

The company's newest directors, Tara Stacom and Domenick Esposito, were close behind with 15,859,436 votes and 15,859,407 votes, respectively.

Longtime Chairman, President and CEO Farooq Kathwari was next with 15,832,466 shares voted in his favor.

The votes for the four each represented about 59% of the 26.8 million shares that were voted at the Nov. 24 annual meeting.

The highest vote total for any of Sandell's six nominees was 10.35 million, or about 38.6% of the shares voted, captured by Ken Pilot, former president of retailer ABC Carpet & Home.

Sandell, who owns about 5.5% of Ethan Allen's stock, issued a statement Tuesday promising to "maintain vigilant oversight" and claimed that more than 50% of the shares not directly or indirectly owned by Kathwari supported the dissident shareholder's effort.

According to the company's proxy statement, Kathwari controls about 11.2% of Ethan Allen's shares.

"Contrary to the company's claims of 'overwhelming' support for the Ethan Allen slate, these voting results demonstrate a far-reaching desire for substantive change from the shareholder base," Sandell's statement read. "This widespread expression of discontent should not go unheeded by the board, particularly considering that any shareholder or group of shareholders has the ability to call a special meeting by written request of shareholders owning 20% of the company's outstanding shares."[1]

There is increasing shareholder agitation and shareholders may be proposing more limits on company control of selecting auditors and determining executive compensation in future years. A knowledge of SEC filings and proxy statements is important to find such proposals, as they should be written about every time a business reporter finds them in a proxy.

TIPS FROM THE PROS

Crain's New York Business senior reporter Aaron Elstein on covering executive compensation:

Companies must disclose the perks they dole out to execs and the dollar value of these items. They can include personal use of the corporate jet, car and driver, help with preparing their taxes, a burglar alarm at their home, a fancy apartment, etc. These goodies are typically broken out in footnotes to the compensation table. Read the footnotes carefully, because this is where this juicy stuff lies.

There is plenty of other information in a proxy filing to interest business readers. Most business reporters immediately turn to the compensation chart of a proxy when they receive it. How much a CEO's salary or bonus rose or fell in the past year is obviously news. The hard part is deciphering the numbers and explaining them to readers, who also want to know this information but do not have access to the proxy, or to investors who have not yet received their proxy.

stock options: A stock option is the opportunity, given by your employer, to purchase a certain number of shares of your company's common stock at a pre-established price, known as the grant price, during a specific period of time, known as the vesting period.

Compensation stories are among the most widely read in the business section. Executives at other companies want to know what their counterparts are making down the street. Employees of the company want to know what their boss is pulling in. And company shareholders want to know whether the executive is worth his salary. This can often be determined by comparing the percentage increase or decrease in the CEO's compensation package in any given year with the percentage increase or decrease in the company's stock price for the same year. What most investors would like to see is an executive's total compensation package—his salary, bonus, stock options and other pay—change somewhat in line with how the company performed for the year. For example, if a CEO's pay increased 75 percent during a year in which the company's stock price fell 40 percent and profits dropped 50 percent, an investor is likely to be upset and could ask questions at the annual meeting.

In recent years, the SEC has made changes to the disclosure requirements of proxy statements, making it easier for reporters to ascertain how much an executive was paid. Previously, a journalist would have to add up each part of the compensation package to obtain the total compensation amount. That sometimes led to mistakes. Now, companies have to disclose a total compensation amount. Still, there can be some differences in how total compensation is reported. The Associated Press, for example, issued guidelines in 2008 in which it said its stories would calculate executive compensation differently from what is provided in the compensation table in a proxy statement.

In addition, the new SEC rules provide more information for reporters. There is better disclosure as to how an executive's bonus was determined and more complete disclosure of all of the stock options that an executive holds. There's also more information about how much an executive would be paid if he left the company and how much he receives in his pension plan.

The proxy is the only place in which public companies annually release executive compensation. It explains who is making the big bucks, how much of a bonus was awarded in the past year and whether stock options were granted. A category called "All Other Compensation" is often the most interesting section.

Figure 9.3 is an example of what one of these charts looks like, taken from News Corporation's 2015 proxy statement. News Corporation is the parent company of business journalism outlets such as the *Wall Street Journal,* MarketWatch.com, Dow Jones Newswires and *Barron's.*

Summary Compensation Table for the Fiscal Year Ended June 30, 2015

The following table sets forth information with respect to total compensation for the fiscal years ended June 30, 2015, June 30, 2014 and June 30, 2013, respectively, for the Company's NEOs.

Name and Principal Position	Fiscal Year	Salary[a]	Bonus	Stock Awards[b]	Option Awards	Non-Equity Incentive Plan Compensation	Change in Pension Value and Nonqualified Deferred Compensation Earnings[c]	All Other Compensation[d]	Total
K. Rupert Murdoch Executive Chairman	2015	$1,000,000	$ -	$2,067,675	$ -	$ 2,000,000	$ -	$ -	$ 5,067,675
	2014	$1,000,000	$ -	$5,019,258	$ -	$ 2,681,333	$ -	$ -	$ 8,700,591
	2013	$ -	$ -	$ -	$ -	$ -	$ -	$ -	$ -
Robert J. Thomson Chief Executive Officer	2015	$2,000,000	$ -	$4,445,521	$ -	$ 3,000,000	$ 475,466	$ 373,280	$10,294,267
	2014	$2,000,000	$ -	$7,215,209	$ -	$ 2,681,333	$ 314,434	$ 255,040	$12,466,016
	2013	$ 992,308	$1,000,000	$ -	$ -	$ -	$ 616,476	$ 52,679	$ 2,661,463
Bedi Ajay Singh Chief Financial Officer	2015	$1,200,000	$ -	$1,654,143	$ -	$ 1,500,000	$ 128,469	$ 156,104	$ 4,638,716
	2014	$1,100,000	$ -	$2,760,596	$ -	$ 1,340,667	$ 80,489	$ 128,009	$ 5,409,761
	2013	$ 655,769	713,425	$ 496,499	$ -	$ -	$ 58,282	$ 163,467	$ 2,087,442
David B. Pitofsky General Counsel	2015	$ 854,808 [e]	$ -	$ 413,531	$ -	$ 750,000	$ -	$ 31,022	$ 2,049,361
Gerson Zweifach Former General Counsel	2015	$ 937,500 [f]	$ -	$1,145,960 [g]	$ -	$ -	$ -	$ -	$ 2,083,460
	2014	$1,500,000 [f]	$ -	$ -	$ -	$ -	$ -	$ -	$ 1,500,000

Figure 9.3 Executive Compensation

TIPS FROM THE PROS

Crain's New York Business senior reporter Aaron Elstein on covering executive compensation:

Obviously executive pay lends itself to outrage, but you can't judge pay in a vacuum. You have to look at how the company fared compared to prior years. How did its stock price perform? And what kind of company is this? By that, I mean is a place run by a founder/entrepreneur rewarding himself for taking a chance years ago? Or is management a bunch of guys milking a business that was successful before they took over? Did the company grow fast—and boost the CEO's pay—based on a merger that isn't panning out? Asking questions like that along the way will give your story depth.

A number of potential stories should jump out at even the first-time proxy reader when looking at this table. For one, the CEO's total compensation declined in the last year. Another story would be that Robert Thomson, the chief executive officer, made twice as much money as the executive chairman of the entire company, Rupert Murdoch, who is the largest shareholder. The compensation committee report before the chart, not shown in Figure 9.3, explains why Thomson is being paid so much money. In this case, the $4.4 million in stock awards was because of the performance of the company.

After reading enough proxy statements, the reporter will begin to establish some patterns. One is that many companies give stock options to their executives as part of their compensation packages. The stock options are a way of providing an incentive to the CEO and other executives to improve the company's performance, which should lead to a higher stock price—and higher assets for the CEO.

chief executive officer: The person with overall responsibility for ensuring that the daily operations of a company run efficiently, and for carrying out strategic plans. The chief executive normally sits on the board.

Consider a fictitious company called ACME Inc. ACME's compensation committee decides to give its executives some stock options. The CEO is granted 100,000 stock options, allowing him to purchase the stock at $25 per share. He typically has a certain amount of time, perhaps 10 years, to exercise those options at $25 per share, regardless of how high the stock is valued. What the CEO wants to do is exercise his options and buy the stock when it is at a price much higher than $25 per share because he will only be paying the prearranged $25 price. He wants to do this because if he can get

ACME's stock price up to $50 per share, those 100,000 shares of stock are now worth $5 million. Mr. CEO will spend $2.5 million to buy those shares at $25 per share, on the basis of the agreement struck with the compensation committee. He has just pocketed a profit of $2.5 million, minus taxes, in this transaction. Many times, executives turn around and sell the stock at the higher price immediately after exercising the options. That is a story for a business reporter.

Of course, the opposite often happens. The CEO and other executives can be unsuccessful in raising the stock price above the option price, making the options worthless. Who would purchase stock for $25 per share if it were trading at $15 per share? However, companies sometimes change the stock option agreement, lowering the price at which executives can purchase shares. This upsets investors and should be front-page news.

It is also significant when the options expire. If the expiration date is coming up soon and the company's shares have not yet reached the option price level, the CEO may seek to find another company willing to purchase the entire company at a price tag above the option price. That way, he or she can exercise the options before they expire.

TIPS FROM THE PROS

Crain's New York Business senior reporter Aaron Elstein on covering executive compensation:

There is a large industry of consultants who help boards set executive pay. Frederick W. Cook, Towers Perrin, Mercer, and Pearl Meyer & Associates are the biggest. Similarly, there are growing groups of shareholders who feel pay has gotten detached from reality—the AFL-CIO, AFSCME, the Carpenters Union, and the like. It's worth trying to get the opinions/input of all these parties, but you should be aware of the agendas each brings. Similarly, there firms such as RiskMetrics, Glass Lewis, and Proxy Governance that advise mutual funds and other big investors how to vote at annual stockholder meetings, and these research firms often have much to say in their reports about a company's pay practices.

It is important to know whether executives are exercising options. If they are not exercising options when the exercise price is below the current price, that is a sign that they feel more comfortable putting their money elsewhere. Later, this chapter examines how to find out if an executive is buying or selling stock. These items are of particular interest because options are a way for companies to pay their executives additional "compensation" in addition to salary and bonuses. Shareholder rights activists also criticize large stock option awards to executives as being excessive because company executives are already being paid multimillion-dollar compensation packages.

Companies also give executives what is called restricted stock. Restricted stock has more limits than stock options. Most companies that give executives restricted stock set limits that the executive cannot sell the stock prior to retirement. If the executive leaves the company before retirement age, the restricted stock is forfeited. In most cases, however, the executive receives dividends paid on the stock, despite the fact he or she does not actually control the stock. The granting of restricted stock and stock options to executives often adds millions of dollars to an executive's compensation package. That is news.

restricted stock: A restricted stock award is a grant of stock by an employer to an employee in which the employee's rights to the shares are limited until the shares "vest" and cease to be subject to the restrictions. Typically, the employee may not sell or transfer the shares of stock until they vest—frequently a defined period of time—and forfeits the stock if the employee's employment terminates before the stock vests.

A reporter should look elsewhere in the proxy for explanations about compensation and why executives are receiving stock options and restricted stock. A reporter's best bet is what is called the "Compensation Committee Report." The compensation committee is composed of board members. This report on executive compensation is usually found with the chart on executive compensation. A reporter should look for the report from the members of the board of directors who sit on the compensation committee and who decide how much or how little executives get paid.

For example, the News Corporation compensation committee report informs readers of the following accomplishments by Thomson:

- Led the execution of the largest acquisition to date for the Company, Move, with early positive results against the strategic plan. Leveraging the power of the News Corp audience, realtor.com® has delivered several months of record traffic and enhanced audience engagement, and is now the fastest growing real estate website in the U.S.
- Provided exceptional leadership as evidenced by the successful and seamless integration of Harlequin and Move and the turnaround of the Dow Jones professional information businesses
- Continued to deliver on strategic plan of globalization and digitization through a series of complementary acquisitions and investments in Australia and throughout Asia that have enhanced the breadth and depth of monetization opportunities across the region
- Continued relentless focus on reducing costs—renegotiated newsprint contracts in Australia leading to significant savings and consolidated

> U.K. headquarter locations for News UK, HarperCollins and Dow Jones, improving collaboration opportunities and positioning the Company for reduced expense in future years. (News Corporation, Form DEF 14A, 2015, p. 24)

Thomson's bonus, while already large in 2015, actually decreased from the previous year. A story written about the News Corporation proxy might begin the following way:

> The chief executive officer of News Corporation, the parent of *The Wall Street Journal*, received a lower bonus in 2015 due to the company's struggles with the changing media landscape, according to a proxy statement filed by parent News Corporation with regulators.

Sweetheart Deals and Board Members

Another eyebrow-raising section of the proxy, normally found right after the list of the members of the board of directors, is a section called "Certain Relationships and Related Transactions." It details business relationships between board members and the company. For example, if a board member is an attorney, this section will detail, in dollar amounts, how much the company is paying his or her law firm in annual fees.

Herb Allen is an investment banker in New York, and his firm Allen & Company does work for the Coca-Cola Company. In this section of the 2015 proxy, the company discloses that relationship:

> Herbert A. Allen, one of our Directors, is President, Chief Executive Officer and a Director of Allen & Company Incorporated ("ACI") and a principal shareowner of ACI's parent. ACI is an indirect equity holder of Allen & Company LLC ("ACL").
>
> ACI has leased and subleased office space since 1977 in a building owned by one of our subsidiaries and located at 711 Fifth Avenue, New York, New York. In June 2005, ACI assigned the lease and sublease to ACL. In 2014, ACL paid approximately $5.5 million in rent and related expenses. In the opinion of management, the terms of the lease are fair and reasonable and as favorable to the Company as those that could have been obtained from unrelated third parties at the time of the execution of the lease.
>
> (Coca-Cola Company, Form DEF 14A, 2015, p. 39)

On its own, this is probably not something worth reporting, given that Allen & Company has done work for Coca-Cola for decades. (A business reporter can look this up by going back and reading old proxies.) Still, it is worth remembering should the reporter run across a story involving Coca-Cola and its investment bankers.

The section in Coca-Cola's proxy detailing its relationships with Warren Buffett's companies is more detailed. Buffett is chairman of Berkshire Hathaway, an Omaha company that owns dozens of companies, from carpet makers to jewelers. Part of the disclosure states the following:

> The father of Howard G. Buffett, one of our Directors, is Warren E. Buffett, the Chairman of the Board, Chief Executive Officer and major stockholder of Berkshire Hathaway. Berkshire Hathaway's holdings constituted 9.16% of the Company's outstanding Common Stock as of March 2, 2015.
>
> Berkshire Hathaway Specialty Insurance Company ("BHSI") is a wholly owned subsidiary of Berkshire Hathaway. In May 2014, the Company and BHSI entered into a one-year insurance contract under which BHSI provides the Company and one of its subsidiaries with insurance covering property on a primary basis. In 2014, the Company and the subsidiary paid an aggregate of approximately $269,000 to BHSI for insurance coverage in the ordinary course of business.
>
> Business Wire, Inc. ("Business Wire") is a wholly owned subsidiary of Berkshire Hathaway. In July 2013, the Company and Business Wire entered into a new two-year services agreement under which Business Wire disseminates news releases for the Company. In 2014, the Company paid approximately $274,000 to Business Wire to disseminate news releases for the Company in the ordinary course of business. This business relationship was in place prior to Berkshire Hathaway's acquisition of Business Wire in 2006.
>
> FlightSafety International Inc. ("FlightSafety") is a wholly owned subsidiary of Berkshire Hathaway. In 2014, the Company entered into a new five-year agreement with FlightSafety to provide pilot training services to the Company and a new three-year agreement with FlightSafety to provide flight attendant and mechanic training services to the Company. In 2014, the Company paid FlightSafety approximately $762,000 for these training services provided to the Company in the ordinary course of business.
>
> International Dairy Queen, Inc. ("IDQ") is a wholly owned subsidiary of Berkshire Hathaway. In 2014, IDQ and its subsidiaries received promotional and marketing incentives from the Company totaling approximately $2.0 million in the ordinary course of business. This business relationship was in place for many years prior to Berkshire Hathaway's acquisition of IDQ.
>
> McLane Company, Inc. ("McLane") is a wholly owned subsidiary of Berkshire Hathaway. In 2014, McLane and its subsidiaries paid approximately $213 million to the Company to purchase fountain syrup and other products in the ordinary course of business. Also in 2014, McLane received from the Company approximately $5.2 million in agency commissions, marketing payments and other fees relating to the sale of the

Company's products to customers in the ordinary course of business. This business relationship was in place for many years prior to Berkshire Hathaway's acquisition of McLane in 2003.

(Coca-Cola Company, Form
DEF 14A, 2015, p. 39)

Again, all of these relationships between Coca-Cola and Buffett's companies seem legitimate. But this section of the proxy is required reading for any business reporter because it could detail business dealings that might raise questions. A reporter will also find interesting transactions such as the one below, which was detailed in Progressive Corporation's 2000 proxy. At the time this document was filed, Peter Lewis was the company's CEO.

On April 23, 1999, the Company sold its corporate airplane, a Canadair Challenger 601–1 A, to a company independently owned by Peter B. Lewis. The airplane was sold to Mr. Lewis for $12.1 million, the fair market value as determined by JetPerspectives, Inc., an independent aircraft appraiser. The net book value of the airplane was $6.9 million at the date of the sale. Operation of the airplane is supported by two pilots and a mechanic, who are employees of a subsidiary of the Company. Mr. Lewis reimburses the Company for the salaries and all other payroll costs of such employees and pays directly or reimburses the Company for all operating and other costs that the Company incurs in connection with the storage, maintenance, use and operation of the airplane. The Company reimburses Mr. Lewis at the rate of $3,567 per hour, the air charter rate for comparable aircraft (based on the quotes obtained from three air charter companies selected by JetPerspectives, Inc.), for his use of the airplane on Company-related business or as a member of the Board of Directors.

(Progressive Corporation, Form
DEF 14A, 2000, p. 5)

TIPS FROM THE PROS

 Crain's New York Business senior reporter Aaron Elstein on covering executive compensation:

Always give the company a chance to explain itself when doing an exec pay story. Call the company, but also reach out to the compensation-committee members of the board. Most of the time, the company and its directors will refuse to talk to you, which of course gives you more room to write on your own. But when they do talk, you invariably hear something interesting.

This seems like a reasonable arrangement, at least at first reading. The statement clarifies the relationship between the company and the CEO in case questions should arise regarding the airplane sale. But an inquisitive reporter may want to make a few phone calls on the value of this model of airplane and the going rate for chartering planes.

Health care provider Aetna Incorporated also disclosed some interesting relationships among board member Leonard Abramson and his relatives in its 2000 proxy statement.

> A subsidiary of the Company paid Richard Wolfson, a son-in-law of Mr. Abramson, $150,469 under an independent contractor agreement for services rendered in 1999.
>
> During 1999, the Company and its subsidiaries paid $7,068,958 to Criterion Communications, Inc. pursuant to a service agreement. Marcy Shoemaker (a daughter of Mr. Abramson) owns 100 percent of the outstanding voting securities of Criterion.
>
> (Aetna Incorporated, Form DEF 14A, 2000, p. 16)

This may be a story. Such financial arrangements smack of nepotism at its worst. And when Abramson resigned from the board, these relationships were reported in an Associated Press story and in a *Philadelphia Inquirer* story. The fourth paragraph of the *Inquirer* story stated the following:

> Abramson's two daughters and son-in-law also were paid more than $18 million by the insurer since 1996, according to the Associated Press, which cited financial statements filed by the company with the U.S. Securities and Exchange Commission.
>
> (Stark, 2000)

Later, the story quotes shareholders criticizing the consulting fee arrangements. Other sections of the proxy can provide clues as to how much power certain board members have. It is important to see which board members belong to which committees. Membership on certain committees, such as the compensation committee, can result in abuses of power.

It is also important for a business writer to review the "Chart of Principal Ownership," which lists the largest shareholders of the company. The list should include the number of shares owned by every board member, every top executive and the largest institutional investors. The more shares owned by a board member, the more power he or she is likely to wield at meetings.

The company CEO or a former CEO should be, typically, one of the largest individual shareholders. In addition, board members should increase their stock ownership annually. A reporter should check the stock ownership chart for the current year with the one from the previous year to determine if board members are buying more stock. If they are not, then maybe they should be asked why. If a board member's stock holdings are going up, that could indicate a bullish future.

This chart is also valuable for another reason. It lists the largest shareholders who are not company executives or board members. Reporters should call them if the company implodes. Sometimes the footnotes of this section contain home addresses for these shareholders, which should help reporters dig up some phone numbers for them.

Insider Trading

Ask the average person on the street about insider trading, and he will make the uninformed comment that it is immoral and that the government should step in and be more aggressive in prosecuting cases. Many people probably know that home maven Martha Stewart was convicted of perjury in an investigation into insider trading of ImClone stock based on a tip she might have gotten from the company's former CEO, Sam Waksal, who stepped down from the company and pleaded guilty to insider trading.

What people do not realize is that more than 99 percent of all insider trading is perfectly legal. And insider trading records are an excellent way for a business reporter to assess what a company executive, board member or investor thinks about a company.

According to the rules used by the SEC to govern investing, an insider is defined as an officer or director of a public company or an individual or entity owning 10 percent or more of any class of a company's shares. In Martha Stewart's case, she would be considered an insider because she allegedly received information from an insider—Waksal—and acted upon that information.

Form 4: A document required by the SEC to announce changes in the holdings of directors, officers and shareholders owning 10 percent or more of the company's outstanding stock.

Those executives, board members and institutional investors are allowed to buy and sell stock in these companies as long as they file a Form 4 with the SEC following the transaction. If an insider buys or sells stock in the open market, he or she must file with the SEC by the tenth day of the month following such a trade. Insider trading becomes illegal when the executive, director or outside investor buys or sells stock in the company on the basis of nonpublic information that is, or could be, considered material in nature—generally anything that would require the company to file a Form 8-K, covered in Chapter 6.

For example, if an executive at Pep Boys told an investor in December 2015 that the company would be acquired by investor Carl Icahn before the deal was announced, and the investor bought the stock with the intention of profiting from this information, the feds would be coming after him or her with handcuffs.

The following is the type of story that most casual business section readers equate with insider trading:

> Investor John D. Weil of St. Louis has agreed to pay $93,424 to settle an insider trading suit brought by the Securities and Exchange Commission.
>
> The SEC alleged that Weil had profited illegally from a tip that Kaye Group Inc., an insurance brokerage based in New York, might be acquired.
>
> Without admitting or denying the allegations, Weil agreed to give up $46,712 in profits and pay a civil fine of an equal amount. Weil could not be reached for comment.
>
> David Horowitz, assistant district administrator for the SEC in Philadelphia, said the NASDAQ Stock Market became aware of suspicious trading in Kaye's stock as part of its normal surveillance process. The NASDAQ then alerted the SEC, he said. According to the SEC, Weil learned in late November or early December of 2000 that another company was interested in buying Kaye Group. The information came from Ned L. Sherwood, a director of Kaye Group.
>
> The SEC says that Weil, who owned 10 percent of Kaye Group's stock, talked regularly with Sherwood about the company, and had assured Sherwood that the conversations were confidential.
>
> Using brokerage accounts in his future wife's name, Weil bought 7,400 shares of Kaye Group between Dec. 28, 2000, and Jan. 17, 2001, at prices ranging from $7.44 to $7.94 a share.
>
> Kaye Group announced on Jan. 20, 2001, that it had accepted a $14-a-share buyout offer from Hub International Ltd., another insurance brokerage. The SEC also accused Rand E. Shapiro of Orlando, Fla., of making $35,804 in illegal profits on Kaye Group's stock. Shapiro's inside information came from another director, Howard A. Kaye, the SEC said. Like Weil, Shapiro agreed to settle the charges, return his profits and pay a fine.
>
> The Kaye Group directors weren't accused of wrongdoing because they thought their conversations were confidential, and they didn't expect anyone to trade on the information, Horowitz said.
>
> The SEC's allegations were included in a civil lawsuit filed Tuesday in federal court in Orlando.[2]

insider trading: Trading in securities by executives, board members or large shareholders. When insider trading is based on privileged information, it is illegal.

These stories are valuable and important to write when covering business news. But the facts for such stories do not come from SEC filings. Instead, they come from an SEC complaint, which is often available on the agency's website at www.sec.gov. Again, virtually all stock trades done by company executives, board members or other investors are perfectly legitimate and typically are not worth writing about. But it is a story if a board member or company executive is selling the majority of his or her stock holdings in the company or buying a large chunk of stock.

There are legitimate reasons for an executive or board member to sell stock. It might be time to pay for junior's college tuition. Or maybe he is buying a vacation home. It might even be time to diversify the investment portfolio and not hold too much of his net worth in one stock. These are all valid reasons for an insider to sell stock. But business reporters should watch for insider selling. When it happens, a reporter should call the company to find out why. If the executive can give a good reason for selling, then it is not likely a story. But if there is no good reason, it might mean that he does not think the price is going to get higher anytime soon. Executives know more about the future prospects of a company than anyone else. Also, reporters should watch for executives buying large amounts of company stock. That could be an indication that these executives think good things about the company's future prospects and believe the stock price is going higher sooner rather than later. Now, where can a reporter find this information? Again, the SEC comes to the rescue.

TIPS FROM THE PROS

Crain's New York Business senior reporter Aaron Elstein on covering executive compensation:

Most companies hold annual "say-on-pay" votes at their annual meetings. Dodd-Frank made them do this. The vote gives shareholders the chance to say whether they approve of the company's pay practices, but really what it's about is measuring how dissatisfied investors are with management. In most cases, the vote is no big deal. The vote is non-binding, which means board members are free to ignore the outcome. But sometimes these votes are very revealing. Citigroup dismissed its CEO a little while after investors voted down his pay package. ISS and Glass Lewis spend a lot of time analyzing pay practices at different companies and recommend how investors should vote, and these are the first places reporters should turn to for insight. Many companies announce the result in a press release, but if they don't, the way to find it is to turn to the company's 10-Q that covers the period during which the annual meeting was held. In there, you'll find an item disclosing the say-on-pay vote along with other matters taken up at the annual meeting. Also, a research firm called Georgeson publishes a useful review every year that contains every shareholder vote taken at annual meetings, including the say-on-pay votes. Finally, if you want to know how a particular mutual fund voted, you can find that out, although not until many months after the fact. The form that funds use to disclose this information is called, dreadfully, an N-PX, and you can find them by searching the SEC's Edgar database.

It should be noted that business reporters might be tempted to act on information they find and buy stock. This must be avoided, because it will likely result in the reporter being fired from his job. No media outlet allows its reporters to actively buy and sell stocks of companies they are reporting on.

The SEC requires executives, board members and other investors to disclose their transactions in a variety of forms. The Form 4 is a two-page document filed by directors, officers or owners of more than 10 percent of the stock in a company. The report contains information on planned purchases and sales of certain equity securities. The form also contains information on the reporting person's relationship to the company. In addition, the form will disclose whether shares were bought or sold, how many shares were bought or sold and the price. The form will also state how many shares the person still owns.

Reading these forms can be valuable because they also typically contain street addresses for the filer. If a reporter is having trouble tracking down a company board member, this form can help. Sometimes, however, executives or board members simply use the company's mailing address when they file Form 4s. Another problem for reporters in tracking these trades is that insiders have until the tenth day of the month following their trades to file their Form 4. By that time, the conditions causing the buying or selling may have changed.

Anytime a reporter is writing a story about a company's strategy or the CEO, it is wise to check insider trading. If CEOs gush about a new product or a change in a company that is expected to produce better results, they should be willing to put their money where their mouth is. If a CEO is not buying his or her own company's stock on the basis of those prospects, a reporter should ask why.

Watching insider trading is also helpful in a broader sense. Wall Street experts who track insider trading want to know if more buying than selling is occurring. If that is the case, it may be an indication that the broader stock market could be headed higher.

The following is part of a story that documents insider trading by investors:

A number of institutional investors have been adding to their positions in Trenwick in recent months, according to SEC filings. During the third quarter, New York-based Jennison Associates LLC purchased more than 1 million shares. Trainer Wortham & Co., another New York-based money manager, purchased more than 686,000 shares. Over the same period, Memphis-based New South Capital Management Inc. added to its position as Trenwick's largest institutional investor, purchasing an additional 457,915 shares. New South, a longterm investor in the company, now owns more than 3.5 million shares.

More recently, Lord Abbett & Co. purchased more than 240,000 shares in the fourth quarter, bringing its total holdings in Trenwick to more than 1 million shares. The Teacher Retirement System of Texas bought 97,000, bringing its total position to 240,000 shares. And Palisade Capital added 43,400 shares to its position.

According to the most recent SEC filings for the firms, only two of Trenwick's top 10 institutional shareholders have lowered their holdings in the past six months. In the third quarter, Reich & Tang sold 51,525 shares, less than 4.0% of its total holdings. New York-based Royce & Associates Inc. trimmed 289,600 shares from its Trenwick holdings in the fourth quarter, but the firm still owns more than 905,000 shares.

Yet as Trenwick's market capitalization nears $1.0 billion, the company still attracts little interest from the sell-side analyst community on Wall Street. Three of the five analysts who follow Trenwick currently give it a "hold" rating.[3]

This is the kind of insider trading activity that readers of business stories want to know about but quite often do not have the time to look up themselves. If reporters can provide more such information in their stories, they will better serve their readers. In addition, they will show company executives that they know the most meaningful measure of performance—whether investors are willing to buy stock. An increase or decrease in these filings can be an indicator of what Wall Street pros think about a certain stock.

There are several other important filings about stock trades worth noting, although they do not directly involve company executives or board members. Investors who are not connected to a company are also required to file documents with the SEC when they purchase and sell company stock.

Schedule 13D: A form filed by anyone acquiring a beneficial ownership of 5 percent or more of any equity security registered with the SEC. The form must also be filed with the exchange on which the stock is traded.

A Schedule 13D is filed when a shareholder or a group of shareholders acquires more than 5 percent of a company's stock. These filings must be made within the first 10 days of the investment. In addition, someone filing a 13D typically wants to effect a change at the company. These are most often disgruntled shareholders. Because investors have to file a 13D when they acquire 5 percent of a company's stock, many times they will purchase shares up to 4.9 percent so that other investors do not know of their interest in the company, which might drive the price up.

There is another form that is also important for business reporters. The SEC notes when institutional investors and professional investors acquire stock in the course of their business and not with the idea of changing the control of the company. When this happens, an institutional investor files a Schedule 13G. A Schedule 13G must also be filed within 10 days of the end of the quarter when the transaction occurred. Even though it is not filed as quickly as some other documents, a 13G can still provide good information.

 Schedule 13G: A form filed by any party acquiring a beneficial ownership of 5 percent of more of any stock registered with the SEC.

How much of a treasure trove are these files? Schedule 13Gs and Schedule 13Ds typically include the name of the investor's company, how many shares were purchased, purchase dates and prices and, quite often, the name and the phone number of someone at that institution who is in charge of the specific investment.

For example, consider the excerpt from the Schedule 13G below. A reporter found this filing while doing research for an article about American Physicians Capital Incorporated, a Michigan-based company. All the reporter had to do was look up the phone number for Greenlight Capital and get David Einhorn on the other end, who was more than happy to talk, even though he had never heard of or seen the publication for which the reporter was writing.

Item l(a) Name of Issuer. American Physicians Capital, Inc.

Item l(b) Address of Issuer's Principal Executive Offices. 1301 North Hagadorn Road, East Lansing, Michigan 48823

Item 2(a) Name of Person Filing. Greenlight Capital, L.L.C. ("Greenlight"), David Einhorn and Jeffrey A. Keswin.

Item 2(b) Address of Principal Business Office, or, if none, Residence. 420 Lexington Ave., Suite 1740, New York, New York 10170

Item 2(c) Citizenship or Place of Organization. Greenlight is a limited liability company organized under the laws of the State of Delaware. David Einhorn and Jeffrey A. Keswin are the principals of Greenlight and are United States citizens.

Item 2(d) Title of Class of Securities. Common Stock, no par value per share (the "Common Stock").

Item 2(e) CUSIP Number.

Item 3 Reporting Person. Inapplicable.

Item 4 Ownership. (a) Greenlight and Messrs. Einhorn and Keswin are the beneficial owners of 990,000 shares of Common Stock.

(b) Greenlight and Messrs. Einhorn and Keswin are the beneficial owners of 9.9 percent of the outstanding shares of Common Stock. This percentage is based upon the outstanding shares of the Issuer equaling 10,000,000 shares, the amount of shares initially offered in connection with the Issuers initial public offering (the "IPO"). Mr. Keswin has been informed that underwriters of the IPO have elected to subscribe for an additional amount of shares causing the outstanding shares to equal 11,450,254 as of December 14, 2000. Based on this revised number of outstanding shares, Greenlight's and Messrs. Einhorn's and Keswin's percentage ownership would be equal to 8.6 percent.

(c) Greenlight has the sole power to vote and dispose of the 990,000 shares of Common Stock beneficially owned by it. As the principals of Greenlight, Messrs. Einhorn and Keswin may direct the vote and disposition of the 990,000 shares of Common Stock beneficially owned by Greenlight.

(Greenlight Capital L.L.C., Schedule 13G, 2000)

The story was a look at American Physicians Capital's strategy for improving its performance. And, likely, the only person better to quote assessing that strategy than an investor who has purchased a large amount of stock in the company is the CEO himself. The valuable information in this filing that allowed the reporter to find Einhorn was the name of his company, Greenlight Capital, its mailing address and Einhorn's name. The reporter obtained the firm's phone number with a quick call to directory assistance.

Writing about company executives, boards and investors involves detailing one of the most fascinating relationships in business reporting. These people are all human, and they are all driven by certain factors. The CEO may be driven by the need to have power or by the desire to provide a good working environment for his employees and a favorable return for his investors. Board members are often driven by the same factors. Investors are driven by one factor—to make money. How the three interact often results in compelling stories.

Notes

1. From "SEC filing: Four Ethan Allen directors each get 59% of shareholder vote," by L. Thomas, December 2, 2015, *Furniture Today*. Copyright 2015 by *Furniture Today*. Reprinted with permission.
2. From "St. Louis investor John D. Weil settles SEC insider trading suit," by D. Nicklaus, December 14, 2002, *St. Louis Post-Dispatch*, p. 2. Copyright 2002 by *St. Louis Post-Dispatch*. Reprinted with permission.
3. From "Trenwick Group's growth spurt: The reinsurer has added new businesses through acquisition and is seeking more deals. Can CEO Jim Billett keep the stock price rising?" by C. Roush, March 2001, *Insurance Investor*, p. 1. Copyright 2001 by SNL Financial. Reprinted with permission.

Key Terms

board of directors	president or chief operating officer
bonus	proxy statement
chairman of the board	restricted stock
chief executive officer	Schedule 13D
Form 4	Schedule 13G
insider trading	stock options

Suggested Exercises

1. Review the organizational charts of two different companies. Write a 500-word analysis of why the organizational structures differ, focusing on job titles and who reports to whom, with emphasis on the relationship between the CEO, president and executive vice presidents or division presidents.
2. Review the executive compensation for a public company. Compare the bonus and salary increase for the CEO and president of the company to the increase in net income and stock price for the same fiscal year. Discuss why there may be a discrepancy between the compensation and the company's performance.
3. Examine a company's board of directors. List the directors who may be considered to have financial ties to the company and those who don't. Discuss whether the financial connections might have a bearing on the decisions made by the board member.
4. Review a list of the top shareholders for a company. Take 30 minutes to determine which shareholders are outside investors, which ones are board members and which ones are current or former executives. Compare the amount of stock held by board members to the amount of stock held by outside shareholders. Discuss whether a large outside shareholder deserves a seat on the board.
5. Examine the insider buying and selling by a single company's executives and board members for the past 12 months. Total the number of shares sold by the entire group to the number of shares purchased. Is the insider trading for the company in the past year a reflection of the company's future performance?

Books on CEOs and Management

Bossidy, L., & Charan, R. (2002). *Execution: The discipline of getting things done.* New York: Crown Publishing.

Charan, R. (1998). *Boards at work: How corporate boards create competitive advantage.* New York: Jossey-Bass.

Charan, R. (2001). *What the CEO wants you to know: How your company really works.* New York: Crown Publishing.

Collins, J. (2001). *Good to great: Why some companies make the leap . . . and others don't.* New York: Harper Collins.

Ellig, B. (2001). *The complete guide to executive compensation.* New York: McGraw-Hill.

Greising, D. (1999). *I'd like the world to buy a Coke: The life and leadership of Roberto Goizueta.* New York: Wiley.

Slater, R. (1998). *Jack Welch & the GE way: Management insights and leadership secrets of the legendary CEO.* New York: McGraw-Hill.

References

Aetna Incorporated. Form DEF 14A. (2000, March 22). (SEC Publication No. 0000914039–00–000119, pp. 15–16). Washington, DC: Securities and Exchange Commission.

Barnhart, B. (2002, January 8). Activist shareholders forcing change. *Chicago Tribune*, p. 8.

Coca-Cola Company. Form DEF 14A. (2015, March 12). (SEC Publication No. 0001308179–15–000041, p. 39). Washington, DC: Securities and Exchange Commission.

Greenlight Capital, L.L.C. Schedule 13G. (2000) (SEC Publication No. 0000941302–00–500113, pp. 1–6). Washington, DC: Securities and Exchange Commission.

McDowell, D. (2002, January 18). Confessions of a securities writer. TheStreet.com. Retrieved Sept. 15, 2002 from www.thestreet.com/funds.

News Corporation. Form DEF 14A. (2015, December 1). (SEC Publication No. 0001567619–15–001147, pp. 25–27). Washington, DC: Securities and Exchange Commission.

Nicklaus, D. (2002, December 14). St. Louis investor John D. Weil settles SEC insider trading suit. *St. Louis Post Dispatch*, p. 2.

Progressive Corporation. Form DEF 14A. (2000, March 16). (SEC Publication No. 0000950152–00–001752, pp. 4–5). Washington, DC: Securities and Exchange Commission.

Roush, C. (2001a, March). Trenwick Group's growth spurt: The reinsurer has added new businesses through acquisitions and is seeking more deals. Can CEO Jim Billett keep the stock price rising? *Insurance Investor*, p. 1.

Roush, C. (2001b, March). Bill Cheeseman enters the fray: The CEO of American Physicians Capital wants to buy other medical malpractice insurers. The line forms to the left. *Insurance Investor*, pp. 6–8.

Stark, K. (2000, June 8). Abramson quits Aetna Inc. board; he sold U.S. Healthcare to the insurer in 1996. *The Philadelphia Inquirer*, p. C1.

Thomas, L. (2015, December 2). SEC filing: Four Ethan Allen directors each get 59% of shareholder vote. *Furniture Today*. Retrieved December 31, 2015 from www.furnituretoday.com/article/526272-sec-filing-four-ethan-allen-directors-each-get-59-shareholder-vote.

Unger, H. (1999, December 7). Coke's shocker: Ivester retiring after 2 years under pressure. *Atlanta Journal-Constitution*, p. 1A.

Valdmanis, T., & Howard, T. (2000, November 22). Coke plan to buy Quaker for $16B stock collapses; Disagreement over price, strategic direction bring startling about-face. *USA Today*, p. 1E.

10

COVERING SMALL AND PRIVATE COMPANIES

A Vital Part of Local Economies

Private and small businesses are the backbone of the nation's economy. Without them, many towns and communities would not exist. They provide stable jobs for millions and help the economy grow—or remain stable when larger companies struggle or go out of business.

Yet read the nation's newspapers, Internet sites and magazines; listen to its radio; or watch its television news, and the bulk of the business coverage ignores small and private businesses. Part of the reason is that many reporters believe that these companies are too small to be making news or that they are not interesting enough.

At first glance, these reporters may be correct. Big companies whose products and services are used by millions around the country—and the world—have a bigger impact on more people. Small businesses do not sell products that have a huge impact.

But if a small business develops a product that is going to have an impact on a large part of the population, it will become one of those big companies. Bill Gates started his company in his garage, and now Microsoft is one of the biggest companies in the world, dominating the computer software industry. Wal-Mart started with one store. Coca-Cola started by selling its soft drinks at one drug store. Ford started by selling its first car. These companies were not created as multibillion-dollar operations with tens of thousands of workers. They began as tiny operations with dreams of becoming something bigger.

TIPS FROM THE PROS

RichmondBizSense.com and BusinessDen.com founder Aaron Kremer on covering small businesses:

Moxie: Entrepreneurs are dreamers and tinkerers who pour their heart and soul into their projects—often at the expense of their families and stable careers. That gives you a tremendous hook, akin to an athlete who has prepared his whole life to make it to the pros.

The other argument against covering small and private businesses in the media is that it is tough to find objective information about them. Virtually no private and few small companies are required to file financial information with the SEC, for example, that would reveal their revenues and profits. When the CEO of a small company says that his or her company's revenues grew by 50 percent in the past year, it would seem that a reporter has no way of verifying that information unless the executive shows him the books. But, there are plenty of ways to find financial information about small and private companies across the country. All it takes is some thinking and research, as this chapter will demonstrate. No company is completely private. And no business, no matter how small, leaves a cold trail. The reporting can be done. Many just do not know how to do it.

 TIPS FROM THE PROS

Public records for private companies. What to look for:

1. **Local government:** Real estate transaction records; register of deeds, health department records, planning department records, property appraiser or tax assessor; civil and criminal litigation.
2. **State government:** Secretary of state's office for incorporation records; Uniform Commercial Code (UCC) filings, economic development records; state legislature; professional licensing boards; state regulatory agencies for insurance and banking.
3. **Federal government:** Consumer Product Safety Commission (CPSC), Environmental Protection Agency (EPA), Equal Employment Opportunity Commission (EEOC) and OSHA for worksite-related records; FTC, Patent and Trademark Office and specific federal agencies for certain industries such as energy and aviation.

There is another, more important, reason why mass communication outlets should likely pay more attention to small and private businesses and the issues that affect their operations. As mentioned earlier, small and private businesses are vital to the economy. Labor Department data showing that businesses with fewer than 250 employees created more than half of the new jobs created since 2010 and most of those new jobs came from firms with fewer than 50 employees. In addition, 46.7 percent of all employees work for a company with fewer than 250 workers. And companies less than a year old are responsible for 23 percent of all new jobs.

Some media outlets—particularly those in large metropolitan areas—virtually ignore businesses that collectively employ more than half of the country's workforce and account for more than half of all private sector output. To be sure, a number of newspapers and other media outlets do have a reporter assigned to cover small business issues. And small-town newspapers, such as the *Statesville Record & Landmark* in western North Carolina, have a business reporter in a community where virtually all news is small business news. But for the most part, business journalism has overlooked many small and private businesses compared with the coverage of public companies and well-known private corporations.

 corporation: The most common form of business organization. The organization is ongoing, and the owners face limited liability.

This is despite the fact that Americans have a higher opinion of small businesses than they do of better-known corporations and labor unions, according to a survey by the American Enterprise Institute in Washington. Ninety percent of Americans have a favorable opinion of small business, according to the survey, and the figure has hovered between 84 and 94 percent for the last quarter century.

In comparison, the latest Harris poll showed that 66 percent of people have a great deal of or some confidence in labor unions. The confidence level for large companies was 72 percent.

Small businesses have been revered in this country for more than a century. When Congress first passed antitrust laws in the nineteenth century, it did so to protect small and private businesses. The U.S. Small Business Administration (SBA) was created in 1953 to aid and assist small companies.

Because of their collective interests, small businesses have grown into a powerful lobbying force in state legislatures and in Congress. The National Federation of Independent Business has 325,000 members and offices in all 50 states. Its lobbyists fight for small business rights with state and federal authorities.

The following story from MarketWatch.com shows how regulatory agencies have catered to small business interests in the past, with one notable exception:

Call it the red tape wars. Rules and regulations churned out by the government are the bane of most small businesses. For more than 20 years, they've fought a running battle with federal bureaucrats over the daunting process of complying with the edicts emanating from Washington.

Make no mistake; small businesses have won a significant round or two along the way. Yet the war continues in all its pencil-snapping frustration. The latest skirmish unfolded last week before the House Committee on Small Business. The target: the Internal Revenue Service.

By way of background, an armistice in the red tape wars was supposed to have been reached back in 1980. That's when the White House Conference on Small Business served as a catalyst for three significant new laws—the Regulatory Flexibility Act, the Equal Access to Justice Act and the Paperwork Reduction Act.

Together they were supposed to insure that government agencies took the concerns into account of anyone afflicted by federal rule making. The Regulatory Flexibility Act, in particular, was key. It exacted a pledge that agencies would study proposed regulations—before they were issued—to assess how they affected small businesses. The goal was to find ways to limit the impact, if regulation hit small firms disproportionately.

TIPS FROM THE PROS

RichmondBizSense.com and BusinessDen.com founder Aaron Kremer on covering small businesses:

Conflict: Business is by definition a competition. So there is built-in drama. Make sure to explain in stories where appropriate how the small business is gaining market share and what their plans may be to expand. One good question that usually gets a good quote is "What is the biggest challenge about what you're trying to do?" You can also try "What keeps you up at night?"

As we all know, no federal agency seems to pile on the paperwork quite like the IRS. Yet when it comes to complying with regulations itself, the nation's tax revenuers have proved to be particularly resistant to change. "If avoidance of the RFA has been the Service's implicit goal, they have been unquestionably successful; but for those who care about the efficacy of the RFA, the overall record has been dismal," said Dan Mastromarco, Principal of The Argus Group, a Phoenix, Ariz., company that provides insurance to small businesses.

Congress last tightened the RFA's legal standards in 1996, following a bruising four-year legislative battle. Perhaps not surprisingly, the IRS triggered the reform effort when it issued supposedly innocuous changes to the payroll tax deposit system. "What they put out as a proposed rule can best be described as gibberish," said former Congressman Andy Ireland, who was involved in the fight. "I couldn't understand it. And, when I went to testify at a hearing before the staff of the IRS Commissioner none of his people seemed to understand it," he told the committee. "Yet these same people were confident that the average small businessperson would have no problem complying."[1]

Writing about small and private businesses can be different than covering large, public companies. For one, many small and private businesses are not seeking publicity to help pump up their stock price. Many of them do not want a reporter poking around, looking for stories. Whereas many public companies have public relations personnel to handle media inquiries, most small and private businesses do not. When a reporter calls, the president or CEO often takes the call.

TIPS FROM THE PROS

The Dirty Dozen: 12 questions for the small or private business owner. Many small business owners are wary of questions from reporters, particularly when they've never been interviewed before. These questions will show the owner that you're genuinely interested in telling readers about his or her company.

1. Where did you get the idea to start your business? How does your background fit into the company idea?
2. How did you fund the business? Did the money come from savings or relatives?
3. How soon after you first opened your doors did your business make a profit? How did you celebrate?
4. What was the hardest obstacle to overcome in getting the business off the ground?
5. Whom do you consider to be your biggest competitor and why?
6. How have you grown the business? Has it been through advertising or customer recommendations?
7. Who is your biggest customer? What would you do if you lost that customer?
8. What is your best-selling item?
9. How would you react if a similar business opened nearby? How could you handle the increased competition?
10. How big do you foresee your company becoming in the next five years? In the next 10 years?
11. What would make you sell your business to another company?
12. How are your employees involved in the day-to-day decision making of the business?

Business reporters do not necessarily have to write stories about what is going on at small and private businesses to write stories that include them. A retail reporter writing about Christmas sales can call the private storeowner as well as the publicly traded department store chains and Wal-Mart. A banking reporter will want to write about how a private community bank is adding branches to compete against Bank of America and BankOne.

Private business owners and executives are sometimes willing to grant interviews to talk about the local and regional economy or to assess issues such as a shortage of experienced workers or how they will be affected by new laws. With each story, the reporter is not writing about the business but is gaining the trust of the small and private business owner or executive. Then, when news specifically about the company merits coverage, the owner will be more likely to open up.

Like most businesses, small and private companies need to understand the role of the media. Many of them expect to receive glowing or positive coverage, and when they do not get it, they are mad. Some of them may even believe that positive coverage is a quid pro quo in exchange for their advertising.

The reporter should make the ground rules clear. With any business story, the job of the reporter and of the media outlet is to inform the public. Some stories are written about small and private businesses if they are unique to the market. The *Door County Advocate* in Sturgeon Bay, Wisconsin, covered the opening of the first car wash in the county north of Sturgeon Bay. But that was because of its uniqueness—it was the only car wash for miles. It should be clear that the media outlet decides what is news.

Stories about small and private businesses can show how they are changing and evolving with the community. The *Southeast Missourian* in Cape Girardeau, Missouri, published a story about the influx of immigrant small business owners and international workers in a front-page story that helped explain to its readers why these businesses were opening around town.

TIPS FROM THE PROS

RichmondBizSense.com and BusinessDen.com founder Aaron Kremer on covering small businesses:

Color: Think about the characters involved and dig up the details that show the reader a glimpse of who they are. Often you can find a gem by asking them what their previous job was. Maybe they were mistreated. Or maybe they hated working for an incompetent boss. We always ask entrepreneurs, "What makes you think the market needs your product?"

Many small business reporters focus on issues and trends instead of profiling companies. They look at how small companies struggle to make it in the business world. They write about the decision to provide health insurance and other benefits to workers and how the cost of doing so can cripple a small operation. They write about the struggle of a small business owner to hand his operation to the next generation after 40 years of running the company. They assess the impact of the new Home Depot on the local hardware stores that have been part of the community for half a century.

Writing about small and private businesses can be fascinating because it forces the reporter to dig deeper into analyzing a company's situation. He or she cannot rely on SEC filings to provide the facts. He or she must interview competitors, customers and clients; assess the market; and look for clues as to why a small business is successful—or struggling to make ends meet.

The reporter should think of him- or herself as a small business. The reporter has revenue—a paycheck—and expenses, such as rent, electricity and gas, just like a small business. What is left over is used to expand operations by buying a new television or some furniture or even a new car. The more money left over from the paycheck, the more the reporter can expand his or her "business." But if there is no money left over, then the "business" is struggling and may have to go into debt to make ends meet. That may mean making purchases with credit cards or asking the bank for a loan to buy that car.

Small and private businesses operate much the same way. And when they struggle, they borrow money, too. If they continue to struggle, they may be forced to go out of business. If the reporter's financial situation continues to flounder, he or she, too, may be forced to go out of "business" and find a new job that pays more money.

Small and private businesses have ups and downs, just like any business. Those ups and downs can be news.

Finding Information

Many reporters mistakenly believe that private companies are just that—private. And while private companies rarely hand out information willingly about their operations, there are plenty of other places to get that information.

Reporters should consider what information would be good to know about a small or private business and then ask the company for that information. The CEO of watchmaker Timex once gave me the private company's revenues and profits for the most recent year because I asked. The largest private company in North Carolina provided me its revenues and profits for each year dating back to its founding in the 1930s. If the business declines to provide the information, then think about where that information might be found.

TIPS FROM THE PROS

RichmondBizSense.com and BusinessDen.com founder Aaron Kremer on covering small businesses:

Source work: The business owners all know each other, even in huge cities. The restaurateur with three spots around town is going to know the coffee shop proprietor, the sausage maker and the brewers. Think about sources in unglamorous fields. For example, we often call a firm in Richmond that installs and rents commercial kitchen equipment. Those guys are first to know every move in the restaurant industry.

Some private companies willingly give a range of revenue and profits to publications such as the local business journal. In other cases, revenue and earnings may be estimated on the basis of knowledge of the company's operations. When reporters use numbers like these, they must make sure to attribute them to the source.

Still, it is relatively easy to find information about small and private businesses if the company is not forthcoming. Government agencies are the best places to look for most of this information. Basic information about small and private companies, such as articles of incorporation, is filed with the secretary of state's office. The articles of incorporation will provide the names of the executives and owners, as well as phone numbers and mailing addresses. That is the first place to start when researching a small or private business. Sometimes the incorporation records may not be up to date, and maybe the state has listed the company as not in good standing. This could be a sign that the business is having financial trouble.

Another good place to find information is local government records. The local building department will have building permit and inspection records, for example. A county clerk or register of deeds will have information about real estate deeds, mortgage agreements and fictitious name registrations. The names may be important when a company is operating its business under one name but is incorporated at the state level under another name.

While at the courthouse, a reporter should not forget to check whether the business has been sued in the past. The reporter should read the lawsuits and check the names of the lawyers suing the company. The reporter should call them and ask about their dealings with the business. If there are a lot of lawsuits against a company in the last few months or year, that could be a sign that the business is having trouble paying its debts. Also check to see if the business is litigious itself and is filing lawsuits against others. Lawsuits can provide information about small and private businesses that may have otherwise gone undisclosed.

Reporters should check the criminal side of the courthouse, too. If a CEO or small business owner has been arrested, that is often news. CEOs and company executives also occasionally find themselves in civil suits unrelated to their business in which information about their company is disclosed. Divorce filings are a prime example. A spouse may be seeking half of the worth of the business and may file detailed information about its financial performance in the filings.

There is lots more information available at the local level. The local health department will have health inspection records and some permits. Health records are important for many industries, such as restaurants. The *Loveland Reporter-Herald* in Colorado, for example, lists restaurant and food service inspections throughout the county every week, ranking them from those that received "excellent" ratings to those that received "marginal" and "inadequate" ratings.

TIPS FROM THE PROS

RichmondBizSense.com and BusinessDen.com founder Aaron Kremer on covering small businesses:

Document work: At both our Richmond and Denver newsrooms, we scour public documents, including civil court cases, building permits, deeds, patents, new business entities and SEC filings for capital raises. Lawsuits are a gold mine because you can quote from them directly, and the lawyers like to make their case in extra inflammatory language, which helps spice up a story.

The planning or zoning department will have information about development permits and bonds posted to guarantee construction. Such information can be helpful for reporters writing about a local commercial or residential developer. In addition, the property appraiser or tax assessor's office can provide the assessed value of a property as well as property and building descriptions.

Local real estate transactions can also be telling for a small or private business. Reporters should check to see if the company has been making any purchases recently. If so, where is the land, and what does the company plan to do with it? If the purchases are near its current location, the company could be planning an expansion. It is also important to check to see if a small or private business is purchasing residential property. If it is, who is living in the houses? If the residents are employees or executives of the company, why are they receiving this special treatment?

Small and private businesses also come into contact with state regulatory agencies that could provide information. In addition to the secretary of state's office, other state agencies that might have records on a business include the attorney general's office, which might have investigated consumer complaints against the business or prosecuted the company, and economic development offices, which have the goal of keeping businesses happy in the state and attracting new companies. If a business has ever received a tax break or other financial enticement, the economic development office would have a record.

The *Hartford Courant* reported that Connecticut officials assisted a small Pennsylvania company seeking state funding to help it expand. In addition, the company helped close relatives of those officials invest in the private company. The value of their investment skyrocketed shortly thereafter. That story came from looking at the state economic development agency.

State licensing agencies are also an important source of information for small and private businesses. They regulate businesses ranging from barbershops to doctors, and many of their records are public information. Fines and suspensions against the medical profession, for example, can be obtained in some cases.

Reporters should also check the state legislature to see if there have been any hearings related to the company or its industry. The state environmental protection agency may have records of pollution on the business, whereas the department of labor may be able to tell whether the company has been laying off workers. The state purchasing office can tell whether the business has any contracts with the state, and if so, for which goods or services.

UCC filings are also important documents that can help tell a story about a small or private business. The UCC has a body of laws that has been adopted in virtually every state in the country. A UCC filing occurs when one business sells something to another business on credit. The business that sold the tractor to the farmer, for example, filed a UCC form showing that the tractor was collateral for the loan. If the business that purchased the tractor fails to pay the loan, the other business can repossess the tractor. UCC forms can show whether a business is borrowing a lot of money to make purchases. This could be a sign that the company plans to expand its operations.

TIPS FROM THE PROS

RichmondBizSense.com and BusinessDen.com founder Aaron Kremer on covering small businesses:

Real estate: The commercial real estate beat has been a beast in both our cities. It also feeds the other beats, because a new brewery, for example, isn't really worth writing about until they've signed a lease. We also run residential real estate stories when someone notable buys a mansion, or when an unusual home hits the market or sells.

State regulators tracking the banking and insurance industries can also be important sources of information, even for small businesses like insurance agencies. They will have financial reports for every bank and insurance company operating in the state. If the bank or insurer is private and not willing to disclose its revenue and profits to a reporter, the information should still be readily available because it has given this information to regulators. Reporters should let the company know they are going to get the information and use it. The company might open up more after the reporter makes a few calls to the state. The same goes for utility companies, such as electricity and water operations. They are regulated by a state public service commission, which keeps financial records.

State tax records can also be valuable. Jim Hoffer, of WABC in New York, searched state tax records and discovered that many Manhattan restaurants owed thousands in back taxes. "From fast food to some of the city's finest restaurants, our investigation found nearly 200 establishments that have collected from their customers a combined total of about $10 million," noted Hoffer. "It's money collected through the 8.25 percent sales tax. But instead of passing it on to the city and state, these restaurants kept it." Armed with this information, Hoffer confronted some of these restaurant owners, all small, private businesses. Many claimed to be working to pay off the debt. One said he used the sales tax as a loan to help make it through the aftermath of the September 11, 2001, terrorist attacks, fully understanding he would pay a penalty (Hoffer, 2003).

Federal agencies might also have information on small and private businesses, depending on their operations. The EPA, for example, issues permits to businesses that discharge environmentally sensitive liquids, and it also investigates spills. The CPSC will have records on a company if it has ever had a product recalled because of safety concerns. (For more information about regulatory agencies, see Chapter 14.)

For employee-related matters, the EEOC and OSHA are excellent places to check for information. These agencies investigate complaints of job discrimination and harassment and unsafe working conditions. If the business has had a worker injured on the job or has ever faced a claim from an employee alleging unfair treatment, there is a record of an investigation into the matter. Check the National Labor Relations Board (NLRB) if the business has unionized workers to see if the company has gotten into trouble for tampering with union votes.

If the company is involved in technology or another specialized business, it may have patents on inventions being used to help it make money. The Patent and Trademark Office will have a record of every patent issued to the company. If the company does not want to talk about its products, this could be a way of getting information about them. However, it may take an engineer or a scientist to help explain what the patent means.

TIPS FROM THE PROS

RichmondBizSense.com and BusinessDen.com founder Aaron Kremer on covering small businesses:

Egos: Small business owners have huge egos, and they all like to think they are the top dogs in town. Use that to your advantage to pick up tips about who may be hurting.

Federal agencies also regulate specific industries. For example, financial information about a credit union is available from the National Credit Union Administration. Many journalists do not know this, rightfully thinking that credit unions are nonprofit organizations owned by the depositors. Yet, many credit unions are very profitable. A reporter should find out the profitability of the credit unions in his or her town. That may be a story waiting to be written.

The Federal Aviation Administration collects information about airports that can be useful in writing a story, particularly for a reporter interested in transportation or tourism. The agency has enforcement information against airlines, pilots, mechanics and others in the industry, as well as a registry of all aircraft owned in the country. The FCC has tons of information about each and every radio and television station in the country, as well as documents on telephone and cable companies.

Reporters looking for information about private mining companies can check with the Mine Safety and Health Administration. And the Nuclear Regulatory Commission has records about operators of nuclear plants. As these two examples show, there is likely a regulatory agency for almost every type of industry. For the reporter trying to write a story about a gun store in town, the Bureau of Alcohol, Tobacco, and Firearms maintains a database of federally approved gun dealers across the country. If the gun store is not on that list, then the reporter has a better story than he or she may have originally thought.

Or maybe a reporter is writing about a small business that has gotten some help from the SBA in the form of a loan guaranteed by the agency. The SBA has a database that details the size of loans, when the loan was approved, whether the loan has been paid or become delinquent, which bank made the loan, the number of jobs the company promised to add to its employee base because of the loan and other information. The SBA also administers a program that encourages the federal government to award contracts for work to small and minority businesses. Similar information is available on these contracts. If the business you are writing about mentions that it has done work for the federal government, a lot of information should be available, including revenue for the company and where the revenue is coming from—even for private businesses.

Other good information about small and private companies is available from other sources. For example, credit reports from companies such as Dun and Bradstreet can be purchased for a fee. These reports can sometimes tell a journalist if the company has had problems repaying its debt.

TIPS FROM THE PROS

RichmondBizSense.com and BusinessDen.com founder Aaron Kremer on covering small businesses:

Think like a business person: We write in a lively tone with details that are valuable to the local business readers. Before sitting down to type, we ask ourselves, "What would a local business person want to know?" We slip in the story details like what the business is paying in rent and who the lender was and if it is looking at more locations. Those details make us a must-read for the local business people.

A private company may have made a debt issue. If it has, then it may have filed information with the SEC. In addition, bond-rating agencies will likely have reviewed the debt issue and issued a rating on the bonds. The rating agency may have also written a report about the company and its financial status.

Small companies do not always have to go through the same steps as larger companies when filing documents with the SEC to become public companies. If it had less than $25 million in revenue or its stock is worth no more than $25 million, the company can file a Form SB-1 to raise $10 million or less. This form allows the business to provide information in a question-and-answer format. A Form SB-2 is used by a small business when it wants to raise an unlimited amount of cash in a stock offering but still requires less disclosure than the SEC requires for larger companies. For example, small businesses have to provide two years of audited financial statements, whereas large companies must provide three years of audited financial statements.

Other sources exist for ferreting out information about a small or private business. If the business has issued a news release about anything, the document should be available from PR Newswire or Business Wire. Reporters should check their media outlet's library to see if it has done a story on the company in the past or should do a broader search on a database such as LexisNexis to check for other articles or mentions. If the small or private business is part of a niche industry with a specialty publication, such as a newsletter or monthly magazine, reporters should check it to see if the business has ever been mentioned. Every little bit helps when you are gathering string on a company that is not divulging any information.

Again, competitors may be able to provide valuable information. Suppliers such as advertising firms and distributors of the company's products or goods can provide information as to what it is like to do business with the company. Public interest groups may also have information. Check with the local chamber of commerce or Better Business Bureau to see if there have been complaints filed against the business.

Another valuable source is employees. They may be disgruntled or unhappy. Although they may not talk on the record about their employer for fear of losing their jobs, they may seek retribution for bad treatment by providing internal documents or company information that could be damaging. Reporters should tread lightly here. If an employee balks, he may go to his superior and tell him that a reporter has been snooping around.

A survey of visitors to Forbes.com resulted in 53 percent of the respondents replying that private businesses should not be required to disclose revenue, profits, assets and employees, whereas 29 percent believed they should. It is unlikely that any laws will be passed requiring private companies to do so. But the notion that small and private businesses are closed doors when it comes to information should be dispelled. Plenty of information can be obtained. It certainly takes some legwork, and most of the legwork may not result in any information that will make it into the story. But the one fact that does makes the story worthwhile.

UCC Code Filings

UCC filings are a source of information for small and private businesses. This cannot be emphasized enough.

UCC filings are some of the best documents available to a reporter, but they are seldom used to tell the story of a business—public or private, big or small—or an individual. That is disappointing because these filings help tell the reporter vital information about a company or a person. A reporter should look at UCC filings each time he or she writes a story about a company or a person.

UCC filings are available from the secretary of state's office in each state. Many of these are available online and can be searched by lender name as well as by the borrower's identity. As mentioned earlier, UCC filings are made with the state to show when money has been borrowed to make a purchase or for another reason. UCC filings show which company or business holds a lien on a corporation or a home. Sometimes, the filing will disclose the amount of the loan and what was used as collateral for the loan. No one would want to buy a house that has a lien on it from a creditor of the previous owner. A UCC filing can disclose this information, and it can tell a business owner how many loans, and sometimes for what amounts, a potential business partner has. Many business owners check the UCC filings of other businesses before they sign a contract. They want to know that the company is going to be able to fulfill its end of the deal.

Uniform Commercial Code (UCC): A set of laws regulating commercial transactions, especially those involving the sale of goods where money is borrowed.

The North Carolina Secretary of State's office explains the usefulness of reviewing UCC filings in the following way:

> This Section provides an essential service to the business community, offering a repository of records of UCC and federal lien documents. It also has the character of a public "bulletin board" with regard to liens against personal property.
>
> Lien information on any person or business may be obtained from the UCC Section upon request. Such information may be used to determine whether a lender would be interested in extending credit to the small business owner to, for example, provide capital for purchasing equipment or raw materials. The small business owner may, in turn, access the Section's records to determine whether to extend credit to customers by taking a security interest in the finished product to be sold.
>
> Without the services offered by the UCC Section, the lender or small business owner might be required to check county lien records in several counties in order to get a true financial picture of the person or business involved in the potential transaction.
>
> (North Carolina Department of the Secretary of State, 2016)

These filings can be helpful in a number of ways. When writing about a business or an individual, reporters can find out how much and to whom the person or company owes money. When *USA Today* researched disgraced former World-Com leader Bernie Ebbers, it pored through UCC filings around the country to get a detailed list of everything he had invested in or purchased during the last decade. That helped show readers where the money he had made from World-Com had gone. Another example of the benefits of looking at UCC filings is illustrated by the *Pittsburgh Post-Gazette* investigation into a church that wanted to redevelop a shopping center. The reporter looked at the church's UCC filings and discovered that banks and other lenders had given it seven loans despite the fact that it had fallen behind in paying its taxes and other debts.

TIPS FROM THE PROS

RichmondBizSense.com and BusinessDen.com founder Aaron Kremer on covering small businesses:

Filter out happy talk and clichés: Nothing kills the flow of a story like jargon. And business people love to heap it on reporters to make their business sound more successful and virtuous. Strip out all the marketing speak. And be suspicious of any business that touts their philanthropy or says they give a pair of breath mints for every breath mint they sell. Stay away from using words like "proprietary" and "value-added." You can always delete "strategic."

There are two main types of UCC filings. The first one is called a UCC-1 and is the original finance statement being recorded for the first time. A UCC-3 filing is a statement that continues, terminates, amends or releases the debt or loan.

UCC filings may seem intimidating, but all they are doing is recording simple business transactions. Reporters should use them to their advantage. When a small or private business owner—or anyone, for that matter— discovers that a reporter has taken the time to look at its UCC filings, he or she suddenly realizes that that reporter is serious about finding information. The *St. Petersburg Times* used UCC filings to track down information about a company providing water to the city of Port Richey. The owner of the company was surprised that she had been found.

Ownership and Structure

Knowing the structure of small or private company ownership is as important as knowing the facts about the business and its operations. The company's ownership will tell you who is calling the shots for the business. If a business is owned by one person, it is likely that he or she is also the president or CEO and is making all of the major decisions for the business.

Sole proprietorships often change ownership structure as the business becomes more successful. For instance, if the small business needs money to expand, the sole owner may decide to sell a stake in his or her fledgling company to investors in return for the cash. These investors now may want a say in how the company operates so as to boost the value of their ownership in the company. Or a business may actually sell itself to its employees. Thus, the employees have a vested interest in how the business performs as well.

A study on private businesses by accounting firm PricewaterhouseCoopers discovered that the typical private company has about 200 employees and annual revenues of about $47 million. For a reporter in a small town, the average small or private company may not be that big. Private companies in larger cities may be much bigger than that, however. About half of the private companies in the PricewaterhouseCoopers survey were close corporations, meaning that the businesses only have a small number of shareholders, usually no more than 50. These businesses also have no ready market for the corporation's stock, and a majority of the shareholders are active in the management of these corporations.

 S corporation: A company that has met the requirements under subchapter S of the Internal Revenue Service (IRS) code. This allows the company to be taxed as if it were a partnership. These businesses must be domestic, have 75 or fewer shareholders, and only one class of stock.

The survey found that about 40 percent of the private businesses are what are called S corporations, which provide the benefits of incorporation but eliminate double taxation, which can occur when the profits of a company are taxed as a corporation and then as income for the shareholders of the corporation. An S corporation is limited to no more than 100 shareholders.

The survey also found that about 4 percent of private businesses were partnerships, such as limited liability corporations. This business structure provides limited liability to the members and also pays taxes like it is a partnership, eliminating double taxation. These businesses are often law firms or accounting businesses. And about 3 percent of private businesses are sole proprietors, meaning there is just one owner of the company.

Other small and private businesses take the strategy of offering ownership in the company to employees through a program called an employee stock ownership plan (ESOP). About 7,000 companies now have ESOPs covering more than 13 million employees, or about 10 percent of the private sector workforce. Employees can receive stock in an ESOP in a variety of ways. They can purchase the stock directly or be given the stock as a bonus. They can also obtain stock through a profit sharing plan in which the profits of the company are divided up among shareholders.

employee stock ownership plan: A plan where the company allows its employees to buy shares of the business. These plans are increasing in popularity with small and private businesses.

ESOPs are commonly used by private companies to allow the owners to sell their stake in the company and to motivate their remaining employees at the same time. In almost every ESOP, all full-time workers above the age of 21 participate in the plan. They receive stock in the company on the basis of their pay rate or another formula. Employees are then vested—which means they then own the stock—within a five- to seven-year time frame. If an employee leaves the company, then the business buys back the stock on the basis of an outside valuation of the shares. Sometimes this valuation can be obtained from the company or from employees.

ESOPs are designed to encourage employees to consider the best interests of the business, but that is not always how it works. Some ESOPs have failed to turn struggling companies around. Between 1994 and 2000, workers at United Airlines

profit sharing plan: A plan where the employees of a company share in its profits. The business typically decides what profits will be shared.

accumulated 55 percent of the stock in its parent company in exchange for pay and benefit cuts totaling $4.8 billion. But critics say that the ESOP eventually failed because it excluded the flight attendants and did not allow employees who owned the stock to vote for directors. And employees who joined the company after 2000 were not allowed to join the ESOP at all, which created a rift between employees. But, other ESOPs have been successful. Simmons, the mattress company, was majority owned by an ESOP for a decade before selling to other investors for a profit. The risk of an ESOP structure to a private business is that the employees are putting all of their retirement eggs in one basket. If the company should struggle and begin to lose money, then the value of the stock in the plan will go down, just as the value of stocks traded on Wall Street declines when a public company performs badly.

The following story illustrates how the ownership structure of a private company can change and the causes behind that change.

> Rogers Manufacturing's employees liked their jobs so much they bought the company.
>
> The floor and truss manufacturer founded by Larry Rogers and headquartered in western Ouachita Parish completed its 15-year employee stock ownership plan this month to become 100 percent employee owned.
>
> Rogers, who started the company in 1981 with eight employees and has grown the work force to 250 with locations also in Ashland City, Tenn. and Mexia, Texas, will remain chairman and active in day-to-day operations. Derek Moody will remain president and the existing management team remains intact.
>
> "I'm very pleased to be able to pass on the company to its employees who's hard work and efforts have contributed to its success," said Rogers, who was honored at the White House in 2012 as an example of "success in rural America."
>
> Rogers Manufacturing provides its floors, trusses and engineered wood products to the construction industry throughout the southeastern United States.
>
> It has annual revenues of about $50 million.
>
> "Nothing is more motivational than each employee having a stake in the company's success," Moody said. "I certainly think this program has made us stronger."[2]

The value of this acquisition is disclosed, even though neither the seller nor the buyer is a public company. Still, the transaction does not say who among the employees will be the largest shareholder.

Changes in ownership structure, such as a shift from a nonprofit company to a for-profit business, merit closer scrutiny. Some businesses have trouble making the change after running themselves a certain way for so long. Many businesses made the switch in recent years from being owned by customers to being owned by stockholders. This change has occurred most commonly in the insurance and banking industries, where savings and loans and insurance companies that were owned by their depositors and their policyholders have converted to a stock ownership structure.

These thrifts and insurers were previously known as mutual companies. A mutual company is one in which the customers have an ownership interest and which is operated for the benefit of the customers. But their ownership ends if they should terminate their insurance policy or withdraw their money from the bank. Some of the largest companies in the country are mutuals, including State Farm and Northwestern Mutual. In the first few years of the twenty-first century, many thrifts converted from a mutual company structure to a public company structure. In such a conversion, the depositors are offered stock in the public company.

Many of the largest insurance companies, including MetLife, John Hancock and Prudential, have also converted from a mutual structure. As part of the conversion, they distributed millions of shares of the new company to their policyholders. These conversions are approved by state regulators, and the process can be lengthy.

TIPS FROM THE PROS

RichmondBizSense.com and BusinessDen.com founder Aaron Kremer on covering small businesses:

Numbers: Get sources to give you numbers. How much money did they raise from investors? How many square feet is their new production facility? How many employees do they think they will hire as they ramp up in town? Even if they won't give you revenue, you can often get a range.

A number of small and private businesses have a unique structure in which their performance is tied to a much larger company. These smaller businesses are called franchises. A franchise is formed by entering into a contractual relationship with a franchisor that already has a product or a service to sell. The franchisee then operates the business under the trade name of the franchise, often with its guidance, in exchange for a fee.

Franchises can take different shapes and forms. They are predominantly used in industries such as fast food for companies such as McDonald's and Burger King, although it should be noted that these companies sometimes also operate locations that they own themselves. Franchises are predominantly privately held businesses, although there are some franchise operations that are publicly traded. A Papa John's pizza store operator, based in Birmingham, Alabama, is an example of a franchise that was at one time publicly traded but is now a private company.

franchisee: A businessman who runs a location of a larger company (the franchisor) in exchange for a fee.

Running a franchise operation requires an up-front amount of money to be paid by the owner. McDonald's requires an initial fee of $45,000 and that the franchise purchaser has at least $500,000 in capital. McDonald's acquires the property for the location and builds the building. The franchisee is then responsible for equipping the building with the kitchen equipment, the seating, signs and landscaping.

Why do franchise owners go into such business operations? For one, all of the decisions about products and operation have been made for them. All they have to do is run the business, executing the plan, to make money.

Franchisees can be important sources for reporters covering the larger company. The parent may make decisions that affect the franchisees, upsetting the franchise owners. Sometimes, the franchisees may revolt against the bigger company and force it to make changes.

According to the International Franchise Association, there are more than 780,000 franchise locations in the country, and they provide 8.9 million jobs to the economy. Franchising is regulated by the FTC, and some states have also passed franchising laws. Many of them are designed to protect the franchisee, requiring the franchisor to disclose the costs associated with the business and make fair assessments of the earnings potential of the business.

Once a reporter knows the structure of the small or private business he or she is reporting about, some questions should emerge. For example, if it is a private company that has sold a stake to an investor to help fuel growth, how does it plan to manage that growth without losing money? If the growth is successful, how big does the company plan to get? If the business is a franchise, does it have plans to add more locations to the business? If the business is a mutual company, is it considering changing its structure? In some of these cases, the structure of the small or private business may be the story.

Profiling a Private or Small Business

Many times a media outlet will profile a small or private business. These stories may seem innocuous, and they are often written as flattering, positive stories that tell how a business is thriving because of its products or services. Many times, these stories can read like advertorials, copy that the business should have probably paid the newspaper to run.

Profiles of small and private businesses, however, do not always have to be this way. Like the business reporters who fell over themselves in the 1990s writing about the latest Internet company to go public and make millionaires of its workers, many reporters writing stories about small and private businesses are not as critical as they can and should be.

Writing about small and private businesses should reflect the local economy. If the economy is going bad in a town because a plant has closed, putting 400 workers out of jobs, then that is going to affect the surrounding small businesses that depend on these workers to spend part of their income buying their goods and services. If things are not going well, the reporter should not sugarcoat it. If a particular industry is suffering, reporters should not buy the story that one small business owner in that industry is telling them when he or she remarks, "We've never had a better season." He or she is probably lying.

The following lead, which focused on the closing of a local bar, from the *Opelika-Auburn* (Alabama) *News,* on April 6, 2015, told the story of the business well:

Wednesday afternoon, John Brandt arranged dozens of merchandise orders on the front bar of the War Eagle Supper Club after going without a single one in the last month. He looked up from his task and surveyed the walls around him, covered from ceiling to floor in car tags, t-shirts and posters.

"It's all kind of brand new to us," he mused. "We weren't expecting it to get out so fast."

Earlier that morning, Brandt confirmed with The Corner News the War Eagle Supper Club would close its doors at the end of 2015 after 78 years. New Year's Eve will be the Supper Club's last night on South College Street.

"My whole adult life has been in this building," he said. "... There are just too many memories."

Brandt started his tenure with the Club as a doorman in the early 1980s and bought into ownership in 1985. The property was recently sold to a new owner, who allowed the Club to continue on its existing lease until the end of the year. Brandt and co-owners Mark Cadenhead and Cory Hattier learned they wouldn't be able to renew the lease four or five weeks ago.

"Nobody wants to see that place go down, but it's out of our hands to be honest with you," Cadenhead, who started bartending in the early '90s and became partners with Brandt in 1996, said. "We were hoping we would be able to renegotiate the lease, but their terms were a little more than we were willing to handle."

He added the Supper Club's last night will be a tough one.

"I've heard many people say that's where they met their wives and their ex-wives and everything else," he said. "It's going to be a sad day when it does close. It means a lot to Auburn alumni."

The Supper Club building was built in 1937 and operated as a brothel after World War II, former owner Hank Gilmer said. The building housed Stoker's Steakhouse in the '50s, and later became a pizza joint under the ownership of H.H. Lambert.

"I've got what is probably the best pizza recipe in the world," Gilmer said. "That's a story in and of itself, believe me."

During the height of the civil rights era, bars and restaurants across the South were transitioning into private clubs to circumvent integration. During that time, in 1961, the Supper Club became a private club and took on its now-iconic name. Gilmer was a member when he was an Auburn student and bought the club, along with his father Henry Jr. and brother Jeff, in 1977.[3]

Stories about small and private businesses are reported for a number of reasons. Maybe the business is new to the town or city and is unique. Maybe the company is in conflict with another company. Maybe the business is fast-growing and adding many local employees. Or maybe the business is struggling and may not be around in six months.

Whatever the reason, reporters should think about small and private businesses the same way they think about larger and public businesses. These companies are just as important to the reader and viewer, and because the stories are being written about a business that probably has not had much exposure, the piece will probably have readers wanting to learn about a company they have not heard about before. In addition, reporters should not forget about these businesses after the story has been written. They could just be headed for bigger fame or notoriety, and journalists will want to be there to report it.

Imagine being a reporter in a small town of about 15,000 people. A few years ago, a chocolate shop opened downtown making truffles and other exotic desserts. The reporter wrote a short story about the shop, and afterward forgot about it. Then, one morning, that same reporter walks into the newsroom to discover that the chocolate shop is on the front page of the *Wall Street Journal*. It is now famous around the world because of its delicious sweets and cannot keep up with its orders for Valentine's Day because of the demand. The owner would like to expand, but he cannot because there are not enough hours in the day to make as many truffles as he needs.

Perhaps the local newspaper did not have that story before the large, national media because the local reporter did not keep in touch with the storeowner or check in regularly just by walking into the store and chatting with the employees. As a result, a great story was missed.

The following lead is from the *Herald-Sun* in Durham, North Carolina, which won first place in a SABEW contest. It is about a private company, but the detail makes the story read as if the business was publicly traded. The reporter followed up on the disclosure that the company was delinquent in paying its loans from a bond-rating agency to discover there were even more troubles than had been disclosed. Armed with the bond-rating agency information, he was able to garner interviews that showed just how serious the problems were.

After rapidly growing into the nation's second-largest privately owned convenience store chain, Durham-based Swifty Serve Corp. is fighting for its life.

The chain, which at one time had more than 600 stores throughout the Southeast, has closed between 70 and 100 locations and cut about 1,000 jobs as it fights the red ink flowing from money-losing stores.

Swifty Serve, like the rest of the convenience store industry, has been hit hard by a shrinking profit margin on gas sales and dropping cigarette sales—two of the core businesses of convenience stores.

The 5-year-old company is talking with lenders to help finance a plan for remaking Swifty Serve, but something has to be resolved "in weeks, not months," said Jeff Hamill, a former 7-Eleven executive who became the company's president and CEO in April.

If something can't be worked out, "I don't know if it's bankruptcy or additional changes we'll have to make," Hamill said from the company's headquarters on Hillandale Road.

Durham developer W. Clay Hamner started building the Swifty Serve chain in 1997 with his longtime business partner, Wayne Rogers. Hamner is best known for playing a lead role in the Treyburn residential development and the retail center Brightleaf Square while Rogers is the actor who played Trapper John in the television series M*A*S*H.[4]

Later in the story, the CEO of this company calls the company a "tremendous opportunity" and the owner of the business is "confident" of the management team. Yet, the reader of this story gets a vivid picture that this convenience store chain is in trouble because of changes in the industry that have affected its performance. This story does not use any specific figures for revenues and profits (or losses) to detail the trouble but cogently explains how competitors are undercutting it in pricing and building bigger stores. Even without the numbers, the writer is able to make a case that the business is in trouble on the basis of the quotes he uses—and the one single number he does have about the delinquent loans from the bond-rating agency.

Other media are able to effectively report about small and private businesses the same way. The *Loveland Daily Reporter-Herald* in Colorado focused on the problems its local travel agencies were having after airlines announced they were eliminating commissions. The *Antelope Valley Press* in California focused on the local minor league baseball team—not as a sport but as a business—and wrote about how the Lancaster JetHawks were trying to boost attendance. Although the team did not cite any numbers, the reporter was able to quote a source within the organization saying that the team had lost money the previous year.

When writing profiles of small and private businesses, reporters should think of them as companies that might be sold, go out of business, or go public in the future, which would put them in the public eye. Because stories have already been written about the company, the reporter's media outlet will have the background to cover future stories about the company more thoroughly.

Small and private businesses like to have stories written about them when they are new and trying to attract customers. But rarely do they want the attention when they are going out of business. Still, these stories can also be important because they might reflect on the broader town or county economy. If a store could not make it in the town, what does that say about the future of similar stores in the area?

Reporting about small and private businesses often requires the journalist to focus on the founder or owner of the business. They are often the ones that control the company. Without that interview, though, where would a reporter turn? If possible, he or she should find out where the founder used to work. Maybe someone there can talk about his or her work habits or business ideas. Maybe he or she was fired or dismissed from the previous job or left the previous employer to start a competing business.

Small and private business owners are often proud of what they have accomplished in building a company from a simple idea. Many of them are extremely protective of their business and want a reporter to recognize the long hours and the tough times they put in to make the business successful, or at least survive. If a business owner is reluctant to give an interview, the reporter must understand why they are leery. One way for reporters to get past the hesitation is to let the business owner see that they recognize the pain that went into building the operation. That does not mean the story should be positive. But a good point to make in most profiles of small and private businesses is how they were started and how they have lasted as long as they have.

Reporters should not hesitate to ask for information. All the owner or president can say is "yes" or "no." Reporters must ask for letters or other documents from companies that do business with the company they are reporting about. Maybe a competitor has a letter or document that would make a good story about the business. Consider the lead of the following story from the *Rochester Business Journal:*

> Excellus Inc. deliberately has sabotaged important Strong Health initiatives and continues trying to subvert the University of Rochester's health system, a top Strong Health executive claims.
>
> In a Jan. 4 letter to Excellus CEO Howard Berman, obtained by the Rochester Business Journal, and Berman's reply three weeks later, reflect a massive rift between Strong and Excellus, the parent of Blue Cross Blue Shield of the Rochester area. They are the area's two most powerful health care organizations.
>
> Berman's response letter contains a point-by-point refutation of the charges in the earlier missive from Steven Goldstein, Strong Memorial and Highland hospitals CEO. Berman also offered to meet with Strong officials to further discuss the issues.[5]

The story is about two private companies. But because the reporter was able to obtain the first letter, the CEO supplied the response letter after being questioned about it. That is how obtaining one document can lead to another.

Writing a story about a small or private business should not just consist of interviewing the owner or the president of the company. That is not going to give the reader or the viewer the balance and objectivity that the story demands. Think of other people to interview that know the business and where other information about the company can be obtained. Putting all of the pieces together will make for a story that tells the complete picture.

Notes

1. From "The battle rages on: Small business squares off against IRS rulemaking," by K. Girard, May 5, 2003, CBSMarketWatch.com. Copyright 2003 by MarketWatch.com. Reprinted with permission.
2. From "Employees now own Rogers Manufacturing; WM company employs 250," by G. Hilburn, December 16, 2015, *Monroe News-Star*. Copyright 2015 by *Monroe News-Star*. Reprinted with permission.
3. From "War Eagle Supper Club to close at the end of year," by S. Falligant, *Opelika-Auburn News,* pp. 1A. Copyright 2015 by *Opelika-Auburn News.* Reprinted with permission.
4. From "Swifty Serve Corp. is in fight for its life; Durham-based convenience store chain has closed stores, cut jobs," by J. Zimmer, September 27, 2002, *Durham Herald-Sun,* p. A1. Copyright 2002 by Durham Herald Company Inc. Reprinted with permission.
5. From "Letter underscores UR-Excellus feud," by W. Astor, March 15, 2002, *Rochester Business Journal,* p. 1. Copyright 2002 by *Rochester Business Journal.* Reprinted with permission.

Key Terms

corporation

employee stock ownership plan

franchisee

profit sharing plan

S corporation

Uniform Commercial Code (UCC)

Suggested Exercises

1. Find a small business owner in your city and conduct an interview. Ask him how he started his business and why. See how much financial information the owner is willing to disclose about the business. If he's not willing to disclose revenues and profits, then ask if there's any financial information that he will disclose, such as an increase in sales or profits.
2. Take the name of the small business whose owner you interviewed and search for information about the business in public records with the secretary of state's office and at the county courthouse. Don't forget to check lawsuits, UCC filings and federal records. After you've collected the information, go show the business owner the information. Is the owner now more forthcoming about providing additional information on the company?
3. Many small companies rely on college students. Find a handful of these businesses—restaurants, bookstores, bars, copy centers—near your campus and ask them what percentage of their business comes from college-age students. What does this tell you about the economy of the town or city in which you're living?
4. Ask other students in the class if they have part-time jobs at small businesses. If they do, ask them if they know the owner of the company and

how often the owner works at the business. If they don't know the owner, how many hours does the manager or supervisor spend at the business?

 ## Private and Small Business Company Books

Gerber, M. (1995). *The e-myth revisited: Why most small businesses don't work and what to do about it.* New York: Harper Business.

Hartley Smith, P. (2003). *Board betrayal: The Weirton Steel story: Failed governance and management hand in hand with Arthur Andersen: An ESOP fable.* Belgrade, MT: Wilderness Adventure Books.

Sutton, G. (2001). *How to use limited liability companies and limited partnerships.* Reno, NV: SuccessDNA Inc.

 ## References

Astor, W. (2002, March 15). Letter underscores UR-Excellus feud. *Rochester Business Journal*, pp. 1, 17.

Falligant, S. (2015, April 15). War Eagle Supper Club to close after 48 years. *Opelika-Auburn News*, p. 1A.

Fitzpatrick, D. (1999, July 21). Petra Ministries battles financial woes; back taxes, lack of experience as a developer raises concerns about the independent church's ability to revitalize the former East Hills Shopping Center. *Pittsburgh Post-Gazette*, p. B-1.

Girard, K. (2003, May 3). The battle rages on: Small business squares off against IRS rulemaking. CBS.MarketWatch.com. Retrieved May 27, 2003 from http//cbs.MarketWatch.com/news.

Hilburn, G. (2015, December 16). Employees now own Rogers Manufacturing; WM company employs 250. *Monroe News-Star.* Retrieved December 31, 2015 from www.thenewsstar.com/story/news/2015/12/16/employees-now-own-rogers-manufacturing-wm-company-employs-250/77421030/.

Hoffer, J. (2003, April 27). Too common restaurant practice is costing New York City. WABC-TV. Retrieved May 28, 2003 from http://abclocal.go.com/wabc/news/investigators/wabcinvestigators_042803restaurants.html.

Kleinbaum, J. (2002, July 7). A minor struggle … JetHawks deal with smaller crowds. *Antelope Valley Press*, p. A1.

McIntire, M., & Lender, J. (2003, April 13). Family ties and hefty profits; as a food company seeks state aid, investments in its stock benefit some close to the circle of power. *Hartford Courant*, p. A1.

Mickelson, C. (2002, April 21). Taking a shine to it. *The Door County Advocate*, p. 6.

Moyers, S. (2002, April 21). Cape's global economy: Business owners from afar take a chance on Missouri. *Southeast Missourian*, pp. 1A, 6A.

North Carolina Department of the Secretary of State. (2016, January 1). *Important notice to UCC record filers.* Raleigh, NC: Author. Downloaded from https://www.secretary.state.nc.us/ucc/thepage.aspx

O'Donnell, J., & Backover, A. (2002, December 12). Ebbers' high-risk act came crashing down on him. *USA Today*, pp. 1B, 2B.

Waite, M., & Glenn, B. (2000, April 2). Well deal unearths murky ties. *St. Petersburg Times*, p. 1.

Zimmer, J. (2002, September 27). Swifty Serve Corp. is in fight for its life; Durham-based convenience store chain has closed stores, cut jobs. *Durham* (N.C.) *Herald-Sun*, p. A1.x.

11

NONPROFITS AND FOUNDATIONS

Operating Like a For-Profit Business

So far, this book has ignored an important segment of the business world, one that is often underreported because of its unique structure. But there are thousands of businesses and other organizations operating like businesses that offer goods or services to the public that are neither public companies nor for-profit private enterprises.

There are more than 1.5 million entities in this country classified as nonprofit organizations by the IRS. Collectively, they account for 9.2 percent of all wages and salaries paid in the United States and 5.3 percent of the gross domestic product, according to the National Center for Charitable Statistics. In addition, charitable contributions by individuals, foundations, bequests and corporations reached $358.38 billion in 2014, an increase of 7.1 percent from 2013.

These nonprofit organizations include everything from the National Council of YMCAs, the American Red Cross and Goodwill Industries International to local child-care centers, homeless shelters, health insurance plans, community health care clinics, museums, hospitals, churches, schools, performing arts centers and conversation groups. They are some of the largest organizations in a town or a community, and often they are some of the most powerful as well. In many cases, these organizations compete against public and private companies. The local YMCA, for example, competes with for-profit workout centers to attract fitness nuts. Nonprofit managed care plans such as Kaiser compete with for-profit companies such as CIGNA and Aetna. Hospitals run by Catholic groups compete against hospitals managed by multibillion-dollar hospital corporations. Many times, the for-profit companies will complain that their nonprofit competitors are taking advantage of their status to undercut them and steal business.

> ## TIPS FROM THE PROS
>
> University of Illinois journalism professor and former executive director of Investigative Reporters and Editors, Brant Houston on covering nonprofits:
>
> Get a complete a list of nonprofits in your area by getting the database of tax-exempt organizations from the IRS or from the database library at Investigative Reporters and Editors, www.ire.org . The database lists all organizations granted tax exemption by the IRS and includes some overall financial information. Specifically, the data includes the organization's name, address, contact person, total annual income, total assets, and codes describing their activities generically. Also, you can do searches at www.guidestar.org/, which collects information on nonprofits. Remember that nonprofits exist on nearly every beat and any topic you can think of.

A nonprofit organization is a corporation formed to carry out a specific purpose, whether it is educational, religious, scientific or community-related. The corporation does not pay any taxes to the state or federal government because of its status. The IRS and state regulatory agencies have determined that the public's benefit from these organizations entitles them to special tax status.

However, forming a nonprofit organization does not guarantee tax-exempt status. The corporation must make a request with the IRS, which will then determine whether the organization merits tax-exempt status. If the IRS agrees, the organization receives the designation of filing financial documents under section 501(c)(3) of the tax code. That is why these companies are often referred to as 501(c)(3) businesses.

Just like public and private for-profit corporations, nonprofit businesses must incorporate with their state's secretary of state's office. And every state has laws and administrative rules governing nonprofit organizations that they must follow. Typically, a state department of justice regulates charitable activities as well. Most nonprofit organizations also have a president or CEO who oversees the day-to-day operations, and they hire and fire staffs that sometimes can total in the thousands. They recruit executives from the for-profit world and often look at the for-profit sector for strategies and tactics that they can adapt to their organizations. In addition, nonprofits are required to conduct themselves in the same manner as many for-profit businesses. They must hold board meetings and keep minutes of those meetings for their corporate records.

They are different as well. Nonprofits are allowed to raise funds from the public and from private business and government agencies. Unlike for-profit businesses, they are not allowed to make political lobbying a significant part of their operations, and they cannot conduct their business in a way that would benefit their directors or officers. And nonprofits are not allowed to distribute their profits to members.

Nonprofits are not actually owned by anyone and cannot be sold. If the directors decide to dissolve the organization, they must pay off all of its debts and distribute the remaining assets to another nonprofit organization. The focus is on the nonprofit aspect of the business. Many people donate their time and money to nonprofits with the idea that these organizations are performing functions for the benefit of the community and are not in existence to make as much money as possible. The money that is made by a nonprofit organization must be used to further develop its programs and services.

TIPS FROM THE PROS

University of Illinois journalism professor and former executive director of Investigative Reporters and Editors, Brant Houston on covering nonprofits:

Research a nonprofit through news stories, its Website and the courthouse. Read news stories going back at least five years, if the nonprofit has been around that long. Go through its Website pages—and its Facebook page if it has one. Check out the previous versions of its Website through www.archive. org/, which archives old Web pages. Often, a previous unpleasant audit or report or an exaggerated claim may not be on the current Website. Check the civil lawsuits at the local courthouse to see if the nonprofit has been sued or is suing. Court records often contain information that is hard to get otherwise.

Despite the function and structure of nonprofit organizations, many are profitable ventures. Some of them are more profitable than their public and private competitors. The American Cancer Society reported $886 million in revenue 2014, a decrease in $85 million from the previous year, which may be why it hired a new CEO for the first time since 1992. Still, its expenses were $857 million, meaning it had an operating profit of $28 million.

It's not the only one. The Salvation Army had $4.1 billion in revenue in 2014 and nearly $3.5 billion in expenses, leaving it with $600 million in profits for the year. Indeed, most of the large nonprofit organizations reported more in revenue than they did in expenses in 2014. The Public Broadcasting Service reported $642 million in revenue and $541 million in expenses for 2014.

Where do these profits go? The same place they go to in most for-profit companies, that is, into making the organization stronger by adding additional services or building new facilities or rewarding excellent employees with higher pay. The point to take away from these examples is that nonprofit organizations can often be as huge—and as profitable—as many for-profit enterprises. Yet the media often looks at these ventures as completely different entities.

This is a mistake. These organizations are major players in specific industries such as health care and insurance. In many towns and cities, they may have the dominant market share for their business. And sometimes, a non-profit organization can violate its agreement with the public by misusing its money or by not adhering to regulatory standards.

The *Seattle Times* reported that local public television station KCTS was suffering from financial woes. Shortly before their report ran, the station's president resigned. The story noted, "Employees, former executives and the station's own paid consultants say [the president] runs the public entity like a private fiefdom" (Phillips and McFadden, 2003, p. A1). Their reporting noted that the station's losses totaled $3.4 million in 2001 even though the president was receiving a $268,000 salary and that the Corporation for Public Broadcasting was withholding funding because it had not turned in financial statements. In another example, the *Journal Star,* in Peoria, IL, documented how the local CrimeStoppers organization was spending 55 percent of its expenses on fundraising, which is a high percentage compared with other nonprofit organizations. Executives at Minnesota Public Radio were widely criticized when it was disclosed that they had personally earned more than $7 million when they sold a for-profit mail-order subsidiary. And the U.S. Food and Drug Administration (FDA) issued a consent decree against the American Red Cross, requiring the organization to improve its method of reporting information about the handling of blood or face severe fines. The decree, in which the American Red Cross neither admitted nor denied any wrongdoing, followed a lengthy battle between regulators and the group.

From these examples, we see that nonprofit corporations are not exempt from some of the same problems and issues that plague the for-profit world. There are still allegations of misuse of money and of disobeying rules governing the business. Such events are newsworthy no matter where they happen.

To be sure, nonprofit organizations offer great services to their communities. They help millions of people live better lives under the principle that their organization should not be making a profit from others. But they are also newsworthy organizations, and they should be covered aggressively by media outlets. However, most media outlets do not have a full-time reporter to cover nonprofits, and many mass communication organizations do not even have a business reporter to cover this sector of the economy.

The reporting and writing tactics for covering the nonprofit world are the same as they are for writing about for-profit businesses. In many cases, the financial performance tells the clearest picture of how well—or how poorly—the organization is performing. And the competition between the two business structures is increasing, as the following *Dallas Morning News* story suggests, leading to the argument that nonprofits should be covered by the business staff:

> The slogan might not have saved the Oldsmobile, but a new upscale concept among Goodwill Industries has left the venerable charity boasting that "this is not your grandmother's Goodwill store."
>
> Indeed, a new superstore approved by the Hurst City Council on Tuesday night will feature 22,000 square feet of retail space, a coffee shop, a high-end used bookstore and a fashion boutique.

"We envision people shopping at Neiman Marcus in the morning and at Goodwill in the afternoon," said David Cox, director of community relations and marketing for Goodwill Industries of Fort Worth Inc. "You will find Mercedes, Lexus and Beamers in our parking lot any day."

The council action cleared the way for a new so-called superstore at 825 W. Pipeline Road. The new store, part of a growing national trend for Goodwill, will be nearly three times as big as traditional Goodwill retail centers and should open in the 33,000-square-foot former Food Lion by July.

The charity isn't forsaking its century-old tradition of selling second-hand clothes and used furniture and appliances to raise money to put the disabled to work. It's just adding a little twist picked up by watching the agency's upscale thrift stores in Portland, Ore., thrive, Mr. Cox said.

"Our mission is still the same," he said. "We're a hand-up rather than a handout organization. We take the money [the stores' profits from the sales] and train handicapped people to work. We give them a job rather than a new shirt."

Indeed, the Fort Worth agency took in $10 million last year, with $6 million coming from its retail sales and salvage operation, said Erin Quillian, director of retail sales.

Dave Barringer, a spokesman for Goodwill Industries International, said the northeast Tarrant County superstore is a first for Texas, but it is following in footsteps of a growing number of the charity's approximately 1,800 stores across the nation.

"The better we compete with the other discounters—from Wal-Mart to Kmart—and add all the bells and whistles the better we will be able to serve our people," he said. "The stores have two main purposes: They are usually funding mechanisms for our other programs, and they often provide work opportunities for our clients as well."

Rod Ginther, president of the Dallas Goodwill, said such superstores were the newest stage of an evolution that has been changing Goodwill's retail operations. Dallas stores have been on a larger scale, with bookstores and other amenities, for 10 years, he said.[1]

TIPS FROM THE PROS

University of Illinois journalism professor and former executive director of Investigative Reporters and Editors, Brant Houston on covering nonprofits:

Check out the board of directors and all of its activities. Get lists of both former and current members of the board of directors, get board minutes if you can, read the bylaws governing the code of conduct of board members, and try to attend board meetings. You should especially watch for the nonprofit doing business with companies owned by board members. Former board members are more likely to speak candidly about the organization.

After reading this story, can anybody question that nonprofit organizations are an important business story waiting to be told? They are expanding, and they're competing more directly with public and private companies. Look at the names of the other retailers mentioned in this story—Neiman Marcus, Wal-Mart and Kmart. These are some of the biggest companies operating today. Yet Goodwill Industries sees itself as fitting in a retailing niche that these others aren't fulfilling.

Foundations

Foundations are similar to nonprofit organizations in that they are entities that are not interested in making a profit. Foundations, in fact, simply exist to give money away, not to make it. But that does not mean they fall outside of the business world.

Many foundations are the result of the profits made by for-profit corporations and the executives that previously ran them or made their fortunes from the company's stock. The largest foundation in the country is the Bill and Melinda Gates Foundation, named after the founder of Microsoft and his wife. The foundation had more than $44.3 billion in assets at the end of 2014, the latest statistics available. Other large foundations read like a Who's Who of the business world, with names such as Lilly, Ford, Johnson & Johnson, Kellogg, Packard, Hewlett, Duke, Getty and Mellon attached to them.

TIPS FROM THE PROS

University of Illinois journalism professor and former executive director of Investigative Reporters and Editors, Brant Houston on covering nonprofits:

Start with the nonprofit's current 990 tax filing, but never stop there. Get at least three years of forms (usually available and free at www.guidestar.org). Ask for its last three annual audits and its budgets if they aren't on the organization's Web site. If they aren't on the Web site and the nonprofit won't give them to you, ask why not? After all, a nonprofit asks the public to subsidize it with tax-exempt status and asks the public to donate to support its operations. Why would a nonprofit not want to be as transparent as possible?

According to the Foundation Center, there are more than 87,000 foundations in the country with more than $798 billion in assets. In 2013, they handed out more than $56 billion in gifts to nonprofit organizations and other individuals and groups.

A foundation is established as a nonprofit organization or a charitable trust, but its primary obligation is different from that of nonprofit organizations such as hospitals and Goodwill Industries discussed earlier. A foundation's primary purpose is to give away money and sometimes equipment such as computers by way of grants to organizations or individuals who request help. By law, a foundation must give away 5 percent of its assets every year to maintain its tax-free status. (Foundations also apply for 501(c)(3) status with the IRS.)

There are different types of foundations. Independent foundations are the most common. These foundations are not associated with a company or a family. Corporate foundations are those connected to a business, quite often a for-profit company that makes grants to the communities in which it operates. Family foundations receive their money from an individual family and its members, and their grants may be tied to family interests. Famous athletes and celebrities also create foundations, and sometimes these organizations can result in stories for the business writer as well, depending on what the foundation is doing with its money. When football star Aaron Rodgers was voted the NFL Player of the Year, his foundation received $30,000 to give to organizations.

Foundations can be considered huge investment businesses. Although they give away billions of dollars each year to worthy causes, they are designed to exist forever. Foundations, particularly those funded by private investments, most likely will never give away all of the money and assets that they have. Foundations invest their assets in stocks, bonds, real estate or other investments designed to build the assets. The money that is given away in the form of grants typically comes from the income and gains on these investments. Therefore, foundation managers, particularly investment officers, watch the stock market and the economy closely. Their jobs are similar to those of mutual fund managers or Wall Street investment pros.

The 2008 stock market drop affected many foundations, as the ups and downs in the stock market and other investments can affect the worth of a foundation's assets. The Robert W. Woodruff Foundation in Georgia, endowed with Coca-Cola stock by founder and former Coca-Cola president Robert Woodruff, saw its asset value fluctuate with the value of Coca-Cola stock. Other foundations gave their money to New York–based investor Bernard Madoff to manage and then lost most or all of their money when it was discovered that Madoff was operating a Ponzi scheme. At least 147 foundations invested with Madoff.

foundation: A nonprofit organization created to give money away. Foundations are required to grant 5 percent of their assets annually.

Foundations have limits on how much ownership they can have in for-profit businesses. The Tax Reform Act states that a foundation cannot own more than 20 percent of the voting shares in a public or private corporation. Some foundations have gotten around this limitation and received a five-year extension to divest by showing regulators that they have made a good-faith effort to sell the stake.

Understanding how foundations work and where their money comes from is important. Foundations can have a major impact on a local economy and business community, particularly if small businesses are receiving grants or funding from foundations to survive. Many times, foundations will give grants to needy business groups that will help minority-owned ventures. Foundations also give money to scientific and research organizations that may be seeking to develop drugs to treat major diseases or illnesses. Their success could spur the drug industry.

The following excerpt from the *Kansas City Star* shows how a local foundation might be affecting the Kansas City economy:

> After deciding last year to phase out small grants for local social service needs, the Ewing Marion Kauffman Foundation has decided this year to boost such small grants.
>
> The foundation, the region's largest philanthropy, has announced a $2.5 million annual commitment in coming years to a special fund dedicated to nonprofit agencies. This money could end up extending Kauffman's traditional support for urban youth, in activities ranging from leadership camps to art classes.
>
> In 2001, Kauffman dedicated about $1.8 million a year in small grants to local nonprofits, according to a *Kansas City Star* analysis of Kauffman's grant-making. So the foundation's new commitment represents at least a 36 percent increase in the total amount dedicated to small grants, those of $25,000 or less.

TIPS FROM THE PROS

University of Illinois journalism professor and former executive director of Investigative Reporters and Editors, Brant Houston on covering nonprofits:

Know in detail what should be filed in a Form 990 (this chapter tells you much of it) and watch for what is not there. For example, if the nonprofit gives out fellowships or scholarships, all those receiving them should be listed. Reporters covering preparations for the 2002 Olympics in Salt Lake City heard that a Salt Lake Olympics-related nonprofit had given out scholarships, but none were listed on the Form 990. With deeper digging, the reporters got the list and saw scholarships had gone to family members of the International Olympic committee, which had selected Salt Lake City as the Olympic host city. Also, pay careful attention to the lack of significant fundraising expenses. Some nonprofits may try to underestimate how much they spend on fundraising, thinking it makes them look better, or they may allocate all the expenses into an "educational" program about the nonprofit.

Kauffman's turnaround on such grants evolved because the foundation figured out how to dispense them while still downsizing, and because the foundation wanted to respond to the worsening economy. Carl Schramm, Kauffman's new chief executive, said foundations have a traditional obligation toward the less-fortunate, and that duty is heightened in bad economic times.

"We see the recession as an opportunity to expand social welfare," Schramm said.

In the nonprofit community, Kauffman's announcement comes at a time when social service leaders are collectively holding their breath. They are waiting to see how Kansas City's philanthropic behemoth will change under Schramm, who took over from longtime civic leader Louis Smith last spring.

Schramm has indicated he wants the foundation to get more bang for its bucks, to basically put more money into fewer programs.

He also has promised that when the foundation's new "business plans" get approved later this year, more money will end up going into Kansas City, not less. Kauffman's new commitment to small grants is the first tangible follow-through of that promise.

So while some nonprofit leaders hailed Kauffman's action, they wondered what will happen with larger grants.

"It's a good move to make a gift to the (small-grant) fund so that pool grows," said Mary Lou Jaramillo, executive director of the Mattie Rhodes Art Center, which gets Kauffman funding. "We're all waiting in the nonprofit community for the direction Kauffman is going."

For years now, Kauffman has fulfilled a role as sort of a societal caretaker. The foundation assumed responsibilities that used to be primarily the province of local governments. These duties ranged from training public school principals to helping to subsidize social service agencies.

In doing this, Kauffman handed out small grants for smaller community needs in two ways. One way was through its Kauffman Fund, held at the Greater Kansas City Community Foundation and administered by a community advisory board.[2]

This story explains how the shift in grant giving by the Kauffman Foundation, which received its funding from its founder's pharmaceutical company stock, is affecting local organizations. Foundations are also major donors to universities and schools. Colleges and universities often undergo major fundraising initiatives and target foundations to make donations. These donations could spur major growth at a local university, leading to the construction of new buildings and the hiring of new employees. When writing about major grants or gifts given by foundations, reporters should assess the local economic impact.

Foundations and their money can also be important to current business executives looking to leave their mark long after they are gone. CEOs and others sometimes create foundations and donate their stock holdings in their companies to these foundations. The ownership transfer of the stock can be traced by checking SEC filings. In addition, a company executive may continue to lease office space for his or her foundation in the company's headquarters even after he or she has left the business. These agreements are also often disclosed in SEC filings.

Foundations, however, are also prone to some of the same issues that nonprofit organizations encounter. They can be mismanaged or misuse their money.

The *San Jose Mercury News* noted that the president of a local foundation lost 25 percent of its assets and fired staff members, while receiving a compensation package that could have faced sanctions if it had been audited by the federal authorities. And the *Chicago Tribune* reported in December 2015 that a Field Museum employee pocketed $900,000 of its money over seven years and is being investigated by federal authorities.

TIPS FROM THE PROS

 University of Illinois journalism professor and former executive director of Investigative Reporters and Editors, Brant Houston on covering nonprofits:

Beware of assuming too much from reading the 990. The salaries can be misleading if a staff member is receiving pay from the nonprofit and from an affiliated organization or another group. For example, if a nonprofit is based at a university, part of the salary for a staff member can come from the nonprofit and part from the university if the employee also does work for the university. The 990 would show only the nonprofit part of the salary. Or a nonprofit can show a steady increase in net assets year after year, but that may be due to more donations to its endowment than to its operating revenue. The problem is that the principal in an endowment cannot be spent, only investment income. That means that if investments go badly, the organization could have a $5 million endowment, but not be able to spend a penny of it, which could result in staff layoffs because of the investment losses.

Foundations are run like businesses, with an eye toward expenses and a focus on where the money goes. They're not actually selling a product or a service, but they are important operations that control billions of dollars in some cases.

The media, with a few notable exceptions, ignores foundations or downplays their coverage to focus on large grants or gifts handed out. While those stories are news, there's more going on within these organizations that merits coverage.

In the next section, we'll see how to find specific financial information for foundations and nonprofit organizations.

Finding Information: The Form 990

The perception among many journalists is that foundations and nonprofit organizations are secretive entities, just like private businesses, and there is no real way to assess their financial performance.

That belief, however, is wrong, just as it is regarding small and private companies. There is plenty of information available for a reporter to gather about foundations and nonprofits. Just like businesses, these groups are required to file documents with the secretary of state's office in the state in which they are located. They may also have to file information with the state office that tracks charities. These documents will help a reporter identify a nonprofit organization's board members and attorney but may not provide much else.

 Form 990: A document filed with the IRS by virtually every nonprofit organization and foundation. The filing discloses revenue, expenditures and salaries for management.

Many nonprofit organizations also receive funding or have contracts with state, city or federal governments. The documents related to these arrangements are public record. Sometimes, the government agency that has the contract or provided funding to the nonprofit organization will also perform an audit on the group to make sure that the money is being spent in accordance with the agreement.

Other groups also keep track of specific nonprofit information. The Better Business Bureau, for example, has a philanthropic advisory service that evaluates the performance of nonprofit organizations. It measures groups on the basis of their management, their fundraising practices, how money is spent and other items. It stipulates that 60 percent of donations must be used in providing services, and no more than 35 percent of a group's budget should be spent on fundraising. Many of its reports on nonprofits can be obtained by going to www.bbb.org/us/charity.

However, any reporter truly interested in finding detailed financial information about a foundation or a nonprofit organization must examine one document that will provide most of what they need. The IRS has required foundations and nonprofit organizations to file a Form 990 since 1942, and it is a public record.

A Form 990 shows how much money the nonprofit organization collected within the previous year, from which sources and how it was spent. These expenses are divided among program expenses, management expenses and fundraising expenses. The Form 990 also details what kind of programs the organization is running and how much it spends on them. In addition, this document provides information about the group's board members and how much its management is paid. There are also disclosures that show if the organization had any transactions in the last year and whether it lobbies.

TIPS FROM THE PROS

University of Illinois journalism professor and former executive director of Investigative Reporters and Editors, Brant Houston on covering nonprofits:

If you think or know the nonprofit gets federal grants, check out whether they have filed what is known as the "single audit" and request it from the nonprofit or from the federal Office of Management and Budget [OMB]. It was easy to find the audits by going to the Federal Audit Clearinghouse Web site at http://harvester.census.gov/sac/, but the site has been down since it was hacked in the summer of 2015 and it is not known when and if it will be open again. But if a nonprofit spends more than $500,000 in federal grant money a year ($300,000 before Jan. 1, 2004), then it must annually submit the "single audit" of its finances to OMB. The audit contains lots of details, including where the grant money came from and if the organization has accounting weaknesses. Cross-referenced with other public records, it can be a rich source of information on how the nonprofit is spending government funds. You can find audits through 2013 from the data library of Investigative Reporters and Editors at http://ire.org/nicar/database-library/databases/federal-audit-clearinghouse/.

The Form 990 should be thought of as the equivalent of a Form 10-Q or 10-K for a public company, with some of the functions of other SEC filings—such as proxy statements—rolled in for good measure. The Form 990 is one of the most all-encompassing financial documents available for a reporter.

Regulations passed in 2000 greatly expanded access to Form 990 documents. Nonprofit organizations are required to provide their three most recent Form 990 filings and their original filing for tax-exempt status to anyone who requests them. They must be made available the same day of the request from the foundation's office or within 30 days by mail. The documents can also be obtained directly from the IRS by using Form 4506A or by writing a letter. The IRS may take up to six weeks to reply, however. Many states also keep Form 990s on file for foundations in their state. Many foundations are also now posting their Form 990 each year on the Internet, making them accessible to anyone. Organizations can be fined for not making their Form 990 filings available to the public.

Most nonprofit organizations must file their Form 990 with the IRS within six months after the end of their fiscal year. However, the document may not be immediately available, as it can take the federal government agency several months to scan it. Nonprofit organizations can also file for extensions, which may delay when the document is filed.

Most religious organizations are not required to file Form 990 documents, and organizations with less than $25,000 in receipts in a year are also exempt. But nonprofit organizations with more than $100,000 in receipts or more than $250,000 in total assets must file a Form 990, whereas nonprofit organizations with receipts less than $100,000 but at least $25,000 and assets of less than $250,000 must file a Form 990-EZ.

Unlike financial statements from companies, Form 990 filings for nonprofit organizations do not offer a comparison with financial figures from the previous year. To make a valid comparison about a nonprofit group's finances, a reporter needs to look at the financial information for several years to analyze the changes through time. A single Form 990 only provides a snapshot of an organization's finances at the end of the year, much like a balance sheet or cash-flow statement for a public company. The Form 990 for the Chapel Hill-Carrboro YMCA near the University of North Carolina shows that the facility had more than $2.3 million in revenue in the fiscal year ended 2013, more than $2.5 million in expenses, liabilities of $265,000 and assets of more than $4.3 million.

The top of a Form 990 looks just like the tax return you file each year. The nonprofit lists its name, address, phone number and Web address. The first part of the document shows the group's revenue and expenses and changes in its net assets. For example, the Form 990 from 2013 for the Better Business Bureau Wise Giving Alliance, the nonprofit group that tracks other nonprofit organizations, listed total revenue of $1.8 million (see Figure 11.1). Its expenses for the year totaled $1.7 million, meaning that it spent almost as much as it took in. Its expenses totaled $930,000 for management salaries and general expenses, or more than its other expenses.

A business journalist should look at these numbers in comparison with the previous year's filings. If expenses rose dramatically and the money being brought into the organization did not, the reporter should examine which expenses rose and ask someone at the nonprofit why this happened. Or if the amount of money that the group took in during the year increased dramatically from the previous year, the reporter should find out why. Was there an increase in government funding? Or did the nonprofit receive more in private donations? These large increases or fluctuations can often be a story.

TIPS FROM THE PROS

University of Illinois journalism professor and former executive director of Investigative Reporters and Editors, Brant Houston on covering nonprofits:

Beware of ratios when comparing program and management costs. An ironic line about the variety in foundations—"if you have met one foundation, then you have met one foundation"—applies to nonprofits. Nonprofit spending can differ greatly depending on the organization and its mission. While a guideline often cited is that a nonprofit should spend two-thirds on delivering its program services and one-third on management, it does not apply across the board. For example, if that were true with a local United Way, which collects and passes on donations, then you would have quite a story since its management costs should be much less than one-third.

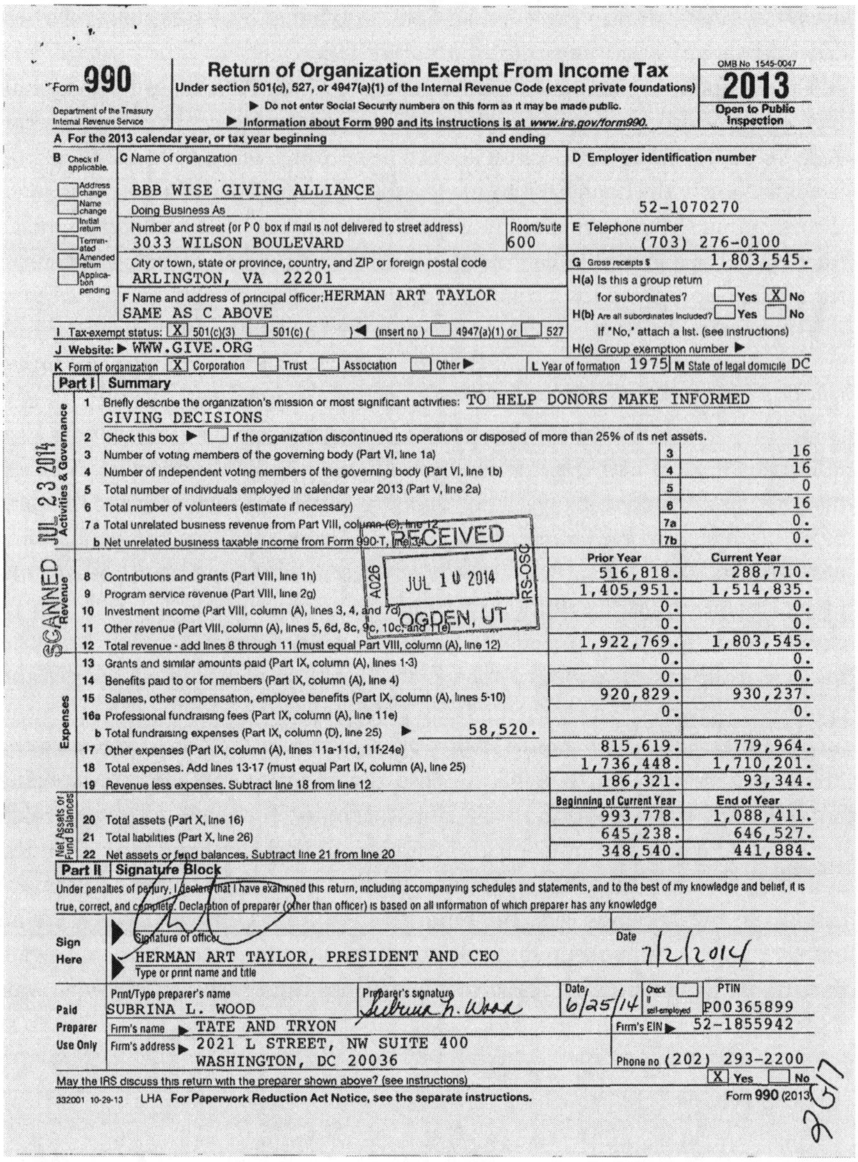

Form 990 — Return of Organization Exempt From Income Tax — Under section 501(c), 527, or 4947(a)(1) of the Internal Revenue Code (except private foundations)

▶ Do not enter Social Security numbers on this form as it may be made public.

▶ Information about Form 990 and its instructions is at www.irs.gov/form990.

Department of the Treasury, Internal Revenue Service — OMB No. 1545-0047 — 2013 — Open to Public Inspection

A For the 2013 calendar year, or tax year beginning and ending

B Check if applicable: Address change / Name change / Initial return / Terminated / Amended return / Application pending

C Name of organization: BBB WISE GIVING ALLIANCE

Doing Business As

Number and street (or P O box if mail is not delivered to street address): 3033 WILSON BOULEVARD — Room/suite: 600

City or town, state or province, country, and ZIP or foreign postal code: ARLINGTON, VA 22201

F Name and address of principal officer: HERMAN ART TAYLOR, SAME AS C ABOVE

D Employer identification number: 52-1070270

E Telephone number: (703) 276-0100

G Gross receipts $ 1,803,545.

H(a) Is this a group return for subordinates? ☐ Yes ☒ No

H(b) Are all subordinates included? ☐ Yes ☐ No — If "No," attach a list. (see instructions)

H(c) Group exemption number ▶

I Tax-exempt status: ☒ 501(c)(3) ☐ 501(c) ( ) ◀ (insert no) ☐ 4947(a)(1) or ☐ 527

J Website: ▶ WWW.GIVE.ORG

K Form of organization: ☒ Corporation ☐ Trust ☐ Association ☐ Other ▶ — L Year of formation 1975 — M State of legal domicile DC

Part I Summary

			Prior Year	Current Year
Activities & Governance	1 Briefly describe the organization's mission or most significant activities: TO HELP DONORS MAKE INFORMED GIVING DECISIONS			
	2 Check this box ▶ ☐ if the organization discontinued its operations or disposed of more than 25% of its net assets.			
	3 Number of voting members of the governing body (Part VI, line 1a)	3		16
	4 Number of independent voting members of the governing body (Part VI, line 1b)	4		16
	5 Total number of individuals employed in calendar year 2013 (Part V, line 2a)	5		0
	6 Total number of volunteers (estimate if necessary)	6		16
	7a Total unrelated business revenue from Part VIII, column (C), line 12	7a		0.
	b Net unrelated business taxable income from Form 990-T, line 34	7b		0.
Revenue	8 Contributions and grants (Part VIII, line 1h)		516,818.	288,710.
	9 Program service revenue (Part VIII, line 2g)		1,405,951.	1,514,835.
	10 Investment income (Part VIII, column (A), lines 3, 4, and 7d)		0.	0.
	11 Other revenue (Part VIII, column (A), lines 5, 6d, 8c, 9c, 10c, and 11e)		0.	0.
	12 Total revenue - add lines 8 through 11 (must equal Part VIII, column (A), line 12)		1,922,769.	1,803,545.
Expenses	13 Grants and similar amounts paid (Part IX, column (A), lines 1-3)		0.	0.
	14 Benefits paid to or for members (Part IX, column (A), line 4)		0.	0.
	15 Salaries, other compensation, employee benefits (Part IX, column (A), lines 5-10)		920,829.	930,237.
	16a Professional fundraising fees (Part IX, column (A), line 11e)		0.	0.
	b Total fundraising expenses (Part IX, column (D), line 25) ▶ 58,520.			
	17 Other expenses (Part IX, column (A), lines 11a-11d, 11f-24e)		815,619.	779,964.
	18 Total expenses. Add lines 13-17 (must equal Part IX, column (A), line 25)		1,736,448.	1,710,201.
	19 Revenue less expenses. Subtract line 18 from line 12		186,321.	93,344.
			Beginning of Current Year	**End of Year**
Net Assets or Fund Balances	20 Total assets (Part X, line 16)		993,778.	1,088,411.
	21 Total liabilities (Part X, line 26)		645,238.	646,527.
	22 Net assets or fund balances. Subtract line 21 from line 20		348,540.	441,884.

RECEIVED — JUL 10 2014 — OGDEN, UT — A026 — IRS-OSC

SCANNED JUL 23 2014

Part II Signature Block

Under penalties of perjury, I declare that I have examined this return, including accompanying schedules and statements, and to the best of my knowledge and belief, it is true, correct, and complete. Declaration of preparer (other than officer) is based on all information of which preparer has any knowledge.

Sign Here ▶ Signature of officer — Date 7/2/2014

▶ HERMAN ART TAYLOR, PRESIDENT AND CEO — Type or print name and title

Paid Preparer Use Only — Print/Type preparer's name: SUBRINA L. WOOD — Preparer's signature: Subrina L. Wood — Date: 6/25/14 — Check ☐ if self-employed — PTIN: P00365899

Firm's name ▶ TATE AND TRYON — Firm's EIN ▶ 52-1855942

Firm's address ▶ 2021 L STREET, NW SUITE 400, WASHINGTON, DC 20036 — Phone no (202) 293-2200

May the IRS discuss this return with the preparer shown above? (see instructions) ☒ Yes ☐ No

332001 10-29-13 LHA For Paperwork Reduction Act Notice, see the separate instructions. Form 990 (2013)

Figure 11.1 The Form 990 for the Wise Giving Alliance

The bottom of the first page of the Form 990 lists the organization's net assets at both the beginning and end of the year. These can be important numbers to assess the future viability of the group. If its net assets are rising, then it is a strong organization. But if the assets are falling or have become negative, this may be an indication of future financial problems. The Better Business Bureau Wise Giving Alliance reported net assets of $1.1 million at the end of 2013, compared to net assets of minus $993,778 at the beginning of the year, according to its Form 990 (see Figure 11.1).

The second page of the document breaks the expenses for the organization down into further categories, including legal expenses, supplies, postage and telephone, rent, printing and publications, and travel. These expenses are broken down for programs, management and fundraising. According to the website www.guidestar.org, many organizations lump most of their expenses into the "Other Expenses" category and detail those expenses in an attachment, even though most of the expenses could be included in a category. Therefore, it would be wise to look at the attachment.

Also pay attention to the amount of money spent on fundraising in relation to the total expenses for the year. Some believe that fundraising expenses should be a small percentage of the total expenses of a nonprofit group. However, fundraising may represent a majority of the expenses for some organizations, particularly new groups or those that are promoting an unpopular cause. If a nonprofit is spending a lot of money on fundraising but its revenue is not increasing, the fundraising has not been effective.

The next section of the Form 990 is where nonprofit organizations can list their accomplishments for the previous year, but it is only about a third of a page and does not provide enough room for many groups to detail what they have done. Part IV of the form is a balance sheet, showing the nonprofit group's assets and liabilities. This can be basic information that may not lend itself to a story. But Part V does draw attention. Part V is where the compensation and expense account allowances of officers, directors and key employees are listed in the filing. In recent years, nonprofit organizations have been offering larger compensation packages to attract managers from the for-profit world. This can provide stories for many media outlets. For example, the Form 990 for the Better Business Bureau Wise Giving Alliance showed that CEO Herman Taylor was paid a 2013 salary of \$246,831 as well as \$18,311 in employee benefits, and COO Bennett Weiner was paid a salary of \$141,531, but their salaries were paid by the Council of Better Business Bureaus Incorporated, not by the Wise Giving Alliance. None of the board members were paid a salary.

Reporters should compare the salaries at nonprofit organizations with those from the previous year. If the salaries have not increased or have gone up only slightly, there is likely nothing to write about. But if the salaries have increased dramatically or a new CEO is making much more than the previous CEO, there may be a story.

TIPS FROM THE PROS

University of Illinois journalism professor and former executive director of Investigative Reporters and Editors, Brant Houston on covering nonprofits:

If the nonprofit gets state money for programs, then see if the state has audited the expenditure of that money and taken any exceptions. Years ago, I looked through audits of a private contractor providing services for the mentally disabled and saw the state had frequently cited the contractor for misuse of funds—cars, swimming pools and other personal expenses—but taken no action.

Reporters should also watch for discrepancies between what is in the documents and what the organization is saying. The beginning of the following *Washington Post* story notes how the Form 990 filings of Jesse Jackson's nonprofit organizations omitted the salary of one of their top executives:

More than 100 pages of tax records and auditors' reports have been released by Jesse L. Jackson as questions mount about the finances of his organizations. But they make no mention of the woman with whom he fathered a child during an extramarital affair even though federal tax law required that she be listed on one form because of the amount of money she earned.

Jackson's tax-exempt Citizenship Education Fund (CEF), which received more than $10 million of the $17 million collected last year by his four charitable groups, failed to list its former executive director, Karin Stanford, on a 1999 Internal Revenue Service form that required the names of all staff members who earned more than $50,000.

Stanford, according to a spokesman for Jackson's Rainbow/PUSH Coalition, earned $120,000 when she resigned in 1999, the year she had Jackson's baby. The controversy surrounding Stanford intensified after it was disclosed that CEF gave her a "draw" of $40,000 against future consulting fees to help her buy a house in California, according to a Sept. 10, 1999, letter to Stanford from a top Jackson aide. Jackson said he gives Stanford $3,000 monthly from his personal funds.

Billy R. Owens, vice president and chief financial officer of Jackson's four interlocking organizations—Rainbow/PUSH Coalition Inc., the CEF, People United to Serve Humanity and Push for Excellence—said today that tax accountants are trying to determine whether they need to amend the IRS Form 990 on which Jackson aides declared "NONE" when asked to list the top five staff members who were paid more than $50,000 by CEF.

"The guys who prepared it are looking at everything to see if there are issues that need amending," Owens said.

The 1999 tax return also did not list the names of any firms or individuals with outside consulting contracts even though Rainbow/PUSH and related groups reported paying nearly $1 million in consulting fees. Owens's "Financial Report to Donors" said the Jackson groups paid $1.3 million in consulting fees last year.[3]

If a reporter finds a Form 990 that does not have all of the information that is required by the IRS, there might be a story. All the reporters in this case had to do was compare public statements with what was reported in the document.

Part VI of the Form 990 shows how much money the nonprofit organization spent on lobbying. Many groups spend little or no money on lobbying public officials. However, if there is a filing in which a large amount of money has been spent on lobbying compared with other expenses, a reporter should check into it. If nonprofit organizations lobby too much, they may put their tax-exempt status in jeopardy.

Part IX of the form is also of potential interest to reporters. This is where nonprofit organizations disclose information about for-profit subsidiaries. Some groups operate for-profit businesses on the side to help them raise money for their programs and services. Check this section to see if the non-profit you are investigating has one of these companies and, if so, how much money it makes.

Each year, thousands of Form 990 documents are filed with the IRS. A recent report by the General Accounting Office, however, suggested that the regulatory agency may not be reviewing all of them to find wayward nonprofit organizations, according to the following *USA Today* story:

Don't count on Uncle Sam to spot potential scams involving charities.

Internal Revenue Service oversight of charities is lagging, even as the number of nonprofits is rising, a federal study shows. Conducted by the General Accounting Office, the investigative arm of Congress, the study found the IRS lacks data to determine the type and extent of possible tax reporting violations by nonprofits. Other findings:

IRS staffing for oversight of nonprofits fell roughly 15 percent in federal fiscal years 1996–2001, even as the number of new charities seeking tax-exempt status grew 9 percent.

The rate at which the IRS examined charities dropped to less than 0.5 percent during the past two years and stands at a six-year low. The IRS does not routinely alert state-level monitors about denials and revocations of charities' tax-exempt status—information the state officials said could be used to help protect contributors.

"The bad apples get headlines after they've cheated people. Clearly, we need to reverse that order," said Sen. Charles Grassley, R-Iowa, ranking minority member of the Senate Finance Committee. "More oversight from the IRS is critical."

Grassley and the Senate panel requested the study after a USA TODAY investigation last year showed some wish-granting charities spend far more on fundraising, salaries and other costs than on their professed mission—fulfilling dreams for seriously ill children. The paper also found that the IRS audits only a fraction of the annual tax returns filed by charities.

The GAO study said the tax agency's examinations have found repeated examples of charities that improperly under-report fundraising expenses or misrepresent spending on fundraising and other costs as part of their philanthropic mission. But the IRS does not know "the extent of misreporting" and "generally has not established results-oriented goals for its oversight," the analysis found.

However, the IRS, coping with multiple oversight and collection missions, plans to study 35 segments of the charity industry to address tax misreporting by nonprofits. The report concluded the IRS should also get reliable data on tax law compliance by charities, expand oversight staffing and improve information-sharing with state charity monitors.

In a written response, IRS Commissioner Charles Rossotti agreed with the general findings and recommendations. But he cautioned that the agency must cope with "considerable resource constraints" and "competing priorities" as it tries to improve oversight.[4]

 Internal Revenue Service (IRS): A federal regulatory agency that collects taxes from businesses and individuals. The IRS also determines the tax status of a business, and reviews documents to determine if a company is in compliance with federal laws.

Business reporters are increasingly reviewing SEC documents for public companies in the wake of scandals at Enron, WorldCom, Adelphia and others. Yet few stories have been written analyzing a nonprofit organization's Form 990 filing in any depth. This area of financial reporting is ripe for aggressive reporters. Their story research does not have to find major misdeeds; the media could simply do a better, more thorough job of writing about nonprofit organizations and foundations.

In addition to Form 990 and the other suggestions on finding information about nonprofits, a number of websites are also available to help a reporter analyze IRS documents. The Guidestar site (www.guidestar.org), mentioned earlier, is far and away the most comprehensive. It helps reporters understand what the numbers mean. A similar site can be accessed at www.grantsmart.org. A third, www.charitynavigator.org, has evaluated more than 1,000 organizations and provides tips and resources.

Acquiring the Form 990 filings of a nonprofit organization shows its management team that a reporter is serious about writing a story that is fair and balanced but that also uses the best information available to provide the most complete picture of its performance (see Figure 11.1).

Blue Plans and Health Care Providers

One industry above all others has seen a number of major nonprofit players. Within the health care industry, major hospital systems, health maintenance organizations, nursing homes and other groups are often nonprofit businesses.

Kaiser Permanente is a large managed care operation that covers more than 10.1 million consumers, resulting in more than $56 billion in annual revenue in 2014. The Catholic Health Association of the United States has more than 600 hospitals, providing care for one out of every six patients in the country. The Veterans Health Administration (VHA) system contains some of the nation's best-known hospitals, including the Mayo Clinic and Cedars-Sinai Health. Many Blue Cross Blue Shield plans across the country are also not-for-profit operations.

TIPS FROM THE PROS

University of Illinois journalism professor and former executive director of Investigative Reporters and Editors, Brant Houston on covering nonprofits:

Build up your nonprofit source base. Nonprofits have enough special accounting and legal twists that you want to get an accountant who audits nonprofits and a lawyer who represents them to help you interpret documents and dissect what people tell you. Get your sources to look at documents on background and give you directions or opinions.

But most important, be ready to sit down with a nonprofit and go over your findings before you finish writing the story so you can catch any errors or misconceptions. If someone is doing wrong, you want to be absolutely right. At the same time, remember that the smaller nonprofits are often created and run by people who care deeply about the mission, but have no management experience or business acumen. Sometimes the story is not malfeasance, but their lack of skills.

Nonprofit health companies exist in every state of the country and in nearly every market. In many cases, they are competing directly with for-profit businesses for patients and members. And in many cases, they hold a dominant market share. In Alabama, for example, Blue Cross Blue Shield has an 80 percent market share in the health insurance industry. Nonprofit health organizations do not worry about making a profit or satisfying shareholders. Their mission is to provide quality health care at the lowest cost available. This is a laudable concept, but in reality these are often huge businesses with billions in revenue and millions in profits. And during the last decade, many not-for-profit hospitals and health insurance companies have converted their ownership structure into that of a for-profit company. Some have even sold themselves to for-profit corporations.

Nonprofit health businesses are run just like other not-for-profit organizations. In many cases, they have tax-exempt status from the federal government, although Blue Cross Blue Shield organizations lost their full exemption from federal income taxes in 1986. They file documents with the IRS reporting their financial performance and executive compensation. St. Joseph's Hospital in Tampa, for example, reported revenue of $832.2 million in 2013 and expenses of $733.2 million in the same year, according to its Form 990. Martha Jefferson Hospital in Charlottesville, VA, reported revenues of $253.7 million and expenses of $238 million for the same year. In many cases, these not-for-profit health businesses are also reporting financial information to state regulators who oversee insurance and health care.

Nonprofit hospitals and other health care businesses have many of the same issues as their for-profit competitors. They must keep costs down to survive.

Strong management can make the overall company better. Acquisitions or expansions help these organizations grow into new businesses and new markets. They also have advantages. Whereas for-profit hospitals and insurance companies can tap the equities market and raise money by selling stock, nonprofit organizations can sell tax-exempt bonds. And studies have shown that for-profit health companies have higher costs. But nonprofits also face problems just like any other business venture. For example, an expansion might not work out as planned, or an executive brought in to turn the business around might fail and be asked to leave, as the following *Boston Herald* story shows:

> Staff at the UMass Memorial Health Care Inc. report a sense of relief that Dr. Arthur R. Russo is leaving the beleaguered hospital.
>
> Hospital directors pushed Russo to resign late Wednesday after his 14-month tenure. He was criticized for his attempts to reorganize the hospital, including cutting a popular liver transplant program at the institution.
>
> He also oversaw more than 200 job cuts and backed an executive who lied on his résumé.
>
> "The mood is much lighter today than it was yesterday," said Dr. Eliezer Katz, head of the liver transplant program, which was ultimately saved. "There is cautious optimism that we will see a change for the better."
>
> The staff has confidence in Dr. Marianne E. Felice, who has taken over as interim chief executive, Katz said. "She has a lot of respect and trust," he said.
>
> A search is planned for a permanent replacement for Russo.
>
> The 761-bed, eight-hospital group lost an estimated $24 million on operations for the just-ended fiscal year, on revenue of $1.07 billion, spokesman Mark Shelton said. The loss would top last year's $9.4 million deficit on revenue of $1.06 billion, he said.
>
> In an attempt to stop the bleeding, officials of the 10,000-employee nonprofit hospital network brought in the Hunter Group, a Florida health care consulting firm. Hunter made a number of controversial recommendations including 500 job cuts and eliminating liver transplants.
>
> The decision to cut the liver transplant program drew criticism from doctors and former patients, who picketed the hospital. Eventually, hospital executives conceded and kept the program.
>
> Russo also backed Michael Greene and kept him on staff after it was revealed that he fabricated his education credentials on his résumé. It's not certain whether Greene will remain on staff, a spokesman said.
>
> A severance package for Russo, who made $680,000, is still being negotiated, a spokesman said. He is expected to stay on and advise Felice through the transition.
>
> Felice is chief of pediatrics at the medical center and a professor at the affiliated University of Massachusetts Medical School. She has been with the center for three years.[5]

In addition, the *Star Tribune* in Minneapolis reported that a number of top executives at nonprofit health care companies in the state were receiving larger compensation packages than disclosed in their operations' Form 990s.

The number of not-for-profit health operations is stable. A General Accounting Office report in December 1997 found that 192 of the more than 5,000 not-for-profit hospitals in the country converted to for-profit status between 1990 and 1996. In 1996, more than 60 converted. Today, the number of nonprofit hospitals is about 2,900 of the 5,686 hospitals in the country, according to the American Hospital Association, about the same as it was in 2009.

In the health insurance industry, nonprofit plans are converting to for-profit status, particularly among Blue Cross Blue Shield operations. The Blue organization in North Carolina filed plans to convert to for-profit status but then withdrew its plans, whereas similar operations in New York, Georgia, Missouri and other states have converted. Some Blue operations, it should be noted, have stated that they will not convert into for-profit companies.

As nonprofit organizations, these businesses belong to the community and their customers. There are no shareholders. But by converting, they are taking that community "ownership" and giving it to stockholders. Many states passed legislation in the 1990s requiring these nonprofit health groups to give something back to the people in exchange for this conversion.

conversion: The process where a company changes its ownership structure, typically from one where the business is owned by customers to one where the business is owned by stockholders.

Now, plans by a not-for-profit health care company to convert to for-profit status must be approved by state and federal regulators. In many cases, public hearings must also be held. The process of the conversion can result in good stories, from the initial filing of the conversion plan to the public hearings, at which consumers are likely to speak about the rising cost of health care and how turning the company into a for-profit venture will increase their medical costs.

Regulators throughout the years have required the not-for-profit health company to set up a foundation with the value of the organization that has been built during its time as a benefit to the community. The valuation of the company—and therefore the amount of money that the foundation receives—can be a sticking point in the conversion plan. In some states, the foundation received a small amount of money only to see the for-profit health care business sold for much more several years later.

In other cases, nonprofit organizations have been criticized for selling themselves for much less than many believe they are worth. One of the issues is that executives of not-for-profit ventures do not have an ownership stake in the entity. CEOs of public companies often own stock and want to sell their companies for the highest price so that they receive as much as possible for their stock. But executives at nonprofits do not have such an incentive.

In some cases, regulators have stepped in and prevented acquisitions of nonprofit health care operations because they felt the price was too low. The California attorney general stopped the sale of a hospital to Columbia/HCA because its offer was $200 million less than competing bids. And the Maryland insurance commissioner turned down a request to sell the not-for-profit Blue Cross Blue Shield operation in the state to for-profit WellPoint. This type of situation—particularly the facts surrounding the scuttling of the deal—is a good story. The companies are also likely to seek another deal, which may result in another story.

Although these nonprofit organizations looking to convert are required to file their financial performance with the IRS, many of them also issue releases showing their performance, just like for-profit companies. They are gearing up for the switch and begin performing some of the functions of a public company.

The following excerpt shows how a reporter analyzed the earnings release from a Blue Cross Blue Shield company in the midst of a conversion process, providing the context through statements from benefits consultants and historical comparisons to show the reader the impact the large profit might have on regulators and other interested parties:

> With its for-profit conversion serving as a backdrop, Blue Cross reported an $85.6 million profit for 2001—the biggest bottom line in the 69-year-old insurer's history.
>
> While company officials described the historic high in terms such as "a continuation of the company's improving operating performance," a health care advocate was more succinct: "Holy moley."
>
> However you describe it, the number indicates more than a good year for the state's largest insurer at 2.5 million members.
>
> "They are simply not acting like a nonprofit company, they are focused on bringing in profits and building the business," said the health care advocate, Adam Searing, who is project director of The N.C. Health Access Coalition in Raleigh. "It makes me think even more they should be allowed to convert."
>
> The large profit—the closest rival was a $75.6 million profit in 1993—also raises the question of why Blue Cross and Blue Shield of North Carolina needed the double-digit premium increases it sought and recently won from state insurance officials, a health benefits consultant in Charlotte said.
>
> "I think that will bring the question from the public—what's really the story?" said Steve Graybill, a senior benefits consultant with William M. Mercer.
>
> Dan Glaser, the chief financial officer at Blue Cross, said premiums are based on medical costs, which have been trending up in recent years. Medical cost trends rose 13.9 percent in 2001 and 8.8 percent the previous year, he noted Tuesday.

Graybill agreed that medical costs are increasing between 12 percent and 16 percent.

"But how do you get to a 33 percent increase on a given product—are they losing their rears?" Graybill asked.

Blue Cross has an array of health plans it sells to employers and other groups, as well as to individuals. A majority of those plans got premium increases that range from 27 percent to 47 percent on average, according to N.C. Department of Insurance information.

The Chapel Hill insurer's 78,000-member HMO, Blue Care, won an average premium increase of 47 percent that goes into effect in July and its 105,000-member Blue Choice plan premium will go up an average of 37 percent in July, according to insurance department information. Other Blue Cross plans that represent about a quarter of the insurer's business aren't going up as much this year, with rate increases varying between 5 percent and 8 percent.

While the insurance department has approved the rate increases, it is keeping an eye on the issue as Blue Cross works through the process of converting to a for-profit company.

"We're looking at is there a comprehensive plan here to raise rates, preconversion," said Mollie Doll, a spokeswoman for the department.[6]

This story ends with the mention that a not-for-profit business bought a for-profit operation. In many states, as noted earlier in the chapter, a nonprofit organization can own a for-profit subsidiary.

If a not-for-profit health care company in a community plans to convert, one of the first steps it will take as part of the process will be to hire a new leader with for-profit experience. That CEO will come into the nonprofit and make changes. The next step is to file their intent with regulators.

Reporters should be on the lookout for any indications that their local not-for-profit health care companies may be thinking about a change. The decision could have broad implications for the community. As a for-profit venture, the hospital or health insurer may raise rates. Also, it now has the ability to raise cash through the stock market and use that money to make acquisitions or to expand its existing operations. And as a for-profit, it could also provide stock options and other incentives to its executives. These moves bear watching.

Attorneys general and labor unions have also begun to criticize the nonprofit status of many health care businesses, according to the Coalition for Nonprofit Health Care. In some cases, they have forced the breakup of a nonprofit, whereas in other cases a divestiture has been forced. Regulators have also threatened to remove the board of a not-for-profit health business.

YMCAs and Other Nonprofits

Many other nonprofit businesses also fall under the radar of most media outlets. Yet they can be a surprising source for news.

Nonprofit organizations and foundations can often make great profiles for the work that they do. They are almost always trying to better their communities or help others. Find the work that they do and the people that they have helped. A *USA Today* profile of a former Cisco Systems executive who started her own foundation to help technology start-ups by women is a perfect example. ABC News profiled how other high-tech executives in the Seattle area have started foundations to help others with the millions they made. The *Chronicle of Higher Education* reported in December 2015 that 32 leaders of private, nonprofit colleges made more than $1 million in 2013.

The relationship between nonprofits and for-profits can also yield interesting stories. The *Wall Street Journal* reported how some entrepreneurial scientists were receiving government grants through nonprofit organizations and then using the money to fund for-profit biotechnology companies.

In some cases, the nonprofit and the for-profit share office space and are run by the same person. These types of connections should raise eyebrows with anyone. And like with for-profit businesses, stories can come from executive salaries, illegal activities, major campaigns to raise money and changes in leadership.

A *Winston-Salem Journal* story focused on the salary of a CEO at a nonprofit health organization. The following is the beginning of that story:

> Carl Armato, chief executive and president of Novant Health Inc., received a 14.4 percent jump in salary during fiscal 2014 to $1.19 million.
>
> The non-for-profit system, based in Winston-Salem but with a major Charlotte presence, released Friday its fiscal 2014 executive compensation figures. It has about 25,000 employees in its four-state territory, including about 5,000 in the Triad.
>
> Armato is in his fourth year as the system's top executive. His salary has risen 70.9 percent since he took over as the top executive Jan. 1, 2012, following the retirement of Paul Wiles.
>
> Armato's incentive compensation increased less than 1 percent to $919,738. Altogether, Armato's core compensation was $2.59 million.
>
> Novant, like most health-care systems serving North Carolina, says high compensation levels are necessary to recruit and retain executives to run "a very complex organization."
>
> Novant said in a statement accompanying the executive compensation chart that "executive compensation must follow very specific checks and balances."[7]

The story then goes on to discuss how Novant's operating revenue rose to $3.79 billion and that hospital management pay has become a hot issue as many of them have cut jobs.

Reporters should check for stories about nonprofit organizations in unusual places. The YMCA in Chapel Hill decided to build a child-care center in a retirement home center recently. The uniqueness of putting young kids with old adults made for an interesting story. Or reporters can check to see if a nonprofit organization is buying land by reviewing local real estate records.

If there is a recent transaction, the reporter should ask what they plan to do with the land.

Covering nonprofit businesses and foundations should be just like writing stories about for-profit companies. In many cases, you are looking in the same places for information—courthouse records, federal filings, lawsuits, etc. Reporters need to look for trends. If all of the nonprofit organizations in the area are seeing their assets decline, reporters should ask why that is happening. Is it because they all heavily invested their assets in the stock market? Or has gift giving slowed? How do they plan to correct the slowdown? Does the decline in assets mean that they will be giving out fewer grants this year? Or is there a foundation or nonprofit group bucking the trend, showing strong growth in its total assets and the amount of its giving while others in the same field or region have seen drops? What is this organization doing that others are not?

Many nonprofit groups also have websites with information about their programs and services. If there is a new program being added, a reporter should interview someone at the organization to find out what the potential is to bring in additional revenue. An executive director or program director might be the first place to start.

Covering nonprofits can be just like any other beat. The reporter has just got to know what to look for and what questions to ask.

Notes

1. From "Goodwill to open megastore: Retail supercenter will be area's largest," by M. Lindenberger, February 15, 2001, *Dallas Morning News,* p. 1N, Copyright 2001 by *Dallas Morning News.* Reprinted with permission.
2. From "Kauffman Foundation will increase small grants to nonprofits," by J. Spivak, January 24, 2003, *Kansas City Star,* p. A1. Copyright 2003 by *Kansas City Star.* Reprinted with permission.
3. From "Missing information noted in Jackson's tax records," by W. Claiborne, March 7, 2001, *Washington Post,* p. A3. Copyright 2001 by *Washington Post.* Reprinted with permission.
4. From "IRS oversight of charities falls behind," by K. McCoy, May 28, 2002, *USA Today,* p. 1B. Copyright 2002 by *USA Today.* Reprinted with permission.
5. From "UMass hospital ousts embattled Russo as CEO," by J. Heldt Powell, November 2, 2001, *Boston Herald,* p. 38. Copyright 2001 by *Boston Herald.* Reprinted with permission.
6. From "Blue Cross racks up record $85.6M profit; as nonprofit eyes for-profit status, question arises about a need for large rate increases," by J. Zimmer, March 20, 2002, *Durham Herald-Sun,* p. C1. Copyright 2002 by Durham Herald Company Inc. Reprinted with permission.
7. From "Novant top executive gets 14 percent salary hike," by R. Craver, December 11, 2015, *Winston-Salem Journal,* p. A13. Copyright 2015 by *Winston-Salem Journal.* All rights reserved. Reprinted with permission.

 ## Key Terms

conversion	foundation
Form 990	Internal Revenue Service (IRS)

 **Suggested Exercises**

1. Go around the class and ask if anyone has ever donated money to a nonprofit organization. If someone did, what made him decide to donate money to that particular entity? Did he think about what his money would be used for? Did anyone consider looking at the financial statements of the organization to see if it was using money properly?

2. Find a Form 990 of a nonprofit organization or a foundation on the Internet. Many groups now post these documents online. Read the filing and, if possible, compare the numbers to the Form 990 from the previous year. Write a 500-word essay analyzing what the document tells you about the revenue for the organization and how the expenses were divided among programs, management and fundraising. Conclude with a statement on the organization's financial condition at the end of the year.

3. Go to a local nonprofit organization and ask for a copy of their Form 990. The next day, report to the class whether you received the form and how easy it was to obtain. Did the organization have the document readily available, or did it take some time for them to find it? Did the organization deny you access to the filing? If so, what reasons did they give? Some suggestions are the local YMCA, a public television or radio station, the local Salvation Army or Goodwill organization or the local American Red Cross.

4. Find a nonprofit organization that has spent a large amount of money recently on fundraising and compare its revenues for the last three years. Did the fundraising have any impact on revenue? Do you think that the fundraising used by the organization was effective? Why or why not? What else could the organization have done to raise money?

5. Look for a local hospital or health insurance plan that is not-for-profit. If you can find one, ask yourself whether it competes with another hospital or insurance plan that is a for-profit company. Can you tell if they're operated any differently? What is the perception among local residents about the differences between the not-for-profit business and the for-profit entity?

 Nonprofit Books

Carver, J. (1997). *Boards that make a difference: A new design for leadership in nonprofit and public organizations*. Hoboken, NJ: Jossey-Bass.

Dowie, M. (2001). *American foundations: An investigative history*. Cambridge, MA: MIT Press.

Drucker, P. (1992). *Managing the nonprofit organization: Principles and practices*. New York: Harper Business.

Weinstein, S. (2002). *The complete guide to fund-raising management* (2nd ed.). New York: Wiley.

Wolf, T. (1999). *Managing a nonprofit organization in the twenty-first century*. New York: Fireside Books.

References

Adams, C. (2001, January 30). Laboratory hybrids: How adroit scientists aid biotech companies with taxpayer money. *Wall Street Journal*, p. 1A.

Claiborne, W. (2001, March 7). Missing information noted in Jackson's tax records. *Washington Post*, p. A3.

Craver, R. (2015, December 12). Novant top executive gets 14 percent salary hike. *Winston-Salem Journal*, p. A13. Retrieved December 15, 2015 from www.journal-now.com/business/business_news/local/novant-top-executive-gets-percent-salary-hike/article_c5259dd8–3262–5557-bb9b-3d4f62026763.html.

Heldt Powell, J. (2001, November 2). UMass hospital ousts embattled Russo as CEO. *Boston Herald*, p. 38.

Howatt, G. (2001, November 30). Health-care executives were paid more than reported; The nonprofit companies vary in their interpretation of an IRS rule on disclosing deferred compensation. *The Star Tribune*, p. 1A.

Johnson, S. (2015, December 11). Former Field Museum employee accused of stealing $900,000 over seven years. *Chicago Tribune*. Retrieved December 15, 2015 from www.chicagotribune.com/entertainment/museums/ct-field-museum-employee-theft-20151211-story.html.

Kambhampati, S. (2015, December 6). 32 Leaders of private colleges earned more than $1 million in 2013. *Chronicle of Higher Education*. Retrieved December 15, 2015 from http://chronicle.com/article/32-Leaders-of-Private-Colleges/234482.

Lindenberger, M.A. (2001, February 15). Goodwill to open megastore; Retail supercenter will be area's largest. *The Dallas Morning News*, p. 1N.

McCoy, K. (2002, May 28). IRS oversight of charities falls behind. *USA Today*, p. 1B.

Nalder, E. (2003, April 27). CEO's rewards at nonprofit. *San Jose Mercury News*, p. 1A.

Okeson, S. (2002, August 4). Stopping crime has "shocking" price tag—CrimeStoppers defends spending 55 percent of expenses on fund-raising. *Peoria Journal Star*, p. 1A.

Phillips, C., & McFadden, K. (2003, April 18). Head of Seattle's public-TV station to step down amid devastating debt. *The Seattle Times*, p. A1.

Shatzkin, K. (2003, May 11). Some foundations spend lavishly on own board members; Most in U.S. pay nothing, but in some cases, fees exceed amount of gifts. *The Baltimore Sun*, p. 1A.

Spivak, J. (2003, January 24). Kauffman Foundation will increase small grants to nonprofits. *Kansas City Star*, p. A1.

Wang, D. (1999, August 4). A boom in giving. ABCNews.com. Retrieved November 29, 2002 from http://abcnews.go.com/sections/tech/DailyNews/hitech_philanthropy 990804.html.

Zimmer, J. (2002, March 20). Blue Cross racks up record $85.6M profit; as nonprofit eyes for-profit status, question arises about a need for large rate increases. *Durham Herald-Sun*, p. C1.

12

BUSINESS NEWS IN THE COURTHOUSE

Use Courts to Find Biz Stories

Given the economic crisis of the past few years, there's no better place than the courthouse, particularly bankruptcy court, to find great business stories. Businesses and individuals have been filing for bankruptcy-court protection in record numbers, and the stories of how they got there are terrific. Bankruptcy cases in recent years have run the gamut from the Phoenix Coyotes hockey team to newspaper owners to the producers of the *Terminator* film series. In the 12 months ended September 30, 2015, the number of bankruptcy cases totaled 860,182, according to the administrative office of the U.S. Courts, with business cases totaling 24,985.

Other courts can also be great sources for business stories. In addition to submitting all of the filings regarding business licenses and deeds for property purchased in the course of business, companies often head to the courthouse to file a lawsuit when they have a dispute with a customer, a supplier, a competitor or an employee. In addition, people who come in contact with a business may also find the need to file a lawsuit against a company.

Litigation as a business tactic and as a way to redress a wrong committed by a company is on the increase; therefore, having an understanding of how the court system is used in the business world is vital to any reporter. Business lawsuits may disclose to the world the first glimpse into a major business conflict or a company's struggles.

The difference between business-related lawsuits filed in federal court and cases filed in state court is simple. Cases are filed in federal court when the company or person suing the business is based in another state. Cases are filed in state court when both the plaintiff and the defendant are based in the same state.

DIFFERENT COURT SYSTEMS

1. **County and state courts:** Will often handle complaints between businesses that are both from the same jurisdiction or complaints by consumers who live in the same county as the business.
2. **Federal courts:** Often handle class action lawsuits filed by employees and consumers against businesses, as well as business litigation against another business when the plaintiff is located in another state from the defendant.
3. **Bankruptcy court:** Part of the federal court system, bankruptcy court handles cases in which a business or individual cannot repay debts to lenders and suppliers.
4. **Small claims court:** Typically covers disputes under $5,000. Any individual or business may use a small claims court, sometimes conducted in the evening for the convenience of the public. Most litigants appear without an attorney.

Some businesses spend a lot of time in the courtroom. In 2000, retailer Wal-Mart Stores Incorporated was sued 4,851 times, or once nearly every two hours, according to a *USA Today* account of its legal tactics. Legal analysts believe that Wal-Mart is sued more often than any other entity in the country except the U.S. government. The Arkansas-based company has recently adopted the strategy of fighting most of the lawsuits against it instead of settling. The plaintiffs run the gamut from shoppers injured while inside one of Wal-Mart's stores to a husband whose wife was abducted in a Wal-Mart parking lot and later killed.

Business executives make decisions every day that can end up in a lawsuit. In fact, some businesses are currently facing lawsuits for decisions made by company executives who have been dead for more than 100 years. Insurer Aetna Incorporated, railroad operator CSX Corporation and bank FleetBoston Financial Corporation were sued by descendants of slaves seeking compensation from these businesses for profiting from slavery. Manufacturers are now facing multimillion-dollar lawsuits for decisions made more than a half century ago to construct buildings with asbestos, later discovered to cause serious illness and death after inhalation.

plaintiff: The individual or business who files the charges in a lawsuit against another party asking for damages or a court ruling.

Other lawsuits may result from less dramatic but nonetheless illegal decisions. A company may decide to build a new product using technology patented or owned by another company without seeking its approval. A manager may share information from a former worker's personnel file with a potential new employer. Or a manager may ask a female job candidate her age and whether she plans to have a baby in the next 12 months. All of these incidents may lead to lawsuits.

Businesses also sue other businesses. One business may enter into a contract with another business to supply it with widgets for a set price. But if the cost of producing widgets goes up, the first company may seek to break the contract because it is losing money under the arrangement. The business receiving the widgets may file a lawsuit seeking to force the company that signed the contract to honor its obligation.

A business may also sue another business if it is owed money and the other company refuses to pay. For example, maybe a company built decks on the backs of houses in a new subdivision for a homebuilder, but the homebuilder believes the decks were sloppily built so it refuses to pay. The deck builder may sue the homebuilder to attempt to collect the money.

Or a business may sue another business if it believes that its proprietary product information is being violated. Companies own patents on inventions and trademarks on brand names so that other businesses cannot use them for their gain. When a company believes another company has infringed on its products, it will file a lawsuit, as happened between two companies, according to the following *Twin Cities Business Magazine* report:

> Manufacturing giant 3M filed a patent infringement lawsuit on Tuesday accusing XPEL Technologies Corporation of replicating a paint protection film it developed to protect vehicles from scratches, stains, bug acids and rock chips.
>
> 3M claims San Antonio-based XPEL, a software developer and manufacturer of XPF Paint Production Film (the product at issue in this case), not only infringed on the 3M's nearly decade-old paint technology, but also "targeted and/or concentrated" sales through dealers located in Minnesota. The Maplewood-based manufacturer of Scotch Tape, Post-It notes and other industrial supplies is hoping the Court will take personal jurisdiction over XPEL in this case.
>
> According to the court filing, 3M said XPEL sold its paint film product to at least nine Minnesota dealers, including Northland Resources, A&L Auto Detail Inc., Bravo Auto Bra, Midwest Clear Bra and Trim Doctor.
>
> 3M's protective film product, developed by Woodbury residents Charlie Ho and Kenneth Halford, is a transparent, multilayer polyurethane film applied over a vehicle's paint job. XPEL has advertised its own product as designed to "protect the leading edge of your vehicle from damage caused by rocks, gravel, salt or insects through the application of a thin and virtually invisible urethane paint protection film."
>
> A spokesperson for 3M said the company "would not comment on pending litigation." XPEL could not be reached for comment.

In its court filing, 3M said it would be seeking damages equal to the sales XPEL gained through infringement, as well as costs to cover attorneys' fees and expenses. A specific dollar amount was not indicated within the filing.

3M was recently picked as a company to watch in 2016 after an RBC Capital Markets analyst told TCB that 3M is poised for "an optimistic 7–10 percent growth" in sales next year in developing countries, and similarly so in other high-growth markets like China.[1]

A business will also file a lawsuit if it believes that another business is interfering with its ability to operate by, for example, stealing its customers. A business such as a bank or another lender may file a lawsuit against another business if that company is not repaying its loan. Or, a business may sue a business in which it is an investor if it feels as if the company in which it has invested is not performing the way it wants.

TIPS FROM THE PROS

Wall Street Journal deputy chief of investigations Jennifer S. Forsyth on covering courts:

Don't diminish the importance of white collar crime. Court coverage usually connotes bloody victims and knife-wielding defendants, but swindlers like Bernard Madoff can wreck the savings of hundreds, even thousands, of investors with a multi-billion dollar Ponzi scheme. People who steal other people's money are big stories with sympathetic victims and there was great drama when he had to face his victims in court. Keep in mind, though, despite Madoff's 150-year prison sentence, many white collar criminals get light prison sentences.

Many business-related lawsuits may not merit even a one-paragraph brief. It is up to the reporter and the editor to decide if the allegations in the lawsuit warrant coverage. The *Washington Post* is not likely to write a story about a small convenience store in Bethesda, Maryland, filing a lawsuit against its potato chip supplier for failing to provide a shipment one month, causing it to lose sales. But that lawsuit may be news in a small town where the store could be one of the few places selling potato chips.

With any litigation involving a business, a reporter should read the entire filing, assessing the seriousness of the allegations and what damages are being sought. Multiple allegations may be mentioned in the original filing. The plaintiffs and the defendants—there can be more than one on both sides—are also specifically identified. In many business lawsuits, the location of the company headquarters is named and an address is given. This can help a reporter find someone to talk to at the company to get a response.

In some corporate lawsuits, a business may ask for a judge to issue a temporary restraining order preventing another company from taking some action that may hurt the business. Many lawsuits simply ask for damages. Some filings may mention a monetary amount as a remedy for damages. This amount should be included in any story about a business-related case.

Important information to be included in any story about business litigation is as follows:

1. The names of the plaintiffs and the defendants and their business relationship;
2. Background on these businesses, which is often contained in the lawsuit;
3. The type of damage alleged in the case. For example, when Liggett Group and Brooke Group, two cigarette makers, sued two-dozen insurance companies, they alleged the insurers were refusing to pay claims to smokers who should have been covered under their policies;
4. When the lawsuit was filed and in which court;
5. History between the two parties of the lawsuit, again sometimes detailed in the initial complaint;
6. Any special considerations, such as permanent or temporary injunctions or restraining orders, sought in the filing.

Writing stories about business-related lawsuits also requires the reporter to call both the plaintiff and the defendant to obtain a reaction. Company executives often will not comment. It is best to go to the public relations staff or the lawyers representing the company. The reporter should try hard to get a comment from both sides to make the story fair. After the original complaint has been filed, the defendant will have a chance to respond to the charges with their own filing. Most of the time, they will deny any wrongdoing. If the case is large enough, their response should also be reported.

Sources When Covering Business Court Cases

1. **The clerk of the court:** He or she will know when lawsuits, depositions and exhibits are filed.
2. **Lawyers:** Talk to the attorneys representing the plaintiffs and the defendants.
3. **Administrative assistants for judges:** They can tell you who is on the judge's calendar, giving you an indication of upcoming rulings.
4. **The plaintiffs and defendants:** Both will want to have their side of the story heard.

Many times, the case will be settled before it goes to court. Settlements and rulings usually come after hearings related to the case in which both sides of the lawsuit argue their point of view. The hearing, as well as the ruling, might be newsworthy, and the reporter should keep up to date on such developments.

There are many hearings involved in court cases that might be newsworthy. Journalists should not just report on the initial filing of the lawsuit and then wait until the trial begins. There is plenty of news occurring between the two.

Employee-Related Litigation

A female worker walks into a break room and finds male workers reviewing nude pictures of other women in a magazine. A male worker wants a job at a restaurant, but the restaurant declines to hire him, saying that they only hire females for the job that he wants. A male supervisor makes suggestive comments to a married female subordinate and asks her out for a drink after work. Another worker asks for training so that she can be considered for future promotions but is denied the opportunity. A factory worker spends 60 hours on the job one week, but is only paid for 40 of those hours. Another worker becomes seriously ill because of the dust inhaled while on the job and has to spend three weeks in the hospital recuperating.

All of the above are examples of incidents that may lead employees to sue their employer to recoup damages suffered while on the job. The number of employee discrimination lawsuits filed in federal courts in the year ended Sept. 30, 2014, totaled 11,937, according to a U.S. Department of Justice study.

Employee lawsuits against businesses make for good stories. They are David versus Goliath all over again. For example, an average employee sues a multibillion-dollar corporation that views him as an ant to be used to increase its profits and improve its productivity. If only employee lawsuits were that black and white. Too often, there are many shades of gray when it comes to employee litigation. Yes, an employee might have been mistreated. But is the company responsible?

To be sure, in thousands of cases workers have defeated their current or former employer and won damages. They file charges and win for not receiving overtime pay, such as what happened to Wal-Mart employees as described in the following excerpt:

> Wal-Mart Stores Inc. agreed to pay employees $4.8 million in back wages and damages, as well as $464,000 in civil penalties, on Tuesday after the U.S. Department of Labor found the company failed to pay overtime to more than 4,500 workers.
>
> While the fine pales in comparison to the $352 million the Bentonville, Ark.-company paid in 2008 to settle 63 suits across the country over allegations it didn't provide workers with proper rest and meal breaks, the settlement highlights the lingering complaints Wal-Mart faces over how it treats its workers.

In this settlement, the Labor Department found that workers employed as Wal-Mart or Sam's Club security guards or as managers in the stores' vision departments between 2004 and 2007 were denied overtime pay when they were incorrectly classified as exempt from the federal Fair Labor Standards Act's overtime laws.

The act mandates employees be paid at least a $7.25 minimum wage, plus time-and-one-half their regular rates for hours worked beyond 40 per week. Some employees, such as executives and administrative workers who are paid a salary of more than $455 a week, are exempt from overtime rules.

Although the suit was resolved only recently, Wal-Mart said it had adjusted its pay practices and reclassified its employees in 2007 when the Labor Department alerted the company to the problem. It has also employed electronic systems to document compliance with state and federal labor laws.

The settlement will award workers payments ranging from $30 to $10,800.

"When the issues resolved today were initially raised in 2007, we took them seriously and fully cooperated with the Department of Labor to make sure they were corrected," said Wal-Mart spokesman Greg Rossiter.[2]

Note the details in this story, such as how much workers will be paid and what the law states. In addition, analysis from a law expert or a business expert would have lent more credence to the writing and helped explain the bigger picture.

Sometimes suits filed by employees against companies begin as one lawsuit by one employee, and then other employees who believe they have been treated in a similar manner join as plaintiffs. Sometimes these suits are classified as class action lawsuits to represent a body of former workers. Cases like this can involve discrimination, harassment or other hiring practices.

TIPS FROM THE PROS

Wall Street Journal deputy chief of investigations Jennifer S. Forsyth on covering courts:

Trials aren't the only activities at a courthouse. In fact, seemingly routine hearings, such as a request for a judge to freeze a defendant's bank account or to order that person not to leave the country, can be a good glimpse into the allegations against him or her. Plus, it's a great chance to meet the players in the case, including government lawyers who otherwise might be reluctant to pick up the phone, as well as family members or associates of the accused or other lawyers tangentially tied to the case who could be valuable sources.

Employee-related cases often require the reporter to dig deeper into the workplace environment. If a reporter is interested in giving readers or viewers a broader picture of what it is like to work at a company, he can review other documents, such as EEOC filings, other lawsuits filed against the company and OSHA records.

Employee-related lawsuits may not always be decided by a trial jury. In December 2002, an arbitration panel ordered stockbroker Salomon Smith Barney to pay $3.2 million to a female stockbroker as part of a settlement of a sex-discrimination class action lawsuit against the firm. The three-member panel's decision was the first to come out of a dispute resolution process for plaintiffs who could not come to terms with the company.

Cases sometimes will be referred to a mediator or an arbitrator to resolve the dispute. Mediation and arbitration are also often used in international business litigation. Many times, one side or the other will suggest this procedure to settle a case as a way of lowering the costs. In addition, employee-related lawsuits often include other documents related to a company—such as employee contracts and internal memos—that may give a better indication of working conditions. These contracts and documents should be read carefully. They might add good color and anecdotes to a story.

mediation: An attempt to settle a lawsuit by an independent third party who attempts to find common points of agreement in order to reach a fair result for both sides.

Those employee contracts can also lead to a business suing current and former workers. Businesses will sue a former employee if they believe that the ex-worker has stolen information or documents and taken them to a new job, particularly if the person is working for a competitor. Many companies use noncompete agreements or clauses in contracts requiring their workers to abstain from working for a direct competitor for a certain amount of time.

Noncompete agreements protect trade secrets. A trade secret can be information that gives a company a competitive advantage because it is not generally known and cannot be readily learned by other businesses that could benefit from it. It can be a formula, pattern, compilation, program, device, method, technique or process that a company has made reasonable efforts to keep secret.

TIPS FROM THE PROS

Wall Street Journal deputy chief of investigations Jennifer S. Forsyth on covering courts:

Companies can be charged with crimes. Most people tend to think of individuals as being indicted, but many companies have faced the same fate. The big accounting firm, Arthur Andersen LLP, effectively went out of business after being indicted for its role in the Enron Corp. scandal. (The firm's conviction was eventually overturned by the Supreme Court but the damage was done.) Indictments against major companies are rare, though many settle with the government in court cases that are approved by a judge. When that happens, the company avoids being charged but its wrongdoing still can cause major reputational harm.

For example, Coca-Cola limits who at the company knows the secret formula to make its famous soft drink. If one of those employees were to leave the company, a noncompete agreement prevents that person from using the formula. (California law excludes noncompete agreements except in narrow instances.)

The following excerpt details a case in which a noncompete agreement became a major story regarding the hiring of an executive by one telecommunications company away from another.

> Sprint Corp. on Sunday said William T. Esrey plans to step down as chief executive and the company has offered the job to Gary Forsee, vice chairman of BellSouth Corp.
>
> BellSouth, however, is trying to block Forsee's move in court. In a brief statement released Sunday evening, Sprint effectively confirmed days of speculation.
>
> The statement said its "independent directors have been evaluating management succession alternatives." It did not say whether the board asked Esrey to leave, or if the chief executive is resigning for other reasons.
>
> The statement said Esrey will be chairman of Sprint "for a transition period." For now, Esrey and president and chief operating officer Ronald T. LeMay will "remain in their current positions with Sprint," the statement said.
>
> LeMay, long considered Esrey's successor, also is expected to leave the company.
>
> Sprint officials declined Sunday to shed further light on an increasingly murky management situation.
>
> "I'm just going to tell you the statement speaks for itself," said board member Irvine O. Hockaday, Jr. "As events progress and it becomes either required or appropriate, even if not required, to offer additional information, that will be done."[3]

Other companies require employees, particularly executives, to sign agreements when they leave the company that set out post-employment guidelines. These agreements may provide the executives a monetary settlement in return for certain conditions, such as not publicly talking to the media about their tenure at the company. Some companies have sued former employees who have broken these severance package deals.

bankruptcy: When a person or company is unable to repay debts. In corporate cases, ownership of the firm's assets are often transferred from stockholders to the bondholders.

On the other side, executives can also sue businesses after they have left the job if the company has not lived up to its side of the agreement. A business can be sued if its executives talk disparagingly about the former coworker, hurting his or her ability to get another job. Or a former executive can sue a company if the business does not uphold the terms of the severance agreement by providing payments or other terms agreed upon in the contract.

Allen Questrom, the former CEO of Federated Department Stores, was widely celebrated for saving the operator of Macy's and Rich's department stores from bankruptcy. But he sued the company after retiring, saying the company owed him more than $45 million in back pay. A judge ruled against his case, and Questrom later became the CEO of rival J.C. Penney.

TIPS FROM THE PROS

Wall Street Journal deputy chief of investigations Jennifer S. Forsyth on covering courts:

Lawsuits can reveal when companies aren't doing right by their investors. These disputes often come in the form of securities fraud litigation, which allege that the company didn't disclose to investors everything it was required to. These suits can be brought as class actions, in which many investors band together. Class actions are unusually transparent: parties must publicly disclose the terms of their settlements, and the lawyers filing the class actions suits are even required to divulge the amount of fees they hope to earn.

Employers can get themselves into trouble by disclosing information about a worker's personal life. In many cases, businesses are not allowed to discuss a former worker's financial status, marital status or other personal issues unless there is a legitimate business reason for disclosing them. And in some states, an ex-worker can sue his or her former place of employment if they give false information to a potential new employer in an attempt bid to interfere with his or her job prospects.

In a majority of states, it is illegal for an employer to "blacklist" a former worker for participating in union activities. The anti-blacklist law can also apply to letters of recommendation, requiring them to be written without false and defamatory statements.

Businesses and Criminal Charges

Bernard Madoff, the now infamous New York investor who pled guilty to defrauding his clients, will likely spend the rest of his life in jail. Former ImClone Systems CEO Sam Waksal was sentenced to seven years in prison after pleading guilty to insider trading charges. Nearly a dozen former executives at rehabilitation hospital chain HealthSouth pleaded guilty to criminal fraud and conspiracy charges, and former company CEO Richard Scrushy currently sits in a Texas prison.

> **class action:** A lawsuit filed by one or more people on behalf of other people who may be in a similar situation. Class action lawsuits may be difficult and are expensive, but they allow people who may not have been able to file a lawsuit individually to band together.

All of these cases involve charges of criminal wrongdoing against major companies and their executives. Increasingly, state and federal government agencies are bringing criminal charges against company executives for defrauding investors, accountants, business partners and others. Crime reporting has never been common in the business world, but sometimes it becomes a major part of the story.

These stories often become front-page news. They are often a major development for a company and signal that the business may be in financial trouble.

The SEC and the Justice Department can launch criminal investigations into public companies suspected of wrongdoing, as they did in June 2003 with Freddie Mac, the mortgage company that ousted three top executives as a result. The Criminal Division of the Justice Department investigates business crimes, such as corporate fraud schemes; financial institution fraud; securities fraud; insurance fraud; fraud involving government programs like Medicare; and international criminal activities, including bribery of foreign government officials in violation of the Foreign Corrupt Practices Act.

> **criminal litigation:** Charges dealing with crimes against the public or members of the public, filed by government authorities.

In addition, the SEC's Division of Enforcement investigates violations of the federal securities laws and prosecutes cases using civil lawsuits in federal courts. It often seeks injunctions, and a person who violates an injunction can be subject to fines or a prison term. Many of its cases involve fraud, such as fraudulent stock offerings, manipulations, illegal insider trading or conduct by brokers in violation of securities laws.

In recent years, the Justice Department has also developed cases directed at schemes such as telemarketing fraud, identity theft and Internet fraud. Justice Department attorneys may also work with other federal agencies to prosecute companies. In June 2003, a manufacturer of heart surgery devices pleaded guilty to hiding malfunctions in its products that may have caused a dozen

TIPS FROM THE PROS

Wall Street Journal deputy chief of investigations Jennifer S. Forsyth on covering courts:

Lawsuits can show whether companies are doing right by the people who work for them. Employees—particularly those who have been fired—often file suits claiming they have been discriminated against on the basis of their race, gender, or age. Discrimination cases often are filed in federal court, which is good news for reporters as federal-court records are easier to access online than state-court filings, though more and more state courts are now going online. Also keep a look out for whistleblower complaints filed at the courthouse. These are brought by employees who claim they were treated poorly because they exposed wrongdoing by their bosses. These suits are on the rise due to federal laws that restrict companies from penalizing whistleblowers.

deaths. Endovascular Technologies, a subsidiary of Guidant Corporation, agreed to pay more than $92 million in civil and criminal penalties. The FDA and the Justice Department handled the investigation of the case.

In addition, the IRS can investigate and prosecute companies for attempting to evade taxes, willfully failing to file returns, submitting false tax forms or otherwise attempting to defraud taxpayers.

So-called white-collar crime cases can result from a number of different areas and do not always have to involve a business executive. Criminal business cases can also involve consumers defrauding companies.

Even small-town newspapers and radio stations can produce compelling stories about business crime, as the top of the following story from the *Lexington News-Gazette* in rural western Virginia illustrates:

> White-collar crime can be as annoying as a bounced check, or as dangerous as a person posing as a paramedic.
>
> In September, Carolyn Kate Smedley was sentenced in Rockbridge County to eight years in prison on 32 counts of forging checks, with five years and four months of that sentence suspended. She was also ordered to make restitution of $4,148.64.
>
> Forged documents allowed a North Carolina man to join not only the Lexington Lifesaving and First Aid Crew, but the staff of Stonewall Jackson Hospital. David Harold Suit, 34, answered about 60 calls between May and July 2001 on the bogus documents. One of those calls was to Interstate 81 when VDOT worker Denny Kegley was struck by a truck. Because Suit said he was certified as a paramedic, he was in charge of rescue squad members on the call. Kegley died at Carlton Roanoke Memorial Hospital a few days later.

Suit received a five-year prison sentence for forging public documents and 12 months for a misdemeanor charge of obtaining property by false pretenses.

Earlier this month the Southwest Regional Crime Prevention Association presented ways local merchants may reduce the risks of these crimes at a day-long seminar at the Virginia Horse Center. More than 60 law enforcement and retail representatives from across the region attended.[4]

As this story notes with excellent examples, white-collar crime is not always committed by business executives. The examples in this story were easily obtainable from court and police records.

There are many other types of criminal cases that involve business. Money laundering, as defined by the U.S. Criminal Code, involves the concealment of the source of money or its destination or the concealment of money gained through illegal activities. In the early 1990s, some banks were accused of helping drug dealers launder money. More recently, some banks are refusing to handle accounts from legal marijuana retailers in certain states.

Reporters should also check the criminal records of many of their sources, particularly if a criminal background might add to the story or shed light on a person's character. For example, say a reporter is covering the election of the new president for the union that represents the workers at Tropicana, the orange juice manufacturer. The reporter checks the criminal records of the two candidates at the courthouse and discovers that one of them was once arrested and convicted of cocaine possession. That should likely be in the story, as well as a response from the candidate.

TIPS FROM THE PROS

Wall Street Journal deputy chief of investigations Jennifer S. Forsyth on covering courts:

Look for interesting companies suing other interesting companies. In 2011, Apple Inc. and Samsung Electronics Co. began a series of legal skirmishes over who owned the patents to the design of smartphones and tablets. This was an epic fight between two companies that together held a sizable share of all smartphones sold in the world, with each company winning in courts in different countries. These kinds of disputes are common between rival companies looking to protect their lucrative products.

It sometimes even pays to check the criminal records of executives, including CEOs. If a reporter is writing a story about how a CEO is mismanaging a company, one of the ways in which he can help describe the CEO's personality is by including his arrest for speeding at 110 miles per hour in a 35-mile-per-hour zone. A CEO of a New Jersey–based company was charged with growing marijuana in the attic of his house. The company placed the executive on a leave of absence after his arrest, and he did not return to his position.

Reporters should not forget about the criminal side of the state and federal courthouses. They are often where the most interesting business stories are found. For example, a criminal case against an insurance agent accused of selling fictitious insurance policies to businesses throughout Tampa caused local businesses to check their coverage more carefully.

Depositions and Exhibits

After the lawsuit is filed and the defendant has issued a reply to the charges, both sides may begin to prepare their cases. Although many business-related lawsuits do not go to trial, the parties and their attorneys must prepare for that likelihood. There will be motions for information or to suppress information from the case. In addition, lawyers will begin taking depositions of key people involved in the case and asking for documents from the defendant. The plaintiff's side will also file documents in the case.

These depositions, or pretrial proceedings in which witnesses are questioned under oath, can yield valuable information and provide the public a glimpse of what might happen once the case goes to trial. The documents, known as exhibits, can help or hurt a case, depending on what they contain.

defendant: The individual or business sued in a civil lawsuit, or charged with a crime in a criminal case.

A reporter should take the time to read through these depositions and exhibits, particularly if they are interviews with corporate executives or documents such as memos written by management. Taken separately, they may not say anything. But together, they could connect a story that paints a picture of a company or business previously unrevealed to the rest of the world.

Depositions can often last several days in complicated business cases, and attorneys for both sides ask questions. A stenographer is present to record the statements. Depositions are used to collect information and facts about the case. Sometimes they are taken to discredit the testimony of the witness if the case goes to trial.

Lawyers often coach a business executive or another person on how to answer questions before a deposition. For many companies, the depositions taken by their executives can help frame the case in their favor or can harm their case, depending on the executive's answers. During the trial, lawyers will look for inconsistencies between the witness's statements and deposition. These incidents can have a significant impact on the outcome of the case.

TIPS FROM THE PROS

Wall Street Journal deputy chief of investigations Jennifer S. Forsyth on covering courts:

Let the bankruptcy courts reveal a whole new world about the local big employer in your town. If a company has to seek bankruptcy protection, something went very wrong with the economy, with that industry or with the way that company was managed—or possibly all three. The courts are there to help sort out who's to blame and to help the company come up with a plan to emerge in better shape. All of it must be done in public, usually in written documents available at the court or now online.

The PBS show *Frontline* went through the depositions given by cigarette company executives in lawsuits filed by state attorneys general in the late 1990s in an attempt to recoup sick smokers' Medicaid expenses paid by the state. *Frontline* found that Geoffrey Bible, the CEO of Philip Morris, the largest cigarette company in the world, (a) denied ever hearing of the committee of counsel, a lawyers' group that met for more than 30 years to discuss tobacco industry strategy; (b) claimed not to have any knowledge of how many teens smoke Philip Morris cigarettes; and (c) claimed not to have ever asked his employees about it. Alexander Spears III, the chairman of Lorillard Tobacco Company, said in his deposition that he did not believe that smoking caused emphysema or lung cancer, that smoking was not addictive and that his company had never done a study to determine if teens smoked its brands.

By using a deposition, a reporter can use quotes and statements made without any doubt as to what was said or who said it. The *Memphis Business Journal* covered the case of some employees who left a local investment bank to go work for another, allegedly taking documents with them that would help obtain business for their new employer. The documents included contact lists and details of bond underwriting transactions not yet completed. According to the deposition of the administrative assistant of one of the employees, her boss ordered her to destroy copied documents.

"Mac was running around like a chicken with his head cut off, going, 'Get everything off the computer,'" said Kelli Feathers in a deposition used in the *Memphis Business Journal* report. "'I don't care what it is. I don't care if it's labels, but get it off because I don't want to give anybody any reason to think that we stole anything, because they can take something and turn it into something else, and I don't want any manipulation going on.'"

Depositions taken in a lawsuit against grocery store chain Supervalu alleging age discrimination show that company executives had discussed making employee information sheets including birthdates available to supervisors. Leland Dake, a Supervalu senior vice president, told another vice president, Randy Wiegand, "Let's do it right so we can get rid of the garbage and save some money," according to Wiegand's deposition, which was reported in the *Minneapolis Star Tribune* (Forster, 2003, p. 1D).

Later in his deposition, Wiegand said that he had another meeting in which he questioned the process. "I told him about my dissatisfaction, dislike, concern for the process that was taking place," said Wiegand. "He quickly got off that subject, obviously, and the meeting wound up very shortly thereafter" (Forster, 2003, p. 1D).

Other documents filed in support of allegations made in business lawsuits can also be helpful to a reporter looking to better understand an issue and disclose to readers an inside look at corporate America. Many business stories have been reported and written solely on the basis of these documents.

When Tyco sued its former CEO Dennis Kozlowski, it added more than 100 pages of exhibits to its allegations. Those documents showed that the former executive had approved a number of perks for himself and other executives paid for by the company, from a $2.5 million Trump Tower apartment in Manhattan to spending nearly $14 million to buy homes for a dozen employees.

Depositions and exhibits may not always be newsworthy. And some of them may be hard to understand out of context. But they can also provide an inside look at developments leading up to a lawsuit, and they can give readers and viewers an idea of what may be said if a case goes to trial.

The entire court system can be viewed as another layer of business regulation. Lawsuits and their related documents are filed as public records to help a company prove itself or defend itself against allegations that may hurt its operations.

Business Gone Bad

Not all companies and corporations are successful. Many of them, including those with the smartest business plans and the best managers, struggle to make money, and some of them actually lose money. This happens to public and private companies.

TIPS FROM THE PROS

Wall Street Journal deputy chief of investigations Jennifer S. Forsyth on covering courts:

It's important to know if a company is expected to survive bankruptcy. So understanding the difference between a Chapter 11 bankruptcy filing and Chapter 7 filing is helpful. Chapter 11 allows a company to shield itself from its debts, and shed some of them, until it can come up with a plan to be a better, more profitable company. A company can operate in Chapter 11 for a very long time, even months. Chapter 7 is called a liquidation, which means the company is simply selling off everything it has and is going out of business. Chapter 11 is sometimes a good option for a company's long-term health; Chapter 7 never is.

What causes the problems leading to a company losing money can be wide and varied. A company could have missed a paradigm shift in its industry that caused competitors to take business away from it. A corporation could have decided to enter a new line of business that led to huge losses. Or a business could have acquired another company, taking on debt and other financial obligations that it is no longer able to meet.

 Chapter 11: A bankruptcy court filing by a company or an individual where the debtor proposes paying off some, but not all, of its debt.

These are just a few examples of why a business can go bad. When a company in dire financial straits can no longer pay its bills and loans in a timely manner, it often files papers with the court allowing it to continue operations but reorganize the money it owes, making those payments more manageable. This is called entering bankruptcy court.

Bankruptcy court is a federal court system, and it is not just for businesses. Individuals can also file with the bankruptcy court. But a bankruptcy-court filing allows a company to have some or all of its debts eliminated or reduced dramatically.

At first glance, such a proposition does not seem fair to the people or other businesses owed money. And many complain bitterly that they will not be repaid what they should receive. But from the perspective of the business in bankruptcy court, going into the court process to eliminate some of its debt allows it to repay some of the money it owes. Without such a process, the people and companies owed money may not have received anything if the company simply went out of business. In addition, the bankruptcy-court process attempts to find a fair method for compensating creditors. Some people and businesses owed money by a company in bankruptcy court receive compensation before others.

Increasingly, bankruptcy filings have become a major story for business reporters. Five of the largest bankruptcies in terms of company assets were filed in 2008 or 2009. Those major companies include Lehman Brothers, Washington Mutual, General Motors and Chrysler. And even when it is a smaller company seeking bankruptcy-court protection, the story can be important to a local town or city. When companies go into bankruptcy court, they typically try to cut expenses by closing locations and firing workers. That can have an effect on any economy.

Understanding how bankruptcy court works and why businesses file for bankruptcy-court protection is important for any reporter, not just those working on the business desk. When businesses file for protection from their creditors, those that are owed money could range from government entities, such as the local school board, to a federal agency that contracted with the business to perform services or provide goods. Or it could be a business that was planning to revitalize a depressed part of downtown.

Bankruptcy courts are located in most major cities in every state. Typically, companies file for bankruptcy-court protection at the bankruptcy courthouse located closest to their headquarters. But that does not always happen. Sometimes, companies file for bankruptcy-court protection in the state where they are incorporated.

Bankruptcy courts operate similarly to other federal courts and to state courts. There is a clerk who handles all of the incoming filings as well as the documents filed in existing cases. It is important for a business reporter to know that these bankruptcy-court filings are considered public record and should be accessible. The U.S. Bankruptcy Code allows a court to prevent public access to filings if they include trade secrets or confidential information about a company's operations, or if scandalous or defamatory information about a person is filed.

The initial filing is an important document because it lists the company's total assets and debts. This list of creditors can be valuable because it often leads to sources willing to talk about how the company has not been paying its bills or is reneging on some sort of business arrangement.

Bankruptcy-Court Filings to Look For:

1. **The initial filing.** It will tell you the name of the company or individual filing for bankruptcy-court protection and the amount of assets and liabilities.
2. **Creditors list.** It lists the name and contact information of everyone who is owed money. Consider this a source list.
3. **Reorganization plan.** A document that details how much creditors will be repaid and whether the company plans to close or sell any operations to cut its expenses.
4. **Judge's rulings.** They are filed for nearly everything, from paying company executives to approval of the reorganization plan.

When a company files for bankruptcy-court protection, its assets are frozen. After the filing, there are hearings to decide whether a company can spend large amounts of money. The beginning of one *Pittsburgh Business Times* story illustrates the typical first day bankruptcy-court structure that details the company and totals its debts and assets for the world to see.

The lead notes that RedZone Robotics Incorporated, a company that designs and manufactures robots to clean hazardous environments such as nuclear plants, filed for Chapter 11, and the second paragraph states in which bankruptcy court the case was filed. The fourth paragraph lists the company's assets and debts. The rest of the story quotes the company's president and mentions that its employment is down.

The reporter actually looked at the court filing to give the reader a sense of the value of the company's assets and the worth of its debt. The reporter also contacted the company to get a comment on the cause of the filing, although the president was not forthcoming. The story, however, does not explain what caused this robotics company to go into bankruptcy court.

The following excerpt from the *Boston Herald* does a good job of explaining what led to a company's downfall. In any story reporting a company's bankruptcy-court filing, the reasons for the problems should be explained prominently.

> Kmart Corp. yesterday became the largest U.S. retailer to seek Chapter 11 bankruptcy protection, a move sources say could trigger the closing of up to 600 stores.
>
> The Troy, Mich., retailer, the second-largest U.S. discount chain, with $37 billion in revenue last year, was battered by weak sales, mounting losses, a disastrous holiday shopping season and the erosion of supplier confidence. It has also suffered at the hand of giant rival Wal-Mart Stores Inc.
>
> Kmart yesterday said all 2,114 Kmart stores will remain open until further notice as it seeks to reorganize under court protection. But it will close a number of unprofitable and underperforming stores this year. Kmart operates 29 stores in Massachusetts, with an estimated 3,000 local employees.
>
> Retail sources said they expect Kmart will close several hundred stores—perhaps as many as 600.
>
> Yesterday, Kmart said it will terminate 350 leases for already-closed stores or for locations that are leased to other tenants, resulting in an immediate savings of $250 million.
>
> The company has 69 stores in New England, with an average of 100 employees each.
>
> Some observers have criticized the chain lately for carrying unpopular merchandise in cluttered aisles, for having outdated inventory technology and not keeping pace with today's consumer demands.[5]

TIPS FROM THE PROS

Wall Street Journal deputy chief of investigations Jennifer S. Forsyth on covering courts:

Look for the free-for-all at the center of every bankruptcy. The company, called the debtor, will likely have a long list of people or companies it owes money to, called creditors. The company will be looking to reduce its expenses and its debt while the creditors will be jockeying to get as much of what they are owed as possible. That means that everyone involved in a bankruptcy is fighting over a limited pot of money. Sometimes, they are also fighting for their jobs, as companies can tear up union contracts or close plants. Likewise, creditors can sometimes force out the company's executives.

The Boston newspaper reporter wrote the Kmart story to reflect how the region would be affected. With any bankruptcy-court filing, it is smart for the writer to note what the company's local operations are and how many workers it employs.

The initial filing helps businesses in an important way. A company's supplier must continue to provide products or other materials to the business in bankruptcy court. Companies in bankruptcy court go through a lot of court hearings as part of the process. There are hearings to determine whether a company should be closing locations or factories. There are hearings to decide how much compensation should be paid to executives and how much in fees should be paid to the bankruptcy lawyers representing the company.

In addition, it is important for a reporter covering a business bankruptcy case to know some other vital parts of what can appear to be a complicated court system. For example, sometimes the decision to file for bankruptcy-court protection is not made by the company but by some of its creditors. This is called an involuntary bankruptcy. Three or more creditors can join together and force a company into bankruptcy court. The company can contest the involuntary filing.

It is vital that a reporter understands who is running the company after it has filed for bankruptcy-court protection. In some cases, the court will appoint a trustee to oversee a company's operations.

It is also important for a company to assess its assets, which can be defined as a resource or item owned by a business that can be expected to benefit its operations. Many times a company in bankruptcy court will look to sell some of its assets to help raise cash to turn its operations around.

When Conseco Incorporated decided to sell part of its operations, reporters from Bloomberg, Dow Jones, Reuters and the Associated Press reported its deal to sell its Conseco Finance unit for more than $700 million to CFN Investment Holdings LLC and its Mill Creek Bank assets to GE Consumer Finance for $310 million. The agreements were reached as part of its bankruptcy-court proceedings in an auction process. They still had to be approved by the bankruptcy-court judge overseeing the case.

A company filing for bankruptcy-court protection should be considered major news, particularly if it is a large company. However, when a company files for bankruptcy-court protection, it often does not mean that the company is going out of business—a common misperception of many readers and even some journalists. Reporters should make sure that their copy clearly states that the company remains in business, if that is the case.

Chapter 11 versus Chapter 7

The U.S. bankruptcy code has many different parts. One section allows companies to seek to reorganize their debt. Another allows companies to simply pay off as much of its debt as it can and close shop.

Chapter 11 court filings are of the former category. This bankruptcy filing allows a corporation, or an individual, to reorganize without having to liquidate all of its assets. The debtor maintains control of the business, unless the court appoints a trustee. The company typically goes into bankruptcy court to come up with a debt payment plan to submit to its creditors. If the creditors approve the plan, and if the court agrees that the plan is fair, then the company is allowed to reorganize its debts and emerge from bankruptcy court.

Chapter 7 court filings, however, are more drastic. When a company files under this part of the bankruptcy law, it means that all of the company's assets will be sold to pay its debts and that the company is going out of business.

A third type of bankruptcy filing that is relevant to business reporters is a Chapter 13, where the company filing repays its debts during a three- to five-year time period.

TIPS FROM THE PROS

Wall Street Journal deputy chief of investigations Jennifer S. Forsyth on covering courts:

Bankruptcy examiners and trustees can be a reporter's aide. These people are hired by the court to take over a business that is liquidating or to investigate whether anyone should be held liable for a company's demise. Examiners often work closely with government agencies that might be looking into wrongdoing. The examiners' reports are a treasure trove of information about how a company failed. And examiners are sometimes willing to talk to the media about their findings.

When a reporter is examining the initial filing of a company at bankruptcy court, one of the first facts he or she should determine is whether the business is filing under Chapter 11 or Chapter 7. The differences between the two are important, and getting this vital piece of information wrong could hurt a company, not to mention severely hamper a reporter's relationship with sources.

Chapter 11 is the most common filing for medium and large businesses, although it is not the most common filing for all businesses. In the 12 months ended September 30 2015, there were 24,985 filings of bankruptcy protection by businesses. Less than 25 percent of all bankruptcy-court filings in the 12 months ended September 30, 2015 were for Chapter 11 protection. That seems like a small amount, but upon examination of the recent cases under Chapter 11, a reporter will discover that there are billions of dollars in assets owned by companies in the process of seeking to reorganize debt while continuing to exist as viable companies. For example, at the time of its filing in September 2008, Lehman Brothers had $691 billion in assets, whereas Washington Mutual had $327.9 billion in assets. It would take thousands of small companies filing for bankruptcy-court protection to equal those amounts.

Chapter 7: A bankruptcy-court filing done by businesses and individuals where the assets are liquidated.

Finding out that a company has filed for bankruptcy-court protection may not be as easy as just going to the courthouse and looking through the filings each day, though that is a good place to start. If a reporter is hearing rumors that a company may be seeking bankruptcy-court protection, he or she should do some background work.

First, the journalist should find out the name of the company as it is incorporated with the state. Sometimes the company's incorporated name may not be the same name under which it is doing business. This is typical for businesses such as restaurants.

Second, the reporter needs to know where the company is incorporated. That will help determine in which bankruptcy court the filing can be found. It is frustrating for a reporter to go looking for an initial filing at one court and not find the document, only to be scooped by another reporter who found the filing at another court. Clerks at the court can often be helpful in cases like this by providing the location where a company has filed. And last, businesses—particularly those prominent in a local community—will file for bankruptcy-court protection at the end of the day or late on a Friday, hoping that the filing will escape notice. Reporters should ask for all of the previous day's filings if they cannot wait around the clerk's office every day until closing time. Other times, however, a company will simply issue a news release announcing that it has filed for bankruptcy-court protection. Life insurer Conseco Incorporated issued a news release about its Chapter 11 filing. This bankruptcy-court protection filing was not considered a surprise by many who followed the company. Some Wall Street analysts, in written research reports, even predicted the company would take such action, and the company also hinted in its SEC filings that it was considering bankruptcy-court protection. Still, the company chose to issue this release at 3 a.m. Eastern time. Because the company's stock was publicly traded, it also filed a form 8-K disclosing the filing. The following excerpt shows how the Associated Press covered the filing and subsequent hearing later that day:

Conseco said Wednesday it plans to make a quick exit from bankruptcy court protection, even though a group of creditors who were late to the table threaten to delay and potentially tangle the insurance and finance company's reorganization.

Conseco, mired in debt from 1990s acquisitions that backfired, late Tuesday became the third-largest U.S. company to file for bankruptcy protection.

The Carmel, Ind.-based company, which employs about 14,000 people and had $8.1 billion in revenues last year, expects to emerge from Chapter 11 protection during the second quarter of next year, if not earlier, the company's lead attorney told a bankruptcy court in Chicago. Banks and bondholders reached a tentative agreement on bankruptcy terms with Conseco over the $4 billion those groups are owed.

But a group of preferred shareholders—who initially were left out of talks begun in August to restructure Conseco's debt, but eventually won a seat under protest—have held out. They continue negotiations with Conseco.

Preferred securities holders carry privileges over owners of common stock in recovering their investments from failed companies, but rank below banks and bondholders. Common stockholders are expected to recover little if any of their investments in Conseco.

Details of Conseco's Chapter 11 plan, which have yet to be filed, must be approved by members of investor groups before a reorganization plan can be submitted for the court's approval. A filing outlining specifics could be submitted within four to six weeks, Conseco spokesman Mark Lubbers said.[6]

reorganization: A process designed to revive a financially troubled or bankrupt firm. It typically involves the restatement of assets and liabilities and communication with creditors in order to make arrangements for maintaining repayment.

Conseco's bankruptcy-court filing, as the above story points out, is unusual for Chapter 11 cases in that the company negotiated with its largest lenders before it actually sought court protection from its debtors. In some cases, a company will take such a strategy, commonly called a prepackaged bankruptcy filing, which means that much of the negotiation that takes place during bankruptcy-court supervision has already occurred. In many of these cases, the time a company spends in bankruptcy court is shorter. To do such a plan, the company must get the approval of a majority of creditors representing two-thirds of its total debt.

Often, however, a company does not negotiate with its creditors before entering bankruptcy court. The negotiations typically occur in the court, often through hearings. Committees of creditors are appointed. These committees are represented by attorneys, who can often be valuable sources, letting a reporter know if the creditors like or disapprove of a reorganization plan floated by the company.

The following excerpt details a case of a not-for-profit company filing for bankruptcy-court protection. The reporter for the *Louisville Courier-Journal* wrote the story the same way it would be written for a private or public company. The reporter lists the assets and debts and the cause of the problems leading to the filing toward the beginning of the story:

When it opened in 1990, the Oxmoor golf and steeplechase development in eastern Jefferson County was another success among the vast holdings of HFH Inc., the Louisville real-estate developer that soared during the golf course and residential building boom in the late 1980s and early 1990s.

Today Oxmoor Golf & Steeplechase Inc., which operates Oxmoor Country Club at 9000 Limehouse Lane, is proceeding through bankruptcy after running up debts to nearly 200 creditors and facing four lawsuits by suppliers seeking to recoup their money.

The not-for-profit corporation filed for protection from its creditors in U.S. Bankruptcy Court for the Western District of Kentucky on July 5, a move that shields its assets while it attempts to reorganize. In a petition entered with the court, Oxmoor Golf & Steeplechase claimed debts of $5 million and assets of $1 million. The debts are the result of escalating rent payments on the land Oxmoor Golf & Steeplechase leases from trusts established by the Bullitt family, said attorney David Cantor, who is representing the club. When HFH experienced financial problems in the mid-1990s, Oxmoor members took over the club's operations.

They inherited a modern clubhouse and a challenging 18-hole golf course—and a 37-year lease with ballooning payments of about $30,000 a month, coupled with $17,500 in monthly mortgage payments.[7]

The story then lists some of the largest creditors for Oxmoor. There are two different types of creditors in bankruptcy-court cases. The secured creditors have claims against the company backed by collateral. This is similar to a car loan or a home loan; that is, if one does not make the payments on one's car or home loan, the loan is backed by the car or home.

The other type of creditors is unsecured creditors. These are creditors with no collateral against their claim. Investors who purchased stock in a public company via a stockbroker fall into this category. Secured creditors are paid before unsecured creditors in bankruptcy cases.

> **secured creditor:** People or companies owed debt that is backed by collateral, such as a car loan or a home mortgage.

The length of a company's stay in bankruptcy court can vary depending on the negotiations with its creditors. Some bankruptcy-court proceedings last for years, whereas others take months. For a reporter, it is important to stay on top of a company's case and its progress, or lack thereof. Some bankruptcy courts now post court hearing times and filings on the Internet. For others, however, reporters need to go to the courthouse to check the docket.

It is also vitally important to know the players, particularly the company's and the creditors' attorneys. Reporters should know the judges as well. Remember the warning about companies filing for bankruptcy-court protection at the end of the day to avoid publicity? Some judges have even allowed filings to be sent to their homes late at night, long after the court has been locked and the lights turned off. Although judges will rarely talk on the record, they and their clerks will often let a reporter know what is happening with a case.

Companies often file for Chapter 11 bankruptcy protection hoping to emerge from the proceedings as a better company that has learned from its mistakes. A number of companies, such as Kmart, seek to become successful after bankruptcy court.

But that is not always the case. A number of companies that look to Chapter 11 to reorganize their debt end up converting their case to Chapter 7 when it becomes apparent that they cannot reach an agreement with creditors or their business deteriorates so much that the best course of action for the creditors is to go out of business. The decision to liquidate is often forced upon the company and its management by creditors or by the court. As with all bankruptcy-court stories, it is critical that the reporter get in touch with the company to get its response to the court proceedings.

In other cases, however, a company will file for Chapter 11 protection and warn creditors that it could convert its case to Chapter 7 liquidation. In a December 2002 interview with the *New York Times,* the CEO of United Airlines warned that the company might switch its Chapter 11 bankruptcy-court case to a Chapter 7.

Many bankruptcy-court experts believe that a company often mentions the possibility of liquidation in an attempt to win concessions from creditors or from employees to lower the company's costs. In the case of United Airlines, the CEO could have been making that assertion to get labor unions to agree to lower wages. Wire reports in March 2003 noted that the company filed in court records that "liquidation is a distinct possibility if United does not achieve its proposed labor cost reductions" (Associated Press, 2003). United Airlines emerged from bankruptcy court and continues to operate today.

When a company begins talking about Chapter 7 even though it has filed a Chapter 11 case, a reporter needs to look at the company's motives. Chapter 7 cases mean the end of the line for a company. By reviewing the court documents and talking to sources, a reporter can write a compelling story about the rise and fall of a company, large or small.

The Reorganization

Companies that enter bankruptcy court with the idea that they will reorganize their debt and terminate court protection rely on building relationships with their creditors to work toward a common goal: coming up with a reorganization plan that allows the business to lower its debt while repaying some of the money owed.

The reorganization plan is vital to the future success of a company. A weak reorganization plan can lead to yet another bankruptcy-court filing. A reorganization plan that gives little or nothing back to creditors often results in investors not wanting to be involved in the new company.

One of the important initial steps taken by a company after it enters bankruptcy court is to find financing from a lender that will allow it to continue to operate while it reorganizes its debt. This decision to provide financing to a company is approved by the court and is often discussed at a hearing.

Securing financing is just one of the first steps in creating a reorganization plan. The plan is developed with a committee of creditors. Some of the creditors may want to be repaid as much as possible and may try to force the company to sell some assets. Other creditors may look to exchange the money they are owed for an ownership stake in the company once it exits bankruptcy court.

A company files a reorganization plan with the court. Reporters should determine the deadline for the plan and make sure to get a copy as soon as it is filed. The plan is likely a story because it discloses for the first time how much money the company is proposing to repay its creditors. A reorganization plan often also discloses whether a company will close locations, fire workers, cut salaries for executives or take other steps to reduce expenses.

Creditors, bondholders and stockholders must accept the reorganization plan. Understand that in most bankruptcy cases, the stockholders typically get nothing as part of a reorganization plan. Then, the judge must approve it.

Reorganization stories should point out how much the company's debt is reduced by the plan. The primary reason a company enters bankruptcy court is an inability to pay. If the debt has not been reduced enough, the company could face trouble down the road.

Interested Parties

When a public company files for bankruptcy-court protection, its stockholders usually get nothing in return. Bondholders often get paid but typically receive less than their full investment.

There are other groups involved with the bankruptcy filing of a company that have a vested interest in the proceedings. Lawyers, accountants, investment bankers, turnaround consultants and even company executives often receive millions of dollars in return for their services in helping steer the company through the legal maze. These interested parties often clash with each other and the company during bankruptcy-court proceedings. Therefore, it is important to understand their roles in the process; often, the relationships between interested parties result in the best stories.

A company lands in bankruptcy court because it is unable to pay its expenses. But bankruptcy court itself can be very expensive. Critics argue that the bankruptcy-court system is flawed, and some of these flaws become apparent during the numerous hearings and motions filed in cases involving companies.

For example, attorneys, consultants and others performing work for companies in bankruptcy court are required to have their fees approved by the judge presiding over the case. These fees can sometimes raise the ire of judges—and readers.

The *Denver Business Journal* noted how much local attorneys, property valuation experts and other consultants were being paid in a story about the bankruptcy case of Colorado's Ocean Journey aquarium. The fees and expenses totaled more than $241,000 for late October and September, including $135,581 paid to its bankruptcy attorney for four months' work.

Bloomberg News went a step further in discussing fees for attorneys. In its exhaustive research, Bloomberg disclosed that the 25 largest bankruptcies in 2001 and 2002 resulted in a total of $235 million in legal fees from the companies' primary law firms as of January 31, 2003. Some of the fees charged by the lead law firm, Weil, Gotshal & Manges L.L.P., in the Global Crossing bankruptcy case included $21,694 for meals, $73,182 for computerized research and more than $24,000 for activities that included composing its fee applications for the bankruptcy-court judge to approve.

The Bloomberg report of the large fees drew criticism from the Texas attorney general, who said he saw "little accomplished" for the fees and that the "creditors and other people who deserve this money are seeing it depleted" (St. Onge, 2003).

Reporters following a bankruptcy case should always look for the filings and motions by attorneys and others working for the company to examine how much they are being paid and whether the services they provide are needed. Often, these filings and motions make interesting stories.

But it is not just attorney fees that draw the ire of those involved. Sometimes, the court-appointed overseers of bankruptcy cases object to money being spent, particularly if they believe that the money could be spent more efficiently elsewhere. This happened in the Conseco bankruptcy and led to stories outlining those concerns by reporters who were vigilant in obtaining the court documents. The executives of a company in bankruptcy court also come under scrutiny. The judge handling their case must approve executives' compensation. Sometimes, a judge will decide that the salary and benefits paid to executives are too much. Other times, the company may go to the court and seek money from its executives. In January 2003, then-bankrupt retailer Kmart demanded that five executives repay loans not approved by the board and fired some of the executives who had received the loans. The story, which came from bankruptcy-court documents, was major news for the mass communication outlets covering the case.

Some bankruptcy-court experts argue that the real winners in any filing are the people hired by the company to turn around its performance, and because they are often paid millions, creditors are hurt. Others argue that without these experts working long hours to salvage what they can from a company in bankruptcy-court protection, creditors, bondholders and shareholders might not receive anything in return. The job of the journalist is to carefully toe the line between these two viewpoints. Reporters who carefully watch a bankruptcy case unfold and document how money is spent go a long way in explaining to their readers this complicated process of reorganization.

It is not an easy job, but with some basic understanding of relationships and how the court works, reporters can help readers understand how they might be affected.

Personal Bankruptcies

As noted earlier in this chapter, public and private companies do not make all bankruptcy-court filings. In fact, more than 70 percent of all proceedings in bankruptcy court involve individuals.

These cases can also be valuable for a business reporter, especially one who is interested in putting a human face on economic conditions in his region. Tracking the ups and downs of personal bankruptcy filings in a region can help a newspaper document its local economy. If more people are seeking bankruptcy-court protection in a three-month time period than they were the same time a year ago, that is a good indication that people are struggling with their finances. They may have been laid off from jobs and are now unable to pay their credit card bills. Or they may have found a job, but one that pays much less than their previous job.

Most bankruptcy courts keep tallies of how many cases have been filed during quarterly and annual time periods. By asking the clerk for these numbers, a reporter has a good start on a story. The reporter can then look through a few filings and write down names of people who have recently filed for protection. After talking to a few of these debtors or their attorneys, the reporter could likely write a story similar to the following one from the *Indianapolis Star:*

> Layoffs, overspending and mortgage debt helped drive a 13 percent increase in personal bankruptcy filings in the southern two-thirds of Indiana in 2002, although the size of the jump was less than half of the 28 percent rise in 2001.
>
> The 32,158 filings in the year ending Dec. 31, up from 28,551 in 2001, "is still a huge increase," said Kevin P. Dempsey, U.S. bankruptcy trustee for Indiana and part of Illinois.
>
> "We're at record levels. It is, by far and away, a record level."
>
> Personal bankruptcy filings in the southern district of Indiana were at twice the national rate during the federal fiscal year that ended Sept. 30: up 15.9 percent versus the U.S. rate of 7.8 percent, according to the Administrative Office of the U.S. Courts. The southern district, which includes Indianapolis, ranked eighth highest in bankruptcy filings during the fiscal year among 75 federal bankruptcy districts. Northern Indiana filings rose 17.5 percent in the fiscal year, or fourth highest.
>
> "Indiana was at or near the top in percentage increases in 2002," Dempsey said. Bankruptcy experts said last year's increase was fueled by the same problems they saw in 2001, including a rise in layoffs during the sluggish economy.

"Indiana has always been a major manufacturing state, and we have lost so many jobs in the past few years," said Indianapolis bankruptcy attorney Mark Zuckerberg. "I think people have held on as long as they can."

"Usually they have used all the resources they have because nobody wants to file for bankruptcy. By the time I see clients, they have no more money to pay their bills," he said.[8]

 trustee: A court-appointed representative who administers the business or estate. Can be assigned if creditors or others argue that the company is unfit to manage its operations.

Like companies, consumers file either under Chapter 11 or Chapter 7, and sometimes, personal Chapter 11 cases convert to Chapter 7 cases. Personal cases go through many of the same steps that business filings encounter, including negotiations with creditors. And personal cases are filed at the same place as company filings. Some states have more filings, however.

One major difference is that unlike corporate cases, there are few lenders willing to give consumers financing to help them make it through bankruptcy court. Bankruptcies can stay on an individual's credit report for up to 10 years.

Personal bankruptcies can also be important sources of information for other stories, particularly stories about companies. Investors who own stock in a company run by an executive who filed for personal bankruptcy in the past would want to know that information. When the *Atlanta Journal-Constitution* asked its retail reporter to investigate the problems at local grocery store chain Harry's Farmers Market Incorporated, the reporter ran the names of its top executives through the computers at the local bankruptcy court. The reporter found that the acting CFO and a vice president of merchandising had been involved in personal bankruptcies.

By reporting these facts, the reporter used the bankruptcy-court cases to call into question the ability of these executives to run a multimillion-dollar public company. If they could not manage their personal finances well enough to avoid bankruptcy court, how would they be able to oversee the spending of millions of dollars on goods and services each week for Harry's?

In some cases, a personal bankruptcy is the precursor to problems at an executive's company, particularly if it is a private company. Many owners of small and private businesses intermingle their personal finances with their corporate operations. When one or the other—or even both, in some cases—start to falter, a bankruptcy-court filing could be looming.

Personal bankruptcy hearings often take up the bulk of a judge's time in court. And although many personal bankruptcy cases are not newsworthy, they do often show the dire financial straits that many people encounter. Sitting in a bankruptcy courtroom for a day will show reporters a side of life they may not have experienced, giving them a broader understanding of how credit cards, loans and other financial instruments can wreak havoc if not used properly.

Notes

1. "3m sues XPEL Technologies for patent infringement," by S. Schaust. *Twin Cities Business Magazine*, December 20, 2015. Copyright by *Twin Cities Business*. Reprinted with permission.
2. From "Wal-Mart to pay $4.8 million in back wages, damages," by S. Banjo, May 2, 2012, *Wall Street Journal*. Copyright 2012 by Dow Jones & Co. Reprinted with permission.
3. From "CEO change near, Sprint says: Esrey stepping down; Forsee offered job, but BellSouth gets court order to keep him," by D. Hayes and S. King, February 3, 2003, *Kansas City Star*, p. A1. Copyright 2003 by *Kansas City Star*. Reprinted with permission.
4. From "Regional seminar here focused on ways of reducing the risk," by M.L. DiBiase, October 31, 2002, *Lexington News-Gazette*, pp. D1–D2. Copyright 2002 by the News-Gazette Corporation. Reprinted with permission.
5. From "Kmart enters bankruptcy; Retail giant Kmart is bankrupt; No immediate loss seen of any of its 29 Mass. stores," by G. Gatlin, January 23, 2002, *Boston Herald*, p. 27. Copyright 2002 by *Boston Herald*. Reprinted with permission.
6. "Conseco promises swift bankruptcy," December 18, 2002, Associated Press. Copyright 2002 by Associated Press. Reprinted with permission.
7. From "Oxmoor club hopes to survive bankruptcy," by M. Green, July 30, 2002, *Courier-Journal*, p. 1D. Copyright 2002 by *Courier-Journal*. Reprinted with permission.
8. From "State bankruptcies go through the roof; area district filings set record and are twice national rate," by C. O'Malley, January 10, 2003, *Indianapolis Star*, p. 1C. Copyright 2003 by *Indianapolis Star*. Reprinted with permission.

Key Terms

bankruptcy

Chapter 7

Chapter 11

class action

criminal litigation

defendant

mediation

plaintiff

reorganization

secured creditor

trustee

Suggested Exercises

1. Discuss spending habits in class. Do your fellow students believe that their spending might cause them problems paying debt in the future? How many credit cards do most students have? Do any of them have car loans?
2. If a bankruptcy-court district is located near your school, attend a hearing. During the next class session, discuss what you saw and comment on the relationship between judges, creditors and attorneys.
3. Pretend that you're shopping in the local Wal-Mart one weekend when you slip on a toy left in an aisle and break your leg. Do you sue the retailer for

the pain and suffering caused by your injury and for lost wages? Why or why not?

4. You're a reporter for a local newspaper, and you're checking the courthouse one day for lawsuits that may be potential stories. You find that a convenience store chain is suing a local doughnut manufacturer to terminate a contract requiring that only its doughnuts be sold at the store's locations because sales have dropped. The convenience store chain wants to start selling Krispy Kreme doughnuts as well. The file includes documents from the doughnut manufacturer that are marked "confidential" and "private" submitted as evidence by the convenience store chain. Do you use them as part of your story?

5. The state insurance department has filed charges against a local insurance company alleging that it doesn't have enough assets to cover its policies and needs to be placed into regulatory supervision. You call the insurance company and talk to the CEO, who tells you that if you write a story about the allegations, the insurer will likely go under because policyholders will get scared and take their money out of the company. He even gets the company's attorney on the phone via conference call, and the attorney makes similar claims. Do you write the story and run it in tomorrow's newspaper?

Top Bankruptcy-Court Cases in U.S. History

Company	Bankruptcy Date	Assets
Lehman Brothers Holdings Incorporated	Sept. 15, 2008	$691.1 billion
Washington Mutual Incorporated	Sept. 26, 2008	$327.9 billion
WorldCom Incorporated	July 21, 2002	$103.9 billion
General Motors Corporation	June 1, 2009	$91 billion
Enron Corporation	Dec. 2, 2001	$65.5 billion
Conseco Incorporated	Dec. 17, 2002	$61.4 billion
Chrysler LLC	April 30, 2009	$39.3 billion
Thornburg Mortgage Incorporated	May 1, 2009	$36.5 billion
Pacific Gas and Electric Company	April 6, 2001	$36.2 billion
Texaco Incorporated	April 12, 1987	$34.9 billion
Financial Corporation of America	Sept. 9, 1988	$33.9 billion
Refco Incorporated	Oct. 17, 2005	$33.3 billion
IndyMac Bancorp Incorporated	July 31, 2008	$32.7 billion
Global Crossing Limited	Jan. 28, 2002	$30.2 billion
Bank of New England Corporation	Jan. 7, 1991	$29.8 billion
General Growth Properties	April 16, 2009	$29.6 billion
Lyondell Chemical Company	Jan. 6, 2009	$27.4 billion
Calpine Corporation	Dec. 20, 2005	$27.2 billion
New Century Financial	April 2, 2007	$26.1 billion
UAL Corporation	Dec. 9, 2002	$25.2 billion

Books on Business and the Courts

Bogus, C.T. (2001). *Why lawsuits are good for America: Disciplined democracy, big business, and the common law*. New York: New York University Press.

Howard, P.K. (2001). *The lost art of drawing the line: How fairness went too far*. New York: Random House.

Olson, W. (2003). *The rule of lawyers: How the new litigation elite threatens America's rule of law*. New York: Truman Talley Books.

Schweich, T.A. (2000). *Protect yourself from business lawsuits: An employee's guide to avoiding workplace liability*. New York: Fireside Books.

 ## Books on Bankruptcy

Baird, D.G. (2002). *Elements of bankruptcy* (3rd ed.). New York: Foundation Press.

Fusaro, P.C., & Miller, R. (2002). *What went wrong at Enron: Everyone's guide to the largest bankruptcy in U.S. history*. New York: Wiley.

Gilson, S.C. (2001). *Creating value through corporate restructuring: Case studies in bankruptcies, buyouts, and breakups*. New York: Wiley.

LoPucki, L. (2006). *Courting Failure: How competition for big cases is corrupting the bankruptcy courts*. Ann Arbor, MI: University of Michigan Press.

Roe, M.J. (2000). *Corporate reorganization and bankruptcy: Legal and financial materials*. New York: Foundation Press.

Swartz, M., & Watkins, S. (2003). *Power failure: The inside story of the collapse of Enron*. New York: Doubleday.

 ## References

Associated Press. (2002, December 18). Conseco promises a swift bankruptcy.

Associated Press. (2003, March 18). United Airlines says liquidation possible without labor cuts.

Banjo, S. (2012, May 1). Wal-Mart to pay $4.8 million in back wages, damages. *The Wall Street Journal*. Retrieved December 30, 2015 from www.wsj.com/articles/SB10001424052702304868004577378381606731206.

DiBiase, M.L. (2002, October 30). Regional seminar here focused on ways of reducing the risk. *Lexington News-Gazette*, pp. D1–D2.

Docherty, N. (1998, May 12). Inside the tobacco deal. Retrieved May 25, 2003, from www.pbs.org/wgbh/pages/frondine/shows/settlement/.

Evans, D. (2003, January 17). Wade Cook financial ordered liquidated by judge. Bloomberg News.

Forster, J. (2003, April 28). Written off: A lawsuit filed by seven former employees of Supervalu Inc. that accused the company of age discrimination has been cleared for trial in August. *Minneapolis Star Tribune*, p. 1D.

Gatlin, G. (2002, January 23). Kmart enters bankruptcy; Retail giant Kmart is bankrupt; No immediate loss seen of any of its 29 Mass. stores. *Boston Herald*, p. 27.

Green, M. (2002, July 30). Oxmoor club hopes to survive bankruptcy. *The Courier-Journal*, p. 1D.

Guzzo, M., Davis, C., & Tascarella, P. (2002, July 12). RedZone files for Chapter 11 reorganization. *Pittsburgh Business Times*, p. 3.

Hayes, D., & King, S. (2003, February 3). CEO change near, Sprint says; Esrey stepping down; Forsee offered job, but BellSouth gets court order to keep him. *Kansas City Star*, p. A1.

Kelly, J. (2003, May 28). Novell says it owns Unix rights, challenges SCO claim. Bloomberg News.

Mason, E. (2002, July 12). Charlesbank sues portfolio firm over accounting issues. *Boston Business Journal*, pp. 1, 53.

Moore, P. (2002, November 18). Ocean Journey dollars flow to handle bankruptcy fees. *Denver Business Journal*, p. A4.

Nilsen, K. (2003, October 18). ArgoMed garners $3.15M in court. *Triangle Business Journal*, p. 13.

O'Malley, C. (2003, January 10). State bankruptcies go through the roof; area district filings set record and are twice national rate. *The Indianapolis Star*, p. 1C.

Parker, V.L. (2002, December 27). Swifty Serve swiftly split up. *The News & Observer*, p. D2.

Perkins, T. (2002, September 20). Report: Duncan Williams staff stole, copied and deleted files. *Memphis Business Journal*, p. 14.

Reuters. (2003, March 5). Conseco in $1 billion deal to sell unit.

St. Onge, J. (2003, February 26). Weil Gotshal reaps most fees on biggest corporate bankruptcies. Bloomberg News.

Wong, E. (2003, December 10). Airline shock waves: The overview; bankruptcy case is filed by United. *New York Times*, p. A1.

13

COVERING REAL ESTATE

Why Land Is Bought and Sold

Every business in the country—and in the world—operates from a central location, often called a headquarters. The business has either purchased that land and constructed a building on the property or leased the property from a real estate company. If its operations become too big for its current location, it purchases or leases a building that gives it more space.

Individuals and families are in the same situation. They live in an apartment or in a house, either renting or buying. If one thinks about real estate this way—that it is the one necessity for every business and every consumer across the country—then writing about the topic does not seem as boring as it might at first glance. Writing about real estate does not involve covering just the buying and selling of homes or the construction of a new industrial park to attract manufacturers and other businesses to an area. Real estate plays a vitally important role in the business world and in the country's economy.

The latter part of the first decade in the twenty-first century showed how important the real estate market is to business and economics coverage. The real estate market has impacted virtually every story in business reporting, from the stock market to lending to personal finance.

Real estate transactions can be small deals for less than an acre of land, particularly for the residential construction of a new home. Other real estate deals can be extremely large, with the ownership of hundreds of acres being transferred to a developer who plans to turn the land into a giant mall or subdivision. Simply put, real estate is a broad-reaching story in business journalism and throughout all reporting.

Retailers need real estate to build their stores. Manufacturers need real estate to build their plants. Farmers need real estate to plant their crops and

TIPS FROM THE PROS

Cleveland Plain Dealer real estate reporter Michelle Jarboe on covering the real estate beat:

Find the personal: People are attached to places. That's easy to see on the residential side, where buyers and sellers have strong feelings about houses and condominiums. It's less apparent on the commercial side. But approaching a piece of commercial real estate—a once-popular shopping mall, a century-old building or a shuttered factory—with an eye on details can bring more readers into your stories. Adding history and trivia can keep an article about a tax-lien sale, a foreclosure, a demolition or a redevelopment from feeling antiseptic. That strategy won't work for every property, of course. There's only so much you can do with a suburban distribution center or a self-storage facility.

allow their cattle to graze. Trash collectors need real estate to park their trucks and to dump the garbage they collect. Even Internet companies need office space to run their businesses.

Others need real estate as well. Towns and cities need real estate to build parks and schools. State governments need real estate to house thousands of employees and offices and to expand public universities and colleges when they outgrow their campuses. The federal government needs real estate for armed forces bases and hundreds of other reasons.

Businesses may also invest in real estate even though real estate is not their primary operation. For example, banks and insurance companies see real estate as an investment that may boost their earnings. Some banks and insurers

 TIPS FROM THE PROS

Cleveland Plain Dealer real estate reporter Michelle Jarboe on covering the real estate beat:

Don't forget debt: When a developer announces a project or hands out slick renderings of a proposed building, ask who's paying for it. From home buyers to real estate moguls, most people borrow to buy property. As the mortgage-fueled financial crisis of 2007 to 2010 demonstrated, debt—the wrong type or amount—can be the downfall of everyday people, seasoned developers and the biggest of banks. Ask about the amount of leverage in a deal and how the borrower plans to manage risk. Ask about what could happen if the purchase, or project, goes south. Real estate is cyclical, and people don't necessarily learn from the past.

invested too much in real estate in the late 1980s and early 1990s and suffered when real estate values, particularly the price for office buildings, plummeted.

There are even companies—public and private—the sole business of which is to buy and sell real estate. Their profits come from the rent they collect from apartment complexes and office buildings. The public companies see their stock prices rise when real estate is in demand and occupancy rates are high, and fall when there is a glut of real estate available.

A real estate investment trust, commonly known as a REIT, is a company that owns and operates real estate properties, such as office complexes, malls, shopping centers and apartments. These companies must provide 90 percent of their taxable income to their shareholders in the form of dividends. There are more than 200 publicly traded REITs with a market capitalization totaling more than $900 billion. There are also private REITs. These companies operate real estate properties in every major metropolitan market.

In addition, there are thousands of other real estate companies that buy and sell commercial real estate. They may only own one piece of real estate, or they may own hundreds. They may even be part of another company.

Reporters writing about commercial real estate transactions typically identify the building being purchased, the significance of the sale, and the new owner and the seller. A *Chicago Tribune* article on the sale of Aon Center, a "trophy tower" in downtown Chicago, noted that the deal was one of the largest transactions in the city's history. The second paragraph named the buyer and seller and noted that the building had 80 stories. And the third paragraph mentioned the price and compared that figure with the original asking price from the seller.

The reporter did some math and told readers the price per square foot of the building later in the story. The reporter also tried hard to pinpoint the actual purchase price for the property. In many cases, that price is available in public records discussed later in this chapter. But in this instance, the reporter had to rely on industry sources to disclose the price. The price of a real estate transaction is probably the most important fact for any major acquisition and should be aggressively pursued by the reporter.

Commercial real estate can be divided into several categories. There is the office market, which primarily includes office buildings in which businesses operate. The National Association of Realtors projected that the vacancy rate for office spaces would ease 0.8 percent to 14.8 percent in 2016 as continued job creation drives demand. The vacancy rate for industrial space is expected to decline 1.4 percent to 9.7 percent, and retail availability to decrease 1.3 percent to 11.3 percent.

In the residential real estate market, home sales have risen in the past few years. Existing home sales were forecast to finish 2015 at a pace of around 5.25 million—the highest since 2006, but roughly 25 percent below the prior peak set in 2005, when 7.08 million homes were sold, according to the National Association of Realtors. The national median existing home price for 2015 will be close to $220,700, up around 6 percent from a year ago.

Still, the number of families owning a home in the United States has declined to 63.7 percent, down from 69.1 percent in 2005.

Indeed, real estate transactions can be viewed as a key barometer of the economy. If total real estate acquisitions increase, the economic growth of a region or the country is also likely strong. But if real estate sales slow, the economy is likely slowing as well. (For more on real estate, particularly new home sales and existing sales, and the economy, see Chapter 4.) However, note that residential real estate activity rises and falls with interest rates, which are tied to the Federal Open Market Committee's decisions on where the economy is headed. Reporters should check with a local mortgage lender to find out how rates are moving in their area.

TIPS FROM THE PROS

Cleveland Plain Dealer real estate reporter Michelle Jarboe on covering the real estate beat:

Know your audience: It's essential to monitor national housing, construction and economic trends. But don't forget that real estate can be intensely local. Home sales and prices might be up nationwide, but the housing recovery in a particular city or region could be much more uneven. Developers might be building nonstop in major markets, but maybe they're holding back in secondary and tertiary cities without the promise of public incentives to mitigate their risks. Talk to real estate agents, researchers, financial consultants and lenders. Swing by open houses and commercial real estate financing forums. Remember that national economists and analysts might be able to comment on your market from afar, but that doesn't mean they actually know what's happening on the street.

Also understand that residential real estate transactions involve different types of loans. A fixed-rate mortgage is one in which the interest rate remains the same throughout the term of the loan, usually 15 or 30 years. An adjustable-rate mortgage is one in which the interest rate fluctuates on the basis of the Fed's moves and sometimes other factors. With the Fed expected to raise interest rates in 2016, adjustable-rate mortgages may become more volatile going forward.

Reporters who follow and report about the activity of real estate in their town, city, county, state or region of the country can help tell readers and viewers how the economy is performing. If there are large commercial real estate transactions occurring in a specific market, business executives believe the market can grow. But if there are large commercial real estate properties for sale for an extended period of time, it could mean buyers of large real estate are betting that the prices will come down and that economic growth could be slowing.

The type of commercial real estate being built or added to a community is also important. Will the new commercial buildings provide office space for corporate headquarters, or will they be for industrial parks where warehouses and manufacturing plants will likely be constructed? The rent paid for office spaces is quite often more than that for warehouse buildings.

Reporters should also watch for any incentives that a local or state government might be providing for new commercial real estate construction. Often, a government entity will offer tax breaks to entice a business to move to its area and build. This is because the new business means more jobs, which will provide an overall boost to the local economy.

TIPS FROM THE PROS

Cleveland Plain Dealer real estate reporter Michelle Jarboe on covering the real estate beat:

Mine records: When buyers, sellers and developers of commercial real estate won't talk to you, public records can be your best friends. The same is true when you're fact-checking what a homebuyer, seller or real estate agent told you. Or when you're trying to figure out if a local celebrity recently bought a high-end house. Familiarize yourself with public filings, including deeds, mortgages, easements, incorporation records, financing statements, disclosure forms and regulatory documents. Monitor local, state and federal court records for real-estate litigation. Keep an eye on public notices, from meeting agendas to comment solicitations to legal bulletins that run in daily newspapers. And reach out to companies that track and compile data, from foreclosures and short sales to the status of bonds tied to bundles of commercial loans. They'll often provide you with hard-to-find documents or figures, as long as you cite the source.

A local government body, such as a city council or county commission, must often approve these tax breaks. A government reporter may not fully understand the ramifications of the tax break and may need help from a business reporter who understands real estate. The following story shows how the *Richmond Times-Dispatch* covered one of these tax breaks for a real estate development:

The Terraces at Manchester, a 148-unit luxury apartment building that opened in August, boasts a rooftop dog park, a club room, a sky lounge and sweeping city views.

And although the lowest advertised rent in the building is $1,200 for a one-bedroom apartment, the building's developers are set to receive $2 million in real estate tax breaks from the city of Richmond through a program intended to encourage the construction of affordable housing.

That's because the way the ordinance establishing the program is written, the building's owners need to rent only 15 percent of their units to individuals who make $41,000 a year or less to qualify.

And they aren't required to offer tenants in that income category reduced rates.

In the case of the Terraces, the developers have said most units rent for an average of $1,300 a month, and rents go up to $2,100. They advertise the building as the "best choice of luxury apartments in Richmond."

Before the building opened, the average rent in Manchester, which has seen a mini-apartment boom in recent years, was $975 a month, according to Integra Realty Resources. The company said the Terraces will push that average up about 10 percent.

A day after a *Richmond Times-Dispatch* reporter first inquired about their use of the program, the developers said they realized they hadn't set aside enough units that would be affordable for tenants who meet the income requirements laid out in the program.

"It turns out, I incorrectly assumed that we had enough," said Robin Miller, who developed the project with business partner Daniel A. Gecker and Mark Purcell of Purcell Construction. "Now that we've gone back through—I told my guys to look at it today—they said no, we don't have enough. So we're going to have to reduce the rents to be able to meet that target."[1]

This story shows the precedent for the approved tax break. Anytime one of these tax breaks has been approved, reporters should see if other developments have received similar deals. If they have not, other real estate developers and their tenants might go asking for a similar break.

Residential real estate can also be important for business, particularly developers, such as D.R. Horton Incorporated, that build subdivisions. But other businesses are interested in the residential real estate market as well. Some technology companies in the Silicon Valley of California had trouble attracting employees during the 1990s because of the high cost of homes in the area. Businesses want their employees to be able to move into a neighborhood or region with which they are comfortable. They also want housing that fits the price range of workers they are hiring.

Residential real estate can also be important to business in other ways. Downtown retailers like to see apartments, townhouses, condos and other residential housing built near downtown so that their shops will be visited. Without residents living near their locations, retailers would close.

But real estate is much more than just the buying and selling of property. As the rest of this chapter details, the actual transaction is just the end of a long process that starts months earlier. Negotiations occur, particularly for commercial space. The buyer or the renter views multiple sites. And, along the way, public documents record much of the process of a real estate transaction.

Residential Real Estate

While most real estate reporters spend the bulk of their time covering the commercial market, writing about deals to build new skyscrapers downtown or about huge buildings being sold, the residential real estate market has increasingly become more important in terms of coverage in the past decade.

TIPS FROM THE PROS

Cleveland Plain Dealer real estate reporter Michelle Jarboe on covering the real estate beat:

Don't omit renters: Residential real estate coverage emphasizes ownership, which makes sense considering that a home is the biggest purchase most people will make. But Census data show that renters make up nearly 40 percent of the nation's households. Watch apartment-market trends, regulatory changes that might impact landlords and tenants, renter demographics and affordability shifts. Talk to renters about whether or not—and why—they plan to buy a house. Attitude shifts driven by the foreclosure crisis, along with movement back into cities, means renters will continue to be an important part of real estate and economic coverage.

Existing home sales topped 7 million in 2005 but dropped to below 5 million in 2014. New home sales have fluctuated as well, dropping to below 600,000 in 2009 but climbing above 1 million in 2014. The fluctuation in existing and new home sales has a big impact on local economies, meaning that reporters should be paying attention to the home sales data in their markets.

In addition to tracking home sales, real estate reporters should also be paying attention to what's happening in the lending market. In the past decade, many banks and lenders created operating units to attract consumers who may not have ever purchased a house before or who may have had a questionable credit history. So-called sub-prime lending, or predatory lending, widely expanded the percentage of homeowners in the country, but many of these consumers ended up having their homes foreclosed and taken away from them when they were unable to make the monthly mortgage payments after their interest rates rose. The question remains as to whether the consumers understood the details of the loans that they were purchasing or whether the lenders failed to properly disclose what documents the consumers were signing.

lender: A financial institution that has financed the loan allowing a buyer to purchase a piece of property.

How residential real estate is financed is important in other ways. Consumers during a tough economy may seek to refinance their mortgages at a lower rate, which lowers their monthly payment. Or they may seek to refinance their loans after the value of their property has gone up, taking equity out of the house to make another purchase, such as a boat or a vacation home. Talk to local lenders to see what trends they're seeing in your area.

Lenders can be a good source for another residential real estate story. In the latter part of the first decade of the twenty-first century, many homeowners found themselves "under water." The term means that the consumers owed more on their mortgage than what the home was worth. This happened when the property values declined shortly after the consumer bought a house by putting little into the transaction as a down payment. As a result, many consumers simply walked away from the homes, which then became owned by the lenders. Many banks and lenders have been trying to unload the real estate they own by selling the property at low prices, further depreciating the average price of a home in the market.

As discussed in Chapter 4, it's important to follow the trends when tracking the residential real estate market. The federal government and the National Association of Realtors both release monthly data that can be the basis of plenty of stories. The government breaks out new home sales by the country's four geographic regions and by price range, for example. If new home sales are rising in your region but falling in the rest of the country, talk to real estate agents and home buyers about why that's happening. If there's a sudden uptick in homes sold at more than $750,000, see if you can find some in your market.

New subdivisions are obviously an important story in the residential real estate market. If the local market has seen a decline in new home sales in recent months or years, then why is a developer planning a new neighborhood? Or if the new development is proposed right next to another new subdivision, what does the competition mean for the older neighborhood?

TIPS FROM THE PROS

Cleveland Plain Dealer real estate reporter Michelle Jarboe on covering the real estate beat:

Put it in context: Stories about new projects, big-deal sales and development dreams gone bust can be compelling. Big egos lend themselves to good yarns. But keep in mind why you're telling those stories. Real estate is an important economic indicator, a yardstick for the health of a city, region or state. Office and industrial leasing speaks to the strength in the job market. Apartment occupancy rates, home sales and housing starts reflect the desirability of a place. Building permits show how enthusiastic developers are feeling—and prospects for construction employment. Tell readers why a project or trend matters. Explain what real estate indicators are saying about a market's growth or decline.

Changes in average prices are also an important story. For most of the 1990s and the first decade of the twenty-first century, home prices rose at a steady rate each year. In markets such as California, Arizona and Florida, the annual increase led to speculators purchasing homes and condominiums with the idea that they could be turned around and sold a year or two later at a higher price. But when the average price began to level off or even fall, those buyers needed to unload their properties fast before they lost money. How do you find these buyers? Scan a county's real estate records and look to see if a name is listed as owning multiple homes. That could be a case of someone purchasing property as an investment.

Real Estate Transactions

The bread and butter of the real estate beat are the multiple transactions that occur each day. If a reporter finds the transactions that will make a difference in his or her community or that have impact on other pieces of property and writes stories about them, he or she will provide a service to readers.

Imagine that a developer has been quietly purchasing property in a specific area of town with plans to revitalize it. He has purchased all of the land for several blocks, except for one property whose owner does not want to sell. By following the previous transactions, a reporter knows that this is the one plot of land that the developer does not have. A visit to that property owner could yield an interesting story.

A developer could be purchasing property for other reasons. The *Triangle Business Journal* researched property records in Raleigh, North Carolina, and discovered that one company owned within a few blocks of the Exploris museum complex 33 pieces of property valued at about $6.9 million. The owner of that development company was Gordon Smith III, the chairman of Exploris. Smith told the paper that he was hoping that plans to revitalize the area would make the property valuable. He suggested erecting sculptures, housing and offices in the area.

Big real estate deals can be considered huge scoops for mass communication outlets. Find out about a deal that a competing media outlet has not reported yet, and they will likely scramble to follow the story the next day.

Steve Cannon, the former real estate reporter for the *News & Observer* in Raleigh, competed with the *Triangle Business Journal*, also located in Raleigh, for real estate news. He said that the best sources for him were commercial real estate brokers who know what properties are for sale, what real estate is about to be sold or leased and who is looking for additional real estate for their operations.

real estate broker: An agent who buys and sells real estate on a commission basis. The broker does not have title to the property but generally represents the owner or the buyer.

The brokers are more in contact with news than the developers are. The developers have their projects, but that pretty much takes most of their time. The broker is always having people knock on the door asking for space. And then the broker knocks on doors looking for space, but those people may say they do not now have any space because they just gave it to another company. The most important sources are the ones who see that big picture, have the historical context, and can see that every deal is part of a larger pattern, that there were things that came before it and things that it would lead to. . . . It's a long process of building up that source list. For a little bit more than a year, I made a point every week, I would try to meet two new people. I would try to have breakfast or lunch with two new people, whether it was a developer, someone in the banking community, or a broker. And from that, you just work the source list over and over again. You call 25 people a week, which covers things pretty well.

(Steve Cannon, personal communication, May 15, 2003)

TIPS FROM THE PROS

Cleveland Plain Dealer real estate reporter Michelle Jarboe on covering the real estate beat:

Consider the gawk factor: People like to look at expensive houses. Unusual houses. On the commercial side, they like to be urban explorers without the risk. Covering real estate, you can take audience members places where they can't ordinarily go. At a time when journalists are rewarded based on online traffic and are expected to be jacks-of-all-trades when it comes to audio, video, blog posts, in-depth stories and social media, property tours can be a valuable sweetener for your stories. They're also great opportunities for face time with brokers, agents, landlords and developers, who might share tidbits that lead to other stories.

In addition to relying on sources, reporters should know that all real estate transactions are recorded at the county courthouse, typically with the clerk's office. They may not be filed for several days after the transaction, however. But for reporters looking for who bought a piece of property and who sold it and for how much, there is no better place. Increasingly, some counties have begun putting this information on the Internet.

Unfortunately, real estate transactions are not always so simple. Sometimes, a company will purchase a piece of property using another name it has incorporated with the state so that no one will know who is buying the property. It can be hard to track who these buyers actually are. Reporters often need to go to the secretary of state's office to look at the incorporation filing for the company and review the names of its executives and its mailing address. The mailing address may be the same as a well-known business in the community, and the executives may be the same executives of a better-known company. That is one way a reporter can discover the actual buyer, or at least get a good hint.

The seller of the property may also be unknown. Sometimes, an attorney or another name that is not well known could be listed as the seller. Again, corporation records can help. Calling the attorney does not hurt either. The reporter should ask him or her whom they represent.

Going to the real estate records may not always be necessary. If the land or building transferring ownership is a major deal, then the buyer or the seller may announce it with a release. Again, the dollar amount changing hands may not always be disclosed. If it is not, get a real estate expert in the community to estimate the price. This can easily be done if the expert knows the square footage of the building or the number of acres and the location of the property. Often, someone from either the buyer's side or the seller's side will disclose the amount off the record.

In addition to the selling price, the acreage and the square footage of the building or the planned building, there are also other important facts that should be in any real estate transaction story. Compare the price per square foot or per acre of the transaction with other similar transactions in the market. If the buyer is paying more—or less—than recent deals, that could be an indication of where the local real estate market is headed. It could also be a significant sign of how much the purchaser covets the property.

Where the property is located and what its current zoned usage allows are also vital facts for an acquisition. If the buyer is not willing to disclose what he intends to do with the property, the reporter should keep calling him after the deal closes until he is willing to talk or should regularly check the local zoning commission or planning commission records to see if any proposals for the property have been submitted.

If the buyer is willing to talk about what he is planning to build on the property, he might already have architectural drawings and other specifications for the building, such as when construction might begin and be completed. As always, reporters should ask for as much information as they can get.

The beginning of the following story from the *Northglenn-Thornton Sentinel* in Colorado emphasizes what the property being acquired will be used for, how much acreage is being purchased and how many square feet of commercial building space will occupy the land:

> The developer of Northglenn's highly successful Marketplace of Northglenn has inked a deal with Thornton to create a regional retail center at Highway 7 and Interstate 25.
>
> Jordon Perlmutter and Co. is acquiring four parcels of land to meld into a 120-acre retail center with an expected 500,000 square feet of commercial space.
>
> Perlmutter's son and business partner, Jay Perlmutter, said the area will be like Park Meadows Mall, with a Highlands-Ranch-size residential area surrounding it.

"This will spawn a whole new economy out there," Perlmutter said. He pointed out that most of the land surrounding the proposed retail center is owned by major residential developers, and thousands of homes are planned for the area.[2]

Note that the lead of this story also tells readers where the property is located. Also, the story explains what the surrounding property might be used for—to build homes.

If an acquirer is making a lot of acquisitions, that should be reflected in the story as well. It does not matter if all of the acquisitions are small; they could reflect a trend by the buyer to purchase specific types of property or to purchase property in a specific area. Reporters should look at the big picture. If the purchaser is making his or her first real estate deal in a market after making lots of deals in other markets, that should also be a signal that the transaction is part of a strategy.

The following is the beginning of a story that reflects the importance of the acquisition:

> The speed at which Madison County snatched up the Florists' Mutual Insurance Co. building shows how great the need is for office space in downtown Edwardsville, real estate experts said.
>
> County Board members approved a plan Wednesday to purchase the 32,000 square-foot building at 500 St. Louis Street. The county will pay $2.23 million and collect rent from the insurance company for about 18 months.
>
> County Administrator Jim Monday said the county made an offer May 17, and the two parties agreed on a purchase price within a week.
>
> The county plans to renovate the building into a criminal courthouse. Commercial developers said the county got a good deal on the property considering that the market for office space in downtown Edwardsville is hot these days.
>
> "There is a lot of demand for space near the public administration buildings, and there is not a lot of new space available," said Phil Polite, president of Amerivest Reality Inc.—a commercial property developer and broker in Edwardsville.
>
> His company is developing the second-story office space in the Manhattan's Restaurant building.
>
> He said the owners just completed their renovations, and they have already leased about 65 percent of the space with other deals in the works.
>
> "Our plan from the beginning was to build space, then advertise for tenants," he said.
>
> "But before we had even hired a contractor, we had two leases in the works."
>
> Polite said he contacted Florists' Mutual two years ago representing a St. Louis firm interested in purchasing a building that size.
>
> But the insurance company was not ready to move.

But Florists' Mutual, led by President and Chief Executive Robert McClellan Jr., signed a deal last year to build a $25 million office park and new headquarters at Illinois Route 143 and Interstate 55.

Before the company put its 30-year-old building on the market, it came knocking at the county's door.

Representatives for the company spoke to County Board members at a buildings committee meeting last fall, Monday said.

County officials looked at purchasing St. John's United Methodist Church on Second Street for a court building but the cost was too high, Monday said.

"It was pretty much public knowledge that we had been talking to people at the church across the street for about five years," Monday said.

Architects who briefly surveyed the Florists' Mutual building said the county could feasibly renovate the structure for courtrooms for about $3 million.

Florists' Mutual said it wanted $2.6 million for the building and the county offered $2 million.

The purchase includes 170 parking spaces, a small house for storage and a fiberoptic cable.

Officials will close the deal by July 15.[3]

This story does an excellent job of explaining the real estate market in this town, the reasons why the purchaser wanted the building, and why the seller was ready to get rid of the property. In addition, note that the last paragraph states when the deal will close, and an earlier paragraph includes the owner's asking price and the purchaser's offer. These are details that add to a story if they can be obtained.

Be on the lookout as well for real estate companies that have been selling property in the past but are now interested in buying buildings and other real estate. The *Dallas Business Journal* noted such a shift by Crescent Real Estate Equities Company. The company decided to sell properties in Omaha and New Orleans to focus on other markets.

There are other real estate records that might help a reporter follow the industry and its players. Realtors and real estate brokers are licensed and regulated by state laws. In some cases, complaints filed against them may be public record. Reporters who believe that a realtor or broker may be in trouble should check these records. Sometimes the story may not be what the brokers are telling a reporter but the broker himself.

Other real estate transaction stories may not necessarily involve a purchase or the sale of a property. Many real estate stories are written about new developments. The approval of a new office complex for construction can also be an important development for a local real estate market.

Real estate transactions and developments can seem difficult to write about. They are often complex deals. The trick is to write the story in a way that the reader will understand.

TIPS FROM THE PROS

Cleveland Plain Dealer real estate reporter Michelle Jarboe on covering the real estate beat:

Get geeky: It pays—in stories about new projects, failed developments, risk and fraud—to understand the tools that developers, builders and homeowners use. Learn about the various financing mechanisms, from tax credits to the federal immigrant-investor visa program, that developers rely on to cut the costs of their projects, secure debt or attract equity. Understanding the nuts and bolts of these programs can help you speak developers' language and detect when someone is flouting the rules or telling tall tales. On the housing-market side, tax abatements and other buyer incentives might explain the popularity of a neighborhood or project—and raise questions about what happens when those perks expire. If you understand how these tools work, you'll do a better job of explaining their broader impacts on local taxpayers and the communities where they live.

"The work that you do to find information can be fairly specialized," said Steve Cannon (personal communication, May 15, 2003). "But the actual writing of the story should not be specialized. It should be important to almost everyone. If it's hard to explain, then maybe I shouldn't be writing it—sometimes I have guys that tell me stuff about how a lease is put together, and it's important to understand that, but I would never write about it."

Zoning and Planning Departments

Before commercial and residential buildings can be sold or leased, they must be built. Local governments typically must first approve the construction plans before dirt is broken and concrete is poured. The government agency responsible for this can be a zoning commission or a planning commission. In some areas, it may take on different names, as well. Zoning and planning departments at town and city governments can be great places for real estate reporters to find news. Often, the submission of plans for a new office building or a new subdivision is the first public disclosure by a developer of its intentions for a piece of property. These plans can be interesting stories. They will often disclose how big the building will be in terms of square footage and when the construction might begin.

zoning: A legal mechanism to regulate the use of real estate. All privately owned land within a jurisdiction is placed within designated zones that limit the type and intensity of development permitted.

The functions of zoning commissions and planning commissions differ in many localities. The zoning commission decides on approved uses for land. An owner of a piece of property on a major street that is currently zoned for residential housing may request by application that the zoning be changed to commercial so that he can sell the property to someone interested in building a gas station or convenience store on the property.

Zoning commission meetings are public, and the commission typically reviews dozens of zoning applications at each meeting. The applicant often makes a presentation before the zoning board, and then the body opens the discussion to allow residents or others to speak. Sometimes, neighbors of the property being rezoned will appear and speak against the proposed rezoning. The zoning commission then votes on the proposal. In many communities, the proposed rezoning then goes before a city council or county commission for final approval.

TIPS FROM THE PROS

Cleveland Plain Dealer real estate reporter Michelle Jarboe on covering the real estate beat:

Don't get overwhelmed: The amount of housing data, in particular, can be daunting. One report highlights home-price appreciation. Another says the market is flat. Every residential price index seems to use a different data set. Sort through the data to figure out what's supportable, what's questionable, what's worth pursuing and what's not. Read and ask questions about the methodology. It's your job to explain not only what a report says but also why—and how the findings relate to, or clash with, what's happening in your coverage area. Your audience will value clear, concise and critical explanations that are jargon-free.

Planning commissions operate in much the same way. An owner of a piece of property may decide that he or she wants to construct a building on the land. Before he or she can begin construction, an application must be filed with the local planning commission detailing the type of building and how it will be built. If the landowner wants to build a car repair center on a piece of property surrounded by homes, the proposal may meet some resistance. Planning commission meetings are also public hearings where residents and others often attend to speak against proposed developments.

The city desk or government reporters at many media outlets often cover zoning and planning authorities. But business reporters should also cover these agencies because of the development and commercial aspects of most construction.

The zoning application process and the planning application process should be followed from beginning to end, particularly for large commercial developments that may mean hundreds of new jobs for an area and new subdivisions that will add hundreds of homes to a community. In some cases, homeowners worried about increased traffic congestion, pollution problems to local creeks and rivers, and overcrowded schools will bitterly oppose these new developments. Millions of dollars are often at stake, however. The developer has likely purchased the land with the specific intent of building a development. If a local agency turns down the plans, the developer is left owning vacant property that cannot be used for the intended purpose.

The following is the beginning of a front-page story about a major development announced in Louisville, Kentucky, before it was filed with the zoning commission and the planning department. Perhaps the developers were promoting their plans before filing them with the local authorities to let them know they were coming.

> The largest piece of privately owned undeveloped property in Louisville, the Oxmoor Farm, would be developed over the next 25 years under a plan unveiled yesterday.
>
> The 450-acre project would contain estate homes, upscale apartments, stores, offices and hotels, attorneys for the farm's heirs said.
>
> The plan would be tied to new roads Mayor Dave Armstrong said he has been working on developing across Oxmoor since he was Jefferson County judge executive in 1994.
>
> Armstrong called the plan "about the best compromise possible. . . . It will be a wonderful and spectacular campus that will blend green space with progress."
>
> About one-third of the land would be protected from development, including the old Bullitt estate and land along two forks of Beargrass Creek and around a small cemetery.
>
> The preliminary plan for 450 acres of the farm includes:
>
> A string of about 10 office buildings, most four to six stories, along both sides of Interstate 64.
>
> A retail area with at least four buildings, each housing several stores, behind Oxmoor Center and serving as an expansion of the mall.
>
> A string of expensive homes on large lots and a retirement center on the east side of the farm, serving as a buffer for estate homes in nearby Hurstbourne and Oxmoor Woods.
>
> A large "commons" in the center of the development, with hundreds of apartments, dozens of small retailers, walking paths, an athletic club and potentially a hotel and conference center.
>
> Officials with the William Marshall Bullitt and Thomas Bullitt trusts, which own the farm, plan to begin discussing the farm's development next week with the Louisville-Jefferson County Planning Commission and to file a rezoning application in about a month.

Because of the project's scope, the commission might need several months to sort out the regulatory issues, said Rick Northern, an attorney for the farm's heirs. The full commission might hear the rezoning case next spring, the trusts' attorneys said.

The board of Aldermen will decide on the rezoning of 405 acres on the farm. Jefferson Fiscal Court would have final say on the rezoning of 45 acres of unincorporated county land.

For now, the entire development plan is conceptual, Northern said. The Planning Commission will be asked to approve a general district development plan. Specific development will proceed as the roads are built and the market demands, Northern said.[4]

Approval of this project is months away, and yet the developer has the local mayor on board. In many cases, zoning and planning requests can be political. Sometimes, politicians want to be known as the ones who approved a great development for the community. They can also use the zoning and planning approval process to force a developer to make other changes, such as improving paved roads in the area or adding sidewalks from a development to another area.

TIPS FROM THE PROS

Cleveland Plain Dealer real estate reporter Michelle Jarboe on covering the real estate beat:

Consider both sides: Higher apartment rents are good for landlords but tough for tenants. Climbing home prices are a boon to sellers but a barrier for some buyers. Rising interest rates can make it harder to purchase a home. But they're also signs of economic growth, which helps the housing market as people find work and save money. It's easy to get caught up in the industry fervor and sales pitches, especially since real estate agents and brokers will be—and should be—some of your most valuable sources. Strive to look at real estate trends from a variety of perspectives to ensure that your coverage is broad, thorough and fair.

Some communities may have additional review boards for construction projects. There may be design review boards that ensure that the new construction is built with a façade that blends in with the rest of the buildings in the area.

The zoning and planning approval processes sometimes hit snags. The body may ask for more information about the project from the developer. Or it may ask for a delay in the hearing to give the developer time to make changes in their proposal to satisfy concerns. If the zoning commission or planning authority delays a vote on a major project, there is usually a reason. Reporters can find out by talking to the commission members, the developer and opponents of the project.

Crain's Detroit Business reported that the Ann Arbor Planning Commission tabled two residential developments because of concerns about providing affordable housing. The story was based on information from the city planner, the director of the planning department and an independent real estate broker.

building permit: An approval by a local government allowing a contractor to construct, expand or demolish an existing structure.

Some local media outlets report all zoning and planning commission decisions, much the same way that they report all real estate transactions and all building permits. The final approval of a development could also be news because it signals government approval. The stories are also important to readers because they may foretell that jobs are coming to the local economy or that a major construction project is about to begin on a road they use for travel that they now may want to avoid.

The following is a story about a residential development that was approved that includes the significance for residents in the area—a connector road:

Preliminary plans for the Smokey Row Estates subdivision have been approved, along with a controversial road that would connect Smokey Row with the Water's Edge development.

The Johnson County Department of Planning and Zoning gave the go-ahead for the 76-lot, 38-acre subdivision to be located 2,000 feet east of Morgantown Road along Smokey Row Road.

The location is adjacent to the south side of Water's Edge in White River Township. Next up for the subdivision—being developed by the Nichols Group LLC, of Scottsdale, Ariz.—is a review by the County Commissioners.

Water's Edge residents have spoken against the connecting street, fearing it would become a shortcut for rush-hour motorists who want to avoid a four-way stop at Morgantown and Smokey Row roads.

Part of the planning department's approval requires a stop sign to be added along the street, which will be called Streamside Drive. The stop sign would be placed one lot south of Water's Edge, according to county planner Joanna Myers.

Water's Edge abuts the northern boundary of Smokey Row Estates. The main entrance to Water's Edge is off of Morgantown Road.

Water's Edge residents had been successful on another front. On June 3, County Commissioners rejected a request by the Nichols Group to rezone 38 acres for Smokey Row Estates from R-l to R-2.

If that request had been granted, 83 homes could have been built on the 38 acres. Plans call for two units per acre, or 76 lots on 38 acres.[5]

Residents of neighborhoods next to proposed developments virtually always come to zoning or planning commission meetings to voice their opposition to a construction project. Many times they have valid complaints, such as increased traffic and overcrowded schools, but other times they just do not want more homes built around their area. Other groups such as environmental organizations may also attend these meetings and voice opposition.

Zoning and planning departments can also be good sources of information for the building permits they issue. A building permit is required for any new construction, demolition, remodeling, expansion or repair to a building. Most city and county governments require that a permit be obtained before the work begins. Without a permit, the contractor and the building owner could face fines.

Building permits ensure that the construction will be done in a safe manner and that the structure will not collapse the next time a strong wind comes through town.

Watching building permit activity can reveal the activity of the local real estate industry. If the number of building permits is increasing in a specific area, the local economy is growing. If the number of building permits is declining, then maybe the economy is slowing.

Often, a local zoning or planning department will have statistics on building permits for an area. Reporters should check these numbers regularly to see if they are showing any trends in construction that may be newsworthy. The following shows how one newspaper noted the fluctuation in permits:

Contractors slammed the brakes on commercial construction last year amid a slowdown that has office, warehouse and apartment vacancies at record levels.

In Wake County, where the Triangle's commercial construction is concentrated, the value of commercial building permits dropped to $210.6 million in 2002, down 61 percent compared with 2001. The decline was even more dramatic in Raleigh, where building permits for new commercial construction declined 74 percent to $102.8 million, according to the Wake County tax assessor.

"Except for college and institutional work . . . we've seen a slowdown in every sector of the market," said Scott Cutler, vice president of marketing for Clancy & Theys Construction Co. in Raleigh, the Triangle's biggest construction company.

"With the broader economy [slowdown] and the tech meltdown, the office market has evaporated, and every other segment has been hit," Cutler said. "Travel and tourism and hotels aren't booming."

Municipalities and the counties don't break down types of commercial projects on the permits. But office and retail construction sectors have been hit particularly hard by the economic slump and a shaky recovery in which businesses are reluctant to add jobs and merchants slow to open new stores. Warehouse construction has ground to a halt.

Commercial construction hasn't fallen as sharply in Durham County, but building permit totals still declined 14 percent to $141.1 million last year, compared with 2001. Together, commercial construction for Wake and Durham counties in 2002 was down 70 percent from the $1.2 billion total value of permits recorded in 2000.

New home construction, which has been bolstered by some of the lowest mortgage rates in decades, also declined in the two counties.

The total value of building permits for new homes in Wake was down 1.3 percent to $1.29 billion last year, compared with permits in 2001. Permits were issued for 9,214 homes last year, compared with 9,467 the year before.

The value of new home permits in Durham County declined 8.5 percent from 2001 to $317 million in 2002. Permits were issued for 2,762 new homes in 2002 compared with 3,643 homes a year earlier.[6]

Although most real estate reporters focus on the commercial side of the business because deals there are often huge, trends in residential construction can be just as important to a local community.

Property Deeds

Property deeds can be helpful to reporters working on a variety of stories. They show who actually owns a piece of property.

A deed is a legal document conveying the title, or ownership, of a piece of property. It contains a legal description of the property being acquired. If there is an error in the legal description, the purchaser may have trouble selling the property later. The deed should also spell the name of the buyer and the seller correctly. If a name is misspelled, this could also cause problems when the property is later sold.

Deeds, like most real estate documents, are public records typically filed with the county recorder. In addition, other documents recorded include mortgages and liens against a piece of property. Each time a property owner refinances a mortgage, a new public record is created.

The availability of property deeds and other real estate records allows reporters to trace the history of a piece of real estate, tracking previous owners and how much a piece of property is worth. Reporters have used deeds to find out other information as well, noted the *News & Observer*'s Steve Cannon.

"There was a property right in downtown on Fayetteville Street mall," said Cannon (personal communication, May 15, 2003). "The people who had the building didn't own the land. They were leasing the land and wouldn't tell me anything about it. But the land lease was filed with the county, and I was able to see how much they were paying for it and how much longer the lease was going to last."

Deeds can be important documents, especially for the lender of the money that allowed the purchaser to acquire the piece of real estate, whether it was a huge office complex or a single-story ranch home. If the owner falls behind in or stops making loan payments, the lender may foreclose on the property. To do that, the lender takes ownership—and receives the deed to the property—and resells it to help pay the loan.

When a property owner falls behind in or stops making payments on his loan, he is considered in default of the loan. Although many real estate loans that go into default do not lead to foreclosures, a default is usually the first step in the process. Real estate lenders such as banks and commercial finance companies will often disclose the default rate for their loan portfolio. If the defaults are increasing, then the lender may have made a number of bad real estate loans.

default: When the owner of a piece of property falls behind in making payments on the loan used to acquire the property, or stops making payments altogether.

A deed can be transferred from the real estate developer to the lender without a foreclosure, as well. The developer may run into financial difficulties and simply transfer the ownership to the lender as a way of satisfying the loans. Many lenders are not in the business of managing real estate properties, so when a deed is transferred to a lender, it is often a major development.

foreclosure: A court proceeding where the property owner's rights are terminated in order to sell the property to satisfy lenders.

Sallye Salter, a former real estate reporter for the *Atlanta Journal-Constitution,* uncovered such a case by reading the deed documents related to Peachtree Center, a downtown complex created by developer John C. Portman Jr. She discovered that the ownership of much of the development had been turned over to two insurance companies who were Portman's lenders. The transfer was recorded in deed documents. Salter's stories became a major disclosure in Portman's struggles to maintain his real estate empire in downtown Atlanta.

In addition, the deed documents can be valuable tools for other reasons; a *Tampa Tribune* reporter used them to determine who actually owned the home of a former corporate executive:

> Corporate raider Paul Bilzerian's trophy mansion in north Hillsborough County is for sale, but he may never see the money.
>
> A federal judge ordered Tuesday that the proceeds of any sale should be frozen until he rules on a contempt hearing against the convicted former chairman of Singer Co. in March.

U.S. District Court Judge Stanley Harris cited Bilzerian's "initial lack of candor" regarding sale of the home as one of the reasons for his order. Bilzerian couldn't be reached Thursday.

No one has made an offer on the 36,000-square-foot home yet, said Bob Glaser, president of Smith & Associates Investment Co. Realtors in Tampa.

"We're still marketing the property," Glaser said.

The 11-bedroom home, considered the largest in the Bay area, is appraised at $3.4 million by the Hillsborough County Property Appraiser.

Bilzerian, in bankruptcy since 1991, was convicted of securities fraud in 1989 for failing to properly report stock transactions. The Securities and Exchange Commission fined Bilzerian and now claims $33 million in fines, plus $29 million in interest.

The SEC asked the judge to hold Bilzerian in contempt for failing to pay the fine and report assets like the Tampa home that could be sold to pay it.

SEC officials discovered Bilzerian's Avila home was for sale when they saw it advertised without a price in January's edition of *Unique Homes,* an upscale home magazine distributed to wealthy prospective home buyers.

"We want him to give a full accounting," said Judith Starr, SEC assistant chief litigation counsel in Washington. In court filings, Bilzerian has denied he owns the home. He transferred ownership to a limited partnership in March 1997, but Starr said there is evidence Bilzerian controls the partnership. The partnership's business address is the same as Bilzerian's home, the deed shows.[7]

The *Fulton County Daily Report,* a daily newspaper in Atlanta that tracks the legal and real estate community, was able to search deed records to show that 8 percent of foreclosures in the area were connected to one developer. Their research and understanding of deeds showed that the developer acquired real estate by assuming the mortgages of the developers who owned them or by purchasing blocks of condos in the same development. Their survey of deed records suggested that the developer secured the funding to pay for the properties by first selling them. But the sales were a sham, according to lawsuits. Deed records show that the mortgages were for higher interest rates than the going market, and that the developer arranged to have the mortgages refinanced at lower rates even before the transactions closed and pocketed the proceeds from the transactions.

All of the details of these transactions were laid out for the reporters to uncover through the deed records and other public real estate records. It took them some digging but resulted in a story that shook the local real estate community. (The story also noted that the developer's $5.1 million home was being foreclosed.)

The government can also foreclose properties if the owner has not paid taxes on the real estate. This can result in a new owner. Public foreclosures such as this are commonly advertised in advance to drum up interest from potential buyers in acquiring the property.

Checking deeds should be the backbone of the work done by any real estate reporter. Quite often, the trip to the local courthouse will not yield a story. But regularly reviewing deeds for commercial and residential real estate transactions will keep the reporter in touch with the market. By tracking the deed activity and looking for trends, the reporter will be able to give his readers insight into a real estate market that another reporter ignoring the deeds might not be able to offer.

Tracking deeds also gives the reporter plenty of examples to pick from to use as anecdotes for stories about residential and commercial real estate. By looking at the deeds on a regular basis, the reporter is able to use these transactions to illustrate broader trends. To be sure, reading real estate deeds is boring work. But it is also the best way to learn about real estate transactions. And reporters will show sources that they are serious about the industry when they call brokers or developers and mention their latest deed filing.

Tax Assessments

Another important place to find real estate information is with the local tax assessor's office. The tax assessor is charged with assessing the value of property throughout his jurisdiction for tax purposes. Those taxes are then collected from the property owners, and the money is used to pay for government services to the community, such as schools, law enforcement, hospitals, road building and maintenance, and parks. The assessed value of a property is a public record available from the tax assessor's office. Increasingly, property values are made available online through searchable databases.

Some property may be exempt from paying taxes. If that is the case, a reporter should find out why, particularly if the property is being used for a commercial purpose.

The tax assessor's office does not set the tax rate. A county commission or city council typically does that. What the tax assessor does is visit the property and estimate the amount for which the property might be sold in a transaction. Owners can contest the assessed value of their property if they believe it is too high.

Typically business and industrial property is assessed at a higher rate than is residential real estate. Often, the property is being used for business reasons that make it more valuable than a home. A $150,000 home may be assessed at 8 percent, meaning the tax bill would be $12,000. But a business building appraised at the same value may be assessed at 15 percent, making its tax bill $22,500.

assessed value: The property value as determined by the county tax assessor for tax purposes.

The assessed value of a piece of property can become an important fact in a real estate story, and it should be looked up for virtually every major transaction. If a purchaser is acquiring a piece of property for $2 million, but the local tax assessor's office only values the property at $1.5 million, what made the acquirer pay 33 percent more than the appraised value? The same question can be asked of the seller if he is unloading a piece of property for less than its appraised value. Of course, not every property will sell for the assessed value, and a sale price slightly above or below the tax assessor's valuation is not likely to warrant a mention. But how much people pay for property is important because that tells how they value it. In addition, whether the taxes on a piece of property are being paid can often become an interesting development, as the following story reports:

> The West Allegheny School District and Allegheny County are embroiled in a dispute over the taxes owed on the Hyatt Regency Hotel property at Pittsburgh International Airport.
>
> The school district has filed a lawsuit against the county in Common Pleas Court seeking to collect $791,777 in real estate taxes it says are owed on the property for 2000 and 2001.
>
> But the county, which owns the land on which the hotel sits, says it doesn't owe the district anything.
>
> The Dauphin County Municipal Authority built the hotel and leases the land from Allegheny County. In 1998, the authority, Allegheny County, Findlay Township and the school district all agreed that the land would not be subject to property taxation. Instead, the parties agreed that the municipal authority would make annual payments of $460,000 to be divided between the county, the township and the district.
>
> But the next step of making such a deal legal never took place, according to West Allegheny Solicitor Ira Weiss. He said the parties would have had to declare the property tax exempt in order for that to work.
>
> Besides that, the $460,000 payments that were supposed to be made instead of taxes weren't made anyway.
>
> In a letter sent to the county last spring, Thomas Smida, solicitor for the Dauphin County General Authority, said there were "insufficient funds" available to make the payment. He said the authority lost an estimated $1.4 million to $3.1 million in income operating the hotel last year. But that doesn't matter to Weiss.
>
> An agreement for payments in lieu of taxes "without the exempt status is a nullity," he said. "The county never took the step it needed to take to get the property declared exempt. The school district believes it is owed this money."
>
> On the county's real estate Web site, the hotel is listed as taxable with an assessed value of $23.8 million.
>
> Weiss said the school district is obligated under law to collect taxes on properties listed as taxable, regardless of the agreement for payments in lieu of taxes.[8]

 lease: An agreement where the owner of a piece of property agrees to allow another party to inhabit the property for a specified period of time.

As this story and others in this chapter illustrate, writing about real estate requires becoming familiar with government records and how local regulatory authorities oversee real estate developments and transactions. It can be argued that nowhere else in business journalism does a reporter have to become as knowledgeable about the inner workings of local government than in real estate. Some real estate reporters might gain more expertise in this area than the reporter covering city hall or the county commission.

Notes

1. From "Luxury apartments get tax break through city's affordable housing program," by N. Oliver, December 5, 2015, *Richmond Times-Dispatch*. Copyright 2015 by *Richmond Times-Dispatch*. Reprinted with permission.
2. From "Thornton lands Perlmutter mall," by N. Bachlet Snyder, December 12, 2002, *Northglenn-Thornton Sentinel*, p. 1. Copyright 2002 by *Northglenn-Thornton Sentinel*. Reprinted with permission.
3. From "Madison County agrees to purchase Florists' Mutual Insurance building," by H. Ratcliffe, May 22, 2000, *St. Louis Post-Dispatch*, p. 1. Copyright 2000 by *St. Louis Post-Dispatch*. Reprinted with permission.
4. From "Development of Oxmoor Farm proposed; plan calls for stores," by S. Shafer and B. Pike, October 13, 2001, *Louisville Courier-Journal*, p. 1A. Copyright 2001 by *Louisville Courier-Journal*. Reprinted with permission.
5. From "Planners give approval for Smokey Row Estates," by J. Thomas, June 26, 2002, *Indianapolis Star*, p. 15. Copyright 2002 by *Indianapolis Star*. Reprinted with permission.
6. From "Drop in building permits tells story of decline," by D. Price, February 5, 2003, *News & Observer*, p. D1. Copyright 2003 by *News & Observer*. Reprinted with permission.
7. From "Court sews up mansion proceeds," by J. Gruss, February 18, 1999, *Tampa Tribune*, p. 1. Copyright 1999 by *Tampa Tribune*. Reprinted with permission.
8. From "Dispute arises over taxes on airport hotel," by M. Belko, October 18, 2002, *Pittsburgh Post-Gazette*, p. C-14. Copyright 2002 by *Pittsburgh Post-Gazette*. Reprinted with permission.

Key Terms

assessed value	lease
building permit	lender
default	real estate broker
foreclosure	zoning

Suggested Exercises

1. Find the real estate records of the home of one of your professors or the dean of your school. In some counties, these records may be available on the Internet, so look there first. Write down how much the home was purchased for and in which year. Also look for the appraised value of the home. What is the difference between the appraised value of the home and the purchase price?

2. Check local real estate records to see if your university has made any acquisitions recently. If you find some, has the university disclosed what it plans to do with the property? Who sold the property to the university? Did this person have any prior connection to the university?

3. Find out when the local city or county government will hold its next foreclosure auction for properties for which taxes have not been paid. Attend the auction. What types of property were sold? Was it primarily commercial property or residential property? See if you can talk to some of the buyers. Who are they, and what was their interest in the property?

4. Attend a meeting of the local zoning commission or planning board and write a 500-word report on the types of properties that went before the council that evening, noting whether there was any opposition to the developments and whether they were approved or not. If some requests were voted down, what were the reasons against the project?

Real Estate Books

Jarsulic, M. (2010). *Anatomy of a financial crisis: A real estate bubble, runaway credit markets, and regulatory failure*. New York: Palgrave Macmillan.

O'Donnell, J.R., Rutherford, J., & Towle, P. (1991). *Trumped!: The inside story of the real Donald Trump—his cunning rise and spectacular fall*. New York: Simon & Schuster.

Pacelle, M. (2002). *Empire: A tale of obsession, betrayal, and the battle for an American icon*. New York: Wiley.

Schachtman, T. (1991). *Skyscraper dreams: The great real estate dynasties of New York*. New York: Little Brown & Co.

Sobel, R. (1990). *Trammell Crow, master builder: The story of America's largest real estate empire*. New York: Wiley.

Tauranac, J. (1995). *The Empire State Building: The making of a landmark*. New York: Scribner.

References

Bachlet Snyder, N. (2002, December 12). Thornton lands Perlmutter mall. *Northglenn-Thornton Sentinel*, p. 1.

Bailey, L. (2002, November 4). Affordable-housing request delays 2 Ann Arbor projects. *Crain's Detroit Business*, p. 17.

Belko, M. (2002, October 18). Dispute arises over taxes on airport hotel. *Pittsburgh Post-Gazette*, p. C-14.

Collison, K. (2003, June 21). Tax break passed for HOK relocation; Architecture firm would move to site in River Market. *Kansas City Star*, p. C1.

Corfman, T. (2003, May 10). Aon Center brings $465 million price; Atlanta firm pays less than expected. *Chicago Tribune*, p. C2.

Gruss, J. (1999, February 19). Court sews up mansion proceeds. *Tampa Tribune*, p. 1.

Nilsen, K. (2003, June 30). Firm called Wood Pile owns 33 properties near museum. *Triangle Business Journal*, p. 1.

Perez, C. (2002, February 1). Crescent is "done selling," ready to spend. *Dallas Business Journal*, p. 10.

Price, D. (2003, February 5). Drop in building permits tells story of decline. *The News & Observer*, p. D1.

Ratcliffe, H. (2000, May 22). Madison County agrees to purchase Florists' Mutual insurance building; Site in downtown Edwardsville will serve as courthouse; price tag is $2.33 million. *St. Louis Post-Dispatch*, p. 1.

Renaud, T., McDonald, R.R., & Ramos, R. (2002, May 16). Deals send $75 million in properties to foreclosure. *Fulton County Daily Report*, pp. 1, 3, 4, 7.

Salter, S. (1995, April 14). Two lenders get more Portman holdings; Downtown complex: Much of Peachtree Center has been transferred to new owners to meet debt agreements. *Atlanta Journal-Constitution*, p. 1E.

Shafer, S.S., & Pike, B. (2001, October 13). Development of Oxmoor Farm proposed; plan calls for stores. *The Louisville Courier-Journal*, p. 1A.

Thomas, J. (2002, June 26). Planners give approval for Smokey Row Estates. *The Indianapolis Star*, p. 15.

14

BUSINESS STORIES WITHIN THE GOVERNMENT

Agencies That Regulate

Throughout many of the earlier chapters, the SEC and its powers in regulating businesses and stocks are discussed, particularly how those regulations can help business journalists do their job in informing the public.

But there are plenty of other federal regulatory agencies that also have a hand in overseeing businesses and corporations. State and local government bodies are also involved in ensuring that corporate America does not run afoul.

Business regulation is the passing of rules, procedures and laws to govern business and industry. Although many business executives might argue that regulation limits their ability to produce a profit, the laws and rules do serve a purpose. Most laws and regulations governing businesses are enacted to protect other businesses, consumers, employees and competitors.

Business regulation has not been around that long in the United States. Most laws governing the business world were not enacted until the nineteenth century, hundreds of years after the first proprietors set up shop and began selling their goods and services to consumers. In fact, it took the misdeeds of some major businesses to lead lawmakers into creating major rules and restrictions on companies. Even worldwide government organizations now play a part in overseeing how businesses operate.

U.S. government regulation of business developed with the Industrial Revolution in the late nineteenth century. As some businesses became bigger and bigger, other businesses wanted protection so that their rights would be covered. In addition, regulation also came about because some companies misused their power. They neglected the working conditions of their employees and attempted to break unions. Some businesses physically harmed and killed their workers.

TIPS FROM THE PROS

Politico news editor Karey Van Hall on finding business stories at government agencies:

Read the fine print. Congress oversees an annual budget process that reaches above a trillion dollars. It's a messy operation that often goes off the rails, with lawmakers instead passing a continuing resolution that extends existing spending levels and policy provisions. But when Congress is able to pull off an annual budget, the legislation is a bonanza for business interests. Spending bills, which are often accompanied by tax bills, are chock full of policy riders and various provisions that can translate into millions of dollars in revenue for solar energy companies, investment banks, oil refiners, dairy farmers and practically every other industry under the sun. The key is to not just look at the headline figures, but to dig deep into the legislation. While earmarks were banned under President Barack Obama, lawmakers still manage to slip in provisions as short as one line that can prop up certain industries and sometimes even a single company.

State politicians tried to regulate businesses, but they were limited in what could be done. States could only pass laws regulating businesses that operated within their borders.

Before the 1880s, the federal government played a minor role in American business. The first major legislation regulating business was the creation of the Interstate Commerce Commission in 1877. The commission regulated the railroad industry, then the major transportation mode for goods across the country. With the passage of the Sherman Antitrust Act in 1890, federal authorities took a major step in regulating business. The law prohibited large trusts of businesses. The law initially had little effect, as the Supreme Court prevented its usage by regulators. But by the turn of the century, the government won out. In 1904, it was allowed to break up Northern Securities Company, and in 1911 the Supreme Court sided with the federal government in its breakup of Standard Oil Company and American Tobacco Company.

Small businesses wanted protection against larger competitors squeezing them out of business by lowering prices. Consumers wanted protection from monopolistic operations raising prices. Not surprisingly, large business opposed this legislation.

Since then, more legislation has been passed at the federal level giving the government more powers. In 1914, Congress created the FTC when it passed the Clayton Antitrust Act, which amended the Sherman legislation by outlawing predatory pricing and making illegal other business tactics.

Other regulators also sprung up. Although the FDA traces its roots back to a single chemist in the Department of Agriculture in 1862, the Federal Foods and Drug Act in 1906 gave it regulatory authority. This act was spurred by Upton Sinclair's *The Jungle*, an account of workers in an unsanitary meat-packing plant.

Franklin D. Roosevelt's presidency saw another flurry of legislation creating laws governing business. Sparked by the October 1929 crash that led to the Great Depression, Congress created the SEC to oversee the stock markets and public companies. The Communications Act of 1934 established the FCC to regulate the radio and television industries. And Congress created the FDIC at the same time to stabilize the country's banking industry.

Federal Communications Commission (FCC): A federal regulatory agency charged with overseeing interstate and international communications by radio, television, wire, satellite and cable.

The Wagner Act of 1935 created the NLRB, which prevented companies from interfering with the rights of workers to organize into unions and to investigate complaints of unfair labor practices. The law also allowed the board to issue cease and desist orders against companies.

TIPS FROM THE PROS

Politico news editor Karey Van Hall on finding business stories at government agencies:

Get your hands on the hot documents. The four most important words to a Washington business reporter are Freedom of Information Act (FOIA). The law allows for the media—and everyday Americans—to get access to complete or partial disclosure of non-public information that is controlled by the federal government. But in practice, FOIA requests turn into a cat-and-mouse game, with overwhelmed agencies relying heavily on opaque exemptions or generally dragging their feet in fulfilling the requests. It's important to know the exemptions—such as privileged communication between federal agencies, and information that could compromise ongoing enforcement proceedings—so as not to draft requests that will be immediately rejected. It also can be helpful to tailor a request, to increase the chances of getting a speedy response. And don't be deterred by an initial rejection. Agencies often claim a blanket exemption, but it's standard practice to file an appeal, and—if the resources are available—to challenge a denial in court. The targets of FOIA requests are almost endless and range from officials' calendars, to communication between agencies on a hot subject, to internal deliberations on a past enforcement action.

Other regulatory bodies have been added throughout the decades. The Department of Transportation was not created until the 1960s, although some of its units have longer histories. The Occupational Safety and Health Act passed in 1970, giving the federal government the authority to set and enforce workplace safety and health standards.

The 1970s, however, saw the beginning of a period of deregulation by the federal government. In 1978, Congress passed the Airline Deregulation Act, which meant that the market would set prices for airline tickets, not the government. Opposed by the industry, the legislation led to a number of new airlines, and a number of airline company failures.

Federal regulation, however, is still alive and well. In 1984, the antitrust laws were successfully used to force the breakup of AT&T just as they had been used 70 years earlier in Standard Oil and American Tobacco. And the FTC took on reviewing all mergers and acquisitions in the late 1970s.

Federal Trade Commission (FTC): A federal agency that works to ensure that the nation's markets are vigorous, efficient and free of restrictions that harm consumers. The FTC enforces federal consumer protection laws that prevent fraud, deception and unfair business practices. The commission also enforces federal antitrust laws that prohibit anticompetitive mergers and other business practices that restrict competition and harm consumers.

State and local government agencies have also had a hand in regulating business for more than a century. States, for example, began regulating utilities near the beginning of the twentieth century. The Oregon Public Utility Commission began as the State Board of Railroad Commissioners in 1887 but was abolished and then recreated as the Railroad Commission of Oregon in 1907. Four years later, its jurisdiction was expanded to include utilities.

Public service commissions and public utility commissions across the country oversee how much electrical companies, water companies and other utilities charge their customers. They also often set limits on how much of a profit these companies can make. Sometimes, these companies can get in trouble with the regulatory agencies that oversee their business. A few years ago a North Carolina utility was found to have made too much money, causing the *Charlotte Observer* to write one front-page story that began the following way:

Federal investigators will review thousands of additional documents in a deeper probe of Duke Power's accounting than the one Carolinas regulators conducted last year, sources close to the investigation say.

Federal prosecutors and FBI agents will scour more than 40,000 documents, including a controversial spreadsheet unearthed during the states' investigation, as they evaluate whether Duke intentionally and inappropriately altered its accounting and committed any crimes, according to sources.

After a 10-month investigation last year, independent auditing firm Grant Thornton LLP said Duke underreported $124 million in regulated profits over three years. Duke changed its accounting methods to fall under the profit margin mandated by regulators, the firm said.

When Duke goes over its allowed limit, utility commissioners can lower the power bills for Duke's 2.1 million Carolinas customers.

Duke says it made unintentional, one-time errors but committed no crime. Duke Power, the Carolinas' largest utility, is a subsidiary of Charlotte-based Duke Energy Corp., which is No. 118 on the Fortune 500 with $15.2 billion in revenue last year.

Federal investigators began their probe after *The Observer* published stories in October about Grant Thornton's allegations of Duke wrongdoing. In February, Duke announced it had received a grand jury subpoena requesting documents related to the Grant Thornton audit.

Days before receiving the subpoena, Duke hired former U.S. Attorney Mark Galloway to represent the corporation. The company also helped assemble A-list criminal defense lawyers for more than a dozen employees. Companies and their employees typically hire lawyers when they learn they're under investigation.[1]

The story later quotes the executive director of the South Carolina Public Service Commission saying that documents he reviewed convinced him there was an obvious effort to underreport profits.

States also play a major role in regulating other industries, such as banking and insurance. Unlike most industries that are regulated by the federal government, regulation of the insurance industry is done on a state-by-state basis. Each state has an insurance commissioner who regulates the insurers doing business in that state. Some states, such as New York, have laws governing

TIPS FROM THE PROS

Politico news editor Karey Van Hall on finding business stories at government agencies:

Know who is getting access. The White House is at the top of the food chain for business interests looking to exert influence in Washington. In a bid for transparency, the White House publicly posts its visitor logs to the main building, as well as to the New and Old Executive Office Buildings, where many of the business meetings occur. Mining these logs is a good way to figure out which industries and their executives and lobbyists have the ear of the president and his or her aides. While the main database—found at https://www.whitehouse.gov/briefing-room/disclosures/visitor-records—can be hard to navigate, other organizations have cleaned up the information and made it much more searchable.

insurance companies that are more strict than other states, forcing some insurers to create separate subsidiaries to do business there or to eschew the state altogether. States also require each and every business that operates in its territory to register with the state. This information can be valuable, and it is discussed later in this chapter.

Last, some counties, cities and towns also have laws and rules that businesses must follow. Developers, for example, must get plans to build a new subdivision approved by a town council or a city commission before they can start bulldozing. Expanding a building to handle the growth of a business also requires a permit.

All of the rules, laws, regulations and other policies that government agencies require of businesses attempt to balance the interest of the public with the need of a business to grow, expand and continue to be a thriving part of the community. Sometimes, a government entity will even try to get legislation passed that will bring new business into the area or improve the quality of existing businesses.

The following excerpt is an example of the beginning of a business story that comes from following bills introduced in a state legislature to change how businesses would operate:

> North Carolina businesses that improve workplace safety could be rewarded with a tax break if Labor Commissioner Cherie Berry has her way.
>
> Berry is pushing for bills that have been introduced in the House and Senate that would give tax credits to companies that voluntarily improve safety in factories, offices, stores and construction sites where several million North Carolinians spend their working hours. The idea, Berry said Tuesday, is to reach smaller employers that don't have a safety director on board or fear that by asking the labor department for help they might be forced to make improvements they can't afford.
>
> "We're trying in this business climate to do as much as we can to promote safety and health and reward businesses that take that step," she said. "It shows that we're trying to reach out, rather than, as in the past, just go out and enforce with that big hammer and club."
>
> Voluntary compliance has been a mission of Berry's since she took office two years ago. One of her first moves was to roll back ergonomics rules that her predecessor, Harry Payne, had sought to make businesses pay closer attention to repetitive stress injuries. Her agency has worked with employers to help them reduce such injuries, reporting strong results in certain cases.
>
> But some question the fairness of the tax credit bills, as well as the timing of such legislation during a budget crisis.
>
> "You don't want to create a system where companies that have already invested in safety get nothing," said John Hood, president of the John Locke Foundation, a conservative think tank in Raleigh. "And now that they're coming in after the law is passed, they get money. The impulse here is commendable, but I would be hesitant to go into the tax code to find a tool to pursue policies other than raising revenue."[2]

public utilities commission: A state agency that regulates water, electrical and telephone companies. In some states, the agency may be called the Public Service Commission.

In addition, many states have recently become aggressive in prosecuting companies for wrongdoing, with former New York Attorney General Eliot Spitzer being a prime example of a regulator filing charges for alleged crimes by business. Following how government regulates business can lead to exciting business stories. Government and business often clash, and that conflict results in good copy.

The rest of this chapter explores how government regulation is an important part of writing stories that explain the ins and outs of business and the economy.

Private Company Regulation

Following the government trail of regulation is important to a reporter who writes stories for the business section, particularly for a writer who spends most of his or her time covering private companies.

TIPS FROM THE PROS

Politico news editor Karey Van Hall on finding business stories at government agencies:

Scour financial filings. Publicly traded companies, broker-dealers and certain private companies must file information about their businesses with the Securities and Exchange Commission. The SEC's EDGAR database provides a trove of information about companies' financials, executive pay, investors, ongoing litigation, and business strategies. Public companies' quarterly 10-Q filings and annual 10-K filing are some of the most rich documents, providing a snapshot of the business's health and future direction. The annual proxy statement, known as a DEF 14A, is another must-read document. While the filing serves as an invitation to shareholders to attend the company's annual shareholder meeting, it also provides business reporters with information on how the company is paying its executives and board members, whether the company has management succession plans, the strength of its auditor oversight, and what proposals investors want the company to consider. Reporters should also pay attention to spot filings known as 8-Ks that provide breaking news about major developments at the company.

Most private companies do not have to report on their financial performance and other major moves to the SEC like public companies do. But knowing and understanding what private companies disclose to government regulators can help a reporter uncover the news at private businesses. Even though it may seem that private companies are reticent in providing information, the truth is that there is plenty of information available if you know where to look.

All companies, public and private, are required to register certain information with their secretary of state's office. Reporters researching any company for an article should look up the company's incorporation records with the state, which will provide the mailing address, phone number and names of officers. This can be important information, for example, if a reporter is writing about a company that has been sued but has been unable to contact anyone at the business for comment. Incorporation records are also required of nonprofit organizations and limited liability corporations such as law firms.

articles of incorporation: A set of documents filed with state authorities for the purpose of documenting the creation of a corporation.

There are plenty of other public records available on private companies at the state level. In every state there are occupational licensing boards that require many businesses, from barbershops to hearing aid providers, to obtain a license before opening shop. These boards may have additional records on the company a reporter may be writing about.

Private companies must also register their business name if that name is not the same name as the corporation. In many places, this is done with the register of deeds office, or a similar courthouse office, at the county level. This is a good place to find out who is the actual owner of a company.

Real estate records are another good place to look for information about private companies. Reporters should check these transactions to see if a company owns any land or buildings. It is also good to check these records under the name of the company president or CEO. This can be done at the county courthouse, or the county in which the business is buying or selling property.

Private companies are also required to disclose information about layoffs and working conditions. These records can be obtained through your local Department of Labor or OSHA office. For example, mass layoffs and firings of workers are typically disclosed to labor regulators, and OSHA conducts inspections on factories and plants, particularly after an accident or death. Obtaining those records can be as easy as one phone call.

State regulators of specific industries also require many companies to file information about their financial performance. Some of these regulatory agencies include those that oversee banks and insurance companies, as well as water and electrical utilities. Private companies document their profits and revenues to these regulatory agencies. Reporters who find out where these records are kept will likely get information that the company otherwise would not be willing to disclose.

Private companies come under the jurisdiction of federal regulators at numerous levels, Even the smallest companies, such as nonprofit institutions and credit unions, are required to file financial information about their operations. For more information about nonprofits, see Chapter 11.

TIPS FROM THE PROS

Politico news editor Karey Van Hall on finding business stories at government agencies:

Spot the enforcement trends. Washington has many eyes and ears on corporate America, from the Justice Department to the Federal Trade Commission to the Securities and Exchange Commission, just to name a few of the agencies with enforcement powers. Washington's investigatory prowess expanded with the creation of the Consumer Financial Protection Bureau in 2011. With limited budgets, the agencies must prioritize their probes. Companies often disclose when they've received a request for information or a subpoena from an enforcement agency. An enterprising reporter can piece together whether these requests amount to a bigger crackdown on an accounting method, hiring practice, or product offering.

All credit unions across the country are governed by the National Credit Union Administration. Credit unions are required to file information to this federal agency on a quarterly basis. The information includes total assets, total loans, total equity and a breakdown of the loan income.

The business reporter for the *Goldsboro News-Argus* in eastern North Carolina regularly reviews this information for the credit union in his town, North Carolina Community Credit Union. By receiving this information, he discovered that the credit union had reported net income of $124,586 in the third quarter of a year, but lost $242,469 in the last three months of that year, a dramatic drop.

Privately owned banks and thrifts are also required to provide financial information to federal regulators such as the FDIC, the Office of Thrift Supervision, and the Office of the Comptroller of the Currency.

The federal government has other agencies that come in contact regularly with businesses. The EPA, for example, has information on companies that handle environmentally sensitive chemicals and products. The FDA has information on food products and drugs sold by thousands of companies. The U.S. Patent and Trademark Office maintains filings of patents and trademarks that a company uses to make its products. Reporters should check these filings regularly to see if businesses they write about have received new patents or trademarks that may help their operations.

Sometimes, private companies run into trouble with these government agencies. In addition to checking for simple financial information and background information about private businesses, a reporter should look for fines and regulatory actions. Unlike public companies regulated by the SEC, private companies do not have to disclose to the government if they want to branch into different business lines—unless, of course, the new business line requires approval of a new product, such as a drug. But "private" companies are not as private as they may seem. With the right research, a reporter can make the operations of a private company as transparent as that of a public business simply by looking at the government agencies that oversee it and following a paper trail. (For more information about private companies, see Chapter 10.)

Insurance and Banking Regulators

Sectors of the financial services industry can be daunting beats for any reporter. Banks and insurance companies touch the lives of virtually every user of mass communication. Most people have checking and savings accounts and automated teller machine cards, everyone has auto insurance, and many people have life insurance policies. Yet banks and insurance companies can be some of the hardest to understand. How do they make money? What do they do with the money that consumers pay them?

TIPS FROM THE PROS

Politico news editor Karey Van Hall on finding business stories at government agencies:

Closely watch the dealmakers. Lobbying is a booming industry in Washington and is the most obvious intersection between the business world and the nation's capital. The Lobbyist Disclosure Act requires lobbyists who meet certain tests—including whether an individual spends more than 20 percent of his or her time lobbying for a single client—to register with the Clerk of the U.S. House of Representatives and the Secretary of the U.S. Senate. The related databases provide helpful information about who companies have hired to wield influence in Washington and how much they are paying their lobbyists. The Center for Responsive Politics' OpenSecrets.org database is a handy and widely used tool for reporters to easily search for lobbyists and campaign contributions. It's particularly interesting to see how much lobbying levels go up and down, depending upon whether a company is seeking regulatory approval for a merger, pursuing a big government contract, or pushing a specific piece of legislation. It's also important to remember, however, that there are myriad trade groups and company surrogates who do not technically meet the definition of a lobbyist but nonetheless hold outsize sway in making sure a company's interests are served by legislation and regulatory decisions.

Unlike most industries, the insurance business is regulated by state insurance commissioners who often, but not always, agree on regulation. In addition, each state has passed laws to govern insurance companies, and these laws are not the same across the country. So the laws that a national insurance company must adhere to in California might not be the same as the laws in Florida.

Insurance commissioners are politicians. Many of them are elected officials who must win a majority of the votes in their state to hold the position. As such, the people holding these positions may not have had much background in the insurance industry. Some of them may view the office as a stepping stone to something greater, such as governor or senator.

Insurance commissioners oversee a multibillion-dollar industry in many states. Insurance companies sell coverage for everything from cars and homes to variable annuities used to invest in the stock market. When an insurance company wants to raise the rate it is charging for coverage in a state, it files a request with the insurance commissioner's office.

These rate requests are public records and could be major stories, particularly if the company holds a large market share in the state. If State Farm or Allstate, the two largest auto and home insurers in the country, want to raise rates in a state, that will affect tens of thousands of readers or viewers.

The following story illustrates how a rate request was written by a business reporter in Florida, one of the country's largest insurance markets:

> Many of the state's Allstate policyholders will see their insurance premiums soar this year.
>
> Florida's second-largest insurer has two statewide rate requests pending with the Office of Insurance Regulation—an average hike of 44.2 percent for individual condo policies and an average increase of 10.3 percent for nonstandard auto insurance policies.
>
> While rates usually tend to be higher in South Florida, Allstate declined to say what the average increases would be in Broward, Miami-Dade and Palm Beach counties.
>
> The company cited rising claims costs as the reason for the requests and expects a decision from the state Office of Insurance Regulation any day now. The company paid out about $1.10 for every $1 it collected in premiums last year, said Kathy Thomas, Allstate spokeswoman.
>
> "Our claims frequency and severity is outpacing the premiums we collected," she said, adding that the insurer has suffered from a rise in water claims, medical costs, repair expenses and auto insurance fraud.
>
> Allstate Floridian Insurance Co., which raised rates 15.7 percent for condos last year, requested another increase earlier this month. The insurer has 203,866 individual condo policies in Florida—60 percent are in Broward, Miami-Dade and Palm Beach counties. An approved hike would go into effect July 30 for new policies and August 24 for renewals, according to documents filed with state regulators.

Allstate Indemnity Co. requested new auto rates in March and hopes to implement approved auto rates May 19 for new policies and June 23 for renewals.

The insurer has 285,523 nonstandard policyholders in Florida, 36 percent of whom are in South Florida. Nonstandard insurance policies have higher rates and are issued to those who don't qualify for standard policies because of poor driving histories, credit problems and high-valued cars, among other risk factors. Allstate's nonstandard auto policyholders saw their rates jump an average 16.5 percent when policies came up for renewal last November.[3]

This story does an excellent job of explaining to the *Sun-Sentinel* readers why Allstate feels the need to raise rates—it paid $1.10 in claims for every $1 it collected in premiums. The story also lets readers know that more than 200,000 south Florida residents could be impacted by the request.

TIPS FROM THE PROS

Politico news editor Karey Van Hall on finding business stories at government agencies:

Know who's writing the legislation. A not-so-well-kept secret is how often businesses have a direct hand in crafting the laws that dictate how their industries operate. In some instances, lawmakers' staff will insert proposed legislative language word-for-word into bills. It's important for business reporters to keep an eye on when lawmakers' reliance on businesses' expertise crosses over into overt influence peddling. One example was how much impact Wall Street banks had over post-financial crisis legislation that attempted to rein in investment banks' excess. As legislation is being crafted, reporters should dig up which companies are hosting fundraisers for lawmakers working on bills, what campaign contributions are being made, and which lobbyists are holding meetings with lawmakers and their staffs.

These rate requests can be checked regularly with any state insurance department. With hundreds of insurance companies operating in most states, it is likely that one of them is filing for a rate hike in one of its insurance lines on almost a weekly basis. In some cases, the entire industry files a rate request. This can happen for workers' compensation coverage or auto insurance policies, for example. The industry has a lobbying group that files requests with the commissioner's office, which then typically gets reviewed by actuaries and other experts. Sometimes, there are public hearings at which company executives and the general public are invited to speak for and against the proposal. The commissioner typically presides over such cases and issues a ruling on the rate request days or weeks after the hearing occurred.

Insurance commissioners are also charged with ensuring that insurers have enough money set aside to pay for claims. This money is often called surplus, and regulators have laws requiring a certain level of surplus to be in an insurance company's bank account. If a company falls below that level, then the insurance commissioner may go to court and ask a judge to allow regulators to take over that company to improve its financial position. This can be called regulatory oversight, or regulatory control.

Insurance companies take the premiums paid to them by consumers and businesses and invest that money. Many of them do not charge enough in premiums to cover their expenses, so they are hoping that their investment income will allow them to report a profit. But if a major storm or natural disaster hits, they could be hit with more claims than they anticipated. Insurers of autos, homes and businesses paid billions in claims after Hurricane Katrina hit Florida and Louisiana in 2005, and life insurers did the same after the September 11, 2001, terrorist attacks killed nearly 3,000 at the World Trade Center and the Pentagon.

Insurance commissioners also work with the industry. Insurance commissioners want companies to offer coverage to as many consumers and businesses as possible. If companies begin to drop policies or decide to withdraw from a state because an insurance commissioner will not allow them to raise rates, then the commissioner may have a problem during the next election. Consumers and businesses want a variety of choices and competition in the insurance market.

The banking industry is regulated in a similar fashion. In fact, states such as Florida regulate banks and insurers with the same elected official. Although banks are not filing requests to raise or lower the rates they charge consumers, they do file information with state and federal regulators that can give an insight into their performance.

Some of the most valuable information available about banks is market share and branch data. A reporter can determine how much money is held in each branch of a bank with thousands of locations, such as Bank of America, from FDIC records. For a reporter in a small or medium-sized town, following this branch data can show who is winning the banking battle in the community. If one branch is gaining market share in the town, while a branch of another bank is losing market share, then there is a story behind those numbers. A reporter should call the banks to find out what strategy the winning bank has been employing, and what new tactics the losing bank is planning to regain deposits.

Surprisingly, few mass communication outlets track bank branch data, although this information helps localize the success or failure of major interstate banks in hundreds of communities across the country. The following excerpt shows how an online news organization that follows the banking industry assessed recent market share changes and branch data in California and New York:

> The United States is more than just New York and California, as most folks who live outside of those areas will be quick to point out. So please forgive

TIPS FROM THE PROS

Politico news editor Karey Van Hall on finding business stories at government agencies:

Catching conflicts of interest. When the president nominates someone to an official position, that individual generally must file a public financial disclosure report and an ethics agreement with the federal government that reveal potential conflicts of interest. These documents—available on the U.S. Office of Government Ethics website—not only show direct conflicts that will force the official to recuse himself or herself from certain business. They also show factors that may influence how that official approaches the new job. If the official has financial enforcement responsibilities, for example, it's helpful to know which banks the official either prosecuted or defended in the past. The official's choice of investments can also inform the mindset with which he or she will approach the new job. Has that person played it safe with mutual funds, or did they aggressively amass hot tech stocks and real estate investments? There are many gray areas when it comes to conflicts of interest, so it's important for reporters to know officials' work and financial histories.

us for being a bit exclusionary in choosing those markets for a quick look at deposit market share trends revealed in the latest available deposit data.

The largest banks and thrifts operating in California had little trouble growing deposits between mid-2000 and mid-2001, based on SNL Securities' analysis of the latest branch deposit data from the Federal Deposit Insurance Corp.

According to the newly updated SNL Branch Marketshare DataSource, each of the eight banks and thrifts with the largest deposit market share in California saw their deposits in the state increase in the 12 months preceding June 30, 2001.

By far the largest increase among this elite eight—which held an aggregate of $324.5 billion in deposits at June 30, or roughly two-thirds of all California deposits—came at Comerica Inc. The Detroit-based bank completed its acquisition of Los Angeles-based Imperial Bancorp on Jan. 30, 2001, and now ranks No. 7 statewide in deposits held. The pick-up of Imperial didn't account for the entire boost, however; the company reported an additional $2 billion in deposits above what it and Imperial reported at June 30, 2000. That represents a 19.6 percent year-over-year increase.

Across Comerica's entire franchise, which stretches from Los Angeles to the Midwest, total deposits increased to $37 billion from $32 billion, the bank said in its second-quarter earnings release issued on July 17. Much of that gain was the Imperial acquisition.

Wells Fargo & Co. added $10.6 billion in deposits, pushing its California market share to 13.9 percent from 12.8 percent a year earlier. The increase widened Wells Fargo's statewide position at No. 2, ahead of No. 3 Washington Mutual Inc. WaMu lost deposits in California a year ago, but it posted a 6.61 percent gain this year to register a 12.2 percent share of deposits.

Adjustable-rate-mortgage lender Downey Financial Corp. raked in new deposits during the last two years, posting a 23.0 percent gain at June 30 to follow the 33.2 percent gain seen in the FDICs prior update. Downey's California deposits increased from $5.5 billion in mid-1999 to $8.9 billion at mid-2001.[4]

Although this story was written about state market share and how that has changed among the top banks in California and New York, a similar story can easily be written for any town or city in the country with competing banks just by reviewing the same data. It may take some addition and subtraction, and following the numbers for a while, but the story will likely be well read and show readers or viewers what is happening in an important industry used by all consumers.

Bank and thrift regulators, like their insurance brethren, are also charged with making sure that banks have enough money set aside to pay off loans and their depositors. Regulators set certain requirements on capital adequacy levels. If a bank falls below these levels, it could be taken over.

Two barometers a reporter should follow in a bank's filings with regulators are its loan losses and loan loss reserves. When a bank starts setting aside large amounts of money to cover loans that have become past due, that could be an indication that the bank's past lending practices were not sound.

Like insurance companies, banks also invest deposits and other money paid to them by consumers. The investment portfolio can be an indication that a bank is engaging in risky business practices. If it is investing in high-risk investments such as real estate ventures in shaky foreign economies or volatile currencies, that can be a sign that the bank is trying to make up for other bad investments. A reporter should always review an investment portfolio to see where a bank—or an insurance company—is putting its money.

State regulators of insurance and banking companies are also involved in approving mergers and acquisitions between businesses. If a merger or acquisition is announced, there might be a hearing by the state regulatory agency that should be attended, or the regulators might ask for public comment.

With a little digging and some knowledge of the documents that must be filed with regulators, a reporter can piece together enough information about a private bank or insurance company that might otherwise go uncovered. These stories can often tell more about a local economy than anything else.

Health Care Regulation

Another industry primarily regulated by state agencies is the health care business. Hospitals, doctors and managed care companies are part of a fast-growing industry that is a vital part of many economies. In many towns and cities, the local hospital is the largest employer. That should be a good reason as to why stories should be written about them.

TIPS FROM THE PROS

Politico news editor Karey Van Hall on finding business stories at government agencies:

Watch the revolving door spin. Officials' tour of duty in the government is often just a stepping stone to a more cushy private sector job with a lobbying firm, trade association, or law firm. Businesses rely heavily on former officials who intimately know how regulatory and legislative decisions get made, and who have the contacts to help make a company's case. President Barack Obama pledged to close the revolving door in Washington, but that proved to be easier said than done. In just one example, a top official responsible for implementing Obamacare then became the health insurance industry's top lobbyist. The still-spinning revolving door provides plenty of business story opportunities, and not only when the jump from government to private sector happens. Officials generally have a cooling-off period, so it's important to keep watch on how closely they're abiding by those restrictions and how they ramp up their activities once that period lifts.

Hospitals, doctors and managed care companies have a symbiotic relationship. Doctors and hospitals rely on managed care companies to bring them large amounts of patients. Conversely, managed care companies rely on doctors and hospitals to treat patients as cost efficiently as possible. Sometimes, these relationships can become strained, as each is out to maintain a level of profitability that is dependent on others.

One of the ways to find stories about hospitals, particularly private or nonprofit hospitals, is through state regulatory filings. Many hospitals are required to file financial information with state regulators, and the rates that some hospitals charge for operations and other services must be approved by a state agency. (In Massachusetts, the state hospital industry was deregulated in the 1980s. As a result a number of hospitals closed.)

Reporters should check to see what agency oversees hospitals in their state, then call or visit that agency to find out what information is available about local hospitals. A reporter may find out that the local hospital is losing money and needs to raise its rates to survive or that the so-called nonprofit hospital has had profits of millions of dollars in recent years.

In many states, hospitals must also receive permission from state regulators before they are allowed to expand and offer new services. In Michigan, for example, a government body called the Certificate of Need Commission approves filings by hospitals across the state asking to build new additions that add beds or services such as cardiac units. The idea behind such regulations is to prevent a glut of hospital services in a certain community. In Florida, the certificate of need process covers new hospital beds as well as the beginning of open heart surgery, organ transplantation, neonatal intensive care, burn services, inpatient psychiatric or substance abuse services, inpatient comprehensive medical rehabilitation, hospice freestanding inpatient beds and skilled nursing.

The certificate of need process in many states also allows consumers, competitors and others to argue against an expansion plan by a competitor, as the following story from the *Cleveland Plain Dealer* shows:

> Without taking a vote, the Parma Planning Commission bounced a controversial proposed 260-bed senior citizen complex back to City Council last night.
>
> After a nearly three-hour hearing attended by 70 persons, the commission said it stands behind its March 9 endorsement of the project proposed by Parma Community General Hospital and Generations Health care, a company formed by members of the Coury family, longtime nursing home operators.
>
> On July 10, residents won at least a temporary victory as council sent the thrice-revised project back to the Planning Commission.
>
> Council did so under the threat of an injunction made by the residents' lawyer, Rodger Pelagalli, who had argued that city laws required any project that has been radically changed since its adoption by the Planning Commission be reviewed again by the panel.
>
> "Residents feel the Planning Commission was just washing its hands of the deal," said Councilman John Stover who said he and others felt the panel should have voted on an array of plan changes since March.
>
> The complex, proposed for vacant land ringing the old Fay Junior High School, would offer a wide range of care, including an Alzheimer's unit.
>
> The old building has been converted to a health education center that would give the proposed senior complex an added dimension, developers have argued. They said they have reviewed alternate sites but ruled them out because of cost.
>
> That drew fire from Ward 5 Councilwoman Michelle Stys, who said: "I'm not concerned about their purse strings. I am concerned about the existing neighbors."
>
> Residents have vowed to continue the fight next month by asking the Ohio Department of Health to not award a certificate of need for the project.
>
> Other opponents, composed mainly of abutting property owners, said the proposal lacks access for emergency vehicles, threatens to overload storm and sanitary sewers, and could erode property values.[5]

Conflict occurs often in the business world, and the conflict a reporter finds in state documents may not always be between business and regulators. Often, another business is also involved, as the preceding story illustrates.

As in the case with insurance company rate requests and bank branch data, few media outlets actively watch certificate of need filings. But in many cases, these documents can be major news, indicating that a health care facility plans to spend millions of dollars. Where is that money coming from? And is that money being spent wisely? Too often, those questions are not answered.

State medical boards can also be a source of business stories. These organizations regulate doctors and surgeons in an area. They can revoke or suspend the license of a doctor if he or she performed an unnecessary surgery or prescribed the wrong medication for an illness. These are public records and can be important information about a business in a town. These boards can also oversee other medical workers, such as nurses and nursing home administrators.

One of the biggest players in the health care business can be the managed care operators. In many instances, these are businesses operated by insurance companies, and often they also come under the regulation of the state insurance department.

Managed care companies generally offer two types of plans to consumers: a health maintenance organization (HMO) and a preferred provider organization (PPO). An HMO provides and arranges for coverage with doctors and hospitals for its plan members for a set rate. The HMO must agree on a set of basic and supplemental health maintenance and treatment services. A PPO establishes contracts with doctors and hospitals, and with those contracts the managed care company provides lower co-payments if its subscribers use one of those preferred providers. Managed care companies charge premiums, just like insurance companies. And the for-profit managed care companies expect to make a profit on the basis of the premiums they have collected. Nonprofit managed care companies often also make a profit on their operations. The financial results of managed care companies can usually be found by asking state regulators, probably with the insurance department.

The following is a story that assessed the financial performance of managed care companies operating in Kansas City:

> Amid rising premiums, the principal managed care companies doing business in Kansas City on the whole enjoyed a spectacular financial turnaround last year.
>
> Eight managed care companies that operate here earned an aggregate net income of $71.9 million last year, compared with an aggregate net loss of $12.7 million in 2001.
>
> The good fortune was not shared by all. Four of the eight big companies were profitable, but the four others reported losses for 2002.
>
> The numbers include results outside the Kansas City area for national managed care companies operating here.

"The HMO industry since 1998 has been focusing on profitability," said Randy McConnell, a spokesman for the Missouri Department of Insurance. "2002 turned out to be a breakthrough year for them on that score."

McConnell said the financial turnaround was largely brought about by HMOs being more selective in choosing the groups they cover, along with "substantial premium increases."

Other numbers pointed to a similar trend. HMOs operating in Missouri earned a record consolidated net income of $167.7 million last year, compared with a $598,287 consolidated net loss in 2001, according to the Missouri Department of Insurance. The numbers include national operating results of some managed care companies.

HMOs operating in Kansas earned a consolidated net income of $93.8 million last year, compared with a $25.9 million consolidated net loss in 2001, based on numbers reported by the Kansas Insurance Department. Those numbers also include the national operating results of some companies.

Beneficiaries of the turnaround included Blue Cross and Blue Shield of Kansas City. Blue Cross earned $31.1 million in net income last year, compared with a 2001 net loss of $6.3 million. The numbers include results from Blue Cross HMOs and PPO networks.[6]

Many of the companies mentioned in this story are private companies, or subsidiaries of public companies that do not break out the financial performance of subsidiaries in their SEC filings. That shows why getting these records from state regulators can provide a better indication of how a local operation is performing in many instances.

The Blue Cross Blue Shield system across the country is one of the dominant managed care players, as are national operators such as CIGNA and Aetna. With Blue Cross Blue Shield plans, each company operates separately, although the plans have been undergoing a consolidation move. When such deals are announced, regulators are typically involved, especially if a for-profit Blue operator wants to acquire a not-for-profit Blue plan. In 2003, Maryland regulators turned down the request by WellPoint, the for-profit Blue company operating in California, Missouri and Georgia, to acquire the nonprofit Blue operator in that state.

Managed care companies watch medical inflation carefully. If the cost of medical goods and services rises too fast, they are unable to keep pace by raising premiums. Many may ask for rate increases from regulators if medical costs start rising.

Water and Power Utilities

All businesses and homeowners pay electricity, water and telephone bills. Some of them also pay a gas bill. What is surprising to many of them is that the rates are regulated by state utility commissions. These regulatory agencies are charged with protecting the consumer by making sure these companies are charging fair rates for their services. In addition, public service commissions also work with the companies to try to make utilities more efficient, thereby lowering the potential for rate increases in the future.

TIPS FROM THE PROS

Politico news editor Karey Van Hall on finding business stories at government agencies:

Track who's getting Uncle Sam's dollars. The federal government doles out almost half a trillion dollars each year in contracts. That can be a windfall, and not just for the defense contractors whose whole business model is shaped around these awards. It can be illuminating to track which companies are racking up certain types of contracts, often because they have mastered the ins and outs of the procurement system and have a heavy lobbying presence in Washington. Federal agencies' inspector general reports are often a good source of information about which contractors are delivering either subpar or dismal services. It's also good to figure out exactly where the flow of money is going. While agencies hail the amount of contract money going to small businesses, often there's a big corporation that is also benefiting.

In addition, there is a federal agency that also regulates some utilities. The Federal Energy Regulatory Commission (FERC) regulates the price, terms and conditions of power sold across state lines and is the federal counterpart to state utility regulatory commissions.

Like their insurance brethren, state public service commissioners must approve any request to raise rates. These rate requests are sometimes accompanied by documents justifying why the electrical company, for example, needs to raise rates. And there is often a hearing to take testimony from the company and consumers before the commission makes its decision.

The filing of these requests, as well as their approval, should be stories, particularly those about rate hikes that affect a large number of consumers. One of these rate requests was covered by a brief item in the *Milwaukee Business Journal,* which noted that Wisconsin Power & Light filed a rate increase with the Public Service Commission of Wisconsin totaling $113.1 million. If the rate increase was passed, the average customer would see a $7.58 increase in their electric bill and a $10.91 hike in their gas bill. Note how this story told the reader how much his or her average monthly bill would increase if the rate request passed. This is information that is vital to any story about a rate request because it tells the consumer how much he or she will be affected.

At many rate hearings, the people are represented by a consumer advocate. Often, the consumer advocate is in a government position with the sole job of protecting the interest of citizens. These consumer advocate offices may often conduct studies on why a utility needs a rate hike. These studies can be important to read and even write stories about. They are public documents that often paint a different picture than the company's rate filing.

Public utility commissions also hold hearings on other matters. They may feel as if the utility has not treated its customers fairly or acted in the public's best interests. When an ice storm hit North Carolina, thousands of residents went without power for as long as a week. Many of them complained that the power companies in the state should have been better prepared to handle the damage and repairs needed to get power restored. Besieged with complaints, the state utilities commission conducted a hearing into the matter while many residents still had branches and trees throughout their lawns.

The following story shows how one newspaper covered the proceeding:

> Duke Power customers, given the opportunity to confront the utility giant at a state Utilities Commission hearing Thursday, lashed out at the company for poor planning, material shortages and unreliable communications after the Dec. 4 ice storm.
>
> Among the 33 people who signed up to speak before the six-member panel was Joe Capowski, a former Chapel Hill Town Council member and an electrical engineer who criticized Duke Power for not doing more to rebuild Chapel Hill's power distribution system after Hurricane Fran in September 1996.
>
> "Duke Power was not born on December 4, 2002," he said before an audience of more than 150 people in Durham's City Hall. "Their efforts, while indeed heroic, were made so by their own management's lack of foresight and learning."
>
> The ice storm brought the state's fourth largest city to "an abrupt and frigid halt," recalled Durham Mayor Bill Bell, who suggested that the commission analyze work reports of Duke Power personnel to see where they were assigned immediately after the storm. Bell has accused the company of not concentrating enough resources in Durham—where 93 percent, or 107,000 of the company's customers, were without power at the peak.
>
> In the storm's aftermath, the information Duke Power supplied "was often too general to give any value to emergency management operations," Bell said.
>
> E.O. Ferrell, a Duke Power senior vice president, said that although the company's "communication with the elected officials and with the emergency centers did not function the way we would have liked," the utility's efforts were hampered by the magnitude of the damage in the western Triangle.
>
> The hearing, requested by Durham officials, was the first in a series of public meetings the commission has scheduled around the state to evaluate Duke Power's and Progress Energy's emergency preparedness in response to hundreds of complaints about utilities' performance after the ice storm. Earlier this week, Duke Power joined CP&L officials at a hearing before state regulators in Raleigh where both companies defended their emergency protocol.

Complaints have poured in from the western Triangle, where 147,000 customers were affected and power-restoration efforts were the slowest in the Carolinas.

One week after the storm, 20,000 remained without power in Durham and 8,100 in Chapel Hill.[7]

No company likes to be in the public spotlight. They dread it when they are dragged before a state regulatory board and asked to answer consumer complaints. A reporter should be there to document it all.

Although most of the reporting on utility commissions focuses on electrical companies, the commissions also regulate water utilities and phone companies in most states, making decisions on rate requests and disputes in those industries. Like other state regulatory filings, utility commission documents are often a gold mine for stories and are frequently unreported because journalists think they contain boring information.

But tracking the dealings of utilities that affect thousands of consumers can be one of the best services a mass communication outlet can provide to its readers or viewers. It can be argued that no other business beat affects as many consumers as the public utilities beat.

Reporters should not forget that many utilities such as energy and electrical companies are also public companies with shareholders. Information from their SEC filings should be used to supplement information contained in state regulatory filings. Also, reporters should be sure to check with the federal agency as well, particularly for energy companies. The recent rise and fall of many energy companies, led by the collapse of Enron, caused the FERC to become involved in many energy company dealings.

Many of these companies also sign long-term contracts to provide power with states and other major customers. If the cost of power should rise or fall, these companies could reap a financial windfall—or face difficulty.

Consumer Product Safety

One of the functions of the government is to protect the consumer. And one of the ways regulators go about this job is to make sure that businesses are producing goods, products and services that are safe for consumers to use. When regulators find out that some product or good could harm a consumer, they may ask the business to change the way it is made. If the product or good is causing people to die or become seriously injured, they may even ask that it be withdrawn from the market.

Consumer Product Safety Commission (CPSC): A federal agency that protects consumers against faulty products. Its jurisdiction covers product safety for more than 15,000 products, and it can force a recall of a product.

Some of the biggest business stories in the last few decades have involved such stories. The question of whether Firestone tires were causing people to crash and die in their Ford Explorers was first reported by KHOU-TV in Houston before it became a national story. Millions of tires ended up being recalled. Ford posted its largest loss ever and ended its relationship with its longtime tire supplier. The story made drivers of sports utility vehicles across the country check their tires and question whether they were driving a safe vehicle.

One of the biggest business stories of the 1980s occurred after drug maker Johnson & Johnson was forced to recall millions of Tylenol containers after seven people in the Chicago area died as a result of ingesting cyanide-laced pills. The ensuing scare caused drug makers around the world to install tamper-proof seals to their packages.

Concerns about the safety of products occur on a regular basis around the world. In the United States, a number of regulatory agencies are charged with making sure the products and goods sold to consumers are safe. The concerns can range from the healthiness of the hamburger at a fast-food restaurant to whether a child can choke on a toy part.

The CPSC was created in 1972 and is the government agency that oversees most products. The products it covers range from adhesives to wood-burning stoves. It does not regulate products such as ammunition, automobiles, cosmetics, drugs, foods, tires and tobacco, which are under the realm of other regulatory agencies.

The CPSC works with companies and industries to set guidelines as to how products should be manufactured so that they are safe. It enforces those standards and can ban products if those standards are not met. The agency also conducts research on potential product hazards, and it can issue a recall or order repairs on a defective product. The agency is run by three commissioners appointed by the president and confirmed by the Senate. One of the commissioners is a chairman, and the agency's 500 employees oversee the safety of more than 15,000 products.

Naturally, some products and the companies that manufacture them fail to meet the CPSC standards. And when that happens, the agency will use its power to protect the consumer. That is when a business reporter is likely to find a story at this agency, particularly if the product is manufactured at a local plant or sold by a company with headquarters located in his or her media outlet's area.

The CPSC remains busy. In December 2015, there were recalls involving KTM off-road motorcycles, Origin8 folding bicycles, Martha Stewart cookware, John Deer's zero-turn lawn mowers, Victorian Trading Company tealight holders, Breville pressure cookers, Carrier air conditions and Focus bicycles. And those weren't all of the recalls for the month. The CPSC's Office of the General Counsel also issues advisory opinions about products that may not need a recall to correct a defect.

Product recalls can be stories for almost any newspaper, Internet site, TV station or radio station because the products are often distributed throughout the country. It is likely that someone in the outlet's audience has a product that has been recalled.

Product recall stories can also be developed by watching trends to see what type of goods or products have been recalled. A reporter from the *Los Angeles Times* spotted such a trend in 2001—the toys that fast-food restaurant chains were giving away with kids' meals were being recalled by the millions because of safety concerns. Fast-food toys accounted for 77 percent of all of the toys recalled.

The CPSC is not the only agency that is trying to protect consumers from unsafe products. Cosmetics, drugs, foods and medical devices come under the watch of the FDA, whereas car seats, tires and vehicles are reviewed by the National Highway Traffic Safety Administration (NHTSA).

The NHTSA is as busy as the CPSC in announcing recalls. In December 2015, it announced recalls involving vehicles ranging from Jeep Cherokees to Audi A3s to Honda motorcycles. In 2010, Toyota Motor Corp. recalled millions of vehicles after it was determined that something in its cars was causing them to accelerate without warning. Major recalls involving thousands of cars or trucks across the country are likely to affect consumers in every state. Although such news may not need to be covered as full stories in many mass communication outlets, they should merit at least a brief mention.

States are also involved in protecting consumers. For example, every state has passed what is known as a lemon law, which allows consumers to return cars and other vehicles that have broken down repeatedly after purchase. Most states have a period where the breakdowns must occur within the first 12 to 24 months of purchase, or within 12,000 to 24,000 miles. If the defect is related to something serious such as brakes or steering, the manufacturer is given one chance at repairing it. If it is another safety-related defect, the manufacturer has two chances to repair the vehicle. The manufacturer is allowed as many as four chances for repair on other defects.

Many other federal and state regulators also act to protect consumers. The FTC, for example, is active in pursuing Internet fraud. State insurance commissioners prosecute insurance agents who sell fake policies. The FCC addresses consumer complaints about telephone companies cutting service without reason and radio stations broadcasting vulgar words. There are even private organizations within the business community that also are involved with consumer protection. The Better Business Bureau also handles complaints against businesses and tracks the number of complaints that a business receives.

Anytime a reporter is writing about a company, particularly a business which sells products to consumers, it is wise to check to see if there are complaints.

Not every consumer is going to be happy all of the time. If there are a handful of complaints about the products being sold by a huge company, such as Wal-Mart or Microsoft, then there may not be a story. But if there are a number of complaints against any company that are all about the same product or the same defect, then there may be a story.

The EPA and FDA

Two other federal agencies that play a vital business regulation role—the EPA and the FDA—are often thought of as focusing on nonbusiness topics. But selling foods and drugs are multibillion-dollar businesses. And increasingly, business practices that affect the environment are coming under closer scrutiny. The FDA was formed more than a century ago, while the EPA was not established until July 1970. Both of them have thousands of staff members charged with regulating numerous companies—many companies that also fall under regulations from other state and federal agencies.

Environmental Protection Agency (EPA): A federal agency whose job is to protect the environment and human health by preventing the release of harmful items into the environment. The EPA can ban the use of certain products, and can fine companies for violating environmental laws.

Rachel Carson's *Silent Spring*, published first in the *New Yorker* in 1962 and later as a book, led to an outcry about the use of pesticides and their effects on the environment. This exhaustively researched reporting can be considered to be what led the federal government to create an agency to protect the environment.

The EPA's job is to protect human health and to safeguard the environment. It carries out its job by enforcing existing environmental laws and setting standards. The agency also sanctions companies that do not meet its requirements and pollute. The EPA is divided into 10 regional divisions across the country, and each region is charged with enforcing the laws.

The EPA has taken measures to ban products sold by companies. In 1972, it banned the use of the pesticide DDT, and two years later it began enforcing the Safe Drinking Water Act. In 1975, the agency banned the use of pesticides heptachlor and chlordane for most household and agricultural uses, calling them a cancer threat to humans. Three years later, the EPA banned ozone-destroying fluorocarbon gases in most aerosol products—such as hair spray and deodorant—produced by large companies such as Allied Chemical, DuPont, Kaiser Aluminum and Chemical, Pennwalt, and Racon.

Superfund: The federal government's program to clean up the nation's hazardous waste sites.

The EPA has also played a major role in the Superfund program and in the cleanup and removal of asbestos from older buildings. The Superfund program has identified sites across the country in which chemicals and other products are polluting the area and has ordered their cleanup, which can cost millions of dollars. Superfund cleanups have caused controversy in industries such as insurance companies, who have to foot the bill to clean up on the basis of old policies. The EPA maintains a list of Superfund sites across the country. If one of them is in a reporter's area, it might be a story.

The biggest environmental issue since the EPA's creation was the spill of nearly 5 million barrels of oil in the Gulf of Mexico in the Summer of 2010. British Petroleum agreed to pay $20 billion in claims for companies and people who were affected by the spill in the surrounding area.

In 1996, the EPA led the phasing out of leaded gasoline, which had been causing illnesses in children. And in 2000, it eliminated virtually all home and garden uses of Dursban—the most widely used household pesticide in the country and a product of Dow Chemical.

Although most of these stories are national issues, the EPA also regulates many businesses in every town and city in the country. The agency conducts thousands of air, water and hazardous waste compliance inspections every year and fines a business if it is found to be violating the laws. The EPA also grants permits to facilities that are allowed to use certain products and dispose of them by approved methods.

If there is an environmental spill in a town or a city, a reporter covering the story should check these records to see if the business had the proper permits and to see if the business had been fined in the past for violating EPA rules. Sometimes, the bigger story can be found in what happened, or did not happen, in the past.

Virtually every company or business dealing with chemicals, liquids or other products that can pollute the environment comes into contact with the EPA. If a reporter suspects a company may be polluting, he or she should check with regulators first to see what those agencies have uncovered.

The FDA plays a similar role with companies that manufacture and produce cosmetics, foods, drugs and medical devices. Its job is also to protect the consumer in many ways. With food products that each of us buy in the grocery store on a daily basis, the FDA ensures that these frozen dinners and packaged meat trays, among other things, are safe, sanitary, wholesome and properly labeled. With drugs, the FDA reviews medical research on the effectiveness of the drugs and approves them for sale to the general public.

The FDA's oversight also includes the safety and labeling of cosmetics; the manufacturing and performance of medical devices; the safety of radiation-emitting products such as microwaves, x-ray machines and sun lamps; and the safety of pet foods, veterinary drugs and devices. All of these products and goods are manufactured by for-profit companies, which means these companies have to receive FDA approval for their products and goods before they can be sold to the public. The labeling must be truthful and not misleading.

The FDA has garnered media coverage in recent years for its role in approving new drugs for pharmaceutical companies, particularly with the increase in the number of AIDS patients in the country wanting medications that can help them combat the illness. The agency's drug approval process has also garnered attention in other ways, such as when it failed to review ImClone's cancer drug Erbitux in 2001, leading CEO Sam Waksal to sell shares in the company before the information was publicly disclosed, resulting in his eventual arrest and prison term.

The FDA's review process can make or break a drug. A pharmaceutical company submits an application to the regulators with research and background on the drug's effectiveness. The agency can review the filing and ask for more information from the drug company, or it can accept the filing, which then places the drug into its review pipeline.

Approval of a drug for public consumption can make or break a small pharmaceutical company. Many start-up drug companies sell stock to investors on the promise that their drugs will be approved by the FDA before their money runs out. Therefore, drug approval for a small company, or drug approval for a major illness, can be an important business story, as the following *San Jose Mercury News* story illustrates:

> Gilead Sciences won Food and Drug Administration approval Friday for Hepsera, its new pill for treating chronic hepatitis B, a devastating illness that can lead to liver cancer, liver failure and death.
>
> The agency action is the Foster City biotechnology company's second drug approval in less than a year and is expected to boost Gilead's newfound profitability. The first shipments of Hepsera should reach wholesalers by Tuesday. The annual cost of the once-a-day pill will be $5,353 per patient.
>
> Only about 50,000 of the estimated 1.25 million Americans infected with hepatitis B are currently being treated, so Gilead is planning an extensive campaign to convince physicians of Hepsera's benefits.
>
> "Wall Street is estimating $30 million in sales the first year," said Gilead Chief Financial Officer John F. Milligan. "We will have to grow the market over time working with physicians, getting doctors used to the treatment."
>
> An FDA briefing paper points out that Hepsera slows the progress of the disease by interfering with the duplication of the hepatitis B virus and that it is effective against viruses that have grown resistant to another antiviral drug, lamivudine or Epivir.
>
> "Today's FDA approval of Hepsera gives physicians and their patients a new weapon in the fight against chronic hepatitis B," said Dr. Eugene Schiff, a liver specialist at the University of Miami and one of the investigators who tested the drug in patients.
>
> Hepatitis B is one of several forms of viral hepatitis. Like AIDS, it is spread through bodily fluids—primarily through unprotected sex and dirty needles.
>
> Gilead will market the drug in the United States and Europe, where the incidence of hepatitis B is more than twice what it is here. Its partner,

GlaxoSmithKline, will sell it elsewhere, including Asia, where there are more than 300 million patients.

Hepsera—the brand name for adefovir dipivoxil—was first developed for treating AIDS. But in the doses required to kill the AIDS virus, it proved too toxic. Researchers showed that in much lower doses, the drug can reverse liver damage in patients with chronic hepatitis B.

Last year, Gilead won approval for Viread, an anti-HIV drug that rapidly became one of the bestselling AIDS treatments and is the cornerstone of the company's profitability.[8]

As any story about a pharmaceutical drug should, this report assesses how much in revenue the new drug will add to the company's financial picture and also evaluates what it will mean to its profits.

The FDA can also file litigation against companies involved in the businesses it regulates, asking them to halt production or dispensing of a product. And it often joins with other regulatory agencies, such as the FTC, to halt misleading advertising of food, drug or beauty products.

An action would be announced in a news release similar to the following one from July 2015:

> The U.S. Food and Drug Administration issued warning letters to three tobacco manufacturers—ITG Brands LLC, Santa Fe Natural Tobacco Company Inc., and Sherman's 1400 Broadway N.Y.C. Ltd.—who describe their cigarettes on product labeling as "additive-free" and/or "natural." The warning letters are for violations of section 911 of the Federal Food, Drug, and Cosmetic Act (FD&C Act).
>
> The action marks the first time the FDA has used its authority under the Family Smoking Prevention and Tobacco Control Act of 2009 to pursue regulatory action regarding the use of "additive-free" or "natural" claims on tobacco product labeling.
>
> "The FDA's job is to ensure tobacco products are not marketed in a way that leads consumers to believe cigarettes with descriptors like 'additive-free' and 'natural' pose fewer health risks than other cigarettes, unless the claims have been scientifically supported," said Mitch Keller, J.D., director of the FDA's Center for Tobacco Products. "This action is a milestone, and a reminder of how we use the tools of science-based regulation to protect the U.S. public from the harmful effects of tobacco use."
>
> The FD&C Act, amended by the Tobacco Control Act, gives the FDA the authority to regulate cigarettes, cigarette tobacco, roll-your-own tobacco, and smokeless tobacco. It also created a process for the FDA to evaluate requests from companies seeking to market their products as modified risk.
>
> Under section 911(b)(1) of the FD&C Act, a "modified risk tobacco product" is "any tobacco product that is sold or distributed for use to reduce harm or the risk of tobacco-related disease associated with

commercially marketed tobacco products." This includes products, the label, labeling, or advertising of which represents implicitly or explicitly that the product or its smoke does not contain or is free of a substance and/or that the product presents a lower risk of tobacco-related disease or is less harmful than one or more other commercially marketed tobacco products.

A manufacturer who seeks to claim that a product poses fewer risks than other tobacco products may submit a modified risk tobacco product (MRTP) application to the FDA with scientific evidence to support that claim. To date, the FDA has not issued any orders permitting the introduction of modified risk tobacco products into interstate commerce.[9]

Just like the CPSC and the NHTSA, the FDA also issues product recalls and safety alerts for products it regulates. These can be food products contaminated with bacteria or other illness-causing organisms such as salmonella, or they may be products with improperly marked packaging that contain ingredients that can cause serious illness or death as a result of allergies.

In each case, reporters should check to see if there is a story for their readership. This is often the case if the product or good has been distributed or manufactured locally, or the company that made the product is located in the area. If local people have become sick or died as a result of the product, it is likely front-page news. The *Detroit Free Press* ran a series of stories in 2001 about how a Sara Lee meat plant shipped tainted meat, killing 15 and making more than 100 sick.

The recall or banning of a food or drug product can be damaging to the manufacturing company. Some fail to handle the situation properly and blame others for their problem. If this is the case with a business on a reporter's beat, he or she should interview industry experts and scientists to find out what went wrong. The regulators will also talk, as likely will the company. But each side will probably have an agenda, and the independent parties may be more objective.

The FCC and FTC

The FCC and the FTC also play important roles in regulating businesses. And both of them have taken high-profile positions in recent years in enforcing and interpreting their laws and regulations.

The FCC's role is to regulate interstate communication by radio, wire, satellite, television and cable. In other words, in a town with a radio station, television station or a cable company, the FCC is involved in overseeing those businesses. The commission is run by five commissioners appointed by the president and approved by the Senate for five-year terms.

Each business that the FCC oversees must have a license from the agency. In addition, the agency handles complaints from consumers and investigates potential wrongdoing. It holds hearings about new regulations for these companies and can fine companies that violate the laws it oversees. The FCC holds auctions, and the winners of these auctions receive the right to broadcast over the bandwidths on which they bid. Winning these auctions can be an important step for a business. A radio station cannot operate unless it has received approval from the FCC to operate on a certain bandwidth.

In mid-2003, the FCC took the step of loosening rules on ownership of media properties. Previously, ownership of television stations, newspapers and radio stations had been limited. But the new rules allow for more cross ownership. To be sure, the FCC wants to maintain competition among the industries that it regulates. Without competition, companies might raise rates. If the FCC is changing the rules for one of the industries it regulates, reporters should check with their local companies to see if it is going to affect them. If the rules cause local companies to make changes, then that could be a story.

The FCC can also be a good resource for reporters writing consumer-related stories about phone bills or wireless phone bills, explaining the different charges.

The FCC also is involved in other issues, such as pushing for more rural telecommunication services and promoting rural health care providers to receive the same rates as those paid to health care providers in urban areas. These are important trends in communities across the country that should be covered as major events for the local business community.

The FCC also regulates telemarketers who make those pesky phone calls trying to get people to accept a new credit card or donate to the local police league. According to the FCC, these calls cannot be made before 8 a.m. or after 9 p.m., and the callers must identify themselves and what organization they are calling for.

In Chapter 7 on mergers and acquisitions, the FTC's role in reviewing deals between companies is discussed. But there are plenty more ways that the FTC becomes involved with regulating business. The care labels on the backs of clothing are the result of FTC regulations, as are the stickers on home appliances showing their energy efficiency. The FTC oversees a wide variety of rules and regulations for businesses that are designed to protect the consumer from unfair and deceptive practices. The agency reviews everything from weight loss advertising to the protection of children online. If an online retailer promises to ship a gift before a holiday but doesn't deliver, the FTC steps in and investigates. If a small business is billed for unordered toner or printer cartridges, the agency will review the claim.

The agency also regulates credit laws, such as the Truth in Lending Act, which requires creditors to disclose in writing certain cost information, such as the annual percentage rate (APR), before consumers enter into credit transactions, and the Consumer Leasing Act, which requires lessors to give consumers information on lease costs and terms. Another credit law that the FTC enforces is the Fair Debt Collection Practices Act, which prohibits debt collectors from using unfair, deceptive or abusive practices, including overcharging, harassing and disclosing consumers' debt to third parties.

Competition and boycotts are also big issues with the FTC. The agency has challenged boycotts by physicians seeking to prevent the establishment of a competing health care facility. And it frowns upon agreements between cable TV companies not to enter a competitor's territory. Price fixing is also banned by the FTC. It encourages competitors to set rates and terms independently. The FTC has the power to charge businesses with lawsuits to prevent them from using what has been interpreted to be unfair or illegal business practices, or it may seek to introduce new rules to outlaw a business tactic that it believes is hurting competition or deceiving consumers.

The top of this story shows how the FTC was going after illegal fundraisers trying to get money from unsuspecting consumers by telling them they were donating to needy causes:

> Federal regulators are going to court—and launching a public education campaign—against fraudulent fundraisers charged with bilking millions of dollars out of donors who thought they were giving to needy veterans, disabled children, police officers and firefighters.
>
> The Federal Trade Commission on Tuesday announced it had charged five operations with fraud. One Florida telemarketer is accused of donors by having its solicitors claim to be firefighters or police officers. One in San Diego falsely said that money raised would benefit veterans, the FTC contends. Another telephone solicitor in Anaheim is accused of raising money for sham non-profits.
>
> In addition to the FTC enforcement actions, law-enforcement officials in 16 states also announced fraud charges Tuesday against what they called sham charities.
>
> "By diverting charitable dollars, these scam artists undermine the public's confidence in legitimate charitable fundraising and injure legitimate non-profit organizations," said Howard Beales, director of the FTC's Bureau of Consumer Protection.
>
> Earlier this month, the U.S. Supreme Court ruled that telemarketers who misrepresent the percentage of a donation that actually goes to charity can be prosecuted for consumer fraud.[10]

The FTC and other regulators went after small companies in this story, not the huge corporations that dominate most business coverage. Many reporters mistakenly think that huge federal regulatory agencies concern themselves only with the biggest businesses. But a large portion of their work is in enforcing the rules against small companies, which may have never been covered by the business media in the past.

Workplace Regulations

In addition to regulating how companies sell products to consumers and how they manufacture these products, government agencies ensure that the workplace is safe for workers and that employees will not be harassed by employers.

The government agencies that oversee workplace-related issues include OSHA, the EEOC and the NLRB. Although federal agencies, they are active in virtually every town and city across the country. OSHA investigates businesses where there have been accidents or injuries on the job. It also investigates job-related deaths. If the business has violated OSHA regulations that led to injury or death, then the company can be fined. Since its creation in 1971, the number of workplace deaths has declined by 62 percent and work-related injuries and illnesses have declined by 42 percent. In 2014, the latest statistics available, there were 4,679 workplace fatalities in the United States, or about 90 per week and 13 per day. In private business, about 30 percent of those workplace injuries were in construction.

Equal Employment Opportunity Commission (EEOC): A federal agency created in 1964 to investigate claims of employment discrimination on the basis of race, color, sex, age, natural origin and religion. Its jurisdiction has since been expanded to include discrimination based on age and disability.

In 2014, OSHA conducted more than 36,100 workplace investigations, with the bulk of those occurring in high-hazard worksites such as construction. State job safety and health organizations conducted another 47,200 investigations. These workplace investigations, and the fines that may occur, are public record, and they can be obtained by asking for them. They are important documents, particularly for journalists reporting about workers who were injured or killed on the job. The following excerpt shows how reviewing OSHA records about a workplace can help tell a better story:

> An Italian man working on equipment at the Case New Holland plant remained in a Lincoln hospital Tuesday, two days after he fell into a tank of poisonous potassium hydroxide and suffered severe burns.
>
> Federal officials said the Sunday accident was the third they were aware of in five months at the Grand Island farm-machinery plant, where a subcontracted worker from Mexico fell to his death Oct. 25.
>
> Gerardo Piazza, 38, was in critical condition at St. Elizabeth Regional Medical Center. He suffered second- and third-degree burns over 80 percent of his body, said Jo Miller, a spokeswoman with the Lincoln hospital.
>
> Piazza, whose family lives in Milan, Italy, was flown to Lincoln Sunday by medical helicopter from Grand Island's St. Francis Medical Center.

He apparently fell into the potassium hydroxide tank about 2:30 p.m. that day but managed to get out and yell for help, Grand Island Police Capt. William Holloway said Tuesday.

He said other workers rushed to Piazza, removed his clothing and rinsed him off with water before Grand Island paramedics arrived to treat him. Only Piazza's head and buttocks were not burned, Holloway said.

Potassium hydroxide, sometimes called lye or caustic potash, is a corrosive acid sometimes used for cleaning. It can be fatal if swallowed and can cause severe burns if it comes into contact with living tissue.

Steve Lee, manager of the Case New Holland plant, did not return telephone messages Tuesday. He said Monday that Piazza's family had been notified and planned to travel to Lincoln. Lee said Piazza was alone when he fell into the tank, which is behind a safety barrier that requires authorization to cross. Plant officials didn't know why Piazza was near the tank, in which parts of combines are dipped before painting. Lee identified Piazza as a project engineer with Comau Geico, a paint-supply firm based in Milan. That firm and Case New Holland, which employs 700 people in Grand Island, are part of the Italy-based Fiat Group.

New Holland NV belonged to that group before merging with Case Corp. in 1999, according to material on Fiat's Internet site. Both firms had deep roots in U.S. farm-machinery production.

The merger formed CNH Global, which announced in July 2000 that it would consolidate its Case IH and New Holland combine production at the Grand Island plant.

Another Fiat company, Comau Pico, and a subcontractor have been fined for safety problems at the plant related to or predating the Oct. 25 fatality, said Bonita Winingham, assistant Omaha-area director for the U.S. Occupational Safety and Health Administration.[11]

Without the background information about the numerous fines and violations, a reader might believe that the most recent accident was an isolated incident. But the story indicates, by using OSHA information, that this workplace may be unsafe for workers and that the company has not done a good job in improving conditions.

OSHA can levy fines on the basis of the seriousness of the violation and whether it is a repeat offense. A violation that the employer willingly or knowingly commits carries a fine between $5,000 and $70,000. A violation in which there is a probability that death or serious physical harm could occur and the employer knows, or should know, of the hazard can result in a penalty of up to $7,000 per violation.

If a company was found in violation of a regulation on one inspection and then found in violation of a similar rule on a re-inspection, it could be fined up to $70,000. Failure to correct a violation can result in a fine of up to $7,000 per day until it is corrected. And violations that have an effect on safety and health, but probably would not cause death or serious injury, can result in a fine of up to $7,000.

A reporter may not get an indication that there is a workplace safety problem at a local company until tipped off by a union complaint or by a lawsuit filed against the company by an injured worker. It is helpful for any reporter covering a large employer to develop relationships with employees to learn about OSHA complaints. In addition, the OSHA website (www.osha.gov) can also be searched for complaints by company name.

The EEOC was created in 1964 and prevents businesses from employment discrimination on the basis of race, color, sex, age, religion or national origin. In 1990, the Americans with Disabilities Act extended the EEOC's regulations to include workers with disabilities. The commission has five commissioners, all appointed by the U.S. president, who serve five-year terms, as well as a general counsel who serves a four-year term.

The EEOC received approximately 88,700 charges of discrimination annually from employees of private businesses in 2014. The agency will then investigate, and if it discovers that there is reasonable cause to believe that discrimination has occurred, the EEOC may attempt to reach a settlement with the company. If a settlement cannot be reached, the EEOC may file charges against the business in federal court.

In 2014, the EEOC filed 167 lawsuits against businesses and settled 144 lawsuits, obtaining more than $22.5 million in damages for workers. These settlements are often newsworthy, and should be reported, as were the following cases in South Florida:

A store manager who alleged she was fired after complaining about sexual harassment that female employees endured from a male manager was awarded $250,000 in back pay and monetary relief after regulators sued her employer.

It was one of three retaliation lawsuits against Florida employers recently settled by the Miami office of the U.S. Equal Employment Opportunity Commission.

"Retaliating against employees for complaining about what they reasonably believed to be employment discrimination is contrary to federal law," said Delner Franklin-Thomas, EEOC regional attorney in Miami.

In Florida, there were 1,725 retaliation filings in 2002, accounting for 29 percent of all discrimination charge filings in the state. Retaliation charge filings with the EEOC nationwide have increased by 33 percent from 17,070 filings in 1995 to 22,768 filings in 2002.

The settlements announced Tuesday were with:

Norstan Apparel Shops Inc., a New York-based chain of women's clothing stores called Fashion Cents. The agency won $250,000 in monetary relief, including back pay and compensatory damages, for a store manager in Tampa. She alleged that she was fired for complaining to district managers about a manager who harassed female workers. Attempts to reach the company president for comment were unsuccessful.

Marine Bank of the Florida Keys. The EEOC charged the bank with allowing a vice president's sexually offensive conduct to go unchecked and with firing a female employee for complaining about the conduct.

The suit was resolved with the bank agreeing to pay two employees $220,000 as well as do annual training at all facilities and comply with EEOC monitoring.

"We take this very seriously," said the bank's president, Hunter Padgett. "We're glad to have the lawsuit behind us. On April 4, we begin the training, and we've made it clear that we will not tolerate those behaviors."

GeoLogistics Americas, a Santa Ana, Calif.-based logistics and freight forwarder, was ordered by a federal judge to pay $100,000 to an employee who alleged that a branch manager in Jacksonville fired her after she complained of discrimination.

She complained that GeoLogistics provided forklift training and certification to male workers, but consistently denied her requests for the training because she is a woman. The court also required GeoLogistics to do annual training for managers and complete reports to the EEOC.

Attempts to reach the company's director of human resources were unsuccessful.[12]

Again, these cases were against small companies, not the big businesses that dominate coverage. To be sure, the EEOC has filed charges against high-profile employers such as Home Depot and Hooters. But again, a large amount of its regulatory work is with small businesses that make up the bulk of the economy.

Reporters should find out where the local EEOC office is in their state. That is where complaints are filed by local workers, and where the investigations begin. If the EEOC is going to take action against a business, it will file its lawsuit in federal court. If a reporter suspects a case is about to happen, he or she should check the clerk's office regularly.

The NLRB also protects workers on the job. It oversees the laws governing relationships between labor unions representing workers and corporations. The NLRB has two basic functions: One is to conduct secret-ballot elections to determine whether the workers at a specific employer want to be represented by a union and which one; the other is to investigate unfair labor practices by employers or unions.

An NLRB official oversees an election. Sometimes the story with one of these elections is actually the events that caused the workers to consider union representation. It might be beneficial to interview some of these workers to ask them about their working conditions and what they believe they will get out of joining a union. There may be pro-union and anti-union workers at the employer. And the employer may also be campaigning actively to defeat the union. Most businesses do not want their workers represented by a union. They believe it brings additional costs to running their operations.

An unfair labor practice can mean a number of different things. It could be a supervisor threatening workers with the loss of their jobs if they join a union or threatening to close the plant or warehouse if the workers vote to join the union. Promising benefits to workers if they vote against the union can also be a violation.

Unions can also engage in unfair labor practices that could lead to an investigation. They may threaten workers with the loss of their job if they do not support the union, or they could refuse to file a grievance against a supervisor if the worker has criticized union officials in the past.

After a charge is filed, an investigation is conducted. If a regional director believes a violation has occurred, the NLRB will attempt to mediate a settlement. If no settlement can be reached, then the case will go to an NLRB administrative law judge who will issue a written decision. Those decisions can be appealed to the five-member board that oversees the NLRB. About 20,400 unfair labor practice charges were filed in 2014. And of those, about one-third were found to have merit. More than 90 percent of those cases were settled.

The relationship between businesses and regulatory agencies can often be adversarial, which makes for good stories by reporters who know how to obtain the details leading to the confrontation. Although regulatory agencies may seem boring at first glance, they play an important role in the business world, setting rules and regulations for how corporate America should operate. Because of that role, they are vital sources of information that should be regularly checked.

Notes

1. From "Fed deepens Duke probe," by S. Choe and G.L. Wright, May 11, 2003, *Charlotte Observer*, p. 1A. Copyright 2003 by *Charlotte Observer*. Reprinted with permission.
2. From "Labor Department tries carrot: It recommends tax breaks for companies that willingly improve safety," by K. Rives, May 7, 2003, *News & Observer*, p. D1. Copyright 2003 by *News & Observer*. Reprinted with permission.
3. From "Allstate seeks premium hikes; condo, auto rates targeted," by P. Patel, April 24, 2003, *Sun-Sentinel*, p. 1D. Copyright 2003, by *South Florida Sun-Sentinel*. Reprinted with permission.
4. From "Research & Analysis: Latest branch data revealed," by M. Saunders, January 28, 2002, SNL Interactive. Copyright 2002 by SNL Financial. Reprinted with permission.
5. From "Planners bounce nursing home plans to council; Parma residents vow to continue fighting proposal," by J. Wagner, July 21, 2000, *Cleveland Plain Dealer*, p. 3B. Copyright 2000 by *Cleveland Plain Dealer*. Reprinted with permission.
6. From "Operating profits," by J. Karash, April 11, 2003, *Kansas City Star*, p. C1. Copyright 2003 by *Kansas City Star*. Reprinted with permission.
7. From "Duke Power assailed at hearing: Customers complain about the utility's planning and actions after recent ice storm," by M. Fishman, December 20, 2002, *News & Observer*, p. B1. Copyright 2002 by *News & Observer*. Reprinted with permission.
8. From "Gilead pill wins approval to treat hepatitis B; FDA says Hepsera slows disease's progress," by P. Jacobs, September 21, 2002, *San Jose Mercury News*,

p. 1. Copyright 2002 by *San Jose Mercury News*. All rights reserved. Reprinted with permission.

9. FTC news release, August 27, 2015.

10. From "Charity fraud alleged by FTC; Agency: firm scammed donors," by J. Boudreau, May 21, 2003, *San Jose Mercury News,* p. 1. Copyright 2003 by *San Jose Mercury News*. All rights reserved. Reprinted with permission.

11. From "Worker falls into tank of poison; An Italian engineer sustained severe burns in an accident at Grand Island's Case New Holland plant," by T. von Kampen, January 1, 2003, *Omaha World Herald,* p. 1B. Copyright 2003 by *Omaha World Herald*. Reprinted with permission.

12. From "3 employer lawsuits settled; regulators take aim at retaliation," by J. Fleischer Tamen, March 19, 2003, *Sun-Sentinel,* p. 3D. Copyright 2003 by *South Florida Sun-Sentinel*. Reprinted with permission.

Key Terms

articles of incorporation
Consumer Product Safety Commission (CPSC)
Environmental Protection Agency (EPA)
Equal Employment Opportunity Commission (EEOC)

Federal Communications Commission (FCC)
Federal Trade Commission (FTC)
public utilities commission
Superfund

Suggested Exercises

1. Ask five people you know if they would file a complaint with the EEOC if they felt they were being harassed or discriminated against on the job. What circumstances would force them to file a complaint? If some answered that they wouldn't file a complaint, why wouldn't they?
2. What type of bad service would it take from your phone company or cable company to lead you to file a complaint with regulators?
3. How would you know if your electrical company or water company was overcharging you? Where could you go to have your bill checked?
4. If you purchased a product that didn't work, what three steps could you take to try to get your money back from the retailer or the manufacturer?
5. Why does the government play such a large role in regulating business? What would happen if the government didn't regulate how companies sold their products or manufactured them?

Books on Business Regulation

Bradsher, K. (2002). *High and mighty: SUVs—The world's most dangerous vehicles and how they got that way.* New York: Public Affairs.

Epstein, R.E. (2008). *Overdose: How excessive government regulation stifles pharmaceutical innovation.* New Haven, CT: Yale University Press.

Hilts, P.J. (2003). *Protecting America's health: The FDA, business, and one hundred years of regulation*. New York: Knopf.

Shapiro, S. (1987). *Wayward capitalists: Targets of the Securities and Exchange Commission*. New Haven, CT: Yale University Press.

Yager, D.V. (1996). *NLRB: Agency in crisis*. Washington, DC: LPA.

 ## References

Boudreau, J. (2003, May 21). Charity fraud alleged by FTC; Agency: firms scammed donors. *San Jose Mercury News*, p. 1.

Choe, S., & Wright, G.L. (2003, May 11). Feds deepen Duke probe. *Charlotte Observer*, p. 1A.

Fishman, M. (2002, December 20). Duke Power assailed at hearing: Customers complain about the utility's planning and actions after recent ice storm. *The News & Observer*, p. B1.

Food and Drug Administration. (2015, August 27). News release. Washington, DC: Author.

Jacobs, P. (2002, September 21). Gilead pill wins approval to treat hepatitis B; FDA report says Hepsera slows disease's progress. *San Jose Mercury News*, p. 1.

Karash, J.A. (2003, April 11). Operating profits. *Kansas City Star*, p. C1.

Kennedy, S. (2001, August 11). Fast-food toys lead in recalls; Kiddie-meal freebies made up 77 percent of hazardous toys recalled last year. *Los Angeles Times*, p. 1.

Madison utility requests $113.1 million in rate hikes. (2001, August 1). *Milwaukee Business Journal*. Retrieved November 25, 2003 from www.bizjournals.com/milwaukee/stories.

Patel, P. (2003, April 24). Allstate seeks premium hikes; condo, auto rates targeted. *The Sun-Sentinel*, p. 1D.

Poling, T.E. (2003, June 4). Big media firms like new FCC rules; Looser regulations have companies discussing mergers, acquisitions, swaps. *San Antonio Express-News*, p. 1E.

Rives, K. (2003, May 7). Labor Department tries carrot: It recommends tax breaks for companies that willingly improve safety. *The News & Observer*, p. D1.

Saunders, M. (2002, January 28). Research & analysis: Latest branch data revealed. SNL Interactive. Retrieved December 23, 2002 from www.snl.com.

Tamen, J. Fleischer (2003, March 19). 3 employer lawsuits settled; regulators take aim at retaliation. *The Sun-Sentinel*, p. 3D.

von Kampen, T. (2003, January 1). Worker falls into tank of poison: An Italian engineer sustained severe burns in an accident at Grand Island's Case New Holland plant. *Omaha World Herald*, p. 1B.

Wagner, J. (2000, July 21). Planners bounce nursing home plans to council; Parma residents vow to continue fighting proposal. *Cleveland Plain Dealer*, p. 3B.

15

PERSONAL FINANCE

Defining Good Coverage

Everybody cares about the money they make, but not nearly enough consumers—and that includes business reporters—pay close attention to where the money goes when they spend or invest it. And with the economic upheaval of the past few years meaning that many of us have less money than we did in the past, it's a hard lesson when we finally sit down with our checkbooks to see how many times we've stopped at Taco Bell on the way home from work or bought a round for everyone on Friday night.

That's where the personal finance reporter comes in. Personal finance coverage is the segment of business journalism that aims to provide advice to readers and viewers on matters related to investing, retirement, savings and other money-related issues. Magazines such as *Money* and *Worth* and websites such as WalletPop focus exclusively on personal finance.

Personal finance has been a growth area in business journalism, but it's also one of the most difficult areas to write about. We're journalists, not financial advisors with training on the differences between types of life insurance policies, and who wants to write about such complicated topics in the first place.

There's an easy answer to that question. We may not yearn to write about these topics, but business news consumers want this information—everything from how to balance a checkbook to the right diversification plan in a 401(k) account—in increasing doses.

For many Americans, the carefree spending ways of the 1980s and 1990s have disappeared. With the stock market drop in 2008, more complicated financial products on the market, and doubts that the Social Security system will be around when we get ready to retire, more consumers are taking their financial matters into their own hands.

TIPS FROM THE PROS

Jennifer Barrett, editor in chief and chief education officer of personal finance news site Grow, on covering personal finance:

Don't forget the personal in personal finance. Any advice you share is much more meaningful, and memorable, if you illustrate it through real stories.

That's good—and bad, especially for the employment of journalists. Many Americans don't have the financial wherewithal to hire a financial planner to help them sort through the maze of products and options that are offered in certain personal finance strategies. These include but are not limited to getting the most out of an employer's benefit options, planning for retirement, using credit with discipline, picking out a mortgage to buy a home, finding a good stockbroker and preparing for who's going to care for their parents.

Personal finance coverage in business journalism can help in these situations. Personal finance reporters have done their job if they can explain these sometimes complicated topics to the average reader and offer prudent advice. Ron Lieber, who covers personal finance for the *New York Times*, says:

> I'm trying to get people reading who wouldn't normally look at a personal finance column. That means using plain English, writing like I talk, avoiding jargon, trying to be funny or deploying mild stunts on occasion, telling stories—instead of giving orders from on high—and redefining personal finance way beyond just investing to topics that hit you in the wallet but you might not expect to be reading about in a personal finance column.

The trick in personal finance reporting, as Lieber suggests, is in how the story is told. Jane Bryant Quinn, the best personal finance writer of the past quarter century, says that she agonizes over how to word her columns. "I will pull back a sentence and ask myself if it's clear," she says about her writing style. "There's a lot of blood behind the keyboard before you see the finished work. You're not doing all of the details that would confuse the readers, but you're including the salient details. And you're using enough explanation to make the experts happy."

Personal finance journalists who are good at writing and explaining, such as Lieber and Bryant Quinn, may be as famous as any business journalist. Jean Chatzky, who used to write for *Money* and *SmartMoney* magazines, now appears regularly on the *Today* show to talk about personal finance issues.

Personal finance has been one of the biggest growth areas of business journalism in the last few years, particularly after the recession began in 2008 and consumers became more concerned with how they spent and saved their money. Fox Business Network launched a weekly personal finance show on Saturdays, as did CNN. The Associated Press rolled out a package of weekly

TIPS FROM THE PROS

Jennifer Barrett, editor in chief and chief education officer of personal finance news site Grow, on covering personal finance:

Speak simply, especially on complicated topics. This does *not* mean dumbing it down, and it's much harder than it sounds. You can't explain something in simple terms unless you have a very good understanding of it yourself.

and monthly personal finance content, and papers such as the *Star-Ledger* in Newark, NJ, and the *Richmond Times-Dispatch* added personal finance coverage. In recent years, personal finance websites such as NerdWallet.com have grown dramatically.

With that growth have come a few problems. Newspapers across the country have been running canned personal finance columns written by a national organization, the Financial Planning Association, under the bylines of local financial planners. (While the content of the columns was fine, the practice of running the same column using multiple writers' names called into question their usage.) And many personal finance publications and writers have been criticized for writing and publishing stories that tout the year's 10 best mutual funds or stocks, which often then underperform the market.

Bryant Quinn derides such coverage as "financial pornography." Deciding what type of advice to offer on the personal finance beat can be tricky and can ruin the reputation of a journalist and his or her publication if the information is wrong.

The issue is the type of journalism being practiced. "Service" journalism in business and economics reporting is stories, graphics, charts and other materials that help readers make decisions with their money. These stories give consumers advice and, done the right way, can increase readership and make readers smarter consumers. But, such journalism is not easy.

Consumer vs. Personal Finance

"Service" journalism falls into two basic categories. One is "consumer reporting," which is journalism that tells readers which products are the most reliable, the cheapest or preferred in comparison to similar products. The best examples are *Consumer Reports* magazine, which accepts no advertising, and product reviewers such as Walter Mossberg of the tech news site Recode. These journalists and publications are experts in their field, with expertise that has been built up from decades of covering the same products.

This type of reporting is not without its problems, though. How can someone, or even a publication, be an expert on every product? In January 2007, *Consumer Reports* was forced to retract a story about the safety of children's car seats. An outside research firm conducted the magazine's testing, which was later refuted by the NHTSA. The tests were supposed to emulate a crash at 38 miles per hour but instead were done to predict what would happen during a crash at 70 miles per hour.

Nearly all *Consumer Reports* stories have been vetted more carefully. The magazine's reputation has remained intact. But the example of the children's car seat article shows the dangers that can arise when a journalist—particularly one whose publication can't hire professional experts to conduct tests—attempts to offer advice on what products are good or bad.

The type of "service" journalism we're going to focus on in this chapter is "personal finance" journalism. This segment of business journalism tells readers how to spend money more wisely, covering topics such as home buying, credit cards, loans, investing and selecting an auto insurance policy.

TIPS FROM THE PROS

Jennifer Barrett, editor in chief and chief education officer of personal finance news site Grow, on covering personal finance:

Read the SEC filings. Companies can spin the news any way they want in a press release, but numbers don't lie.

Beyond helping individuals, such stories sometimes have a broad impact on consumers. In 1990, I wrote a story for the business section of the *Tampa Tribune* about how the state's largest health insurer, Blue Cross and Blue Shield of Florida, had denied coverage to a Cuban native living in Tampa because he didn't speak or read English, meaning he couldn't read the company's policies to understand what he had purchased. After the story ran, the company announced the next day that it would begin developing programs to help Spanish speakers purchase policies. All it took was one article and some phone calls by a reporter to the state insurance department.

What made this story so effective in presenting a personal finance problem—a large group of consumers unable to find proper health insurance coverage—was a real person experiencing the problem first-hand. Pedro Valdes had paid the first two months of his health insurance premiums, but then the company refunded the money when it discovered that he couldn't understand English. All good personal finance stories start with a person whose experience illustrates the broad point that the story is making.

Some personal finance writers use the simple Q&A format, asking their readers to send in questions, which they then research and answer. For example, Steve Bucci answers questions on Bankrate.com from readers about dealing with debt. One recently asked:

> Does anybody ever refinance a second mortgage? Our original mortgage is at 5.625 percent and we are fine with it. Four years ago, I took out a second mortgage when my husband went to graduate school, and I was faced with paying all of the bills by myself. The second mortgage is at 12 percent interest, and I feel as if we are not making any gain. We have incurred other credit card debt since then but are able to make payments, although things are very tight. Please offer advice. Thank you.
>
> Carla[1]

The beginning of Bucci's answer made it clear what he thought about Carla's debt situation. He wrote,

> and most importantly, stop it, stop it, stop it or you'll go blind. Stop what, you say? Stop adding debt to your credit cards! If you are making purchases with credit that are not paid in full each month, it is likely you are living beyond your means. It is very difficult to become financially secure if you don't learn how to live within, or, it is hoped, well below, your means.

Others use these personal examples to help tell their story, presenting an individual's situation as a lead anecdote to help entice the reader into learning more about the topic. Chris Taylor, writing in *BusinessWeek* about how to switch financial planners, used the example of 48-year-old Thomas Keating, of Wareham, MA, who had been slowly moving his investments to a new planner after his individual retirement account, or IRA, started to lose value.

TIPS FROM THE PROS

Jennifer Barrett, editor in chief and chief education officer of personal finance news site Grow, on covering personal finance:

Do the math. Twice. The last thing you want to do in a personal finance article is get your numbers wrong.

After Taylor introduces Keating to his readers, he then gets to the heart of the matter:

> Shaken to the core by a market gone wild and scrutinizing performance and fees like they never had to do in a raging bull market, investors are

more open than ever to getting a financial second opinion. A recent survey by consulting firm Oliver Wyman found that the number of affluent investors looking to switch advisers has tripled in one year. According to Spectrem Group, a scant 36 percent of millionaires think their advisers performed well during the market turmoil of the past year or so.

By giving an example of how someone—an average, everyday guy just like you and me—switched financial planners, Taylor hooked readers into a story that otherwise might have been deadly boring. Sometimes in personal finance writing, the writer will also circle back to his personal anecdote near the end of the story, giving his or her readers closure on the decisions the consumer made and the results.

How do you find such examples to include in your stories? Ask your nonjournalist friends. If you're writing about balancing checkbooks, do your friends have issues in this area? Or do they know someone who does? Publications will sometimes ask readers to e-mail them for specific stories. A graphic with an e-mail address can be placed in the paper or magazine or on a website.

Laurie Winslow, a reporter for the *Tulsa World* in Oklahoma, wrote the following solicitation for examples, which appeared in her newspaper and on its website, for a story she was working on:

The Tulsa World Business section wants to hear about the inventive ways people are cutting costs and adjusting budgets during these economically hard times. Of course, there are the common saving techniques—dining out less, setting the thermostat higher in the summer and lower in the winter, or using coupons. But what unusual, interesting or fun strategies are you using to make those dollars stretch further? Inquiring minds want to know. Readers are invited to send us their savings suggestions by Aug. 21. We'll publish and share some of the submitted ideas, along with the names of those who sent them, so that others can put the tips to use.[2]

Chuck Jaffe, who has written about mutual funds for MarketWatch.com and the *Boston Globe*, collects names of readers who have contacted him about past stories. The list contains their e-mail addresses and other contact information. When Jaffe needs a consumer example for an upcoming article, he simply sends out an e-mail to his list explaining what he's writing about and asking those who have experienced the topic to reply back. As Liz Pulliam Weston, who writes a personal finance column for MSN Money twice a week, states, "People are so hungry for solid, uncomplicated personal finance advice that they're often willing to offer themselves as sources just so they can get some answers."

Good personal finance stories also use statistics to back up the thesis of a story. If you're writing about consumer spending, look for numbers on the Bureau of Labor Statistics home page, which can be found at www.bls.gov/home.htm. Numbers can tell your readers about the significance of what you're writing. The website also has data on how much people earn depending on age, sex, ethnicity and employment. If you can't find the data that you're looking for on this site, look somewhere else. There's plenty of data available to fit any personal finance story, from mortgage statistics to credit card fraud.

Here are some other tips when reporting and writing personal finance stories:

1. Don't write about yourself. Use yourself and your personal experiences to come up with story ideas, but avoid writing about personal experiences for a number of reasons. First, your experience may not be typical of what a broader audience is experiencing. Second, if you divulge too much information, you may open yourself up to fraud. And third, first-person stories often come across as the writer talking down to the consumers that he or she is trying to help. It may sometimes work in a less formal format, such as WalletPop, where Bruce Watson wrote about the time he and his wife were surprised by a large restaurant bill—the waiter had given them a $315 bottle of wine, not the $36 bottle they had ordered—and how they tried to negotiate with the manager.

2. Let the experts do the talking for you. It's the professionals who know more about the specific topic, whether it's picking life insurance policies or picking colleges for junior. As a journalist, you have the ability to write about a number of topics and to do it with authority. But you're not an expert on all of these areas. Very few of us can be. Find the experts in the field and let them be the voice that speaks to the reader or the viewer. These experts will be more comforting to the personal finance consumer as well.

TIPS FROM THE PROS

Jennifer Barrett, editor in chief and chief education officer of personal finance news site Grow, on covering personal finance:

Read the fine print. 1) Your readers probably won't, so you can provide a service just by relaying what you discover in plain English. 2) There are good story ideas buried in there.

---

3. Don't rely on just one expert. Make sure you interview a variety of experts on a topic from different angles. They may be telling consumers to do something that would enrich themselves. For example, an insurance agent could recommend a policy from which he or she receives the largest commission payment, but a fee-for-service personal finance planner, who is paid a flat rate, might recommend another policy that is more suited to the person's financial situation.

Even if you trust your source, report the caveats. Does he own the stock he's recommending? Did she give bum advice at the market's peak? Incorrect forecasts and other honest mistakes should not disqualify your source as long as they are acknowledged.

4. Give the reader something to take away from the story. This can be the pros and cons of a topic. For example, if you're writing about the best way for a person to save for retirement via a 401(k) plan, you could write about the pros and cons of stocks vs. bonds. Ideally, this could be something that the reader or viewer might cut out and save or print off your website.

5. Don't let the article seem as if the journalist is giving the advice. We're not financial planners. We quote the experts who give the advice. Make sure the story is clear about where the advice is coming from. Too many personal finance stories appear as if it's the writer who knows everything and is making a recommendation to the reader or viewer without really knowing the consumer's specific situation.

6. Don't imply that the consumer will have certain results. Articles or headlines that appear to tell readers that they will be able to beat the market if they invest the way the author suggests are one of the biggest problems in personal finance writing. What happens when that advice is wrong? The consumer will likely turn away from your media outlet.

7. Use charts and graphics. Because personal finance is complicated, concepts can often be better explained using graphics. Graphs and charts are also a good way to show the significance of personal finance strategies, such as beginning to save at an early age. Charts can also be used to give readers a checklist of what they need to do. Writing about buying a new home? Make a chart of the 10 things the buyer should do before signing the contract. Charts are also good for investment stories. They can include names of mutual funds, stocks and bonds that your experts recommend.

8. Never, never be absolute. There are no statements made in the fields of economics and finance that cannot be contradicted with equal authority and truthfulness, given the right circumstances. This is especially true when writing about markets and taxes. Use words like "typically" or "usually." One example: Business journalists usually report a trend toward lower interest rates as good news. It's true that the value of fixed income securities, such as corporate bonds, usually increase when interest rates decline in the market (unless, for example, the corporation unexpectedly declares bankruptcy on the same day that market rates decline). But for the retiree living on interest income, lower interest rates are terrible news. On another plane, it's now conceded that the recession that began in 2008 was caused, in part, by low interest rates that prompted speculative bubbles in housing and other assets. If you don't hedge your statements about economics and finance, readers will love to nitpick you to death.

Like many business beats, personal finance reporting requires specific knowledge to perform at the level that readers and viewers expert. But it can be one of the most rewarding types of writing, as your stories have a more direct impact on your consumers than does anything else in your publication or on your website. All it takes is an interest in the field. Read as many books about personal finance as you possibly can. Journalists can't be experts in everything, but they do need to know enough to smell a rat or a fishy explanation.

Ron Lieber was a business journalist with little experience in personal finance when he was hired to be part of the launch of the Personal Journal, part of the *Wall Street Journal,* in 2002. He had spent time at *Fortune* and *Fast Company* before that. "I arrived with a passion for, among other things, frequent flier miles," said Lieber. "From there, it was a half step to writing about the credit card industry. I just sort of took it from there, wandering into employee benefits and banking and other areas that hit you in the wallet."

With that last sentence, Lieber sums up what all personal finance stories should focus on: what hits you in the wallet.

Personal Finance Topics

Now that we've discussed the importance of and the strategies behind personal finance reporting, let's take a look at some of the different coverage areas and issues that a business journalist should know. While personal finance often focuses on investing, there are many other areas where stories can provide great information.

Kathy Kristof, who writes a personal finance column for *Kiplinger's Personal Finance,* says that the issue today is deciding what to write about. "Anything that hits your pocketbook, from grocery shopping to working and investing, fits," said Kristof. "So the big challenge is to either zero in on a handful of topics that you can learn well enough to become a true expert—or find a way to be a jack-of-all-trades, and still be an expert."

TIPS FROM THE PROS

Jennifer Barrett, editor in chief and chief education officer of personal finance news site Grow, on covering personal finance:

Make sure every quote you use is worthy of being a pull quote. Anything else can be paraphrased.

It's obviously difficult for even the most advanced personal finance reporter to be knowledgeable in every field. And to make that point clear, here's a test of basic personal finance knowledge. This should help you assess your strengths and weaknesses in covering personal finance.

Write your answers on a piece of paper and see how you do.

1. What are three ways in which investors can assess a stock relative to another stock?
2. What are three differences between mutual funds and hedge funds?
3. What is the main difference between investing in stocks and investing in bonds?
4. What are the two basic types of mortgages that a consumer can use to buy a home?
5. Why does a homeowner typically refinance his or her home mortgage?
6. What are the two basic types of health insurance coverage offered by most employers?
7. What's the biggest difference between whole life insurance and term life insurance?
8. How should an employee invest the money he or she is putting into a 401(k) account?
9. How many times a year can consumers request a free copy of their credit report?
10. Name two government agencies to contact if you've been a victim of identity theft.

Now, here are the answers. Be honest in grading your work.

1. P/E multiple, P/B multiple and the net profit margin.
2. Mutual funds may advertise, while hedge funds may not. Hedge funds "short" stocks, while most mutual funds do not. (To "short" a stock means to borrow the stock, sell it and hope the price declines before the borrowed stock must be repaid.) Hedge fund managers typically collect a percentage of the profits of their investments as a performance fee in addition to a management fee. Most mutual fund managers do not collect a separate performance fee.
3. Owning stock gives you a small ownership in the company. Owning bonds gives you no ownership.
4. Fixed-rate mortgage and adjustable-rate mortgage.
5. A homeowner typically refinances when interest rates for comparable new mortgages have declined well below the interest rate on their current mortgage.
6. Indemnity plans and managed care plans are the two basic types of health insurance.
7. A whole life policy covers a person until they die. A term life policy covers the person for only a certain period, such as 10 years.
8. For most investors, a 401(k) should have a diversified portfolio, with some money in stocks, some money in bonds, some money in a money market account, and some money in another investment, such as real estate or commodities.

9. A consumer can request his or her credit report three times a year—once from each of the credit rating agencies. Watch out, though. Requesting your credit report too many times can lower your credit score.
10. The FTC and the Social Security Administration.

OK, let's assess how you did. Here is my grading scale:

0 to 2 correct: You're reading this book for a reason, right?
3 to 5 correct: You never worried about the details when it came to spending money.
6 to 8 correct: You pay attention to your finances, but you need to sharpen your skills.
9 to 10 correct: What are you doing here? You already know everything.

I'm guessing that most of you fall into the lower two categories, which means that reading this chapter will do you some good, both personally and professionally. It's details such as these answers that make or break personal finance reporters. The more hard-core, specific information they can provide, the better. So, let's get started.

Investing and the Markets

The rise of personal finance journalism began with the deregulation of interest rates that banks could pay on savings accounts. With inflation running high at that time, ordinary individuals were eager to learn how to capture the highest available rates and assess the outlook for interest rates. After inflation was tamed, a boom in the stock market in the 1980s and 1990s drew millions of ordinary Americans into the stock market. At that same time, employers began dropping traditional pension programs, in which they invested on behalf of employees and paid retirement income from the pension fund. Instead,

TIPS FROM THE PROS

Jennifer Barrett, editor in chief and chief education officer of personal finance news site Grow, on covering personal finance:

Know your audience. What are their needs? Their challenges? The money topics that matter most to them?

employees were offered tax-advantaged retirement savings accounts, such as the 401(k) account, for which employees—not their bosses—made investment decisions. Ordinary people thereby were "empowered" to save for their own retirement, although few knew the ropes. If you look back at the personal finance media, many got their start during this time period. CNBC started in

1989, and *SmartMoney* began publishing in 1992. MarketWatch.com got its start in 1994, and TheStreet.com launched two years later.

Throughout the twentieth century, the number of individual investors increased dramatically. By 1999, more than half of all U.S. households had some sort of investment in the markets. These investors turn to the business and financial press for knowledge about their investments and for clues about where good investments might exist.

Trillions of dollars in investments are traded each day in the markets—stock, bonds, commodities and currencies. Knowing how to write about these investments in a way that the average person can understand is not an easy task. Consumers of personal finance news want to know whether investments are cheap or expensive and where they can take action to improve the performance of their portfolio.

Many personal finance magazines, newsletters, television shows, websites and blogs accomplish this through interviews with professional money managers who give the journalist their opinions about stocks they like and don't like. A money manager may think that bank stocks are currently cheap and may recommend that investors purchase these for their portfolio. They may also think that stocks of retailers have gotten too expensive and should be sold. Readers or watchers of this story then have to decide if they trust this money manager enough to take his or her recommendations.

The personal finance reporter should be questioning the money manager's rationale during the interview. If some stocks are cheap, why? The money manager should be able to back up this assertion by saying that the P/E ratio or P/B ratio of the stocks is low compared to the overall market. Both of these ratios compare the current stock price to a fixed number—the EPS of the company, or the company's book value per share.

For example, if Company A's stock is trading at $30 per share, and the company earned $3.00 per share during its most recent four quarters, it is trading at a P/E ratio of 10. The personal finance reporter can compare this number to an index of the overall market—such as the Standard & Poor's 500 index, which may be trading at 18 times earnings, or to other companies in Company A's industry, which collectively are trading at 15 times earnings—to show the reader that this stock is cheap compared to other stocks. P/E ratios also may be calculated based on future earnings, as estimated by stock analysts.

TIPS FROM THE PROS

Jennifer Barrett, editor in chief and chief education officer of personal finance news site Grow, on covering personal finance:

Readers should finish your story thinking that they either learned something new, or learned to look at something—or think about something—in a new way.

The same technique can be used to explain how a stock may be too expensive. Let's say that a company's shares are trading at $50 a share, and the company's book value—or the value of its assets divided by the number of outstanding shares—is $10. That means that this company is trading at five times its book value. But if the overall market is trading at 1.8 times book value and other companies in this industry are trading at 2.5 times book value, a personal finance reporter can make a good argument that the stock is expensive.

The same reporting techniques can be used for other investments. A reporter can check out a mutual fund's performance for the last year or the last five years and compare those numbers to other mutual funds using a similar investment strategy—such as buying stocks of small companies or buying stocks of companies based in Latin America. Because hedge funds are largely unregulated, numbers and comparisons are harder to come by. Hedge funds require that their investors have a lot more wealth than most mutual fund investors hold, so fewer readers may be interested in hedge funds.

Hedge fund: An investment vehicle typically offered to institutional investors and individuals with high net worths. Hedge funds differ from mutual funds in that they do not advertise publicly for investors and the manager typically gets a share of investors' profits, a share known as the carried interest.

Personal finance stories related to investing can also look at different strategies. A reporter covering the personal finance beat must become a student and, ultimately, an objective critic of these concepts but never an advocate. Should an investor consider put or call options as part of his or her portfolio? Stock options convey a right to buy or sell stock at a specific price during a specified period. And what about short selling, which is when an investor makes money when the price of a stock falls instead of rises? Here's how that works: An investor borrows shares of a stock from a broker and then sells them on the open market. They make money if they can buy back the shares at a lower price. If an investor shorts 1 million shares of a $10 stock, they put $10 million in their wallet. If the stock drops to $8, the shares are now worth $8 million. The investor can buy back the shares and profit $2 million. Of course, there's always a risk in investing. If the stock rises to $12 a share, the investor has to pay $12 million to buy back the shares and loses $2 million.

Put or call options: An agreement that gives an investor the right but not the obligation to purchase or sell a stock bond or commodity at a specific price at a specific time.

Personal finance stories about investing can also take a look at other concepts, such as buying stocks at the time of IPO or when a private company goes public by selling stock on the market. Many investors advocate buying only stocks that pay dividends, which are cash or shares of stock that companies pay their shareholders on a regular basis. The investor can make money two ways: the dividend payments and, hopefully, gains in the stock price.

Investment stories can also look at the people in the investing business. The recommendations of analysts, for example, can be examined to see who is providing better advice for their clients. Some personal finance media will match analysts against each other, with one recommending a stock and the other telling investors to avoid it. Other personal finance publications focus on profiles of mutual fund managers that examine their investment strategies.

TIPS FROM THE PROS

 Jennifer Barrett, editor in chief and chief education officer of personal finance news site Grow, on covering personal finance:

Studies and surveys are good hooks, but don't rely on them. They're only part of the story.

Then there are the other investments beside stocks. A personal finance reporter can look at bonds from a number of perspectives, including whether they're a good buy when the issuer's debt rating gets raised or lowered. While most consumers are limited in their knowledge of the commodities market, they know the financial impact on their wallet when they go to purchase a gallon of gas or a jug of orange juice—two products traded every day. Writing about commodities from a personal finance standpoint helps explain to the reader or viewer why prices are rising or falling and can help them make informed decisions with their investment portfolios and with their family budgets.

There are countless other personal finance stories to write about investing. The only limit is your imagination. When writing about investing, however, remember this: You're not doing your consumers any favors if you're advocating heavy trading. That only helps the brokers who receive the commissions on such actions. The best investors are the ones who have held their stocks, bonds, commodities or something else for a long time.

Benefits

Personal finance coverage also extends into benefits, such as health insurance, life insurance, disability coverage and other options that employers offer their workers as an incentive to stay with or join the company.

Most employers offer some form of health insurance to their workers. Personal finance reporting regarding this benefit typically discusses the most effective option for the employees. Most health care plans have open enrollment periods near the end of the year, when consumers can change their options, raising or lowering the price they're paying, typically through some sort of payroll deduction.

In an indemnity plan, the employee chooses which doctor or other health care provider they use. Because their options are unlimited, the cost is typically higher. But with a managed care plan, such as a health maintenance organization or a preferred provider organization, the insurer has negotiated a flat rate for visits. The downside for some consumers is that they have to go to the doctors in the plan, or they will pay more.

Health maintenance organization: A managed care form of health insurance where the insurer has contracts with physicians and other medical care providers, guaranteeing them a certain number of patients. In return, the health care providers charge a flat rate to patients.

Choosing the health insurance option offered by an employer is almost always a financially smart move because it will likely limit the health care expenses that employees have to pay. In most cases, the insurance premiums the employee pays to an employer-sponsored health insurance plan are tax deductible. But what many employees don't realize is that they can affect the amount they pay by picking certain options. A personal finance reporter can perform a valuable service for such consumers by explaining these options, such as the pros and cons of a flexible spending account or whether the consumer should opt for add-on coverage for items such as dental care, eye care and even pet insurance.

Personal finance journalists also frequently write about life insurance. While some employers offer life insurance as a benefit, many consumers need to consider purchasing policies as part of their overall financial strategy. Explain to them the advantages and disadvantages of the different types of policies and the costs associated with each one. When would a whole life insurance policy be more advantageous than a term life insurance policy?

There are also plenty of other types of insurance to write about when it comes to benefits. Disability insurance helps pay for an employee's bills, such as their rent and electricity, when they are injured and can't work. Many employers offer such a benefit to their workers, and it's relatively cheap, yet few take advantage of the offer. There's also long-term care insurance, which can pay for nursing home care and other expenses when a person retires. The downside to such coverage, of course, is that the premiums will be wasted if the person dies before they need such care.

Personal finance reporting can even take a look at types of insurance, such as auto and home coverage, that few, if any, employers cover. But stories about how to get the most out of such policies—without increasing the price—can be just as valuable to consumers. Many consumers don't fully understand what their auto or home policy does and does not cover. You can explain to them how, for example, to get a rider—a special insurance policy provision that provides additional benefits—on their home policy to cover their baseball card collection or their prized art collection.

Retirement Planning

TIPS FROM THE PROS

Jennifer Barrett, editor in chief and chief education officer of personal finance news site Grow, on covering personal finance:

Get out of the newsroom and talk to people. Real people. In person. Their struggles and triumphs will remind you why you do this and inspire better stories.

As questions arise about the long-term viability of the Social Security system and companies struggle to properly fund their pension plans, personal finance journalism has been taking a closer look at how consumers are planning to pay for their retirement years. The August 17, 2009 issue of *Fortune* magazine took a long look at the problems of Social Security and what it might mean for every American.

Currently, the biggest retirement planning story is the employer-sponsored retirement plan known as the 401(k). Named after a section of the IRS code, a 401(k) plan allows an employer to take money out of a worker's paycheck (before taxed) and put it in a retirement account. The employer will often match the money up to a certain amount.

How does this work? Let's say you're writing a story about a consumer who makes $1,000 a week. This person opts to have 10 percent, or $100, a week put into the 401(k) plan. His employer matches the first 6 percent, which means it is putting an additional $60 in every week. That's money that's essentially given to the employee by the company. In addition, the worker's taxed income decreases to $900, which means he is paying less in taxes every week. If he keeps the money in the 401(k) plan until reaching retirement age, he can withdraw it without having to pay taxes. However, if he takes it out early to purchase a home or do something else, he has to pay taxes and penalties.

401(k) plan: A retirement plan available in the United States where workers can deduct a portion of their pay and have that money placed in a retirement savings plan. With a 401(k) plan, the workers then choose how that money will be invested.

The catch—and what many personal finance reporters focus on—is that the employee has to pick where the money is invested. The employer will typically provide a number of options, including company stock, mutual funds with various investment strategies, money market accounts and bonds. What is the employee to do? Many of them look for advice from personal finance journalists, who regularly advise them to diversify their investments. Some former Enron employees learned this the hard way when the company collapsed and the stock price fell to nothing. They had put all of their 401(k) into the Enron stock options.

Personal finance journalists write about retirement planning strategies, such as checking your 401(k) statement every quarter to make sure the investments are performing, and provide guidelines on when a consumer should consider changing their investment portfolio in the plan. They also write about how workers can take their 401(k) plan when they leave their employer and how they can roll the money from the plan into their new employer's 401(k) option, or invest it in an IRA.

individual retirement account (IRA): A retirement account where people can invest money on a pretax basis and let it compound tax-free. Withdrawals from the account are taxable.

Other topics to write about in this area include IRA accounts and Roth IRA plans. Consumers can save additional money outside their 401(k) by putting money into an IRA. The contributions may be tax deductible based on income and tax-filing status, and the money is withdrawn when the person stops working and their tax rate is lower. With a Roth IRA, distributions are tax-free at least five years after the account has been established. That's the kind of information that personal finance reporters love to provide to readers.

The Big Purchase

Most consumers, at some point in their lives, will purchase a house. And for most consumers, it's the largest purchase they will ever make, which lends itself well to writing about it from a personal finance perspective.

There's the age-old question of buying vs. renting and which is more advantageous for a consumer at certain ages. There's also the issue of mortgage interest payments being tax deductible and the appreciation of the value of a home in terms of helping a family create value. In recent years, a hot topic was using equity loans on a home to pay off higher interest loans, such as credit card debt. Indeed, writing about the buying, selling and refinancing of a home is full of personal finance angles.

fixed-rate mortgage: A mortgage where the interest rate will not change during the course of the mortgage. The interest rate does change with an adjustable-rate mortgage.

Personal finance writers can also explore the advantages and disadvantages of fixed-rate mortgages and adjustable-rate mortgages. The former is preferable to home buyers who plan to stay at the location for a long time, while the latter can work well for someone who plans to sell the home in three to five years. Adjustable-rate mortgages can also be preferable to first-time buyers needing to establish credit. Another consideration is an option adjustable-rate mortgage, where the interest rate rises every month. These are more risky, and consumers should be made aware of how expensive such deals can be.

Then there's the length of a loan. Should a buyer go for a 30-year or a 15-year term? Again, both have plusses and minuses, depending on the consumer's financial situation.

In recent years, the concept of sub-prime mortgages has gained prominence, as they were one of the reasons for the economic meltdown in 2008. Lenders gave home loans to consumers who otherwise might not have qualified for a mortgage. In doing so, they often didn't perform enough due diligence on the customer's ability to repay the mortgage, and they also may not have explained what the consumer was purchasing well enough for buyers to understand the risk of losing their homes. Now, mortgage lenders have tightened their restrictions on who qualifies for such loans, making it a great personal finance story.

 refinance: A process whereby a borrower replaces an existing debt obligation with a new one, typically at a lower interest rate. The most common type of refinancing is with a home mortgage.

Another personal finance topic related to mortgages is whether to refinance the loan when interest rates fall. Refinancing costs money, but it can cut the amount of the monthly payment, and consumers can take some equity out of the home if they need money for another purpose.

Let's not forget the scams out there in home purchasing—and in other areas of personal finance reporting. One of my former students, Andrew Dunn, wrote this story while interning on the business desk of the *Charlotte Observer*. It's about a company that told consumer Ruth Barbour it would buy her house but never did. Dunn writes:

> Like others across North Carolina, she fell victim to a type of mortgage scheme that's become more common as businesses target homeowners

desperate to get out of their houses. The major Charlotte players include a man who spent time in prison for mortgage fraud. One lawyer studying the trend estimates several thousand people have been taken in. The businesses, which say they buy and close on homes quickly, have captured the attention of state regulators and legislators, who are now considering legislation that would make tracking these cases easier. "A lot of homeowners are facing foreclosure, and they're very vulnerable," said N.C. Rep. Jennifer Weiss, a Wake County Democrat who is cosponsoring legislation to track the cases. "There are a lot of unwary folks out there who are being taken advantage of."[3]

Buying and selling a house can be one of the most frustrating experiences for a consumer, and there are personal finance journalists who focus solely on writing about real estate. Their expertise is in explaining the process in a way that anyone can understand, telling consumers what to watch out for, what to push for and what to resist.

Credit Scores

One of the issues that determines whether someone can purchase a house is their credit history, yet few people—including some personal finance writers—fully understand how a person's credit score is determined. That makes it a great personal finance story in virtually any publication.

credit report: A record of an individual's history in terms of borrowing and paying off money. Lenders use a credit report to determine whether to give a person a credit card or lend money to a person who has applied for a loan.

A credit report is a record of a person's credit activities. It lists any credit card accounts and loans the person may have, the balances and how regularly the person makes payments. It also shows any action because of unpaid bills. There are three companies—Equifax, Experian and TransUnion—that collect this information. They tabulate the information and create a score for that person. The score is based on five categories—payment history, amount owed, length of credit history, new credit and type of credit used.

What many consumers don't realize is who can get their credit score. Obviously, creditors who are considering granting a loan to a person can obtain his or her score. But so can others. Employers considering someone for a job, a promotion or a reassignment can acquire a credit report, as can insurance companies considering a consumer for a new policy or a renewal. Government agencies can review a credit report to assess someone's financial status for government benefits, as can a potential landlord or anyone with a legitimate business need for the information. Scared yet? I bet many of you wish you knew what your current credit score was and who has been looking at it.

And that's the point of personal finance journalism. You want to provide information that tells the reader something about their lives that affects them but which they don't know. You want to arm them with the details they need to make themselves better.

Budgeting and Spending

The fastest growing area of personal finance reporting, particularly in the last few years, has been content related to people's everyday lives, such as taking control of their day-to-day expenses and providing tips on how not to overspend.

These personal finance stories range from tips on what to do to lower your family's tax bill at the end of the year to saving for junior's college. They include stories on how to negotiate with a credit card company to lower your annual interest rate and stories on money makeovers, where the personal finance journalist takes a consumer's financial situation to a professional financial planner and then writes about the advice.

Reporter Mai Hoang, of the *Yakima* (WA) *Herald-Republic,* wrote about shopping for clothes on a budget right before the start of the school year. She talked to shoppers about their strategies and got advice from experts. Her story included a box of tips to consider while shopping and what to do while standing in the checkout line.

Sue Stock, a former retail reporter for the (Raleigh) *News & Observer,* took budget awareness to the next level. She wrote a blog called "Taking Stock" where she chronicled her savings each year using coupons and sales and compiles a list every week of where local coupons can be found and used. One blog entry stated,

> One of the most common things I hear from non-couponers is that it simply takes too much time to use coupons. All the clipping and sorting makes people feel like it's too much of a commitment. Well here's my answer. If you can devote one to two hours a week to clipping, sorting and reviewing the sales fliers, you will be able to save a substantial amount. Probably at least $20 a week. $20 a week is more than $1,000 a year. And those are post-tax dollars, too, so that's some real money.

AP business reporter Sarah Skidmore took some data from a survey and expanded the topic to provide some advice on how to negotiate lower prices. About 72 percent of American consumers have asked for a lower price on their purchases in the past few months, according to consumer survey organization American Research Group. And they were successful about 80 percent of the time. So Skidmore provided six recommendations on how to haggle with class that were picked up by papers across the country. Her suggestions, based on advice from negotiating experts, included being polite, practicing your pitch and using your leverage as a shopper.

Conclusion

Remember that personal finance stories can be about virtually anything. Just because something wasn't mentioned here doesn't mean that it can't be a personal finance story. In 1993, I wrote a story for *BusinessWeek*'s "Personal Business" section about collecting baseball cards. Later that year, I wrote another story about buying and selling exotic cars. While these may not seem like your basic personal finance stories, they were extremely popular with readers. The baseball card story was so popular that I was invited to appear on CNBC to discuss the topic.

Notes

1. From "Refi second mortgage to pay off card debt," by S. Bucci, July 27, 2009, Bankrate.com. Retrieved August 12, 2009 from www.bankrate.com/finance/debt/refi-second-mortgage-to-pay-off-card-debt.aspx.
2. From "Business section seeks your money-saving tips: We'll publish them in a few weeks," by L. Winslow, August 15, 2009, *Tulsa World*, p. E2.
3. From "Home scam stings owners: Businesses advertise as buyers. They take over a home's title but not the mortgage, and some can leave distressed owners in foreclosure," by A. Dunn, August 16, 2009, *Charlotte Observer*, p. 1D. Copyright 2009 by *Charlotte Observer*.

Key Terms

401(k) plan
credit report
fixed-rate mortgage
health maintenance organization

hedge fund
individual retirement
    account (IRA)
refinance

Suggested Exercises

1. Write out a basic budget for yourself, listing your expenses and your income—even if the money comes from your parents. Then total up the two categories. When you are done, swap your budget with another classmate and talk about how each of you can lower your expenses. What are some money-saving strategies that you're not implementing?
2. Pull out the last few statements of your credit card bill and review your purchases. Are there items on the statements that you've barely used? If so, what does that say about your credit card habits?
3. Find statistics that detail what percentage of U.S. consumers pay off their credit cards each month and compare that to a quick survey of your classmates. Do you or do you not pay off your credit card statements every month? What does that say about your personal finances?

4. Near the end of the semester, go back and take the personal finance quiz in this chapter again. Did you do better or worse the second time you took the test? Why do you think your performance changed?

5. What type of personal finance stories do you think college students would be most interested in reading about? Who would you interview for those stories, and how would you write them? Come up with a short, one-page story pitch to your instructor or an editor and present it to them.

 ## Books on Personal Finance

Brokamp, R., Gardner, D., Gardner, T., & Yochim, D. (2002). *The Motley Fool personal finance workbook: A foolproof guide to organizing your cash and building wealth*. New York: Fireside.

Kobliner, B. (2009). *Get a financial life: Personal finance in your twenties and thirties*. New York: Fireside.

Murray, N. (2001). *The new financial advisor*. Suffolk, NY: Nick Murray Co.

Opdyke, J. (2006). *The Wall Street Journal complete personal finance guidebook*. New York: Three Rivers Press.

Swenson, D. (2009). *Pioneering portfolio management: An unconventional approach to institutional investment, fully revised and updated*. New York: Free Press.

 ## References

Bucci, S. (2009, July 27). Refi second mortgage to pay off card debt. Bankrate.com. Retrieved August 12, 2009 from www.bankrate.com/finance/debt/refi-second-mortgage-to-pay-off-card-debt.aspx.

Dunn, A. (2009, August 16). Home scam stings owners: Businesses advertise as buyers. They take over a home's title but not the mortgage, and some can leave distressed owners in foreclosure. *Charlotte Observer*, p. 1D.

Hoang, M. (2009, August 9). How to stretch your fashion dollar. *Yakima Herald-Republic*, p. 1B.

Skidmore, S. (2009, August 13). Smart spending: 6 ways to haggle with class. The Associated Press. Retrieved August 16, 2009 from www.philly.com/philly/business/personal_finance/081309_haggle_with_class.html.

Stock, S. (2009, August 15). Managing your coupons and your time ... *The (Raleigh) News & Observer*. Retrieved August 16, 2009 from http://projects.newsobserver.com/ taking_stock/ managing_your_coupons_and_your_time.

Taylor, C. (2009, July 6). Thinking of switching financial planners? It can be a difficult, even emotional decision. Here are some things to consider before breaking up with your current adviser. *Business Week*, pp. 58–59.

Watson, B. (2009, August 4). Financial mistakes by experts who should know better. Walletpop.com. Retrieved August 13, 2009 from www.walletpop.com/blog/2009/08/04/live-blogging-our-first-300-wine-a-shock-and-not-in-a-good-wa/.

Winslow, L. (2009, August 15). Business section seeks your money-saving tips: We'll publish them in a few weeks. *Tulsa World*, p. E2.

INDEX